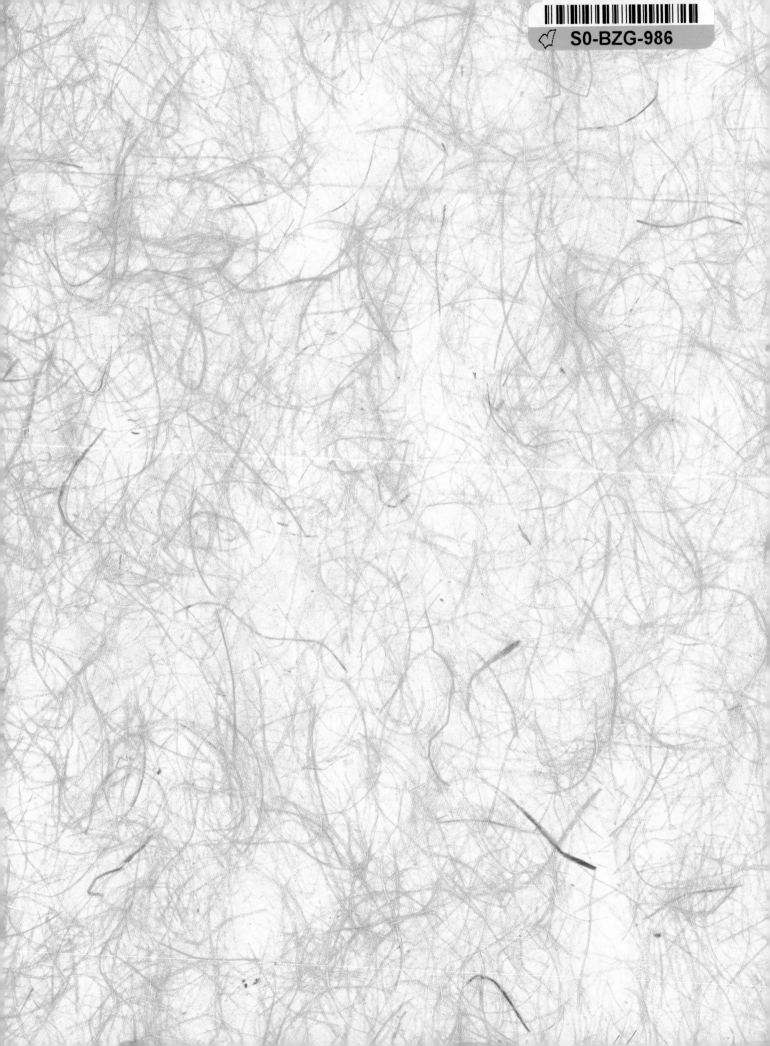

Porcelain and Pottery Shoes

Anne Everest Wojtkowski

Schiffer Publishing Ltd

4880 Lower Valley Road, Atglen, PA 19310 USA

Designed by Joseph M. Riggio Jr.
Type set in Bernhard Modern BT/Souvenir Lt BT

ISBN: 0-7643-1980-9
Printed in China
1 2 3 4

Published by Schiffer Publishing Ltd.
4880 Lower Valley Road
Atglen, PA 19310
Phone: (610) 593-1777; Fax: (610) 593-2002
E-mail: Info@schifferbooks.com

For the largest selection of fine reference books on this and related subjects, please visit our web site at **www.schifferbooks.com**
We are always looking for people to write books on new and related subjects. If you have an idea for a book please contact us at the above address.

This book may be purchased from the publisher.
Include $3.95 for shipping.
Please try your bookstore first.
You may write for a free catalog.

In Europe, Schiffer books are distributed by
Bushwood Books
6 Marksbury Ave.
Kew Gardens
Surrey TW9 4JF England
Phone: 44 (0) 20 8392-8585; Fax: 44 (0) 20 8392-9876
E-mail: info@bushwoodbooks.co.uk
Free postage in the U.K., Europe; air mail at cost.

Dedication

A project such as this should be mostly fun, and mostly it has been just that. The five most important people in my life made this possible. This effort is dedicated, *with the deepest love and a profound sense of gratitude for their endless good-natured support, to them:*

Tom, my husband, who drove with me far and wide searching for additions to my collection and who successfully pretended he didn't notice all the mailing boxes and the infusion of miniature shoes of every description as they filled every nook and cranny in our home;

Tom, Jr., my son, who installed the several computers on which I wrote this book, all the peripheral equipment I added as I went along, and then spent uncountable hours backing up my files, diagnosing problems as they occurred, and debugging the system when it was needed;

Marcella, my daughter, who has antiqued with me since she was eight, has an eye for the authentic articles matched only by my late mother, did so many thoughtful things when I needed to be enmeshed in the shoe business, and who enthusiastically supported and critiqued this project as it progressed;

Jeffry, my son-in-law, who spent several snowy winters laughing with me as we trudged our way through antique shops in four states while his wife was in residency, who has been my French translator and reference book searcher, and who has developed an eye that led to some memorable finds; and

Kerry, my daughter-in-law, whose kindness and superb acting skills have prevented her new mother-in-law from determining her real thoughts about a person whose home is the repository for some 3,000 miniature shoes.

Acknowledgments

Early in this project, I met three people who became very important to its completion. They are named in the order in which I met them: Wendy Lankester, originator of ceramic historic shoe series, preeminent figural shoe designer and modeler, artist, writer, and researcher who shared her research on English factories that made figural shoes; Michael Osterwind, who traveled to Thuringia on two occasions, acted as translator between the author and many German factories and museums, and who made numerous contacts to expedite materials being awaited from German sources; and Ruth Brady, who allowed me to set up shop in her kitchen every two weeks for two years as I photographed the shoes in her collection while she shared her best chocolates with me. Special thanks are also extended to Millie Mali for advisories from Rhode Island and Cathern James for boxes from Alaska.

Many people and organizations generously allowed me to photograph their collections, sent photos to me of pieces that filled in holes in my own collection, or in other ways aided this project. They bowled me over with their anxiousness to be helpful. I shall always be thankful for their kindness and generosity. Those whose contributions are mainly narrative are listed in the References. Those whose contributions are primarily photographic in nature are listed below:

Ashmolean Museum, Oxford
Bennington Museum, Bennington, Vermont
Berkshire Community College Library
British National Archives
Clark Art Institute
Förderverein Thüringer Porzellanstraße e.V.
The German Doll Company
Keramik-Museum Mettlach
Porzellanfabrik Martinroda
Rijksmuseum, Amsterdam
Royal Bayreuth Collectors' Club
Schlossmuseum, Arnstadt
Sotheby's, London
Spode Museum Trust Collection
Trustees of the Wedgwood Museum
Victoria & Albert Museum
V & A Picture Library

Florence Aalbers
Mary Anderson
Helen Beasley
Ann & Dennis Berard
Lee & Harold Berman
Susan Bickert
Mary Wallace Bocking
Ruth T. Brady
Larry Brenner
Karen L. Church
Mike & Kathy Clum
Robert Copeland
Patsy Crouch
Rosemarie De Bruin
Jason Dennis
Dorothy & Richard Earle
Sheryl L. Elghanayan
Maria Franson
Les Gardner
Tim Gaudet
Mario Gauthier
Herbert W. George
Dale Graham
Ethel Greenblatt
Trescott Haines
Susan Hartman
Sandy & Chuck Heerhold
M. Holland-Moritz
Cathern James
James D. Kaufman
Andrea Koppel

Barbara Kuhlman
Wendy Lankester
Kathryn M. Lapkin
Anne C. Lewis
Marc S. Lewis
Millicent S. Mali
Beatrice Massey
Randy Merritt
Piotr Maciej Olszanecki
Brigitte Osterwind
Michael Osterwind
Harriet R. Rothman
Diane C. Ryan
Helga Scheidt
Roland M. Schlegel
Stephen Smith
Ken & Judy Stockwell
Richard Stockwell
Pia D. Stratton
Jane & Tim Sullivan
Marcie Thueringer
Colleen & Paul Toland
Janice Vogel
John B. Watson
Bonnie B. Weitzman
Patricia J. Westlund
Judith White
Abe Yalom
Libby Yalom
Milton & Doris Zorensky
Jeffrey Zuehlke

Contents

Introduction

The hunter-gatherer instincts are alive and well. The daily need of our ancestors to collect berries and hunt animals for survival has been replaced by our desire to accumulate man-made objects that intrigue and amuse us. How else could I possibly explain to anyone why I have over 2500 miniature shoes made from porcelain and pottery, another 350 made from glass, and an undetermined number made from metals, wood, and various mystery materials?

Figural shoes made from every material known to humankind have been created for at least four centuries. Sandal and foot-shaped vessels have been found in Egypt and other locations dating to approximately 2000 BC. Boot and sandal forms have been unearthed that were created by the ancient civilizations of Central and South America. European museums have shoe and boot shaped vessels dating to the 16th and 17th centuries. Wendy Lankester wrote a carefully researched pair of articles on the history of the figural shoe in 1985 for the British periodical *Antique Collecting*. In about ten pages she wrote the most concise evolution of figural shoes encountered by this author.

Many proposals have been made to explain the symbolism of the shoe in figural form. To some, the shoe represents liberty and freedom because slaves of old went barefoot. To others, the shoe represents control; a father giving one of his daughter's shoes to his son-in-law was a symbol of passing off his authority over her. The symbolic message of the shoe that has survived to this day is its representation of good luck. It was long the practice of a young man to give his fiancé a small replica of a shoe as a good luck symbol. This custom was adopted by the upper class in the late 1700s when the fad of exchanging porcelain shoes erupted after a life-sized print was published in 1791 of the Duchess of York's elegant shoe that led to an exact scale model of her shoe in china. It was a mere 5-3/4" long, but its small size caused a large obsession with giving and acquiring porcelain shoes. Again in the late 1800s it became the rage for young men to give their fiancées a figural shoe as a love token. This prob-

ably can be attributed as the primary reason that so many of them are found in today's secondary market.

Among the embossed, die-cut cardboard ornaments manufactured in the Dresden/Leipzig area of Germany from 1880 to the mid 1920s were shoes like the one in Figure 1. This shoe was featured in a 1901 German catalog as a wedding and shower favor, with its silk crepe bag in the opening of the shoe filled with candy or small gold-colored paper coins. After a wedding, the shoe was often hung on a Christmas tree as a symbol of luck for the New Year in having a successful marriage. Postcards of this era also can be found with the shoe as a good luck symbol; an example is shown in Figure 2.

Figure 2. The implied message of both the shoe and the four-leaf clovers in this c.1909 postcard is, "Good luck in the New Year."

Figure 1. Lady's embossed, die-cut cardboard 4"-long slipper candy container given for luck as a wedding and shower favor. The remains of the silk bag once held candy or small, gold-colored paper coins. Listed in a 1901 German catalog, it was sold until the mid-1920s as a good luck party memento.

In explaining the shoe as a good luck symbol, a favorite story is told. When a couple would marry, they would say to the oldest person in the tribe, "We hope that we can follow in your shoes because you have lived such a long life." This sentiment has been attributed to the tradition of attaching old shoes to the bumper of a wedding car. Some have traced the shoe as a good luck symbol back five centuries. The shoe as a good luck icon can be traced back at least to the 16th century in the written word:

> "Now for good lucke,
> cast an old shooe after me."
> —proverbs of John Heywood (1497-1580)
> Part I, Chapter IX, the earliest collection of
> English colloquial sayings; first published in 1546.

Figural shoes are also one of the oldest categories of collectibles. I received a dozen good luck shoes for my twelfth birthday in 1947 from my mother. She knew several people who had long had their own shoe collections. The shoes she gave me were made of glass, metal, and porcelain. For years, the eleven shoes shown in Figure 3 sat on this whatnot on the wall of my bedroom. The twelfth was a cast iron high button shoe on a base that was propped against my bedroom door.

Figure 3. Start of a shoe collection, 1947: two Victorian pattern glass slippers, two metal boots, and seven German porcelain shoes from various manufacturers. Such a dated record is important because it places an outside time on the age of the collectible.

It is common for shoe collectors to have shoes in their collection made from such varied materials as leather, archaic jade, fabric, various kinds of wood, and even carved coal in addition to the more common materials. And, over the years, I added shoes to my starter collection made from a wide variety of materials. The easiest to identify were the Victorian glass shoes I found. Glass shoes primarily made in the United States and England during Victorian times constitute a favorite category for shoe collectors. Ruth Webb Lee pioneered research into glass shoes in her 1944 publication, *Victorian Glass*. Her initial work was expanded in scope, research, and organization by Libby Yalom, whose *Glass Shoes 2* is the contemporary authoritative reference on glass shoes. Shoes of high-content silver were also usually easy to trace to their origins, especially if hallmarked. Shown in Figure 4 are some uncommon Victorian glass, sterling, and wooden shoes, all of which add interest to a collection of this delightful figural.

As my collection grew, I became aware that I had an enormous number of porcelain and pottery shoes, most of which had no marks to identify their manufacturer and seldom to mark their country of origin. By far, the largest number of figural shoes has been made in porcelain and pottery. Yet I could not find a reference for them. Then, some years ago, I saw something that provided me with an idea of how to track down at least the country of origin for some of the unmarked shoes in my collection.

What I saw were three souvenir china shoes marked "Made in Germany", which I immediately recognized as having come from the same molds as three unmarked shoes I had that were decorated with floral appliqués and hand-painted details but had no mark indicating their origin. One of the three souvenir shoes had come from the same mold as one of the original twelve given to me by my mother, the one on the far right of the middle shelf of the pictured whatnot in Figure 3. I had grown to believe over the years that this bisque shoe with the rose appliqué was German, but I could not prove it. Now I could. This simple observation based on the mold details was the beginning of a journey whose goal has been to attempt to bring some small amount of order to and classification of porcelain and pottery shoes.

Figure 4. Assortment of uncommon glass, wood, and sterling shoes against a backdrop of Florette pattern satin glass made by the U.S. firm, Consolidated Lamp and Glass Company, c.1894. Left to right: 2-5/8"L hand-carved cap toe wood oxford, China, c.1920; 2-7/16"L sterling slipper w/heavily embossed geometric pattern and floral appliqué, late 1800s; 3-3/4"L pink threaded glass slipper w/rigaree appliqué, prob. England, late 1800s; 6-1/8"L pair of matched, hand-carved silky oak T-strap shoes w/original pin cushions, England, c.1920; pair of 833 silver, hinged strap slippers w/pierced and beaded rims and embossed scenics, the smaller 4-1/8"L and the larger 4-9/16"L, The Netherlands, c.1891; 4-3/4"L x 3-1/2"H cranberry glass boot w/crystal appliqués of flower, leaf, and rigaree, England, c.1880; 5-5/8"L x 2-7/8"H cased glass spatter shoe w/crystal appliqué of leaf and rigaree, England, c.1890; 6-3/4"L 800 silver, pierced vamp curled toe slipper w/triple tie appliqué and heavily embossed figurals, Continental hallmark, late 1800s; 5-5/8"L cased and frosted rubina heeled mule, prob. Italy.

Little could I have foreseen the tortuous paths that would be taken as this project progressed. When I started this trek, I had about 500 porcelain and pottery shoes in addition to those made from other materials. As I write, the number of porcelain and pottery shoes has more than quadrupled … perhaps even to the vicinity of 2500, though I long ago stopped counting. The acquisitions were made to help me clarify theories, expand on the holdings of particular manufacturers that had been identified, and provide better defined models for the scale sketches being made to aid in the classification of some of these shoes. I even found myself purchasing marked pieces such as plates, vases, and cups that had similar décors to shoes I was trying to identify. Sometimes, my family wondered on just what topic I was writing.

The challenge has been to try to categorize porcelain and pottery shoes by manufacturer according to similarities in mold design, décor, and other characteristics and then try to identify the manufacturer of as many as possible of these categorized groups of unmarked shoes. Most of the unmarked shoes came from German porcelain factories, especially in Thuringia (formerly east Germany). Since the wall went down in 1989, more information about the old Thuringian factories is becoming available, making it probable that the origins of many of the unidentified porcelain shoes may be found. With a project of this nature, the job is never done, but I have had fun making a start at the task and hope that others may wish to use this work as a starting point for further research.

Historic Shoes in the Collections of The Rijksmuseum, Amsterdam, The Netherlands

Figure 5. Blue and white glazed faience shoe with applied bow, 15.5cm x 8.5cm (6-1/8"L x 3-3/8"H), c.1650-1670.

Figure 9. Pair of glazed faience shoes with applied bows, 13cm (5-1/8"L each), c.1740-1760.

Figure 6. Pair of glazed faience mules, 23.0cm (9"L each), c.1700-1725.

Figure 10. Glazed blue and white faience shoe, 21.5cm (8-7/16"L), c.1740-1770.

Figure 7. Glazed faience mule, 13.9cm x 3.5cm (5-7/16"L x 1-3/8"H), c.1700-1730.

Figure 11. Pair of blue and white glazed faience mules, 11.2cm (4-3/8"L each), c.1750-1775.

Figure 8. Glazed faience mule, hand-painted "AS" on inner sole, 18cm x 5.5cm (7-1/16"L x 2-1/8"H), c.1720-1750.

Figure 12. Pair of glazed faience mules, 11.5cm (4-1/2"L each), c.1750-1780.

Figure 13. Pair of glazed faience shoes with crossed flaps and recessed heels, 13.0 cm (5-1/8"L each), c.1750-1790.

Overview
Historic Shoes

Figural shoes are a delightful art form that has long been collected, but which especially flourished in Victorian times and after World War II (WWII). It is from these eras that so many examples are found in the secondary market, though manufacture of them has been continuous from about the mid 1800s. To keep the size of this book within reason, a decision was made to limit the shoes shown within this book to those manufactured up to roughly the period between WWI and the Depression, with only a few exceptions. So many factories closed during the period from WWI through the Depression years that this sad time in the world's history inadvertently provides a natural break between the figural shoes made prior to and after this time. Shoes manufactured after this interval would comprise a worthy subject for a second volume.

Human history is not orderly, so there is not a clear demarcation between the figural shoes made prior to, say WWI, and after, say, the Depression. There is considerable overlap. But if generalizations may be made, it would be fair to say that for the collectible shoes made prior to, say, WWI, the bulk of porcelain versions were made in Germany and England and the bulk of pottery shoes in France. If the same gross generalizations were made about shoes manufactured from, say, the 1920s to the present, it would be fair to say that most pottery shoes were made in the Netherlands and the United States and most porcelain shoes in Japan, with other Asian nations entering the porcelain market in the late 1900s.

Shoes made from the 1600s to the early 1800s provide an historic context for the shoes found today in the secondary market, and they allow us to trace the evolution of the figural shoe form. Most of these early shoes can be found only in museums or in the collections of wealthy people.

The Rijksmuseum in The Netherlands has one of the finest collections of early pottery shoes. It is assumed that all of them were made in Dutch factories. They are shown in Figures 5 to 13 and have been arranged in chronological order by the year(s) in which the Rijksmuseum believes them to have been made.

Several English museums and the Williamsburg Museum in Virginia have in their collections a form of English delftware shoe that has a number of variations. A matched pair of English delftware shoes made in Bristol that were sold by Sotheby's, London on 14 April 1966 are shown in Figure 14. They are 4-1/8" long and are dated 1729. A 4-1/2" long pair similar to these was hammered down at a Christie's of New York auction on 25 January 1993 for $7,150, and one of them was broken and had been repaired. They had an overall pattern of stylized flowers and husks. The underside was inscribed, "EH/Dec.r 16/1768". Two contemporary versions of these shoes are shown in Figure 15.

Figure 14. Matched pair of English delftware shoes sold by Sotheby's London in 1966, made in Bristol, 4-1/8"L, c.1729.

Figure 15. Two contemporary replicas of English delftware shoes of the 1700s. On the left is a copy of a 1729 shoe in the Williamsburg Museum in Virginia; it was commissioned from a manufacturing company in Taiwan by the Williamsburg foundation and sold by them in the 1990s. On the right is a copy of a shoe made at Bristol in 1729; it was commissioned from Princess Royal by Compton & Woodhouse (both British firms) and sold by them in 1994. Each was sold for about $35.

Three other variations illustrate the variety of the hand-painted artistry found on shoes of this genre. Figure 16 shows a shoe held by the Victoria and Albert Museum. It differs in several respects from the Sotheby's pair shown in Figure 14. The V & A shoe has a much more elongated toe and the top of the tongue is curved. The floral patterns are also significantly different. Similar variations can be found in the two shoes of the same type held by the Ashmolean Museum at Oxford; they are shown in Figure 17.

Figure 18. Two 18th century pottery shoes sold by Sotheby's London at auction in 1994, that on the left for $7,730 and that on the right for $44,160.

Figure 16. English delftware shoe in collections of Victoria and Albert Museum, London; made in Bristol, c.1729.

Figure 17. 18th century English delftware shoes in the collections of the Ashmolean Museum, Oxford.

It is impossible to place a value on shoes held by museums unless similar examples come up for sale. For their size, the rarest of them extract big prices. Early English pottery shoes come on the market occasionally, and bring high bids. One of the two shoes shown in Figure 18 that was hammered down at a Sotheby's London auction on 15 November 1994 may hold the record. The c.1710 English delftware shoe with the diagonal blue and red stripes against a tin-glazed ground brought £4,830, or $7,730 at the exchange rate on that day. But it was the final price of the Fazackerly shoe that left everyone breathless. It went for £27,600, or $44,160. Some explanation may be necessary. *Fazackerly* is a palette of blue, yellow, red, and green done in motifs similar to the shoe in Figure 18. This shoe was advertised in the Sotheby's catalog for this auction as "An unrecorded dated Liverpool delft 'Fazackerly' shoe, inscribed 'E. K. 1760' ... " that "...appears to be the only known Liverpool delft shoe." Of additional interest was the catalog's notation that "These delft models of shoes were made to be given as gifts and occasionally to commemorate a marriage. The earliest examples date from around the end of the seventeenth century."

Of the shoes made since the late 1800s, by far those that are most sought after are the Royal Worcester models that were patterned with pierced work and embellished by the master of reticulation, George Owen. He was so secretive about the techniques he used to achieve the meticulously crafted piercing of the green ware pieces that he is reputed to have allowed only his son to work with him; and his son was not permitted to actually see how he did the work. His son would usually cast the piece. Then the ambidextrous Owen would lock himself in a room and proceed, starting it is believed at the top of the piece and working downward, with intricate precision. Over the years that he freelanced with Royal Worcester, he made some of their most memorable works, including vases and other decorative pieces. A 7-3/4" long Royal Worcester shoe with pierced work by Owen, signed by him and date coded 1919, sold at auction at Sotheby's on 18 March 1982 for $7,679 (including buyer's premium). Were it to come on the market today, it could be expected to fetch two, three, or more times this amount. It is shown in Figure 19. Owen used a blank cast from Royal Worcester shoe model #439. (See *Royal Worcester* in the manufacturer's section for the blanks of this shoe and the one following.)

Figure 19. Royal Worcester c.1919 shoe with piercing, appliqués and décor, by George Owen, sold by Sotheby's London in 1982 for $7,679.

Owen also produced the pierced Royal Worcester shoe shown in Figure 20 that he created in 1907 from a blank cast from Royal Worcester shoe model #763. It was sold at auction by Sotheby's, London on 14 December 1972. In both Owen shoes, note not only the precise reticulation but also the beading he applied on the rims and in various locations on the vamps. Every bead had to be individually formed, painstakingly affixed in regimental formation, and accomplished in a manner that would withstand kiln temperatures close to the melting point of some of the porcelain ingredients. On the 1907 shoe, the rim beads are graduated, like a golden string of pearls. Owen's staggering craftsmanship has had more than a few technically oriented people searching for the means he used to accomplish his masterful pieces.

Figure 20. Royal Worcester c.1907 shoe with piercing, appliqués and décor by George Owen.

The Manufacture of Porcelain and Pottery Shoes

Porcelain and pottery shoes have been manufactured because the public was anxious to buy them for a host of reasons. From the manufacturers' viewpoints, they presented both challenges in the manufacturing procedures and the opportunity to more efficiently use kiln space. It is expensive for the fuel and labor to fire up a kiln and maintain it at specific temperatures. Small shoes could fit in between the irregular spaces of the bases of candelabra, bowls, vases, and other large decorative pieces. This made the kiln utilization more efficient and it diversified the product line of the manufacturer. If there were a market demand for such figurals, then manufacturers would respond with the products. But the irregular shape of figural shoes gave rise to special fabrication challenges and resulted in products that have caused some collectors to raise questions:

Why is it possible to see through some shoes when held up to the light and not others?

Why do two shoes that look like they came from the same mold have different measurements?

Why is there glaze on the shanks of some shoes but not on the bottoms of their heels or on their soles?

Why is there a seam along the middle of the bottom of many shoes?

Why did some of the paint come off a shoe when it was washed?

Why was it impossible to remove original shoelaces with metal aglets from a shoe?

These questions and more can be answered if there is a rudimentary understanding of the processes by which porcelain and pottery shoes are manufactured. Porcelain and pottery have some characteristics in common as well as others that distinguish one from the other. An understanding of these similarities and differences, and the methods used to make shoes from the two materials, will not only help the collector figure out the answers to the above questions, but will also help to distinguish one manufacturer's product from another, aid in the identification of unmarked shoes, and lead to a better appreciation of these objects. What follows on the manufacture of porcelain and pottery is just sufficient for the purposes of this book. Collectors desiring a full treatise on the manufacture of porcelain and pottery can find excellent books in public libraries and good information on the Internet.

Composition

Pottery is a general term that usually refers to wares formed from soft clays that are fired at relatively low temperatures in very large ovens called kilns to harden the shape. Also called *earthenware*, pottery is opaque and porous. It needs a coating called a *glaze* to make it waterproof. Typically, pottery is made from indigenous clay. Additives may have been mixed in to provide special characteristics. Fragments of pottery have been found in Egypt that are more than thirteen centuries old. Porous pottery may be called simply that, pottery. Other types of pottery are *faience* (also, faïence and the German, fayence), *majolica*, and *terra cotta*, although such terms usually imply certain specific characteristics. For example, use of the term *faience* means not only that the

piece is made from pottery but also that it typically has a particular opaque white glaze called a tin-glaze applied. Stoneware is a denser, harder ceramic that is fired at a higher temperature.

Porcelain is a material that was invented by the Chinese and whose formula they closely guarded. It can be traced back to the 6th century AD. After tiring of the cost of purchasing Chinese porcelains, Germany developed its own in 1708 in Meissen. This event initiated an industry that has been important to the economy of Germany and resulted in objects important to collectors. After its invention in Germany, the secrets of making porcelain spread across Europe and then throughout the world.

Porcelain is made from (1) kaolin, or China clay, which gives the ware its white color and fine texture; (2) feldspar, or China stone, which allows vitrification and permits the ware to achieve its translucent quality after being fired at very high temperatures; and (3) quartz, which provides the compound after its first firing with the ability to achieve more even drying and withstand distortion. If you hold up porcelain to the light, you generally can see through it, which is not true of pottery. *Bone china* and *vitreous china* are forms of porcelain. The distinctions between them and between soft paste and hard paste porcelains are ignored for the purposes of this book.

Pottery and porcelain together are referred to as *ceramics*. In this book, "ceramic" is the term used to indicate the material from which a shoe is made if it is not obvious whether it is porcelain or pottery, or if the shoe clearly is not porcelain or earthenware, but some other intermediate material. Ceramic is also the term used when referring collectively to porcelain and pottery.

So-called cold cast "porcelain", or cold cast ceramic or resin shoes, are not covered in this text at all. They are neither genuine porcelain nor genuine ceramic because they have not been kiln-fired.

Mold Design

Ceramic objects can be formed by *"throwing"* the raw, elastic material on a potter's wheel, by *molding* using a mold for one surface and a profile tool for the other surface (as with cup bodies and plates), or by *casting*. Two sizes of a rare shoe made by molding are shown in Figure 21. Note that their bottoms show the protruding ridge usually found on the bottoms of cups and plates. Casting porcelain or pottery is the method typically used when the object is irregularly shaped or difficult to make by another method. Nearly all the shoes shown in this book have been cast. However, because they were cast in forms called *molds*, it is common practice for some to talk about "molding" shoes when the forming method was actually casting.

Figure 21. Pair of cobalt souvenir shoe pipe rests in two sizes. They are rare for two reasons: they are not plentiful and they were molded, using a mold for one surface and a profile tool for the other, whereas nearly all figural shoes are made by casting.

The process of creating a shoe begins with the designer, who often makes a sketch of the shoe as a first step. A three-dimensional model is then sculpted from clay, wax, or some other appropriate material. What is important in the modeling stage is that the material used for modeling be easy to manipulate into the often complex shape of a shoe and be an easy material on which to create whatever designs the sculptor wishes in the form of surface relief work.

It is also important during the design stage to avoid or reconsider design features that are known to cause production difficulties at any stage of the fabrication. Design features that will impede the easy removal of the newly cast shoe from the mold or cause it damage during removal cannot be allowed. For economic and production reasons, the designer may choose to avoid features that are known to be susceptible to failure during kiln firing or which require unusual supports during firing to prevent their collapse. Shoes with straps, for example, are especially vulnerable to failure during firing, and such shoes are uncommon. Shoes with portions of their rims that protrude

Figure 22. A Conta & Boehme shoe whose exceptionally high vamp medallion made its fabrication challenging.

significantly above the rest of the rim and are not supported in any way are also vulnerable to collapse during firing and are uncommon as well. An example is seen in Figure 22, which shows a rare porcelain Conta & Boehme shoe whose vamp medallion is exceptionally high and not structurally supported within the design of the shoe to withstand the high temperatures of kiln firing.

Fabrication

A *master block mold* is created from the sculpted model. It is a reverse impression of the design and is used to make the *master case mold*. The master case mold is used to create the *working block molds* that are made from plaster of paris. The shoes in collections are actually cast in the working block molds. Working molds generally can be used for only twenty to forty castings before their detail becomes too degraded and worn away to use further. Enough working molds must therefore be produced to supply sufficient shoes to fill an order. Figure 23 illustrates the degradation of mold detail that occurs after the mold is used a number of times.

The raw materials for the ceramic are cleaned and mixed with sufficient water to produce a mixture called *slip*. The slip is poured into the plaster of paris working mold to its top. The plaster mold immediately begins to absorb water from the slip adjacent to it, causing parts of the slip nearest the mold to adhere to its walls. The longer the slip is left in the mold, the thicker the material adhering to the walls. The length of time necessary to build up sufficient thickness in the shoe casting depends on whether the slip is porcelain or pottery. Only several minutes are required for porcelain; considerably longer is required for pottery. After the proper thickness has been obtained, the remaining liquid slip is poured off, leaving a thin-walled reproduction of the mold design. (The remaining slip is not usually thrown out, but used for other purposes, as for smaller castings.) The shoe casting may be left in the working mold for several hours to set up, or cure, and to allow it to shrink slightly away from the walls of the mold. The sections of the working mold are then carefully separated and removed and the newly cast shoe is said to be in its *green ware* stage. This attribution does not refer to its color but to the fact that it is unseasoned. Figure 24 shows a working block mold used in 1997 in the Martinroda Porcelain Factory (Friedrich Eger & Co.) for a porcelain boot. The newly cast boot can be seen still contained within the right side of the mold.

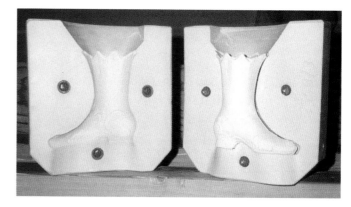

Figure 24. A working block mold that has just been opened, showing the newly cast green ware shoe resting within the right side of the mold.

Porcelain and pottery shoes are nearly always made in a two-piece mold, as the one from the Martinroda factory. This will result in a visible seam on the outside wherever the mold sections come together. After removal from the mold, excess material along the seams as well as at the rim is removed with a sharp tool, by sanding, and/or by polishing with a wet piece of material or a wet sponge. The piece is also dipped in water to remove any excess particles. It takes time, which translates into money, to sponge off all the excess material along the seam lines so that the joint becomes invisible. Some factories did not have their workers devote much time to seams that would not be noticed once the article was positioned for display. This is why the seam line is much more visible on the bottoms of some shoes.

Casting a shoe in a two-piece mold also results in the inside being hollow down to the bottom of the heel. German and Japanese shoes were generally made this way, as were English crested china shoes. Most French faience shoes and most high-end English shoes such as Coalport and Royal Worcester were made with applied heels. This required a separate mold to make the heel, and a separate process to attach the heel to the main body of the shoe, requiring addi-

Figure 23. The details in a working block mold degrade after it is used to cast twenty or more shoes, as illustrated in the shoe on the left whose detail is not as sharp as that of the shoe on the right, which was probably cast early in the life of a working block mold.

tional labor and cost. In these shoes, air would be trapped inside the attached heels. During kiln firing, the trapped air would be heated, raising its pressure. Without a means to escape from the heel enclosure, the pressurized air could cause the heel to blow up during high temperature firing. A tiny steam hole often can be located in a shoe with an applied heel, especially in the older ones. It was one means for allowing the pressurized air to escape and avoid the risk of failure during firing. Unless otherwise noted, shoes in this book are hollow on the inside down to the bottom of the heel. Figure 25 shows a shoe with an applied heel that has an unusual additional feature – a section overlapping the shank to provide additional structural strength.

Figure 26. *Wedding cake shoes* of Galluba and Hofmann, illustrating how the name was derived: extruded slip appliqués have been applied in a manner similar to the icing décors of fancy cakes.

Figure 25. Royal Worcester mule with applied heel. The fitting together of the heel to the front portion of the shoe body is unusual because the joint of the separately molded pieces was designed to be an overlapping one, as visible in the ridge in the first photo. This design feature strengthened the shank of the shoe by providing a double thickness at a location vulnerable to collapse during kiln firing.

Appliqués

Many shoes, especially those made from porcelain, are found with flowers, leaves, figurines, and other items attached to them that were not formed in the original casting of the shoe. These are called *appliqués* and are hand-formed, cast, or in some other way made separately. Floral appliqués on shoes have generally been hand-formed, with each petal, leaf, twig, and bud individually made. Leaves can also be made in single-sided press molds or extruded from a metal nose with an appropriately shaped opening, much like the decorating tips that are used to apply frosting to birthday and wedding cakes. While the shoe is in the green ware stage, the appliqués may be attached with a liquid slip mixture specially blended to result in a secure weld after kiln firing or they may be applied directly on the green ware pieces.

Galluba and Hofmann is famous for what have come to be known as "wedding cake shoes". The factory produced shoes with extruded appliqués of shirring, starflowers, and other décors that are exactly like the icing décor on fancy cakes. Figure 26 shows examples of G & H wedding cake shoes with applied slip décors.

A fairly unique example of appliqués can be found on shoes and novelty items made in Germany and referred to as Elfinware. The designation derives from a factory bottom stamp of this name found on some pieces. Figure 27 shows examples of Elfinware shoes. It was apparently the intent of the designer of these items to create a representation of woodland moss with tiny flowers throughout. Examination of 19th century groups of figurines in naturalistic settings made by such great porcelain manufacturers as Meissen and Sitzendorf often can be found with tiny flowers throughout a grass or moss-like setting, which may have been the inspiration for Elfinware. The "moss" is actually a liquid slip mixture that has been forced through a sieve. The extruded material is carefully removed with a sharp tool and is attached to the surface of the green ware like any other appliqué. This extruded material, painted green at a later stage in production, is referred to as *moss* by collectors and as *bocage* by potters.

Figure 27. Porcelain shoes with appliqués of sieve-extruded slip applied and painted to look like moss.

Appliqués and hand painting make individual ceramic pieces unique. Choices in colors and in the locations of appliqués result in differences between the end products. Thus, some make the argument that wares with hand appliqués are "one-of-a-kinds".

Kiln Firing, Glazing, and Painting

After the casting is air dried so that it can be handled without fear of damaging it, the piece is ready for firing in a kiln, which is just a very high-temperature oven, as shown in Figure 28. How high the temperature in the kiln is for a first firing depends on whether the object is pottery or porcelain and whether there is to be more than one firing. Pottery is generally fired to a high of about 1400°F. Porcelain and stoneware need to be brought up to about 2700°F during one of their firings to cause the proper fusing of their ingredients.

Depending on the decorations, porcelain objects may be subjected to, say, three kiln firings, with each accomplishing a different part of the décor. At one stage a coating may be applied called a *glaze*. It may serve any one of many purposes, such as to make the piece non-porous if made of pottery or to protect the décor beneath it. There are numerous variations in the order in which a piece may be decorated and fired. In addition, special techniques have been developed for applying certain finishes, like the enamels for which Longwy is noted. For the purposes of this book, knowing all the technical details is unnecessary. However, some or all of the following may be of interest to the reader:

•Temperature and timing are critical in the production of a perfectly formed piece of pottery or porcelain. If the temperature is allowed to rise too high, or remain there too long, the piece may be deformed, however slightly. This is especially true of thin-walled porcelain. The rim opening of a shoe will tend to broaden if it is subjected to excess temperature. In porcelain, shrinkage in size from the green ware stage to completion of the firing is typically 15% to 20%. Two shoes coming out of the same mold with slight differences in casting wall thickness and differences in firing time and temperature will have slightly different amounts of shrinkage. The resulting products will not have the same measurements. Older shoes were fired in kilns that were wood fueled where it was difficult to achieve consistent temperature.

•When the green ware piece is fired in a kiln but left unglazed, the resulting ware is called *bisque*.

•The composition of pottery and the temperature to which it will be fired result in pottery being porous. One purpose of glazing pottery can be to make the piece non-porous so that, for example, it can hold liquids. Any material used for a glaze, then, must be made of a different composition, one that is non-porous. Such a glaze not only will have a different chemical composition from the earthenware body, but it also will have different thermal characteristics. This means that during cooling the glaze may not shrink as much as the pottery body, resulting in a wrinkled glaze, or it may shrink more than the body, resulting in a glaze with cracks all through it. Some potteries, like Dedham and Longwy, have used the unmatched shrinking between the pottery and the glaze on purpose to produce an interesting effect referred to as a *crackle glaze*. To other potteries, especially American factories, the challenge has been to find a glaze whose cooling characteristics match the pottery body, producing a smooth glaze surface.

• Once it has been fired to about 2700°F, porcelain is non-porous. At that temperature, the feldspar is molten, much of the quartz has melted, fusing with the feldspar, and the kaolin has mulled within the mixture. The result is a material that is upwards of 60% glass, making the product translucent and allowing light to pass through it but not liquids. If porcelain is glazed, then, the purpose is connected in some way with the décor.

Figure 28. A contemporary kiln in the Martinroda factory of Friedrich Eger. On the right of the photo is the very thick edge of the insulated door, indicative of the high temperatures reached inside the kiln. Barely visible on the second shelf, front row, fourth from the right, is a shoe.

•Decorations may be painted directly on the air-dried green ware before being glazed and fired, as the early Chinese porcelains were made. More typically, porcelain is given a first or *biscuit* firing (producing *bisque*), then the painting applied and over-coated with glaze after which it is subjected to a second firing to affix the décor. The chemistry and thermal characteristics of certain colors may require multiple firings, with each being at a lower temperature to accommodate those characteristics.

•Glazes used on porcelain are generally just watered-down porcelain slip, with perhaps a small portion of additives that do not substantially change the material's thermal characteristics. Since the thermal characteristics of the glaze match those of the body of the object, it is rare to find glazed porcelain with a crackled finish.

•Glazes are ordinarily transparent after firing. In the cases of the earthenware bases of majolica, faience, and delftware, the pottery is coated with a lead-based glaze to which tin oxide has been added to produce an opaque white (unless color is added) glaze. Coating non-white pottery with a tin glaze produces a good surface on which to paint the décor because this glaze prevents the color of the clay from bleeding through during firing.

•*Rockingham* glaze is a mottled brown coating placed on pottery, not porcelain. In this country, Rockingham is not the name of a product of a specific pottery. If and only if the Rockingham glazed piece was made in Bennington, Vermont, then is it properly called *Bennington Rockingham*. If the piece was not made by one of the Bennington, Vermont factories it is erroneous to call it Bennington anything. It is also erroneous to refer to brown-glazed porcelain as "Rockingham".

Before explaining what a Rockingham glaze is, it should be mentioned that the meaning of Rockingham in the United States is very different from its meaning in Great Britain. There, it refers to wares made of both soft paste porcelain and pottery in Swinton, Yorkshire, England at a specific pottery established in the late 1700s under the direction and patronage of the Marquis of Rockingham. During poor economic times, when demand for the factory's expensive porcelain declined, the factory workers kept revenues coming in by producing an inexpensive brown-glazed pottery for household use. In the mid 1800s, English potters were recruited to work in American potteries. When they became involved in making similar brown-glazed pottery, they inevitably referred to it as Rockingham, and the name became part of the American pottery lexicon even though the American glazes and pottery composition were different.

Typical glazes are transparent and colorless. Any color evident would have been applied to the body of the piece before glazing and is simply showing through the transparent glaze. A distinguishing characteristic of *Rockingham* is that the color is mixed in the glaze. The fundamental component of a Rockingham glaze that gives it the brown color is manganese. To enhance the richness of the tone, a small amount of umber may also be mixed into the glaze.

•Colored glazes, other than Rockingham, can be produced by introducing metallic oxides. Iron oxide will produce green or gray-green, ferric oxide will produce yellows and browns, copper will produce red, etc.

•If the décor is applied over the glaze, i.e., without having the glaze to protect it, the décor will be subject to scratching.

•If some or all of the décor is applied and not fired in a kiln to set it, it can wash off with time. This is referred to as *cold-painting*. On some older shoes, gold trim has been applied in this way. It can be discerned by its dullness. Time has usually seen much or all of it worn away.

•Most contemporary porcelain is decorated by underglaze transfer prints or decalcomania (decals). Colored tissue-paper prints are applied to the unglazed ware. When the tissues are soaked off, the designs are left on the surface. Then the piece is glazed and kiln fired. In the case of decalcomania, the design is applied to the surface of the object and becomes integral with it during firing; when an object with a decal is placed under the right lighting conditions, the broad outline of the decal can be seen.

• Glazing is generally applied by dipping the piece into a tub of it. This causes the bottom of the piece to be glazed. Were it then placed on a shelf or tray in a kiln, the piece would stick to the tray after the glaze melted and cooled, making it impossible to remove. There are two common ways to prevent this from occurring. In one, which was frequently used in older porcelain or pottery wares, each piece was laboriously mounted on at least three stilts. These were cone-shaped devices that held the piece off the kiln tray, but could easily be broken off after the piece was cooled, leaving only tiny marks where the tips of the stilts had been. In some older pottery shoes, the process of removing whatever was used to raise the piece above the kiln tray left significant scars, as seen in the shoes in Figure 29.

• A faster way was developed to prevent the bottoms of glazed objects from sticking to the kiln shelf or tray during firing. Prior to being placed directly on the tray, the portions of the bottoms that would rest directly on the tray are wiped or sponged clean of glaze. This is why the shanks of shoes are glazed. No one intentionally coated just the shanks with glaze. It is what remains after the bottoms of the heel and sole were wiped clean of glaze. The time saving in this process comes from eliminating the job of balancing hundreds of objects on stilts on shelves or in trays and inserting them in the kiln without their slipping off their precarious perches.

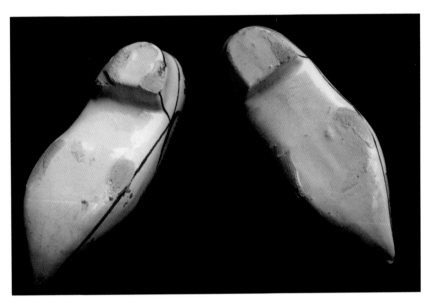

Figure 29. Fully glazed bottoms of French faience shoes showing large chunks broken off the bottom of the shoe during removal of the devices used to hold them above the kiln tray.

Techniques Used to Simplify Labor Intensive Production

Because German factories produced so many shoes, they provide a good study of the techniques developed to find less labor intensive ways of accomplishing what at first glance appears to be the same job. Factories are in business to produce quality goods while at the same time making money. Designers and production people are always looking for ways to simplify the fabrication process. The less labor required to make a product, the less money needs to be charged for it, and the company can stay competitive or even increase its profit margin. Figure 30 shows two rare Royal Bayreuth children's shoes. It is not their rareness that is of interest for this discussion, but the strap button and vamp bow on each. On the shoe on the left, the button and bow were molded in separate operations and attached as appliqués, all fabrication operations adding to the labor cost of the shoe. In contrast, the shoe on the right has been designed to incorporate the button and bow as a part of the mold, i.e., in one casting; the shoe emerges from its mold with the protrusions already in place to represent the button and bow. From prior discussions, it may be obvious why both of these are rare. The protruding ankle straps of their designs spell potential failure at every step of the fabrication process, from trying to remove them from their molds without breaking off the straps, to having to support the straps during kiln firing, to preventing them while in a nearly molten state from collapsing from their own weight, to trying to get them decorated and to market without accidentally snapping off their vulnerable straps.

Figure 30. Two rare Royal Bayreuth children's ankle strap shoes. The button and bow on the left hand shoe have been applied while those on the right hand shoe are in-mold, reducing fabrication time.

It has been noted that only kiln-fired porcelain and pottery are treated in this text. The manufacturing processes for these are much more difficult and exacting than such contemporary fabrication processes as those involved in cold-cast "porcelain" and resin and the other names by which such products are popularly called. Although cold-cast ceramics are not treated in this text, they do offer the ability to create forms not practical with kiln-fired ceramics.

For example, the ballet slipper with the free-flowing "satin" ties shown in Figure 31 is a cold-cast contemporary piece. Creating the satin ties would never have been attempted in kiln-fired porcelain for three reasons: the number of molds required to form the ties; the complex supports required to keep the ties in place in the kiln so they would not droop during the high temperature vitrification; and the

susceptibility to breakage of the porcelain ties extended outward from the slipper. Figure 32 illustrates the manner in which a Royal Bayreuth designer dealt with the problem of a kiln-fired porcelain slipper with looping straps … a sock was incorporated into the design.

Figure 31. Contemporary cold cast resin ballet slipper with free flowing "satin" ribbons, possible with this non-kiln-fired technology.

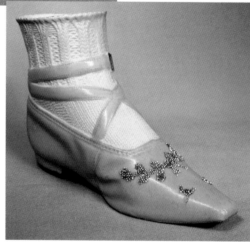

Figure 32. Kiln-fired porcelain Royal Bayreuth slipper, c.1900, whose creative designer incorporated a sock to support straps that would otherwise have collapsed at high temperature.

Weiss, Kühnert & Company specialized in another type of mold modification. They produced a pair of Dutch shoes with in-mold grapes, one held by a Dutch boy and the other by a Dutch girl. Each of the children was made separately, with the heads, arms, legs and bodies cast in individual molds, then assembled and applied to the Dutch shoes. The process was extremely labor intensive and, therefore, costly. But it was apparently a popular design. Figure 33 shows two sizes of the original versions of the boy holding the shoe and a smaller version illustrating what the company did to preserve the concept but simplify the fabrication process. For the smaller version, the piece was redesigned to incorporate the boy as a part of the shoe mold, i.e., the piece was cast with the boy and shoe as a single mold by eliminating spaces between legs, between the arms and the body, and between the body and the shoe. Careful sculpting of the original mold, and equally careful choice of painting décor provides the illusion that the boy is separate from the shoe. The technique of incorporating a figurine as part of the shoe also was used by Weiss, Kühnert for their clever animal shoes, as will be shown shortly.

Figure 33. Weiss, Kühnert products: two figurines on the right holding shoes as originally designed and, on the left, the mold modification made to achieve the same motif that incorporated the boy as a part of the shoe mold to reduce the labor intensiveness of the original design.

One of the largest manufacturers of figural shoes a hundred years ago was the German firm of Galluba & Hofmann. One of their specialties was piped-on, extruded slip in the form of shirring, starflowers, teardrops, shells, and other shapes that could be created with liquid slip extruded through an appropriately shaped nozzle. So many of their shoes have survived to our day that one can only extrapolate to gain an idea of the volume of their production. At some point it evidently occurred to the company that a significant amount of labor and cost could be saved if the hand-applied décor could be incorporated into the mold. On the left in Figure 34 is a G & H shoe with hand-piped-on starflowers whose purpose was to frame a vamp medallion. On the right is a G & H shoe whose model was retooled to incorporate piped-on starflowers, then put through the master and working mold process to produce working molds within which the starflowers were a part of the casting. It is a simple matter to confirm which G & H shoes have been so modified. Examination of the inside will show the negative impression of the starflowers, an as-cast characteristic. Shoes with hand-applied appliqués will not exhibit this negative image on the inside. In addition, G & H marked their modified shoes with a letter beside the 4-digit model number, usually an A.

The G & H factory modified the molds for many of their shoes and boots. The typical modification consisted of piping on slip starflowers or beads to the vamp in a way that would allow them to frame a transfer print of angels, florals, or locations for souvenir china. A new mold was made with the starflowers or beads as a part of it, thus eliminating the labor needed to hand apply this décor. Such modifications were designated by adding an A after the four-digit number of the particular model. A few variations to this designation scheme have been found and they are noted on the list of G & H shoes in the manufacturer's section of this text. Illustrations typical of these mold modifications are shown in Figure 35, where the original boot designs are on the left and their modifications on the right.

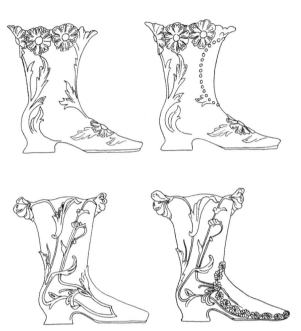

Figure 35. Sketches of the in-mold designs of original and factory-modified Galluba & Hofmann boots, illustrating a method devised by the factory to reduce labor costs in the finishing stages. Upper boots: on the left, an original "Daisy" boot; on its right, a factory-modified "Daisy" boot with in-mold beading whose shank-impressed model number now has an added "A". Lower boots: on the left, an original "Sweet Pea" boot; on its right, a factory-modified "Sweet Pea" boot with in-mold starflowers whose shank-impressed model number now has an added "A".

Other modifications to molds are evident if both sides of the shoes are examined. In Figure 36, the shoe on the left is believed to have been the original design. One side of the model was obviously redesigned and retooled to produce the second shoe because their back sides are identical. Figure 37 illustrates a similar process. Here, the shoe on the right is believed to be from the original design.

Figure 34. Two Galluba & Hofmann shoes, the one on the left showing hand-applied starflowers and the one on the right showing modification of the mold to incorporate the starflowers into the casting process. The negative image of the in-mold starflowers on the smaller shoe can be seen on the inside of the shoe in the lower photo.

Figure 36. Modification of a shoe design to create a new model while using the same backs for both.

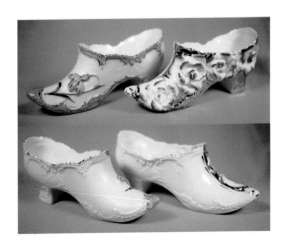

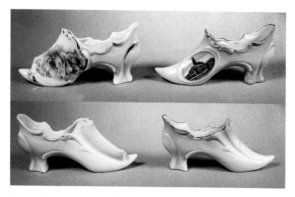

Figure 37. Another modification of a shoe design to create a new model while using the same backs for both.

Figure 39. The well-known snowdrop shoe, illustrating three probable forming offs that began with the largest shoe.

A great deal of effort is involved in designing and modeling a shoe for production. The Germans took advantage of the shrinkage of porcelain during kiln firing to create several sizes of the same shoe design. The largest shoe would be modeled and all the molds created. When a green ware shoe was given its first firing, about 15 to 20% shrinkage typically would occur. This reduced-in-size shoe would be used just like a sculpted model, with the necessary molds made from it, which would ultimately produce a shoe the next size down. The process could be continued to as small a final size as desired. This process is called *forming off.* Figure 38 shows two Weiss, Kühnert shoes, the smaller probably formed off the larger. It is also a good example of another advantage of incorporating figurines into the design of a shoe to allow the composite to be achieved in one casting – it is a simple process to form off the larger shoe and get not only the shoe but the birds as well in the same casting. Figure 39 shows four sizes of a shoe well known to collectors, the snowdrop shoe. The three smaller sizes probably were formed off the largest.

A *blank* is a piece that has been cast and taken through its first kiln firing but left undecorated. Many factories supplied decorating shops with blanks. Figure 40 may illustrate this. The shoe on the left is a marked RS Germany shoe. The one on the right is unmarked and presumed to have been purchased from the RS factory by a decorating shop. What is apparent, however, is that the smaller version probably was formed off the larger.

Figure 40. A marked RS Germany shoe on the left with an unmarked shoe on the right, probably formed off from it and presumed to have been sold as a blank to a decorating shop.

Figure 38. Pair of Weiss, Kühnert animal shoes, the smaller probably formed off the larger.

Dating the Period of Manufacture

The best source of information on shoes, like any other product, is found in old catalogues of company products. The author was fortunate to obtain this kind of data for shoes made by Villeroy & Boch; Coalport; Weiss, Kühnert; and a half-dozen or so shoe models from Arnstadt, allowing others from this company to be deduced. Bottom marks of the manufacturing company, if they exist, alongside authoritative texts on marks can also aid in a determination of the age of a piece. Photographic evidence, where it exists, can also be beneficial. For example, the cover of *Hobbies* for October 1953 (shown in Figure 41) is very helpful because one knows that every shoe on that cover was made before that date. And, since they are portrayed as being "old", it can be assumed that most of them would predate, say, WWII. In fact, there are many shoes on this cover familiar to collectors as having been made in the decade or two on either side of 1900.

The middle row has three Galluba & Hofmann shoes and a pair of Ilmenau shoes. Below this row there is a Royal Bayreuth rose tapestry low cut ladies oxford. On one end of the same shelf is a pair of Conta & Boehme boots and a bootjack on a base. There are a number of Weiss, Kühnert shoes including the Dutch Boy with Dutch shoe on the top shelf, the clowns in their tramp shoes on the middle shelf, a rooster shoe on the shelf below, and a strap shoe on the bottom row. Also in the bottom row are an Arnstadt boot with pig in a dust cap and a Goss Princess Victoria baby shoe. Readers are invited to see how many others they can spot. Most of the porcelain and pottery versions are pictured elsewhere in this book.

There are numerous clues in and on each shoe that can help date it. They range from the manufacturing methods used to any marks that may be present, short of a unique manufacturer's mark that in itself can be dated. Among the helpful markings are those that appear on souvenir shoes made for particular, dated events. Observation suggests that most German souvenir shoes were not originally intended for this purpose but rather were adapted from existing molds when souvenir china became popular. Thus, when a German souvenir shoe is found with a date, as "St. Louis World's Fair 1904", this usually indicates that the originally designed shoe was first produced **before** that date.

Catastrophic events have tended to interrupt the flow of porcelain and other goods that might be classified as luxury or novelty items. In particular, the two world wars slowed the manufacture of porcelain and pottery to a trickle, and what was made was primarily utilitarian. In fact, these two wars have inadvertently provided boundary points in ceramic shoe design because the consumer design demands

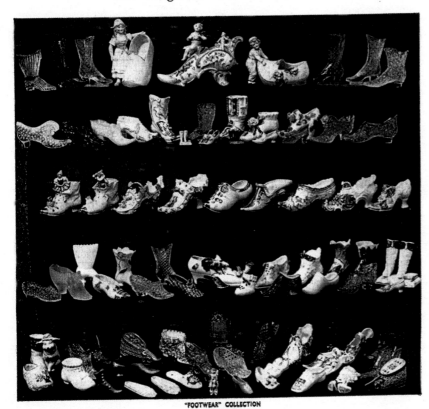

OCTOBER *Hobbies* 1953

The Magazine For Collectors

"FOOTWEAR" COLLECTION
(See page 80)

Figure 41. This *Hobbies* cover can place an outside date on the shoes illustrated.

before and after each were significantly different. Though there are exceptions, careful observation of ceramic shoes made before and after each war will often provide one clue toward the identification of the era in which an unmarked shoe may have been made. Lest anyone think that no porcelain was being produced in, for example, the United States as WWII was in its midst, Gannon dispels that with his report on the fate of the freighter *Bristol City*. She was torpedoed and sunk in early 1943 by the German U-boat 358 as she was making her way to New York City with a 2500-ton cargo of kaolin. The "china clay" described on her manifest comprised the majority of *Bristol City's* 2864-ton gross registered tonnage, though its intended use is unknown.

Shoes occasionally are found with a hand-written date on them. Sometimes it is accompanied by a name. It is assumed that this usually indicates the date of a gift and the name of the giver – or purchaser if bought for oneself. Often, such a date is a good gauge of the age of the shoe, but it must be consistent with the period in which the shoe is believed to have been made.

When trying to date a shoe, the following may be helpful. Note the word *helpful*. These are not rules, but guidelines. It is only the summation of all the information able to be gathered that can lead to a conclusion that may be defensible. Further, where acts of the U.S. Congress are concerned, their implementation took place over a period of time.

Guidelines

•**British Registry marks can be found on some of their registered ceramics and other decorative arts wares beginning in 1842.** Occasionally, a shoe can be found with a British registry mark. From 1842 to 1883, the mark consisted of a diamond shape surmounted by a circle with coded information within that told the exact date of registration and had a parcel number that could be matched to a manufacturer on a master list in the British Public Record Office. Since 1884, the registry mark consists of "Rd No" followed by a number; alternatives are "Reg.", "Rd.", or "Registered" with a number. The numbers are sequential. For example, numbers 1-19,999 were issued in 1884; 20,000-40,799 were issued in 1885; etc. Finding a British registry mark on a Royal Bayreuth shoe allowed the author to track down some interesting information about the shoe, including the fact that it had been registered in 1899, thus placing an approximate date of manufacture for the particular model.

•**The German Patent Law was passed 25 May 1877.** Items marked "Geschutzi" (patented) will post date 1877.

•**Wares marked "Made in" for importation into Great Britain are c.1887 – present.** Beginning in 1887, British law required wares coming into their country to be marked "Made in" plus the name of the country of origin. *Note date U.S. required this marking.*

•**Wares marked with the country of origin, as "Denmark", or "Germany", or Nippon"** (The word for Japan), **will generally date a piece to 1891 or later if made for importation into the United States.** The United States McKinley Tariff Act of 1890 that took effect on 1 March 1891 required that "…all articles of foreign manufacture … shall … be plainly marked, stamped, branded or labeled in legible English words, so as to indicate the country of their origin…" It is this piece of federal legislation that caused items imported into the United States that may not have been previously marked to now bear a mark that specified the country of origin. For Japanese items, the Japanese word for its country, Nippon, was used. Wares made earlier than 1891 can be found marked with the country of origin, so 1891 is simply a benchmark. Just as important, wares made substantially later than 1891 for import into the United States can be found unmarked! Thus, the absence of "Made in *Some Country*" or "*Some Country*" does not mean that the piece was made

prior to 1891. Shoes and other souvenir china made for the 1904 St. Louis World's Fair, for example, are often found with no mark whatsoever, including most of the shoes made for this event by Galluba and Hofmann. Also, shoes made for export to countries that did not require the country of origin to be marked and that have subsequently found their way into the United States or England cannot be assumed to be pre-*some specific date* because of the absence of the country-of-origin backstamp.

•**"Carlsbad" items produced for export also bearing "Bohemia" were made pre 1891; bearing "Austria", 1891-1918; bearing "Czechoslovakia", 1918-1993.**

•**The German Design Patent Law was passed 1 June 1891 and took effect 1 October 1891.** Items marked "DRGM" or "D.R.G.M." (Deutsches Reich Gebrauchs Muster) will post date October 1891.

•**Souvenir china with a Wheelock mark was made between 1895 and c.1920** when the company stopped importing souvenir china and specialized in other import china.

•**The year in which Quimper, France faience factories first added the word "Quimper" to their marks generally has been accepted as 1904, though this may have occurred as early as 1895.**

•**"Déposé", the French word for "registered", first appeared c.1900.** *See also "DEP", below.*

•**Souvenir china with the Roth name (JONROTH) and "Germany" as part of the backstamp were made c.1910 to no later than the 1930s.** John H. Roth & Co. did not renew business with its German suppliers after WWII.

•**The © symbol for copyright used to indicate registration with the U. S. Copyright Office is c.1914-present.**

•**"Bone china" as a part of a backstamp first appeared about 1915.**

•**DEP** (depose, French word for registered) **found on wares usually places their manufacture between about 1900 and 1918.** DEP (**dep**osited with the patent office) found on German wares also usually dates the piece between 1900 and 1918.

•**Wares with "Foreign" as their identifying mark usually were made in Germany immediately after WWI.** Because the British were reluctant to buy anything German following the end of WWI, some German manufacturers marked their items "Foreign", and sometimes incorrectly "Austria" or "Czechoslovakia". Some shoes can be found with an impressed mark "Foreign" on a straight line. Saxony is one factory known to have done that. A few shoes have been found marked "Foreign" that are known to have been made in the 1990s; this is an exception to this guideline.

•**Wares marked "Czechoslovakia" were made from about 1918 to 1993.** The Hapsburgs/Austrians ruled Bohemia for about three centuries, until the end of WWI, when the Austro-Hungarian Empire was dissolved. In 1918, Bohemia became independent of Austria. It joined with Moravia and Slovakia to form the country of Czechoslovakia on 28 October 1918. In 1948, three years after the end of WWII, Czechoslovakia became a satellite of the Soviet Union. In 1993, three years after the collapse of the Soviet Union, Czechoslovakia split into the Czech Republic and Slovakia, and their wares are now so marked.

•**Wares marked "Made in" may have started appearing in the United States as early as 1914, but in general most items bearing this designation are believed to have begun to appear beginning in 1921.** *Note date Great Britain required this marking.*

•**The word "Nippon" for the country of Japan was not allowed to be used unless also accompanied by "Japan" on US imports from Japan after 1921.** A US Treasury Department Decision of 1 March 1921 ruled that the "Marking of Japanese merchandise with the word 'Nippon' [was] not in compliance with the law" because "Nippon" is a Japanese word. Effective six months after the date of the decision, products coming into the United States from Japan had to be marked with the English word for the country, "Japan", although the word "Nippon" could accompany it. Therefore, Japanese products marked "Nippon", but not "Japan", are generally gauged as having been made between 1891 and 1921, unless other information about the item modifies the time period.

•**The use of "22 carat" in a bottom mark dates the piece to after the 1930s.**

•**Wares marked "U.S. Zone" or "U. S. Zone Germany" were made in Germany between 1945 and 1949. Wares marked "West Germany" or "East Germany" were made from 1949 to 1990.** At the conclusion of WWII in 1945, the Allies divided Germany into four occupation zones, one occupied by each of Great Britain, France, the United States, and the Soviet Union. "U. S. Zone" and "U. S. Zone Germany" marked merchandise was made in U.S.-occupied Germany from 1945 to 1949. In 1949, the three zones occupied by Great Britain, France, and the United States became the Federal Republic of Germany, known as West Germany. The Soviet zone became the German Democratic Republic, or East Germany, and remained under the control of the Soviet Union until it collapsed in 1990, when Germany was reunified.

•**Wares marked "Occupied Japan" are post 1946.** Japan bombed Pearl Harbor, Hawaii on 7 December 1941, thrusting the United States into a war with them. No new imports from Japan entered the United States during WWII. After the defeat of Japan, the United States occupied the country from 2 September 1945 until 28 April 1952. On 15 August 1947, the Japanese ceramics factories were permitted to send their products abroad, but they had to include in their backstamp the phrase "Occupied Japan". A US Customs Bureau decree of 18 February 1949 made it acceptable for Japan to mark its merchandise "Made in Occupied Japan", "Made in Japan", or "Occupied Japan". Given those choices, it is unlikely that many companies continued to use "Occupied" much longer. Nevertheless, it is fairly safe to say that an "Occupied Japan" piece was probably made between 1947 and 1952.

•**The ® registered symbol for a design legally registered with the U. S. Patent and Trademark Office has been used from 1949 to the present.** Although this symbol has only been used since 1949, trademark registration began in 1881.

•**Paper labels on imports are usually post WWII.** Although paper labels were used on some imports prior to WWII, the technology of applying them was in its infancy and they were subject to falling off with little provocation. This often resulted in the US Customs Bureau requiring importers to replace the labels with indelible ink backstamps. Improvement in the technology of applying paper labels allowed them to be used once again beginning in the 1950s.

Mold Design

The shape of the shoe and its in-mold designs can provide clues about its age. The design of many shoes was influenced by the style of the period. Rococo themes of scrolls, cartouches, and just over-decoration can be found in many Victorian era shoes. Tiny blue forget-me-nots also are often found on Victorian era shoes, the implied messages being those of love, or friendship, and luck. These themes were found on Victorian objects other than figural shoes, as seen on the postcard in Figure 42.

Trying to date a shoe by its mold design is susceptible to misinterpretation because once a design is made, it can be produced at any time thereafter. This provides one rule for dating that is truly valid. It is unlikely that any figural shoe was made *prior* to any real look-alike shoe on which it was patterned.

An antique dealer once sold this author a pair of "authentic" Jackfield Pottery high shoes that may have been intended as match holders. They had all the correct Jackfield characteristics: red clay base, lustrous gloss black glaze, some gold trim, and signs of age. They were unmarked, of course. Jackfield had decorated with oil colors and gilt, but had not refired their pieces to make the trim permanent. It would be very unusual to find any surviving pieces with much remaining gilt. That was a fit, too. The design included the nice touch of ribbed gussets on their sides, a feature that simulated elastic while serving as a striking surface for matches. They were a great find because all Jackfield Pottery is scarce, and the factory's dates of operation, 1713-1784, would make these among the oldest of the collection. They sat on a table near my desk for several days. Something about them was bothersome. The shape of the toe did not look like an 18th century shape. Finally, all the books came out. Delving through them and looking at 18th-century shoe shapes accidentally turned up an unassailable fact. Elastic side gussets were patented by J. Sparks Hall in 1837. The moral of the story is that all the elements of an unmarked shoe must be examined to attempt to place a date of manufacture on it.

Figure 42. A c.1900 postcard carrying the dual messages of luck, represented by the shoe, and love or friendship, represented by the forget-me-nots.

Identifying Unmarked Manufacturers' Products

Sketches

Of great interest to shoe collectors is a determination of the factory of origin. So many shoes are unmarked that such a determination is not often possible at first glance if at all. As I began the task of trying to organize unmarked shoes so that I could classify them by similar characteristics and so that the copies could be discerned from the originals, I began to make scale sketches of many shoes. These proved so helpful that I have included those that I made in the main body of this book alongside the descriptions of the illustrated shoes in the hope that they may prove useful to collectors. Sketches were generally not deemed necessary where the shoe is usually found well marked.

Sketches are especially useful when even the most careful photography fails to bring out mold details, either because the details are not sharp or because they have been obscured by layers of paint and glaze and can only been seen with a magnifying glass transcribed to the sketch. Dimensioned scale sketches help in focusing on the details of what was molded into the shoe, i.e., the in-mold detail, as well as the general shape. Sketches prove valuable to:

• See design similarities that help to group shoes by similar characteristics and that may aid in identifying the manufacturer of an unmarked shoe, as illustrated in Figure 43;

• Determine the original mold design from its modifications and copies, as illustrated in Figure 44;

• Distinguish similar shoe types from one another, as for example, Dutch shoes. Royal Bayreuth and Goss sabots are unique, and once seen are unlikely to be confused with other Dutch shoes. But sabots from other manufacturers are often similar to each other. Their shapes and dimensions must be carefully observed to identify an unmarked Dutch shoe. Another example can be seen in Figure 45, where three quilted baby bootees are shown that might at first glance be assumed to come from the same manufacturer. An examination of the sketches of them shows that they have different designs and proportions, making it unlikely that they were made by the same manufacturer.

• Help readers determine when shoes they have are a match to what is illustrated in this book.

Figure 43. Sketches of the in-mold detail of six shoes never found with a manufacturer's mark. It is impossible to examine the details of these six shoes without noticing their similar characteristics: art nouveau themes, proportions between the various parts of the shoe, and the floral design elements. The convergence of these characteristics in each shoe strongly suggests a high probability of their being made by the same manufacturer.

Figure 44. Galluba & Hofmann large Clover & Swirls shoe. In the photo, the left shoe has hand-applied star flowers. The matching sketch, shown below this shoe, shows only what is in-mold, and therefore does not show the starflowers or anything else that may have been applied after casting. In the photo on the right is the same shoe where the original mold was modified to incorporate the starflowers in-mold. Therefore, the sketch of this shoe, shown below it, reflects this in-mold characteristic. Note that the sketch does not show the row of starflowers down the center of the shoe on the right. They were applied after casting and are not a part of the modified mold design.

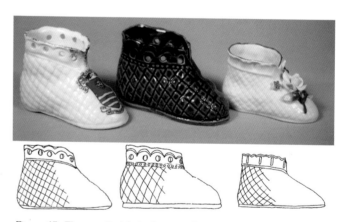

Figure 45. Three quilted baby bootees that appear with a cursory glance to have been made by the same manufacturer. Examination of the sketches shows them to have different design elements and proportions. They were made by three different manufacturers.

The most beneficial aspect of the sketches for readers may be that they illustrate exactly where to take measurements to determine whether a shoe in their collection is a match in size and/or proportions for one in this book.

Some cautions need to be expressed about the sketches to relieve my mind of any criticism of inaccuracy, for which I of course bear full burden. The sketches are exactly that, SKETCHES. They are **not** engineering drawings. The shape and proportions of the shoe outline are fairly accurate because it is clear where the shoe ends and the surrounding air begins, a rather evident observation. It is the design details that have been eyeballed.

First of all, I had to work from the example that I happened to have, usually a single example. If the shoe from which I produced the sketch was made at the end of the useful life of a particular mold, the in-mold details will not be sharp, and I may either not have been able to see them clearly even under magnification or perhaps not see them at all.

Second, painting and glazing on top of the in-mold detail will soften detail edges. If the paint or glaze is thick, much detail will be lost. The observation of in-mold detail is further complicated if it cannot be determined whether a painted detail is following an in-mold line now obscured by the paint or whether the decorator was just embellishing the design in the mold. An extra glob of paint inadvertently left on a critical part of the in-mold design by a decorator hurrying to complete an order may completely mask the detail attempted to be detected.

Occasionally, sketches will be found whose outlines are partially dashed. Generally this indicates either that the actual outline could not be discerned because it was obscured by appliqués or that it was desirable to show a part integral to the shoe but it was applied to the shoe in a separate operation.

Mold Design

Just as with trying to date a shoe or boot, its shape and the in-mold designs on it can often provide valuable clues when trying to determine who made it.

The Major German Manufacturers of Porcelain Shoes

By far, the largest numbers of pre-Depression porcelain shoes in the secondary market are German. They often are found with no mark whatsoever, including no country of origin. A substantial effort has been made trying to track down the source of as many as possible of these German porcelain shoes. Since most of them were made in the German state of Thuringia, it may be helpful to the reader to discover that in the time since the reunification of East and West Germany in 1990, a special project has been initiated in Thuringia pertaining to their historic place in the manufacture of porcelain. Thuringia was formerly a part of Soviet-occupied East Germany. Until 1990, it was nearly impossible to do any original research into its porcelain factories.

A century ago, Thuringia was the heart of the German porcelain industry. Among those to whom the industry can be traced there was Georg Heinrich Macheleid (1723-1801), who received permission on 8 September 1760 to found a porcelain factory in Sitzendorf. It was moved in 1762 to Volkstedt. By 1800, there were twelve porcelain manufacturers in Thuringia. By 1900, the number of porcelain factories had grown to 110, more than in any other German region. Growth was spurred by the abundant presence of kaolin-rich soils, quartz sand, and gypsum. The native dense forests provided easily accessible fuel for the kilns, and the many rivers provided the power necessary for the operation of the clay mixing and processing mills. The thriving Thuringian porcelain industry was severely curtailed by WWI and the worldwide economic crisis brought on by the Great Depression that began in 1929. WWII, Soviet occupation of East Germany, and the nationalization of porcelain factories into very large combined collectives under government ownership reduced the number of surviving factories even more. By the time the Soviet Union collapsed, East and West Germany reunified in 1990, and the remaining factories returned to private ownership, only a few of the once vibrant network of porcelain companies had survived.

In the spring of 1992, the museum in Eisfeld proposed establishing a "Porcelain Road" in Thuringia in a memo that it sent to the management of a few Thuringian porcelain companies, the tourist association Thueringer Wald in Suhl, and the federal museum Schloss Heidecksburg in Rudolstadt. The concept of a "Thuringian Porcelain Road" was to present the artistic and technological accomplishments associated with Thuringian porcelain by organizing a travel route that would provide visitors with easy access to sites of former and current porcelain manufacturing as well as museums. Work was officially begun on 8 September 1992. A map showing the sites available as of 2002 is shown in Figure 46. Material for this book on many Thuringian factories was derived from extremely accommodating people in the companies and museums during two trips along the Thuringian Porcelain Road in 1997 and 1998. The Road winds 340km (about 200 miles) from Weiden north to Coburg. Along it are numerous museums, local exhibition rooms, and factories that have their own outlet stores for bargain purchases. At the museums, visitors can learn about the history and production of German porcelain as well as see exhibits of the beautiful wares produced over two centuries of porcelain production in Thuringia.

Figure 46. Map of modern day Thuringia showing the Thuringian Porcelain Road, a travel route coordinated by a coalition of towns and factories that provides visitors with an organized way to access sites of former and current porcelain manufacturing as well as museums.

Marks

Many references on German porcelain refer to certain "Made in Germany" and "Germany" marks as generic, implying that they were used by many factories. Generic is a term that has especially been applied to millstone marks, those comprising a pair of concentric circles within which is some version of "Made in Germany". Observation has led this author to believe that many of these marks are not generic at all, but just "unknown" in terms of what specific factory used them. Whenever certain marks have been encountered on a shoe, the shoe has always been one that could be attributed to a group of shoes known from their designs and décors to have come out of the same factory, although the factory name may not yet have been identified. This observation may be of great help in aiding the reader to group their shoe collection by manufacturers, even though the name of that manufacturer awaits discovery.

Major German Manufacturers

For production volume and/or breadth of designs, the big six of German porcelain shoe manufacturers were Royal Bayreuth, Galluba & Hofmann, the Ilmenau Porcelain Factory, Arnstadt, Weiss Kühnert, and an unknown company dubbed Factory X by this author. The designs and décors of the highly collectible Royal Bayreuth have been so often copied that an effort has been made in the following paragraphs to establish identification criteria and sort through some of the more commonly misidentified copies. The examples of products by the other five in the illustrated central section of this book should provide the collector with sufficient information to identify them.

Royal Bayreuth Shoes

The shoes made by the Bavarian firm known in the United States as Royal Bayreuth are in demand by collectors, are usually unmarked, and have been among the most copied of shoes. Further, Bayreuth is often attributed for shoes they did not make. Therefore, it seems appropriate to devote some effort to spelling out the criteria one looks for in identifying a Royal Bayreuth shoe and in identifying some of the shoes most often mistaken as having been made by the Bayreuth factory. The analytical process involved may also be useful to the student of shoes who wishes to establish criteria that distinguish the products of other shoe factories.

To date, over fifty different shoe models have been identified as Royal Bayreuth, each in distinguishable lefts and rights. Many of these models were made in numerous décors as well as different color combinations. The earliest of them probably go back to about 1885. They all look like miniature versions of real shoes, including fabric shoelaces with metal aglets if the real shoe from which the miniature was modeled would have required them. It is important to emphasize that the shoes identified as Royal Bayreuth in this book, some of which are not known to ever have been found marked, are **believed** to have been made by the factory based on all the characteristics unique to the factory's shoes and the combined wisdom of many Bayreuth shoe collectors—including the author, who has been collecting them for nearly forty years.

Royal Bayreuth shoes fall into three categories: tapestries, sabots, and figurals. A representative of each is shown in Figure 47. While all porcelain and pottery shoes in this text can be referred to as "figurals", the term used when referring to RB shoes is chosen to distinguish between the tapestries, sabots, and "all the others". In general, the characteristics to look for in authentic RB shoes are the following:

• thin porcelain.
• always shaped like real shoes that were manufactured from the late 1800s to the early 1900s.

• distinguishable lefts and rights.
• distinctive details in the figurals like stitching detail, perf, and broguing where they would be found on a real shoe. In figurals, which usually are not marked, these are especially important to look for as are other key details like the factory's usual painting of the insides and bottoms in a light tan to look like new leather, and its typical color combinations that include, but are not limited to, gloss brown and matte camel, gloss and matte black, and matte ivory with peach trim.

Figure 47. Representative members of the three general categories of Royal Bayreuth shoes. From the left, a tapestry, a sabot, and a figural are illustrated. The tapestries derive their name from the textured surface on them. The sabots are all the same shape but can be found in numerous décors. The figurals look like the real shoes that would have been worn in the years around 1900. Technically, all three could be called "figurals". However, if a RB shoe has a woven, textured surface, it automatically falls into the category of "tapestry". Likewise, if it is a RB sabot, it automatically falls into that category. All others are classified as RB figurals.

Many German factories chose to make a shoe design in several sizes as a routine practice. Royal Bayreuth is not one of them. With rare exceptions, the factory made only one size in a shoe. One of the exceptions is shown in Figure 48 where a typical size RB shoe is shown along with its unusual miniature version. A second exception is shown in Figure 49 where a typical size RB sabot is shown along with an uncommon smaller version.

Figure 48. A Royal Bayreuth 11-button figural shoe alongside an unusual smaller version of the shoe, the latter an exception to the factory's habit of generally making a shoe in only one size.

Figure 49. A Royal Bayreuth nursery rhyme standard size sabot alongside an uncommon smaller version with a hunt scene.

Although RB did not normally make the same shoe in multiple sizes, there is evidence that the factory may have formed off of some of their standard line of shoes to produce blanks that they may have sold to others to decorate. Such a shoe is shown in Figure 50. It is a small version of a well-known RB shoe that has the same in-mold details, but has other features that are atypical for RB. Two of these stand out. The glaze is not one known on recognized RB shoes, and there is a four-digit number, 1772, impressed into the right side of the heel.

Figure 50. A 3-15/16"-inch long shoe that apparently was formed off of a larger Royal Bayreuth shoe and may have been sold as a blank to a decorating shop.

Occasionally, a shoe is found that apparently has been formed off an authentic Royal Bayreuth shoe by some unknown factory. Examples are shown in Figures 51 and 52.

Figure 51. An authentic but unmarked Royal Bayreuth spat on the left, with an unmarked fake on the right. The fake has give-away details such as the thick rim, filled-in strap at the buckle, peculiarly-shaped buttons, and the lack of hand-painted stitching details.

Figure 52. An authentic, marked, contemporary Royal Bayreuth shoe on the left and its unmarked pretender on the right. Like the RB shoe, the copy has decal décor, but is smaller and has only four pairs of open eyelets aside the open vee.

Royal Bayreuth appears to have modified the molds of some of their shoes and made blanks for decorating shops. Figure 53 shows a well-known RB shoe in brown and its counterpart decorated by Franziska Hirsch. Except for the shape of the opening between the seven sets of open eyelets, all the in-mold details of the shoes are the same. Ironically, the hand-painted Hirsch shoe is somewhat more valuable in today's market because of its meticulous detailing in the Dresden mode. In 1997, Herold of the Bayreuth factory supported the supposition that the factory sold shoe blanks in this translation

from the German: "…a great number [of shoes] were produced and sold in solid white and then decorated and fired in small shops. We have never kept track of these beautifications and designs." It has been the author's experience that contemporary factory personnel, especially those in German factories, often do not possess the institutional memory to provide answers to questions pertaining to things that happened a century or more ago. In this case, however, the evidence clearly supports the response.

Figure 53. A brown lace-up shoe from the Royal Bayreuth factory and a version of the same shoe sold as a blank and decorated by the Dresden decorating shop of Franziska Hirsch.

Evidence also suggests that RB made different molds for the same design shoe. The 4 x 4 (four pairs open eyelets, four pairs grommets), two-tone, swept back toe cap, ladies high tops in Figure 54, for example, would both be described the same verbally. Yet they are clearly from different molds. Another example is the ladies low-cut tapestry oxford. It is known in both blunt toe and tapered toe versions, as seen in Figure 55. The men's dress oxford can be found with and without in-mold stitching on its sole. Possibly, the original molds were lost in the devastating fire that leveled the factory in 1897. Whatever the reason, variations in the molds occur in some RB shoes of the same basic design. This often is not evident until two shoes are compared side by side. For collectors trying to match up a left with a right, or vice versa, it is important either to have the two shoes together to see if the molds are a match, or to have accurate measurements and descriptions of the critical design features. It becomes especially important to have the two shoes together to match the colors because so many variations of shades of colors exist. What is referred to as RB camel color, for example, can vary from a light shade to almost orange.

Figure 54. Two Royal Bayreuth ladies high top shoes of the same design but cast from different molds.

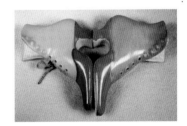

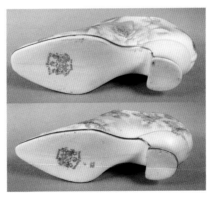

Figure 55. Bottom views of two Royal Bayreuth rose tapestry, ladies oxfords. The blunt-toe version, above, may be the older design. The tapered-toe version, below, is always slightly longer than the blunt-toe version. Both shown have the Bayreuth blue mark usually found on tapestry oxfords and high-tops.

Royal Bayreuth shoe collectors are always happy to find shoes with original laces. These laces are of a woven material with metal aglets, or tips. The author once asked the factory if they might have any spare shoelaces in a back room that could be purchased. They responded with astonishment and claimed that the factory **never** put shoelaces in their shoes! Not for one instant was it plausible to the author that the importers, distributors, or retailers placed all those shoelaces in all those shoes. They came out of the factory that way. This is just another example of institutional memory being lost because there have been several generations of people in the factory between the time the shoes were made and now.

The author has many RB shoes with their original laces. Several of them are laced in a peculiar way. It appears that the lace was often, but not always, started at the top, threaded through the holes all the way to the bottom, and then brought back to the top open hole all the way from the bottom. This suggests that they had a device, perhaps a large curved needle with a large eye like those used on canvas, which allowed the rapid threading of the cloth lace through the holes. The cloth lacing material was probably contained on a roll, as shown in Figure 56. When the shoe had been laced, the end attached to the roll was cut, and the metal aglets were crimped on to the raw ends to prevent them from raveling. The supposition that the metal aglets were crimped on the lace ends after the shoe was laced is supported by the fact that on some Royal Bayreuth shoes, the aglet will not fit through the eyelet. Thus, it could not have been laced with the aglet already in place. The holes for the open eyelets were usually drilled after the shoe was cast, but while it was still in the green ware stage. Burrs can be felt on the insides of many shoes with open eyelets.

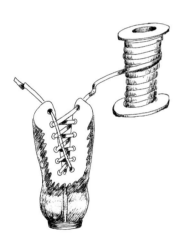

Figure 56. Sketch of method that may have been used to lace Royal Bayreuth lace-up shoes. Using a curved tool with a large eye, a scheme such as shown in this sketch would have allowed the rapid lacing of a shoe whose small eyelets would have made the operation difficult and time-consuming if done in the conventional way.

The credence of the factory's contention that RB shoes were not provided with laces as a part of the factory finishing operation was further eroded when the documents submitted for a British registration were tracked down. There is a RB men's shoe commonly referred to by collectors as "the white buck" because it resembles the white bucks worn by college men of the early and mid 20th century. Some of the RB versions can be found with a rectangular box on the bottom within which is "Rd No 335843", which is a British Registration mark. The number code was traced and it was found that the shoe had been registered in the British Commissioner of Patents Journal on 27 March 1899 to Porzellanfabrik Tettau, Vormals, Sontag and Sohne, Tettau, Bavaria, Germany. When copies of the sketches submitted by the factory were acquired, it was discovered that one of the cut-away drawings showed another version of what would be considered a bizarre lacing scheme if the manner in which the job was performed had not already been deduced. Some of the submitted sketches are shown in Figure 57. They are of interest for a number of reasons. Among them are the illustrations of the painted inner sole

found on this shoe as well as the typical light tan painting of the inside to imitate real leather. Both are characteristics found on certain RB shoes and not on shoes made by other manufacturers of that era, except in the few instances where a company was trying to imitate **all** the design elements of a RB shoe.

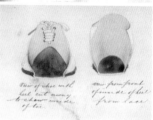

Figure 57. Sketches submitted to the British Registry in 1899 by the Royal Bayreuth factory. The bottom left sketch of the inside of the shoe illustrates the result of using the time efficient manner devised by the factory to lace up the shoe.

Royal Bayreuth shoes were so popular with the public that it was inevitable they would be copied by other factories. Some of the copies were deliberately painted in RB color schemes. Others were simply created to look like a RB shoe. In Figures 58 to 65 are some of those shoes that are commonly misidentified as Royal Bayreuth.

Figure 58. On the left is a Royal Bayreuth Victor shoe. In the middle is a shoe made by Schmidt Victoria. On the right is a shoe made by Carl Scheidig that is often misidentified as Royal Bayreuth, especially when it is found with the same color combination found on the RB shoe from which it was copied. The Scheidig shoe usually has an impressed "3586" on the right side of its heel, and it is longer than the RB shoes, as is the Schmidt Victoria version.

Figure 59. Comparison of Royal Bayreuth ladies high top, on the left, with two versions of a Saxony shoe. While a cursory look suggests that the smaller shoes may have been formed off the RB shoe, their backs reveal the most obvious difference. The RB shoe has a narrow, triangular back seam, while the Saxony back seams are a pair of parallel lines.

Figure 60. Four boots from the Schmidt Victoria factory, three of which were intentionally painted in RB colors. Those on the extreme left and extreme right have Schmidt Victoria marks. The other two are unmarked but come from the same molds as the marked boots of the same size.

Figure 63. A Royal Bayreuth shoe on the left and a shoe inspired by it on the right. The men's oxford on the right can be found in at least two sizes, the other being smaller and close in size to the RB. Shoes from this unknown factory are referred to in this book as DGCWs (Dip Glazed Chalk Whites). On some of them, stitching detail was painted on to make them resemble Royal Bayreuth oxfords.

Figure 61. A Czechoslovakian shoe, on the left, that was inspired by the Royal Bayreuth shoe, on the right. The Czech shoe has been painted a light tan on its inside and bottom, characteristics often found on Royal Bayreuth figural shoes, but it is a "straight", whereas Royal Bayreuth shoes come in distinguishable lefts and rights.

Figure 64. Two sizes of DGCW men's oxfords. Just visible on each is the characteristic band of glazing on the inside, below which the shoe is unglazed. The larger of these two is the same shoe as that shown in the previous illustration, but in a gloss brown glaze thinned at the rim and eyelet edges.

Figure 62. A Royal Bayreuth shoe on the left and a shoe inspired by it on the right. The shoe on the right is double-walled, i.e., a second casting with an oval-shaped bottom has been fitted inside the shoe casting and the two connected at the top rim during the green ware stage. The intention apparently was to provide a regularly shaped container that would allow the shoe to be used to hold something, as toothpicks or a small bouquet. Several features of this shoe make it unlikely that it was made by RB. Prime among them are the fact that the in-mold detail of shoe seams is poorly defined, painted trim details are atypical of RB, and the double-walled form itself is an anomaly in RB shoe products. On the other hand, it is a well-constructed shoe whose open flaps required technical skill to form. This shoe is reported to have been seen with an "Austria" bottom mark.

Figure 65. A Galluba & Hofmann textured Peony boot that is often misidentified as a Royal Bayreuth tapestry piece. The texture was achieved in-mold, i.e., designed into the mold and achieved during casting. The texture on RB tapestries was achieved in-kiln, i.e., coarse material was laid over the surface of the green ware piece and then kiln-fired, which burned up the material but left a fabric-like surface ready to be decorated.

Souvenir Shoes

Some shoe collectors specialize in Royal Bayreuth shoes. Others collect only miniature shoes, perhaps because space is at a premium in their homes. The category of souvenir shoes will receive attention here because it provides insight into their production as a category and because they provide so many clues to otherwise unidentified shoes, especially those made in Germany.

Souvenir china, view china, pictorial souvenir china, and scenic china are four terms for the same items. Souvenir china is any ceramic piece carrying an image and/or name of a location or scene that was made and purchased primarily as a memento of a place visited. To this day, such pieces can be purchased new all over the world. In this book, however, souvenir china refers to those items manufactured from the late 1800s to the early 1900s.

Although they were produced for *everyday* use, the historical blue china made in Staffordshire, England beginning about 1820 probably originated the concept of presenting scenes of various countries on inexpensive ceramics. Historical Staffordshire dinnerware is now contained primarily in private collections and museums. But the souvenir china made c.1900 is available in the secondary market and much of it is affordable. The earliest of them tended to be small, making it easy for a tourist to fit it in a pocket, handbag, or suitcase. The fact that so many have survived for about a century in such remarkable condition is partly due to the high quality of their fabrication, even though they were mass-produced. It is also partly due to so many of them having been put away in drawers or trunks for a century.

The biggest market for souvenir china made about a century ago was the United States, due largely to several aggressive American importers and distributors. The two primary firms were C. E. Wheelock & Co. (1888-1971) and John H. Roth & Co. (1909-present), whose trademark was JONROTH. Both were located in Peoria, Illinois. Wheelock imported and distributed souvenir china from 1895 to about 1920. Roth went into competition directly against Wheelock. He imported and distributed German souvenir china from about 1910 until the 1930s.

In the first decade of the 1900s, Wheelock had up to fifteen salesmen on the road at a time. Typically, they would visit a local storeowner and interest him in ceramics that displayed appealing local scenes for the tourist trade. As a selling point, an offer would be made to place the merchant's name and town on each piece. Scenes for the pieces were often selected from a rack of postcards. Orders from the importers/distributors were sent to Germany or England because America did not have an extensive ceramics industry c.1900. The German wares were hard paste porcelain and the German factories were the source of souvenir china shoes (really, souvenir *porcelain* shoes).

The German factories produced finely detailed steel or copper engravings from the postcards or whatever other sources of views had been provided, scaled and sized for the pieces that would be decorated. Color (black, for souvenir china) was spread on the heated engraving, the excess carefully removed, and tissue paper placed over the engraving. The paper and engraving were passed through a press to impress the engraved image onto the paper. The images on the tissue were carefully cut out by hand and positioned before being rubbed down on the ware, using something like a stiff bristle brush lubricated with soft soap. Some souvenir china was decorated with the single color applied from the engraving transfer process. If the scenes were to be colored, they typically were painted directly on the porcelain by local artisans following the lines of the transferred engraving. A subsequent kiln firing affixed the view. Thus, colored German view china usually has scenes enhanced with hand-painting that are about a century old and that document the way the nation looked in that age. They are genuine historic artifacts whose value increases with time.

Many German souvenir china shoes show evidence that they were never originally intended to be used in this way. Rather, they were adapted for this purpose, and in some cases the molds were modified to take on scenes. There was a large demand for porcelain shoes in the late 1800s that caused many German factories to design molds for them. When the souvenir china craze hit a bit later, many German factories simply used molds already on hand to take on the scenic transfers, as the shoe shown in Figure 66 illustrates. The in-mold beading wanders through several areas of the picture. It strains the imagination to believe that a shoe designed for the express purpose of showcasing a scene would ever be designed with an in-mold pattern going through the space reserved for the view. The observant collector will often find this occurrence in souvenir shoes. It does not lower the value of the piece, but is simply a record of the enterprising factories.

Figure 66. German souvenir china shoe illustrating the adaptive reuse of a mold originally designed for some other décor than a scene on its vamp.

Figure 67. Three Worlds Fair souvenir china boots from the same German factory.

Most souvenir china is marked with at least the country of origin. Matching marked souvenir china shoes to unmarked porcelain shoes from the same mold allowed the author to identify the country of origin of a number of shoes whose country of origin could not previously be certain.

To souvenir collectors in general, it is the scene and its craftsmanship that are the primary factors in determining its value. Collectors from other fields search for particular topics such as occupations, lighthouses, ships, and railroads. Scenes from small towns are avidly pursued. Shoes with scenes sought by crossover collectors will automatically have a higher than normal value. The primary color of a souvenir piece also influences value. Cobalt blue and the uncommon brown, plum, and green are highly valued, so shoes in these colors have a premium on their value.

Worlds Fair souvenirs comprise a subset of souvenir china. Some collect only mementos of these fairs, making any shoes from them more valuable than the same shoe with a scene less in demand. Figure 67 shows three Worlds Fair souvenir china boots from the same German factory.

Inspirations, Modifications, and Fakes

Of considerable interest to some collectors is the evolution of figural shoe design. Many shoes were inspired by earlier designs. For example, some of the much-hunted Royal Worcester shoes appear to have been motivated by models preceding them. The pair of shoes in the collection of the Rijksmuseum in Amsterdam shown in Figure 68 may have stimulated the design of the Royal Worcester shoes shown in Figure 69. This fact does not detract from the value of the Royal Worcester shoes, for they are avidly collected because of the quality of their décor and craftsmanship.

Figure 68. Pair of faience shoes, c.1750-1790, in the collections of the Rijksmuseum, Amsterdam, The Netherlands.

Figure 69. Pair of English porcelain shoes, c.1873, manufactured by Royal Worcester, Worcester, England.

Inspirations for shoes knew no boundaries between countries and were not limited to the Japanese, who are most often thought of as having gained their main post WWII design motivations from older European wares. Following are two illustrations that demonstrate how good ideas were borrowed by German factories.

Figure 71. The Meissen crushed-heel slipper on the left has inspired numerous copies, one of which is the contemporary German shoe on the right that carries a Dresden mark but can be found marked in other ways.

A number of examples can be found where American Victorian glass shoes may have served as the models for porcelain shoes that are believed to have been made later. What suggests that some of the glass shoes were made earlier is the detail in them. The less distinct detail in the porcelain models suggests that they were the copies. Two examples of glass and porcelain shoes with the same design are shown in Figures 72 and 73. A third example of similarity between glass and porcelain shoe mold design is illustrated in Figure 74.

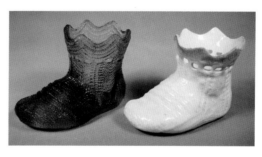

Figure 72. The amber glass bootee with knitted pattern by the King Glass Company of Pittsburgh, c.1880s (3-5/8"L x 2-5/8"H), may have been the inspiration for Heubach's porcelain baby bootee (3-1/2"L x 2-1/2"H), though the reverse could be true if the Heubach bootee can be dated earlier.

Figure 73. The attached pair of amber glass baby shoes by the King Glass Company of Pittsburgh, c.1880s, may have been the inspiration for the pair of porcelain baby shoes on the right, believed to be German.

Figure 70. The Gien, France c.1875 spade-toe heeled slipper on the left may have been the inspiration for the Conta & Boehme, Germany c.1900 spade-toe slipper on the right.

Figure 74. The porcelain shoe on the left came from the Charles Ahrenfeldt decorating studio. The factory that supplied the blank has yet to be determined. The c.1880s two-piece milk glass shoe of unknown manufacturer on the right has the same dimensions and proportions on its lower body and its rear quarter latticework is identical in shape and nodes to that on the porcelain shoe. Who was inspired by whom is a matter for speculation.

During the Victorian period, there were many shoes made in various metals, from sterling silver to brass to white metal. Figure 75 illustrates a brass shoe that may have been the inspiration for the porcelain shoe shown with it.

Figure 75. The 5-1/2" long heavily patined brass shoe with hand-tooled detail and leather laces on the left may have been the inspiration for the uncommon shoe on the right made of tinted porcelain with detailed white porcelain appliqués that mimic in every detail the proportions and detail of the brass shoe.

There are certain shoe shapes that need to trigger a healthy skepticism when encountered. One such shape is shown in Figure 76. The exquisitely decorated version on the left is well identified with an impressed mark that makes it plausible that it came from the factory identified. The beautifully hand-painted version to its right has a mark associated with a factory that was in existence in the second half of the 1700s. It is difficult to believe that this shoe is that old, though it certainly appears to date from the 1800s, and has significant value for its décor. But it is unlikely that it came from the factory implied by the bottom mark. Accounting for all the décors and marks found on this shape shoe presents a dilemma unless its mold was passed around to numerous factories over several centuries. This same shoe shape has cropped up in a very nice Italian renaissance décor on a white ground with a bottom mark that reads "VRBINO", under which is "1600". It can also be found in a Longwy type décor with a fake Longwy mark. The version seen done in this way has a turquoise ground with pink flowers and is shown in Figure 77. The worth of such a Longwy fake is strictly in its decorative appeal.

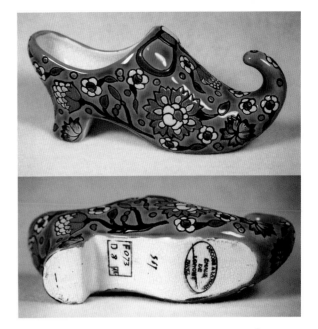

Figure 77. Fake Longwy contemporary clog manufactured by the Faïence de Saint-Germain-sur-Morin77 in France. The bottom mark, which includes "ÉMAUX DE LONGWY FRANCE" might lead an unsuspecting buyer to believe that the piece was made by the factory in Longwy.

Another shoe shape that crops up with various marks, most of which are suspect, is shown in Figure 78. The illustrated shoe is very well crafted and the hand-painted lady in a garden is well done. These qualities will set the value of the piece, not its mark, which is almost certainly a fake Perrin signature. This particular mark consisting of a capital V and a capital P that share an upright line is a mark that can be found on numerous items that did not come out of the Perrin factory. Cushion warns, "The marks of this factory are much copied on forgeries." (pg. 33)

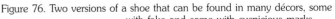

Figure 78. A shoe shape that can be found in many décors, often with marks that are suspect.

Figure 76. Two versions of a shoe that can be found in many décors, some with fake and some with suspicious marks. Left: a meticulously decorated version with hammered metallic trim and cobalt interior with the impressed mark of Vieillard & Co. that appears to be from that factory; right: a tin-glazed version with skillfully hand-painted scene with standing lady that has a suspicious mark like that used by the Veuve Perrin factory.

Over the years, certain types of décors became popular and invited imitation. The list is too long for a book of this nature, but there are memorable examples like delftware, the blue onion pattern, and the straw flower pattern. Certain factories have become known for certain patterns, and differentiating the authentic from the imitation often requires extensive study and experience. An example out of the mainstream is shown in Figure 79. It appears to be an unmarked piece from the elusive Chaumeil faience works in Paris, France (See *Chaumeil* in manufacturers' section) because it has so many of the characteristics of this pottery. Included are the loop-and-dot pattern, the two-tone orange and yellow fleur de-lys, the black ermine tails, and the green fire-breathing salamander, motifs found in many of the châteaux of the Loire. Even the coarse crackle glaze suggests a fit. But the bottom dispels any question about the piece. The clay is not red and the inscription marks it as a souvenir made for sale at Chaumont-sur-Loire. Novelties like this sabot were made to be sold in souvenir shops outside many of the châteaux. This one probably was made in Desvres.

Figure 80. Glazed white ceramic copies of piked-toe German slippers made by unknown manufacturers. L-R: unmarked, 5-1/2"L x 2-5/8"H; unmarked, 5-5/16"L x 2-5/8"H; gold shield paper label with green printing, "Knox/Imperial/Hand/Painted", 4-3/16"L x 2"H.

Figure 81. Glazed white ceramic unmarked copies formed off Galluba & Hofmann boots by unknown producer, probably 1950s-1960s. L-R: form-off of G & H Daisy boot, 4-1/16"L x 4"H; form-off of G & H Peony boot, 3-3/8"L x 3-5/16"H.

Figure 82. Four of the numerous copies of the Galluba & Hofmann Bear Claw slipper. These are unmarked, white ceramic, and probably made in the 1950s or 1960s. L-R: 4-11/16"L x 2-3/16"H; 4-3/16"L x 2-3/16"H; 4-7/8"L x 2-3/8"H; and 4-7/8"L x 2-5/16"H.

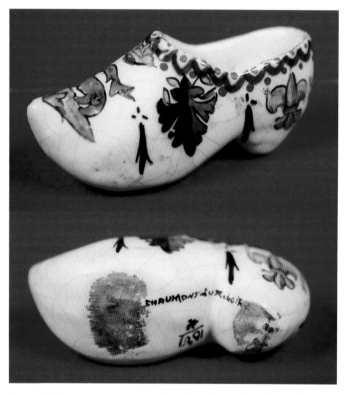

Figure 79. French faience sabot with pattern that imitates the motifs found on many Alcide Chaumeil wares.

Collectors will need to be alert to shoes that have been modified by amateur ceramicists. Their value will depend on whether the enhancement makes the piece of more interest and whether it is of interest to the individual collector.

There are large numbers of shoes in the secondary market that are copies of c.1900 German shoes. Some of the copies are porcelain, but most are of a white pottery or ceramic. Typically, they are unmarked. Most were probably made post WWII. Some appear to have been directly formed off an original German shoe. With the exception of souvenir shoes, where the view portrayed is collectible, these shoes have little but decorative value. By far, the most copied shoes were originally made by Galluba & Hofmann. Common examples are shown in the following three illustrations.

Fakes are anything designed to intentionally fool the prospective purchaser. They are the aggravation of every collector, and shoe collectors have their share of fake shoes with which to contend. In this section are some of the more flagrant examples—those with fake marks intended to trick the purchaser into believing something has been found when it is nothing but a phony piece that will distress the buyer when its identity is uncovered. In particular, this section deals with those shoes that began appearing somewhere in the 1970s or 1980s and continue to be found in importers' catalogs. Unfortunately, they are also showing up in the secondary market, often passed off as something they are not. Originally, they may have been manufactured in Japan or Taiwan. Some or most may currently be from China.

One of the most elegant shoes ever designed is the Royal Bayreuth high top tapestry shown in Figure 83. It is 4-1/2"L x 3-1/2"H. In Figure 84 are four shoes of the same shape, but larger. They are all about 5-3/4"L x 4-1/16"H. And every one of them has a fake mark, from R.S. Prussia to Meissen. Brand new, these were still selling in American importers' catalogs of the 1990s for a little over $10 each. The décors on the shoes with the fake R. S. Prussia and Limoges marks may actually have been inspired by authentic wares. Figure 85 shows an authentic Limoges, France plate with a hand-painted daisy motif. Beside it is a contemporary shoe with a similar design, made in China, but carrying a misleading bottom mark.

Figure 83. Royal Bayreuth high top tapestry (textured surface) shoe.

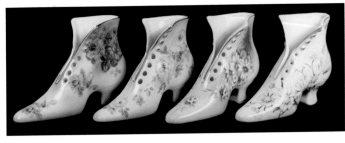

Figure 84. Four contemporary high top glazed (smooth, shiny surfaces) shoes with fake marks. From left, they have a fake R. S. Prussia mark, another fake R. S. Prussia mark, a fake Meissen-type mark, and a fake mark with "Limoges" as a part of the logo.

Figure 85. This hand-painted antique porcelain plate made in the town of Limoges, France may have been the inspiration for the floral pattern on the shoe, which has a misleading "Limoges China" mark that can lead to a belief that the shoe is French. The shoe is contemporary and believed to have been made in China.

Similar to the four with fake marks shown in Figure 85 is the shoe shown in Figure 86. In this shoe there are in-mold design features that include grommets, a bow, and horizontal laces. The shoe has a fake Nippon wreath mark, as shown. To the unwary buyer, the mark would indicate that the shoe was made between 1891 and 1921, when a bottom mark bearing the word "Nippon" was acceptable under United States importing laws. However, the shoe was probably made in Japan in the 1980s or 1990s. The only genuine Nippon shoes seen by the author are all shaped like small Dutch shoes.

Figure 86. Contemporary porcelain shoe with fake Nippon mark, 5-11/16"L x 4"H.

Figure 87 shows another pair of contemporary shoes, one of which has a fake R. S. Prussia mark. The other, from the same mold, has a legitimate 1987-copyrighted decal label on its shank and a paper label indicating it was made in Japan and suggesting the origin of the shoe with the fake mark.

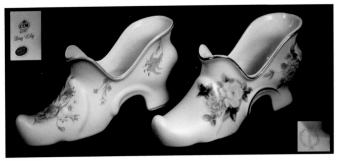

Figure 87. Two shoes from the same mold, the one on the left with a legitimate 1987 © decal mark and a "Made in Japan" paper label, and the one on the right with a fake R.S. Prussia mark.

Certain Galluba & Hofmann shoes are among the most copied of all shoes. In the section of this book that illustrates shoes, their descriptions, and values, there is a large section on Galluba & Hofmann products. Shoe collectors will recognize many there, and will likely have some in their own collection. The beautiful proportions of these shoes and the lovely Art Nouveau in-mold designs on many of them have been too tempting to resist for many manufacturers since the 1900s. Once the originals have been studied, it is easy to spot the copies. They have been made in both porcelain and various ceramic materials, often coarsely detailed and crafted. One particular example of a G & H copy that should be pointed out because it bears a fake R. S. Prussia mark is shown in Figure 88. The authentic G & H large Geranium slipper is on the left. The copy with the fake mark is on the right.

Figure 88. An authentic Galluba & Hofmann large Geranium slipper on the left with a copy of it on the right that is sporting a fake R. S. Prussia mark.

Once the reticulated George Owen shoes in the Historic Shoes section are seen, it is easy to spot the imitations and know precisely from what these shoes were copied. The market has been flooded with shoes like those shown in Figure 89. In a 1999 American importers' catalog, they were boxed in cartons of twenty sets of three shoes per set at a price of $35 per set, or a little under $12 each, brand new. They are believed to have been made in China.

Figure 89. Assortment of contemporary reticulated shoes copied from a famous George Owen shoe. These were sold through a 1999 American importers' catalog for just under $12 each. Some of them sport misleading marks, as shown.

Among the most egregious appropriations of an artist's work is one seen in Figure 90. On the right is a shoe sold through the San Francisco *Museum of Jewelry* catalog beginning in about August 1996. In a call to this company, the author was told that the shoe was made in China, though confirmation of this has not been able to be made through an additional source. Wherever it was made, it is a fake Gainsborough Collection *Sophie* shoe, an authentic version of which is shown on the left. Fortunately, the Gainsborough shoe is always so marked and the two shoes are easy to tell apart. The authentic Gainsborough Collection shoe has an applied porcelain silver buckle and the porcelain is a brilliant clear white. In the fake, the buckle is in-mold, and the porcelain has an off-white gray tone. Intriguing in this tale is the fact that the Lankester mold for *Sophie*, a distinguishable "right", disappeared years ago from the English factory commissioned by Lankester to cast it. The *Museum of Jewelry* fake Lankester is an exact replica in its size, in the unique indentations on the heel counter, and in its décor. And even though the *Museum of Jewelry* advertised "pairs", all turned out to be distinguishable "rights". The manufacturer was apparently unable to market "lefts" because there was no Lankester mold for a left.

Figure 90. An authentic and so marked Gainsborough Collection shoe on the left with its copy on the right. The authentic shoe has an applied silver buckle, while the fake has an in-mold buckle.

Lefts, Rights, Mates, and Straights

Most porcelain and pottery shoes manufacturers made shoes known as *straights*, i.e., the shape of the shoe had no distinguishing curves that would identify it as intended for either the right foot or the left foot. It is usually easiest to see whether a shoe is shaped to wear on the left or right side by looking at its bottom. With the exception of a few manufacturers such as Royal Bayreuth and Longwy, which only made sabots and made them in only one size, very few manufacturers who made distinguishable lefts and rights made **both** lefts and rights. In Figure 91 is a pair of Royal Bayreuth sabots, one a left and the other a right. Note the off-center vamp peak that emphasizes the one-sidedness of each. In addition, these hand-painted sabots have asymmetrical vamp décors. On each, the blue floral vine trails to the inside of the vamp, again emphasizing the one-sidedness of each shoe. *Mates* are a pair of shoes that are not shaped like a distinguishable left or right, but have some other feature that suggests that there is a mate. Notable among these features are those shoes that are straights, but can be found with buttons on the left side and with buttons on the right side. These are referred to as mates. In this text, unless otherwise stated, shoes are assumed to be straights.

The designers at Royal Bayreuth not only initiated miniature porcelain shoes that looked just like the shoe fashions of the era, but they memorialized the advent of lefts and rights in real shoes. Real shoes made on lasts that were shaped for the asymmetrical curves of each foot were first made in 1818. But they continued to be made by hand, making them available to only the wealthy. Machines that stitched shoe parts together quickly and cheaply were in operation by the mid 1800s, but the first practical lasting machine was not designed until 1883, so it was the end of the 1800s before nearly everyone could afford a pair of shoes. It is not clear whether it was the manufacturers who were slow to provide women with distinguishable lefts and rights, or whether it was the women who were slower to adopt them. But women's real shoes continued to be made as straights until about 1900. The availability of real shoes in lefts and rights for the general populace may have been an additional reason for their figural representations to be of such intrigue to buyers of the turn of the last century.

Figure 91. Pair of Royal Bayreuth sabots, one a distinguishable left and the other a distinguishable right. The off-center vamp peaks emphasize the one-sidedness of each shoe.

Shoe Slang

So many figural shoes are unmarked and their manufacturers unknown, that a sort of slang has evolved to quickly describe them. The following terms are examples.

•**Cabinet shoes.** It was common to design Victorian pieces to be used in cabinets or on mantles, where only one side would be visible. This led to the production of pieces decorated on only one side. Catalogs of the period referred to them as *cabinet* pieces, or *mantle* pieces. For example, on page 224 of the Spring 1903 Butler Brothers wholesale catalog, the heading for a figurine was described as "Imported China Mantel or Cabinet Ornament".

•**Church key shoe.** Along the side rims of some shoes is a vertical protrusion whose outline resembles a portion of an old-fashioned church key, and which has provided a quick way to verbally describe the particular shoe.

•**Crushed heel slipper.** Some people slip on their bedroom slippers never fully inserting their feet, resulting in the rear being crushed flat against the inner sole as shown in Figure 92. This shape ceramic slipper has been made famous by Meissen and has been manufactured by many other companies.

Figure 92. Trade card dated 1883 illustrating a "crushed heel slipper". A porcelain Meissen crushed heel slipper may have been the model for this artist's rendering.

•**DGCW.** An acronym for the Dip Glazed Chalk Whites. The shoes with this designation probably all came from the same factory, though its identity is unknown. Most of the shoes have been dipped upside down in the glaze, then righted for the remainder of the glaze application on the outside. This has resulted in a band of glaze along the inside of the rim, below which the shoe is unglazed. When care-fully washed to remove any grime, the porcelain is found to be fine-grained, very white, and chalky to the touch.

•**Fantasy shoe.** They are the large shoes generally found with one or two angels perched on them that are so elaborate they would be worn only in someone's fantasy.

•**Gangster shoe.** There is a group of shoes apparently made by the same, although unknown, manufacturer. Several of them feature spats with green shoes, like those worn by well-dressed dandies and gangsters of the early 1900s. Until the manufacturer of these shoes is identified, the nickname is a convenient way to refer to this group of shoes.

•**Gold face.** Reducing the labor intensity of hand-decorated, mass-produced novelties coming out of German factories about a century ago was achieved in many ways. One was to paint only the front of a piece, usually in gold, which gave rise to the designation, "gold face". This is especially found on souvenir wares.

•**Normandy shoe.** Coalport used this term to designate a clog-like shape with a tapered toe, high back, and medium height, broad heel. The Germans made a large number of shoes similar to this shape in the late 1800s, although their versions usually had ruching around the rim and the toes more pointed. The author has found it a convenient term to designate all such shaped shoes, with or without the ruching.

•**PGGP.** This acronym stands for the Part-Glazed Granular Porcelain shoes. Their décors and the characteristics implied by the acronym suggest that they all may have come out of the same factory, as yet unidentified. The acronym provides a handy way in which to refer to them as a category.

•**Snow shoe.** Edible sugar dolls were made in the early 1800s to be used as Christmas decorations and treats for children. The first permanent versions of these holiday decorations were believed to have been commissioned by the confectionery company, Johann Moll, and made in the early 1890s by Hertwig & Company of Katzhutte, Germany, although other companies would soon join in the production of what became known as Snow Babies. Snow babies peaked in the period from 1906-1910. These miniature bisque creations had a pebbly white covering made from tiny particles of porcelain. A hand-powered "snow" machine was recently found in the Kister porcelain factory in Scheibe-Alsbach. It has been reported that factory seconds were carried in wooden boxes to the machine where they were ground into very fine particles called *grog* that was then applied to dolls and other figurals to simulate snow. It should come as no surprise that shoes covered with this white granular surface should be dubbed "Snow shoes".

•**Wedding cake shoe.** Shoes with piped-on slip appliqués extruded from a nozzle with an opening shaped appropriately to produce shirring, stars, and other décors that are exactly like the icing décor on fancy cakes.

Assessing Value

The value of a shoe is affected by such criteria as who made it, when it was made, its rarity, whether it is a cross-collectible, and many other factors. Prime among the factors is its condition. Many shoes, particularly porcelain shoes from certain manufacturers with lustre or gilt can show extensive wear of the painted décor. If they were left on open shelves or on a table, it is likely that these decorative shoes were washed at least once per year and may have been handled at other times as well. Over a hundred years—the typical age of many figural shoes available today—the amount of washing and handling could be substantial and probably accounts for the extreme wear found on some shoes. Excessive wear of the original décor affects the value of the piece significantly. Figure 93 shows three versions of the identical shoe, with the leftmost having experienced the greatest amount of wear to the gilt trim and the rightmost experiencing the least. The version on the extreme right, with no gilt wear, is the most valuable. The middle shoe, with some wear, would be valued somewhat less, perhaps ten to twenty percent less than full value. The shoe on the extreme left would have perhaps half or less than the value of one with no appreciable wear. Most of these decorative shoes should be placed in glass cabinets where they can be seen and enjoyed, but where they will not be handled excessively. Such storage not only greatly retards dust accumulation but keeps them protected from incidental damage and breakage.

Figure 93. Three shoes showing how wear affects value. The shoe on the left has about half the value of the one on the right.

Supply and demand are the major economic controls that affect value. Generally, the higher the demand for an item and the fewer there are of them, the higher the value. The reverse is also valid. You may have a shoe that is the only one known to exist. But if no one wants it, it has no value. Rarity, then, is a factor only if there is a demand for the item. The value is often extremely difficult to determine, especially if the piece is rare. The director of a well-known company in England related a pointed example to the author in a letter of 12 July 1996 when asked questions about the value of certain objects. He responded, "As to current market values, ... it is just too difficult and the legal dangers to us of customers claiming they have been misled as to value is too great. Last week here in the UK, at

9:30 in the morning, the curator of the Victoria and Albert Museum stated on the radio that a casket containing the relics of St. Thomas à Becket was worth £1,500,000 and that the Museum was devoting all its purchase fund money for the year to buy it. By 2:30 that afternoon Lord Thompson of Fleet Canada has spent £4,500,000 buying it. Who are we to understand 'current market values'? Value, like beauty, is in the eye of the beholder/purchaser."

The ability to identify the manufacturer of a shoe will often affect its value. Royal Bayreuth, Meissen, Royal Worcester, and Coalport shoes are valued because of the manufacturer, who in turn is valued because of the quality of the products produced. Even if the manufacturer cannot be identified, a quality product will be valued. But a shoe by a known manufacturer will usually be more in demand because there are collectors who specialize in the products of specific manufacturers.

If the manufacturer is not known, the primary criteria that affect value are the quality of the painting and the craftsmanship. Exceptionally skillful hand-painted décors will increase value. Exceptional craftsmanship also will generally increase value. Among the craftsmanship issues to be considered are 1) mold design, both the in-mold pattern and the complexity of the assembly; 2) care taken in casting, firing and glazing; 3) painting, as in the Conta & Boehme match striker boots hand-painted with designs versus those without this added decoration; and 4) appliqués, as in Elfinware shoes with and without moss, and Royal Bayreuth ladies cap toe oxfords with and without beading. Figure 94 illustrates four shoes of the same basic mold design that have widely divergent values resulting primarily from the expertise required to create the décor.

Figure 94. Four porcelain shoes of German or Austrian origin illustrating some of the factors that influence value. All were cast from similar molds about 1900. The slipper on the right is the least valuable because it has none of the hand-done finish work of the others. The shoe on the left and the shoe third from the left are the most valuable: the shoe on the left has a pierced vamp and extensive hand painting, even on the vamp straps, with its value further enhanced by being a marked Hirsch, a decorating studio whose works are in demand; the unmarked shoe third from the left has a high comparative value because of its reticulation, burnished gold ground with hand-tooled diamond pattern, and immaculate hand-applied enamel beading ("jewelling") in the mode of Coalport and Royal Worcester.

Mysteries

Mystery stories are among the most popular genres of novels. It should be no surprise, then, that nothing intrigues a collector quite so much as an unidentified piece in their collection. A great deal of time has been spent trying to track down the elusive manufacturers of certain groups of shoes, including Factory X. What follows might be characterized as a progress report on two of the many puzzlers other than Factory X and an invitation to readers who may have more satisfying answers or, even better, the solutions. Additional puzzlers can be found interspersed among the categories in the central section of this book.

Elfinware

A large group of porcelain novelty items was produced in Germany whose distinguishing characteristic is an appliqué of green-painted, sieve-extruded slip made to resemble moss with tiny blue forget-me-nots arranged around the rim of the piece, and other tiny flowers applied elsewhere. Typically, a small rose is centered on the piece and it is often surrounded by lilacs. Various American references give the production period as approximately 1920 to the 1940s. Wendl (German) cites 1900 to 1920 as the production period. In a 1998 John Bly article in a periodical published in Great Britain, the manufacturing period was estimated to have been "late 19th century" by John Sandon, head of European Porcelain and Ceramics at Phillips. Although manufactured in great quantity, these pieces exhibit exceptional craftsmanship and are valued collectibles in this era. The generic name apparently derives from the fact that some pieces can be found with *ELFINWARE* stamped on the body along with *GERMANY*, as on the small moss-less fan box in Figure 95, shown with a von Schierholz piece with the same types of appliqués. Note that "ELFINWARE" and "GERMANY" appear to have been put on together, with a single stamp. This contradicts German factories that have claimed that any mark bearing the word "Elfinware" must have been placed on a piece in America because it is not a German word. The mark may have been at the direction of an American importer, but it was placed there in a German factory.

Figure 95. Small porcelain box on right with typical "Elfinware" mark. Beside it is a porcelain basket with similar décor made by von Schierholz.

The basic mold shapes on which the elaborate appliqués were placed can also be found without the "moss". The appliqués on mossless pieces can range from all the other flowers typically found to a combination of the central rose and some floral decals.

Elfinware experts have been talked with and rigorous investigations have been made in an effort to identify the manufacturer of Elfinware. The experts with whom the author has communicated, some having searched for over thirty-five years, have been unable to make the identification. The author may be no closer to the source of these delightful, labor-intensive pieces.

On two trips into Thuringia, the author's husband and German friends asked at every factory and museum they visited whether anyone could identify the source of Elfinware. No one could do so. Wendl has reported that porcelain items with blue forget-me-nots were produced by Wagner & Apel in Lippelsdorf and Schmidt in Schleusingen. And the author has noted that the unusual method of producing the forget-me-nots was used on some pieces made by von Schierholz. Von Schierholz pieces can also be found that have the same type of lilacs as those found on Elfinware pieces, as shown in Figure 96.

Figure 96. Von Schierholz footed, reticulated bowl with applied lilacs and branches; shield and three oak leaf factory logo.

However, the only Elfinware pieces the author has found with identifiable factory marks are the two shown in Figure 97. They appear to have been made post WWII. The mark belongs to Reinhold Voigt, Porcelain Factory Gräfenroda-Ort, a factory located in Gräfenroda, Thuringia, Germany that was in business from 1919 to c.1972. While the production period of the factory appears to be in the right time frame, the author has not yet been able to make a satisfactory match of the Voigt basic mold shapes to the mold shapes of Elfinware known to have been produced pre-WWII.

Figure 97. Two Elfinware type shoes from the Reinhold Voigt factory in Gräfenroda.

A pair of Elfinware, moss-covered small shoes was purchased from England, both of which had a smeared blue stamp on their heels that might be a manufacturers mark. The mark could be a capital "S" followed by a period. If so, this mark was used by G. Greiner & Company of Schauberg, Bavaria, Germany about 1894 and perhaps as late as 1927. Röntgen reports that they produced decorative porcelain and gift articles as well as toys and household porcelain. Unfortunately, what remained of the factory was sold over half a century ago to a company that specializes in compound and blasting technologies, a company unlikely to have retained any institutional memory of the products made in an earlier time. The current owners of the old factory did, however, have a c.1894 catalog that they copied and sent to the author. It showed only simple dinnerware being made at that time.

An intriguing route the author took that may turn out to have been a detour is reported here. It may provide a subsequent researcher with data that may, or may not, prove useful. In the United States, *Elfinware* was registered by Breslauer-Underberg, Inc. of New York City on 2 January 1947 under the name, Elfinware, Inc., of New York, New York, for use on miniature porcelain boxes, trays, dishes, and other items, claiming use of the name Elfinware since 15 May 1945, made in *Germany*. A search of the New York City records department in 1998 turned up several documents. A County of New York Certificate of Partnership was issued on 15 January 1940 to Martin S. Breslauer and Henry Underberg doing business as Breslauer-Underberg with a business address at 225 Fifth Avenue, New York. A second Certificate of Partnership was issued on 31 December 1947 to Henry and Charlotte Underberg, doing business as Breslauer-Underberg at the same address. It is assumed that Breslauer either died or sold out his interest. On 23 December 1963, a Certificate of Discontinuance of Business as Partners was issued to the Underbergs. It recorded that the business was dissolved on 20 December 1963. The two sons of the Underbergs were located. One of them recalled that during WWII his father used a Trenton, New Jersey firm to make their porcelain. (This is apparently the company that produced the American porcelain that can be found with the Elfinware name incorporated in its mark.) Before WWII, the son recalled, his father imported porcelain from Meissen, Dresden decorating firms, and Schierholz, but did not know the source of the Elfinware. His

father had passed away in 1993 at the age of 94. The Schierholz reference was obviously intriguing, but cannot be pursued from this source, and current managers of the Schierholz factory successor claim that the company did not make Elfinware. But, of course, current personnel at the Royal Bayreuth factory claim it did not put shoelaces in all those Royal Bayreuth shoes at the factory.

Shoe collectors often encounter a small boot with a fluted, paneled top whose bottom is stamped *Elfinware*. It is believed to have been manufactured by the Porcelain Factory Martinroda Friedrich Eger & Co. (1900-present). The boot is sometimes found with the type of color transfers found on Breslauer-Underberg wares manufactured in New Jersey. Although what connection there is between the two companies, if any, has not yet been determined, it is possible that Breslauer-Underberg commissioned these boots from Martinroda shortly before the United States entered WWII. But at this time, no evidence has been found to suggest that the Martinroda factory produced the Elfinware with moss.

Needle-nose Cabinet Shoes

The needle-nose cabinet shoes are a group of porcelain slippers whose length is exceptionally long for their widths, whose toes come to long tapered points, that were decorated on one side only for placement in a cabinet or on a shelf, and whose porcelain is of very high quality. This group of shoes most often can be found with embossed floral designs or, on occasion, transfer portraits.

The Hunt for the Manufacturer of Napoleon Portrait Shoes

To date, the author has seen the portrait shoes with transfer images of Queen Louise of Prussia, Josephine, Hortense, Marie-Louise, and Madame Récamier (Jeanne-Françoise-Julie-Adelaide Récamier). Three of these five women were related to Napoleon Bonaparte. Josephine and Marie-Louise were married to him and Hortense was the daughter of Josephine. Madame Récamier was one of the most celebrated beauties in Napoleon's time and had a Paris salon where receptions were given for the cream of Paris society, including Napoleon's brother Lucien and one of Napoleon's generals, Bernadotte. At one point, Madame Recamier had rejected the advances of both Napoleon and Lucien. Queen Louise, the last of the five, was referred to by Napoleon as "my beautiful enemy", although he was insulting to her when he met her. Although the relationships of these five women to Napoleon vary greatly, their portraits are referred to herein for convenience as the Napoleon portraits and the shoes on which they appear as the Napoleon portrait shoes. Three of the portraits are shown on shoes in Figure 98, in the four sizes in which the shoes are known.

Figure 98. Four sizes of needle-nose cabinet shoes with Napoleon portraits.

On the shoes, the name of the person portrayed is found in script just below the portrait. A manufacturer's mark has yet to be found on any of the Napoleon portrait shoes or on any shoe related to them, such as those with the heavily embossed flowers. But a "GERMANY" mark is occasionally found on the bottom of the heel of these shoes. The mark is semicircular, in the 12 o'clock position, and appears to be a partial millstone mark … at least that was the original thought.

For some years, plates, vases, and other porcelain pieces have been hunted that have the same transfer images and a manufacturer's mark. One found is the portrait plate of Queen Louise shown in Figure 99. It was made by C. Tielsch & Co. of Altwasser, Silesia, Germany (pre 1918, when Tielsch became part of Hutschenreuther). Of interest is that the bottom of the plate has an owner-applied notation that the plate was received in 1905. Other pieces have been found with the sought after transfer prints. They were made by Franz Anton Mehlem of Bonn, Germany; Zeh, Scherzer & Co. of Rehau, Bavaria, Germany; and Erdmann Schlegelmilch of Suhl, Thuringia, Germany. All of these companies apparently purchased the transfers from the same source because they all appear to be identical images.

While the transfers on the pieces from all the companies are the same images as on the cabinet shoes, the images are much larger on the pieces found thus far—except for a plate that has been found that was made by Tielsch. It is shown in Figure 100. What is interesting about this plate is that the small portraits surrounding the central image of Josephine are not only identical to the transfers on the shoes, but they also are the same size. On both the shoes and the plate, the very small script identification of each woman is located in the same place below the portrait. On the back of the plate there are both the Tielsch mark and an intriguing "GERMANY" mark. It is semicircular and in the 6 o'clock position, leading to the speculation that if the shoes were made by Tielsch then the "GERMANY" mark found occasionally was not simply a piece of a larger millstone mark, but the complete mark. All of this is a bit thin to make a declaration about the manufacturer of the Napoleon portrait and related shoes. At this point, however, Tielsch would seem to be a contender as the originator of these shoes.

Figure 99. Portrait of Queen Louise on plate made by C. Tielsch & Co.

Figure 100. C. Tielsch *Josephine* portrait plate with small images around its rim of Napoleon, Josephine, Marie-Louise, Hortense, and Madame Récamier.

Part II

Shoes, Boots, Slippers, Clogs, Sabots, Sandals, and Other Footwear

On the following pages are photographs of shoes that can be found in the secondary market by collectors. Although a few are very rare, and some will take aggressive searching if they are to be found, most are accessible.

Many porcelain and pottery shoes are unmarked. Where I believe unmarked shoes to be attributable to a specific manufacturer, I have made that designation. In this case, it is my best assessment at this time. Where a piece is marked and that mark is consistent with the age, products, and décor of the factory identified by the mark, the mark has been assumed to be genuine. In all cases, designations of factory have been made by me and I take responsibility for any errors that future evidence may prove I have made. It is uncomfortable and indeed treacherous to climb out on the fragile limb called educated guesses, but I have believed it to be slightly more beneficial than detrimental if collectors are to be aided in furthering their own research.

In many cases, I made full-scale sketches of the shoes to study in-mold details, shape, and design features. Where I made such sketches, I have included them in reduced scale for whatever assistance they may provide to collectors, who are directed to the first part of this text (see page 22) for an explanation of how they may prove helpful as well as some disclaimers about their use. Where shoes are consistently found well marked, such sketches usually were not made.

The dimensions given are the measurements for the shoe photographed; variations can be expected because casting and kiln-firing were not an exact science when these shoes were manufactured. Abbreviations used are "L" for "long", "H" for "high", "LOA" for "length overall", "HOA" for "height overall", and "OD" for outside diameter.

Other abbreviations used are "HP" for "hand-painted", "prob." for "probably", "pos." for "possibly", and "MIG" for "made in Germany".

If a specific date is provided in the description, it is the date for the shoe actually pictured. For example, Royal Worcester shoe model number 439 was first introduced in 1874 but continued to be made in succeeding years. The particular Royal Worcester shoe model 439 pictured in this text has a date code that shows it was made in 1886. Therefore, the description reflects that with a "c.1886" notation.

An enormous number of shoes in the secondary market were made from the late 1800s to the beginning of WWI. Most are unmarked in a way that allows dating them. Many, however, have characteristics that allow an approximation of their date of manufacture. **Generally, my use of "c.1900" means "turn of the last century" or from roughly 1880 to 1915, and for some factories into the 1920s.** If characteristics allow shading that one way or the other, that has been done by noting "late 1800s" or "early 1900s".

Many shoes carry a mark that is the painter's mark. It is usually numeric. When the description says that a piece is unmarked, it means that there is no mark indicating either the country of origin or the manufacturer, although there may be painter's marks or other kinds of factory numeric codes. Where there is a number on a piece believed to be a model number, that is given. If a mark has been cropped from a bottom photo of the piece and shown with the shoe itself, it is because bottom marks provide one clue toward the identification of an item. Many marks are hard to discern because they are smudged, faint, partially missing, or some combination of these. They have often been provided regardless because the experienced eye learns to fill in the missing parts and derive valuable information about the piece.

ROYAL BAYREUTH: Tapestry

The Royal Bayreuth factory in Tettau, Germany, is known to have made two forms of porcelain shoes with a tapestry finish: a woman's oxford in both a blunt and tapered toe, and a 4 x 4 (four pairs in-mold grommets, four pairs open eyelets) lace-up high-top shoe. The tapestry finish was achieved by pressing moistened coarse fabric onto the shoes while in their green ware stage and firing them up for their first kiln operation. The fabric burned away, leaving the woven impression that served as the surface for the décor that would then be administered. The factory installed fabric shoelaces with metal aglets in both types of shoes. The background for the rose patterns was often made by airbrushing color over a template of leaf or daisy shapes. For convenience, a small clog is included with the tapestry shoes. It is often erroneously referred to as a tapestry piece. However, its stippled surface was achieved in-mold, not in-kiln. The model from which the molds were made was given a textured surface by repeatedly indenting the surface with a tool with a hemispherical end(s). When the working molds were made, this resulted in the indentations seen in the finished product. RB shoes shown herein were made probably between c.1885 and WWI or possibly into the 1920s, unless otherwise noted.

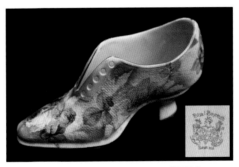

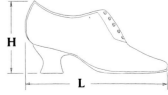

Porcelain woman's oxford, blunt toe, *Pink American Beauty Rose* tapestry pattern; blue mark on sole, "Royal Bayreuth" and logo; a "left"; 4-5/16"L x 2-1/2"H. Royal Bayreuth, Germany. $500.

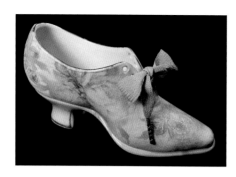

Porcelain woman's oxford, blunt toe, *Apricot and Pink Roses* tapestry pattern; unmarked; a "right"; original shoelace; 4-15/16"L x 2-1/2"H. Royal Bayreuth, Germany. $450.

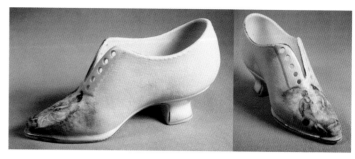

Porcelain woman's oxford, tapered toe, rare *Colonial Curtsy Scene* tapestry pattern; blue mark on sole, "Royal Bayreuth" and logo; a "right"; 5-1/16"L x 2-5/8"H. Royal Bayreuth, Germany. $1,100.

Porcelain woman's oxford, tapered toe, *Yellow Roses with Pink Border Roses* tapestry pattern; blue mark on sole, "Royal Bayreuth" and logo; a "left"; 5-1/4"L x 2-5/8"H. Royal Bayreuth, Germany. $450.

Porcelain woman's oxford, tapered toe, rare *Prince and His Lady* tapestry pattern; blue mark on sole, "Royal Bayreuth" and logo; a "left"; 5-1/16"L x 2-5/8"H. Royal Bayreuth, Germany. $1,100.

Porcelain woman's oxford, tapered toe, very rare *Sterling Silver Rose* tapestry pattern; blue mark on sole, "Royal Bayreuth" and logo; a "right"; original shoelace; 5-3/16"L x 2-5/8"H. Royal Bayreuth, Germany. $2,500.

Porcelain woman's oxford, tapered toe, uncommon *Japanese Chrysanthemum* tapestry pattern; blue mark on sole, "Royal Bayreuth" and logo; a "right"; original shoelace; 5-1/16"L x 2-1/2"H. Royal Bayreuth, Germany. $800.

Porcelain woman's 4 x 4 (four pairs in-mold grommets, four pairs open eyelets) lace-up high-top shoe, uncommon *Triple Rose* (also, *White Rose*) tapestry pattern; blue mark on sole, "Royal Bayreuth" and logo; a "right"; 4-1/2"L x 3-1/2"H. Royal Bayreuth, Germany. $900.

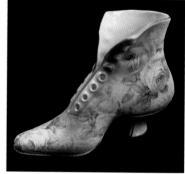

Pair of porcelain women's oxfords, tapered toes, uncommon *Violets* tapestry pattern; green mark on soles, "Royal Bayreuth" and logo; the "right", 5-3/16"L x 2-5/8"H and the "left", 5-1/16"L x 2-5/8"H. Royal Bayreuth, Germany. $800 each.

Porcelain woman's oxford, tapered toe, uncommon *Christmas Rose and Cactus* tapestry pattern; blue mark on sole, "Royal Bayreuth" and logo; a "left"; 5-1/16"L x 2-5/8"H. Royal Bayreuth, Germany. $800.

Porcelain woman's 4 x 4 lace-up high-top shoe, *Double Pink Rose* tapestry pattern; blue mark on sole, "Royal Bayreuth" and logo; a "right"; original shoelace; 4-9/16"L x 3-1/2"H. Royal Bayreuth, Germany, $650.

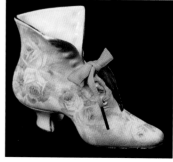

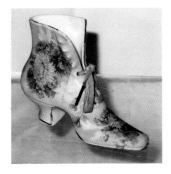

Porcelain woman's 4 x 4 lace-up high-top shoe, rare *Japanese Chrysanthemum* tapestry pattern; blue mark on sole, "Royal Bayreuth" and logo; a "right"; original shoelace; 4-3/4"L x 3-9/16"H. Royal Bayreuth, Germany. $1,200.

Porcelain woman's 4 x 4 lace-up high-top shoe, very rare *Sterling Silver Rose* tapestry pattern; blue mark on sole, "Royal Bayreuth" and logo; a "left"; 4-11/16"L x 3-1/2"H. Royal Bayreuth, Germany. $2,500.

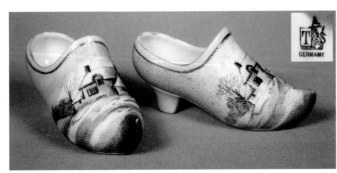

Pair of porcelain clogs, *House with Arched Dormer Winter Scenic* stippled texture pattern; underglaze green "T" mark and lion logo on shank; a "right" and a "left", each 3-1/2"L x 1-3/4"H. Royal Bayreuth, Germany. c.1891-1902. $350 each.

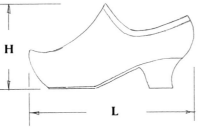

Porcelain clog, *Triple Peaked Roofs Winter Scenic* stippled texture pattern; underglaze green "T" mark and lion logo on shank; a "left", 3-1/2"L x 1-3/4"H. Royal Bayreuth, Germany. c.1891-1902. $350.

Porcelain clog, *Steeple Winter Scenic* stippled texture pattern; underglaze green "T" mark and lion logo on shank; a "right", 3-1/2"L x 1-3/4"H. Royal Bayreuth, Germany. c.1891-1902. $350.

ROYAL BAYREUTH: Sabots

Royal Bayreuth sabots are uniquely shaped and were made in distinguishable lefts and rights. Thus, even though they occasionally are found unmarked, RB sabots are easy to identify. It is extremely unusual to find this sabot in anything other than the standard size; only a few have been found in a smaller size. On many of them, airbrushing was used to obtain finely graduated colors.

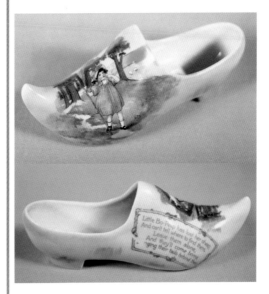

Porcelain sabot, Nursery Rhyme Series, *Little Bo-Peep*; blue mark, "Royal Bayreuth" with logo; a "left"; 5-3/8"L x 2"H. Royal Bayreuth, Germany. $500.

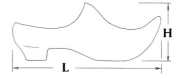

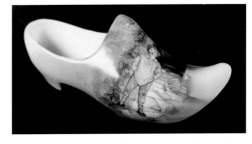

Porcelain sabot, Nursery Rhyme Series, *Jack and the Beanstalk*; on the back side in a rectangular frame of twigs and leaves, *With all his might and main/Jack chopped the beanstalk down/The Giant with a cry of rage/Came tumbling to the ground*; blue mark, "Royal Bayreuth" with logo; a "right"; 5-3/8"L x 2"H. Royal Bayreuth, Germany. $500.

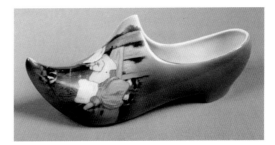

Porcelain sabot, Sunbonnet Babies Series, *Sunday – Fishing*; blue mark, "Royal Bayreuth" with logo; a "left"; 5-3/8"L x 2-1/8"H. Royal Bayreuth, Germany. $650.

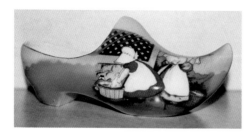

Porcelain sabot, Sunbonnet Babies Series, *Monday – Washing*; blue mark, "Royal Bayreuth" with logo; a "right"; 5-3/8"L x 2"H. Royal Bayreuth, Germany. $650.

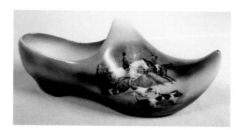

Porcelain sabot with *Hunt Scene* (two horses with riders, six dogs); a "right"; unmarked. Royal Bayreuth, Germany. Shown is standard size: 5-3/8"L x 2-1/16"H; $250. Also known in small size, 4"L x 1-1/2"H; $300.

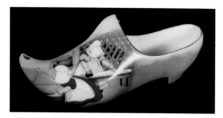

Porcelain sabot, Sunbonnet Babies Series, *Tuesday – Ironing*; blue mark, "Royal Bayreuth" with logo; a "left"; 5-3/8"L x 2"H. Royal Bayreuth, Germany. $650.

Porcelain sabot with overall pattern of tiny multi-color florals; blue mark on shank, "Royal Bayreuth" with logo; a "right"; 5-3/8"L x 2-1/16"H. Royal Bayreuth, Germany. $200.

Porcelain sabot, Sunbonnet Babies Series, *Wednesday – Mending*; unmarked; a "right"; 5-3/8"L x 2-1/16"H. Royal Bayreuth, Germany. $650.

Porcelain sabot with green malachite and gold borders and hand-painted spray of blue flowers and green leaves; pearl luster inside; blue mark on sole, "Royal Bayreuth" with logo and upside-down "Bavaria"; gold letters *M.T.L.* on shank, assumed to be initials of artist; a "left"; 5-5/16"L x 2-1/8"H. Royal Bayreuth, Germany. c. 1900. $400.

Porcelain sabot, Sunbonnet Babies Series, *Thursday – Scrubbing*; blue mark, "Royal Bayreuth" with logo; a "right"; 5-3/8"L x 2"H. Royal Bayreuth, Germany. $650.

Pair of porcelain sabots, Royal Bayreuth, Germany. Standard size with hand-painted pink roses and blue pansies on pearl luster ground; blue mark on sole, "Royal Bayreuth" with logo and upside-down "Bavaria"; a "right"; 5-7/16"L x 2-1/8"H; c. 1900; $350. Small size with hand-filled transfer crest of "Clevedon"; unmarked; a "right"; 4-3/16"L x 1-5/8"H; $100.

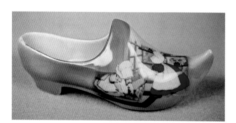

Porcelain sabot, Sunbonnet Babies Series, *Friday – Sweeping*; blue mark, "Royal Bayreuth" with logo; a "right"; 5-3/8"L x 2-1/16"H. Royal Bayreuth, Germany. $650.

Pair of matched porcelain sabots in rare patterns, the left-facing in the *Peering Lady* and the right-facing in the *Shawl Lady*; each, 5-3/8"L x 2"H. Royal Bayreuth, Germany. $500 each.

Pair of matched porcelain sabots in rare, asymmetrically hand-painted *Rose and Forget-me-not* pattern; blue mark on sole, "Royal Bayreuth" with logo and upside-down "Bavaria"; the "right" and "left" each measure 5-5/16"L x 2"H. Royal Bayreuth, Germany. c.1900. $400 each.

ROYAL BAYREUTH:
Figural Men's

Royal Bayreuth men's shoes look just like the real shoes worn in the years around 1900. The porcelain versions typically have striped back straps; elaborate in-mold stitching and perf detail that is often emphasized with hand-painted detail; and open eyelets where fabric shoelaces were threaded through at the factory. They are typically painted a light tan inside and on the sole to resemble new leather, and often have painted inner soles. Glazes range from high gloss glaze to matte, with the latter being somewhat more frequent. They were made in distinguishable rights and lefts. The period in which they were made is generally believed to be from about 1885 to about 1915, and possibly into the 1920s. Many of the more common models were made over a number of years. They are rarely marked, making it difficult to determine the order and year in which they were introduced. The presence of a mark does not affect the value because collectors recognize them with or without a mark.

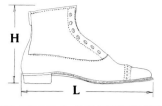

Porcelain man's 7-eyelet cap-toe ankle shoe; unmarked; a "right"; 4-11/16"L x 2-11/16"H. Royal Bayreuth, Germany. $200.

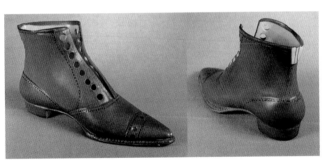

Porcelain man's 8-eyelet cap-toe ankle shoe with pointed toe; unmarked; a "left"; 4-13/16"L x 2-11/16"H. Royal Bayreuth, Germany. $200.

Porcelain man's riding boot with side straps; unmarked; a "left"; 3-1/2"L x 4-9/16"H. Royal Bayreuth, Germany. Rare. $500.

Porcelain man's ivory matte 8-eyelet cap-toe ankle shoe with pointed toe; unmarked; a "right"; 4-9/16"L x 2-11/16"H. Royal Bayreuth, Germany. $200.

Pair of porcelain matched riding boots with wide cuffs (speckled salmon); unmarked; a "left" and a "right", each 3-1/2"L x 4-3/4"H; inside of each boot is vertically "stitched". Royal Bayreuth, Germany. Very rare. $1,300 for matched pair.

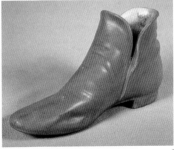

Porcelain man's 5-eyelet wing tip ankle shoe with pointed toe; unmarked; a "left"; 4-5/8"L x 2-5/8"H. Royal Bayreuth, Germany. $225.

Porcelain man's Faustian, or Romeo, bedroom slipper; unmarked (marked versions have been found in both this camel color and in black); a "right"; 5-3/16"L x 2-13/16"H. Royal Bayreuth, Germany. $400.

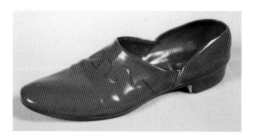

Porcelain man's opera slipper in brick red; unmarked; a "left"; 5-5/16"L x 1-3/8"H. Royal Bayreuth, Germany. Rare. $500.

Porcelain man's 5-eyelet cap-toe oxford; unmarked; 5-1/8"L x 2"H. Royal Bayreuth, Germany. Rare. $375.

Pair of matched porcelain men's 4-eyelet cap-toe dress shoes; purple mark, "Royal Bayreuth" with logo; the "right" and "left" each measure 5-1/8"L x 1-15/16"H; original shoelaces. This shoe is the one believed to be shown in black in Montgomery Ward catalogs from 1903-1906. See, for example, the fall/winter 1903-1904 Montgomery Ward catalog #72, page 32, where they sold for 22¢ each, or $2.40 per dozen. The shoe was advertised as a "toothpick or match holder". Royal Bayreuth, Germany. $175 each.

Porcelain man's 5-eyelet cap-toe oxford with stacked heel and upturned toe, two with original shoelaces; all are unmarked; this model always has a painted, pinked-edge brown innersole; all are 5 to 5-1/8"L x 2"H. Royal Bayreuth, Germany. Camel and black colors: $150 each; rare green, $200.

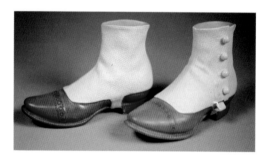

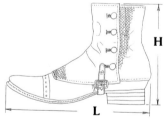

Pair of porcelain men's spat shoes with applied buttons and protruding strap; unmarked; 5-1/8"L x 3-1/2"H each. The spat appears to have been modeled on top of the man's 5-eyelet cap-toe oxford in the previous picture ... the shoe portion of this spat has the same shape, dimensions, and in-mold detail. Royal Bayreuth, Germany. $250 each.

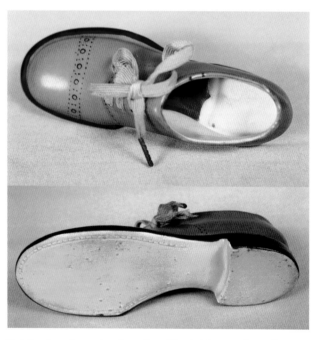

Details of man's cap-toe dress shoe. The inside view shows the as-cast color of the white porcelain, the typical light tan used to paint the insides of many RB figural shoes, and the painted brown innersole found on this shoe. The stitching detail on the sole of the shoe is often barely visible if the shoe was cast toward the end of the working mold's useful life.

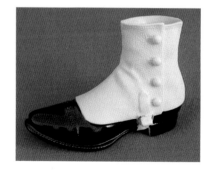

Porcelain man's spat shoe with applied buttons and protruding strap; unmarked; 5-1/8"L x 3-1/2"H. Royal Bayreuth, Germany. $250.

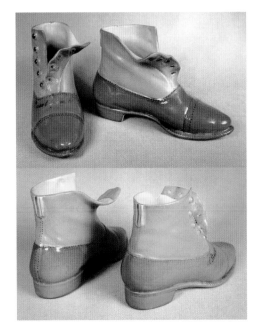

Porcelain man's lawn tennis shoe with reddish brown sole, light tan inside and brown glazed inner sole; unmarked; a "left"; 5"L x 2"H; can be found with or without "2681" impressed into the shank. This shoe originally was sold as a souvenir. Royal Bayreuth, Germany. $250.

Pair of porcelain men's unbuttoned, 5 side-button ankle shoes in two-tone matte camel and gloss brown; unmarked; the "right", 4-3/8"L x 2-15/16"H and the "left", 4-1/2"L x 3"H. The "right" originally was sold as a souvenir. Royal Bayreuth, Germany. $300 each.

Porcelain man's lawn tennis shoe with reddish brown sole, light tan inside and brown glazed inner sole; unmarked; a "right"; 5"L x 2"H. Royal Bayreuth, Germany. Uncommon color combination. $300.

Pair of porcelain matched men's Victor (the real-life, higher top woman's version was called a Victoria shoe) 3 x 3 (three pairs in-mold grommets, three pairs open eyelets) ankle shoes with protruding back straps in two-tone matte camel and high gloss brown; green mark, "Royal Bayreuth", with upside down "Bavaria"; for each, the shoe is 4-3/4"L x 2-5/8"H and including the strap is 5"L x 2-15/16"H. The fabric shoelaces are not original but are an appropriate replacement, being of the older type with metal aglets. This shoe probably was made over a number of years beginning about 1900; a souvenir version has been seen marked "Brockton Fair 1907". Warning: this shoe is often found with the protruding strap broken off, carefully ground down, and sold as though it came from the factory this way; a shoe with this kind of damage has little value. Royal Bayreuth, Germany. $175 each with protruding strap.

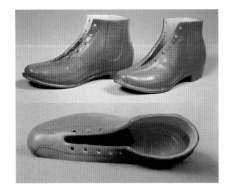

Pair of porcelain matched men's 6-eyelet bicycle shoes, gussets on both sides, stacked heels notched on inside corners; inside painted tan with inner sole part white-glazed and part brown-glazed; unmarked; the "right", 4-3/4"L x 2-1/2"H, and the "left", 4-13/16"L x 2-1/2"H. Royal Bayreuth, Germany. $250 each.

Porcelain man's Victor 3 x 3 ankle shoe with protruding back strap in two-tone matte and gloss black; unmarked; shoe is 4-3/4"L x 2-5/8"H and including strap is 5"L x 2-15/16"H; original shoelace. Royal Bayreuth, Germany. $175.

Porcelain man's 6-eyelet bicycle shoe, gussets on both sides, stacked heel notched on inside corner; inside painted tan with inner sole part white-glazed and part brown-glazed; unmarked; original shoelace; a "left"; 4-7/8"L x 2-1/2"H. Photo of sole shows it painted, with in-mold stitching detail. Note the notched inside corner of this bicycle shoe. Royal Bayreuth, Germany. $250.

Pair of porcelain matched men's white bucks with reddish brown soles, light tan insides and brown glazed inner soles; the "right", 4-15/16"L x 1-15/16"H and the "left", 5"L x 2"H. Can be found unmarked, with a Royal Bayreuth c. 1900 blue mark, or with a British registry mark "R^dN° 335843" for the year 1899. Royal Bayreuth, Germany. $200 each.

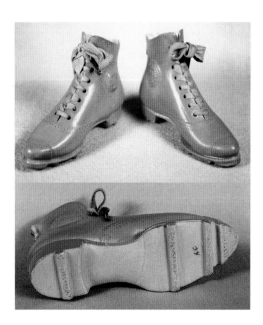

Pair of porcelain men's matte pumpkin 8-eyelet football shoes with in-mold raised pads on ankles on each side, embossed "Stevens Patent Nº11519/THE BOOT"; original shoelaces; unmarked; each is 4-9/16"L x 3-5/16"H. Royal Bayreuth, Germany. Rare. $500 each.

Pair of porcelain matched men's 7-eyelet cap-toe ankle shoes, the "right" with an original shoelace; unmarked; each is 4-3/8"L x 2-3/4"H. Royal Bayreuth, Germany. $175 each.

Porcelain man's 7-eyelet cap-toe brick red ankle shoe with original shoelace; unmarked; a "left"; 4-3/8"L x 2-3/4"H. Royal Bayreuth, Germany. $175.

Porcelain men's matte khaki 8-eyelet field hockey shoes with in-mold raised pads on each ankle, embossed "Hockey Boot"; original shoelace on the "left"; unmarked; each is 4-11/16"L x 2-3/4"H. In the shoes shown, the in-mold arch-height "padding" is on the inside of the "right" shoe, but on the outside of the "left" shoe. Royal Bayreuth, Germany. Rare. $500 each.

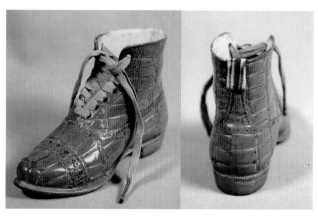

Porcelain man's 7-eyelet cap-toe tan alligator shoe with original shoelace; unmarked; a "left"; 4-7/16"L x 2-7/8"H. In addition to the usual hand-painted stitching and perf detail, a tool was used to remove the tan paint along the alligator pattern lines to emphasize the in-mold pattern. Royal Bayreuth, Germany. Rare. $400.

Pair of porcelain matched men's 7-eyelet cap-toe ankle shoes in two-tone matte and gloss black glaze with original shoelaces; unmarked; each is 4-3/8"L x 2-13/16"H. This mold can be found in several colors and was used as the foundation mold for the alligator and lizard shoes in the following illustrations. Royal Bayreuth, Germany. $175 each.

Porcelain man's 7-eyelet cap-toe green alligator shoe; inside is painted light green; shoelace is not original; unmarked; a "left"; 4-7/16"L x 2-13/16"H. In addition to the usual hand-painted stitching and perf detail, a tool was used to remove the green paint along the alligator pattern lines to emphasize the in-mold pattern. Royal Bayreuth, Germany. Rare. $400.

Pair of porcelain men's 7-eyelet cap-toe tan lizard shoes with original shoelaces; unmarked; each is 4-1/2"L x 2-7/8"H. Royal Bayreuth, Germany. Rare. $400 each.

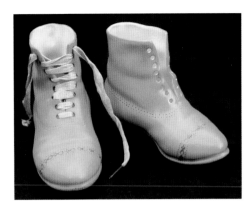

Pair of porcelain matched orange matte 8-eyelet cap-toe large-size men's work boots, one with an original shoelace; blue and white striped back straps; unmarked; the "right", 4-15/16"L x 3-7/16"H, and the "left", 4-13/16"L x 3-3/8"H. Royal Bayreuth, Germany. $150 each.

Porcelain man's two-tone matte gray and gloss black 8-eyelet cap-toe large-size man's work boot; unmarked; a "right"; 4-7/8"L x 3-3/8"H. Has been seen with the c.1900 blue mark, "Royal Bayreuth" with logo and upside-down "Bavaria". Royal Bayreuth, Germany. $150.

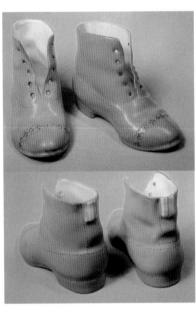

Pair of porcelain matched orange matte 5-eyelet cap-toe small-size men's work boots; unmarked; the "right", 3-3/4"L x 2-5/8"H, and the "left", 3-13/16"L x 2-5/8"H. Royal Bayreuth, Germany. $150 each.

Porcelain man's matte green 8-eyelet cap-toe large-size man's work boot; unmarked; a "right"; 4-7/8"L x 3-3/8"H. Rare color. Royal Bayreuth, Germany. $200.

Pair of porcelain matched two-tone matte and gloss glazed black 5-eyelet cap-toe small-size men's work boots; unmarked; both are 3-3/4"L x 2-5/8"H. Royal Bayreuth, Germany. $150 each.

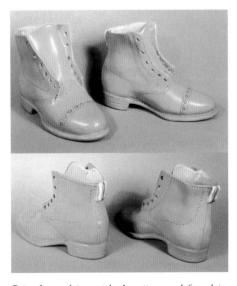

Pair of porcelain matched matte camel 6-eyelet-flap cap-toe men's work boots; unmarked; the "right", 4-5/8"L x 3-1/4"H, and the "left", 4-9/16"L x 3-1/4"H. Royal Bayreuth, Germany. $175 each.

Porcelain 7-eyelet cap-toe man's tramp shoe with intentional openings in the body of the shoe; unmarked; a "left"; 4-9/16"L x 2-13/16"H. Can be found in a high gloss glaze, as shown, and in a matte glaze. Royal Bayreuth, Germany. $300.

ROYAL BAYREUTH:
Figural Girls' and Women's

Royal Bayreuth girl's and women's shoes look just like the real shoes worn in the years around 1900. The porcelain versions mimic real shoes with such details as elaborate in-mold stitching and perf detail that is often emphasized with hand-painting; open eyelets where fabric shoelaces were threaded through at the factory; and, often, light tan painting of the inside and on the sole to resemble new leather. The factory produced a number of women's shoes that featured enamel micro beading. Glazes range from high gloss glaze to matte, with the latter being the most common. They were made in distinguishable rights and lefts. The period in which they were made is generally believed to be from about 1885 to about 1915, and possibly into the 1920s. Many of the more common models were made over a number of years. They are rarely marked, making it difficult to determine the order and year in which they were introduced. The presence of a mark does not affect the value because collectors recognize them with or without a mark.

Porcelain child's ankle-strap shoe with in-mold bow and strap button; unmarked; a "left"; 4-1/2"L x 2"H. Royal Bayreuth, Germany. Very rare. $550.

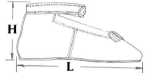

Porcelain girl's ankle-strap shoe with in-mold vamp ornament, strap button, and textured sock; unmarked; a "left"; 4-5/8"L x 3"H. Royal Bayreuth, Germany. Very rare. $1,100.

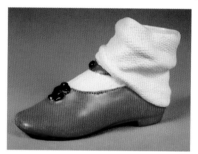

Porcelain woman's t-strap shoe; unmarked; a "left"; 5"L x 2-3/16"H. Royal Bayreuth, Germany. Rare. $800.

Porcelain child's ankle-strap shoe with applied bow and strap button; unmarked; a "left"; 4-3/4"L x 2"H. Royal Bayreuth, Germany. Rare. $400.

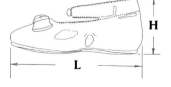

Porcelain 8-eyelet lace-up wing-tip woman's high-top shoe; unmarked; a "left"; 4-1/4"L x 3-3/8"H. Royal Bayreuth, Germany. $250.

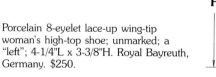

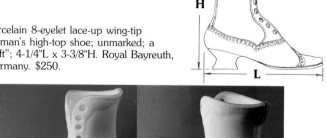

Pair of porcelain 8-eyelet lace-up wing-tip women's high-top shoes; unmarked; the "right", 4-3/16"L x 3-38"H, and the "left", 4-3/16"L x 3-7/16"H. Royal Bayreuth, Germany. $225 each.

Pair of porcelain 9-eyelet lace-up high-top women's shoes with original shoelaces; unmarked; each is 4-3/4"L x 3-7/8"H. Royal Bayreuth, Germany. $225 each.

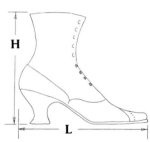

Pair of porcelain matched 5 x 4 (five pairs in-mold grommets and four pairs eyelets) wing-tip high-top women's shoes with original laces; hand-painted raised white enamel stitching and perf detail; impressed old Tettau "T." and "3831"; the "right", 4-5/8"L x 3-7/8"H, and the "left", 4-11/16"L x 3-7/8"H. The c.1885 old Tettau "T." mark suggests that this may have been one of the first shoe models produced by the factory. Royal Bayreuth, Germany. Very rare décor in this uncommon form. $400 each.

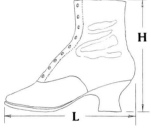

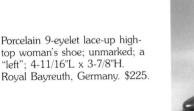

Porcelain 9-eyelet lace-up high-top woman's shoe; unmarked; a "left"; 4-11/16"L x 3-7/8"H. Royal Bayreuth, Germany. $225.

Porcelain 9-eyelet lace-up high-top woman's shoe; unmarked; a "left"; 4-7/8"L x 3-7/8"H. Royal Bayreuth, Germany. $225.

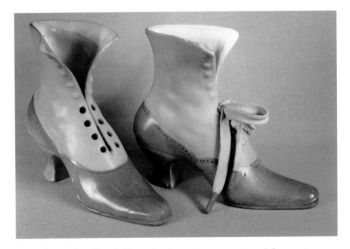

Pair of porcelain 5 x 4 (five pairs in-mold grommets and four pairs eyelets) wing-tip high-top women's shoes; shoelace is not original; unmarked; each is 4-1/2"L x 3-3/4"H. Royal Bayreuth, Germany. Uncommon form. $275 each.

Pair of porcelain matched 4 x 4 (four pairs in-mold grommets and four pairs eyelets) flared high-top women's shoes with swept back toe cap in two-tone matte and gloss black; blue mark, "Royal Bayreuth" with logo and upside down "Bavaria"; the "right", 4-5/8"L x 3-1/2"H, and the "left", 4-3/4"L x 3-9/16"H. Royal Bayreuth, Germany. c.1900. $165 each.

Porcelain 4 x 4 flared high-top woman's shoe with swept back toe cap in two-tone matte camel and gloss brown with original shoelace; unmarked; 4-5/8"L x 3-9/16"H. Royal Bayreuth, Germany. $165.

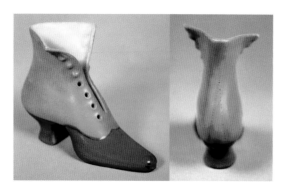

This shoe is identical in its in-mold design to the previous two except for the variation in the swept back toe cap: it is pointed in the center of the vamp; blue mark, "Royal Bayreuth" with logo and upside down "Bavaria"; 4-5/8"L x 3-1/2"H. Note the back seam that is characteristic of the flared high-tops: it is tapered to a point at its top. This design feature has not been found on copies of this shoe made by other manufacturers. Royal Bayreuth, Germany. $165.

Porcelain 11-button, scalloped side closure high-top shoe in two-tone matte camel and high gloss brown; unmarked; a "left"; 5"L x 3-3/4"H. Royal Bayreuth, Germany. $250.

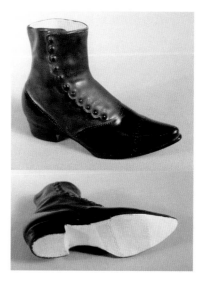

Porcelain 11-button, scalloped side closure high-top shoe in two-tone matte and high gloss black; unmarked; a "right"; 5"L x 3-3/4"H. Note in-mold stitching detail on sole of this model. Royal Bayreuth, Germany. $250.

Pair of porcelain small-size matched 11-button, scalloped side-closure high-top shoes; unmarked; each is 3-15/16"L x 3"H. These appear to have been formed-off the standard size. Royal Bayreuth, Germany. Rare. $700 for the pair.

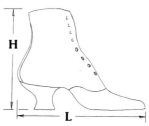

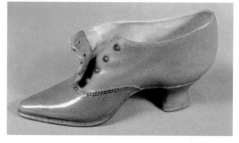

Porcelain unbuttoned and scalloped side closure, 4-button woman's shoe in two-tone camel matte and high gloss brown; unmarked; a "left"; 5-1/4"L x 2-11/16"H. Royal Bayreuth, Germany. Uncommon. $450.

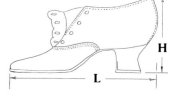

Porcelain center-buttoned triple strap woman's shoe with in-mold vamp ornament; unmarked; a "left"; 5-3/16"L x 2-9/16"H. Royal Bayreuth, Germany. Uncommon. $450.

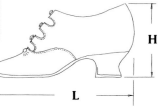

Porcelain center-buttoned triple strap woman's shoe with in-mold vamp ornament; unmarked; a "right"; 5-3/16"L x 2-9/16"H. Royal Bayreuth, Germany. Uncommon. $450.

Pair of porcelain matched double-buttoned triple strap women's shoes in brick red matte and gloss black; unmarked; each is 5-1/16"L x 2-1/8"H. Royal Bayreuth, Germany. Rare. $1,100 for the pair.

Porcelain double-buttoned triple strap woman's shoe in Bayreuth ivory and peach; unmarked; a "right"; 5-1/16"L x 2-1/8"H. Royal Bayreuth, Germany. Rare. $550.

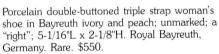

Porcelain 5-eyelet wing-tip woman's oxford; unmarked; a "left"; 5-5/16"L x 2-9/16"H. Royal Bayreuth, Germany. $250.

Porcelain 5-eyelet wing-tip woman's oxford in Bayreuth ivory and peach; unmarked; a "right"; 5-3/8"L x 2-5/8"H. Royal Bayreuth, Germany. $250.

Pair of porcelain 5-eyelet wing-tip women's oxfords in ivory matte and gloss black with peach inner rim band; unmarked; shoelaces not original; each is 5-1/4"L x 2-9/16"H. Royal Bayreuth, Germany. $250 each.

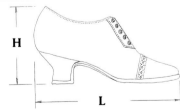

Pair of porcelain matched 5-eyelet cap-toe women's oxfords with original shoelaces in Bayreuth matte camel; unmarked; each is 5-1/8"L x 2-5/8"H. The factory used this mold for a wide range of décors, many shown in the following illustrations. Royal Bayreuth, Germany. $185 each.

Porcelain 5-eyelet cap-toe woman's oxford with original shoelace; blue mark, "Royal Bayreuth", with logo and upside down "Bavaria"; a "left"; 5-1/8"L x 2-5/8"H. Royal Bayreuth, Germany. c.1900. $185.

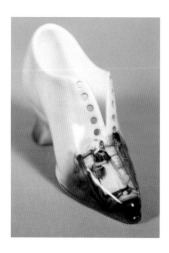

Porcelain 5-eyelet cap-toe woman's oxford with *Dutch Children on Pier* pattern; blue mark with "Royal Bayreuth" and logo; 5-1/4"L x 2-5/8"H. Royal Bayreuth, Germany. Rare. $550.

Porcelain 5-eyelet cap-toe woman's oxford in cobalt with scroll and lace pattern in gold; unmarked; a "right"; 5-1/8"L x 2-5/8"H. Royal Bayreuth, Germany. Uncommon. $275.

Porcelain 5-eyelet cap-toe woman's oxford in cobalt with geometric lace pattern in raised white enamel micro beads; shoelace is not original; a "right"; 5-5/16"L x 2-11/16"H. Royal Bayreuth, Germany. $275.

Porcelain 5-eyelet cap-toe woman's oxford in matte green with scalloped gold rim and rim lace in raised white enamel micro beads; unmarked; a "left"; 5-1/8"L x 2-5/8"H. Royal Bayreuth, Germany. Uncommon. $275.

Pair of porcelain 5-eyelet cap-toe women's oxfords in royal blue with geometric lace pattern in raised black enamel micro beads with original shoelaces; unmarked; each is 5-1/4"L x 2-5/8"H. Royal Bayreuth, Germany. $550 for the pair.

Porcelain 5-eyelet cap-toe woman's oxford in white ground with florals covered with a glass-like granular surface, similar to coralline, with original shoelace; unmarked; a "right"; 5-1/4"L x 2-11/16"H. Royal Bayreuth, Germany. Uncommon. $350.

Porcelain 5-eyelet cap-toe woman's oxford in cobalt with scroll and lace pattern in raised white enamel micro beads; unmarked; a "left"; 5-1/16"L x 2-5/8"H. Can be found with blue mark, "Royal Bayreuth" and logo. This shoe is often found with souvenir gold script indicating the place where it was purchased originally. Royal Bayreuth, Germany. $150.

Porcelain pastel mint green woman's evening slipper with pieced vamp ruff and in-mold buckle, both with raised white enamel micro beads; unmarked; a "right"; 5-1/4"L x 2-11/16"H. Royal Bayreuth, Germany. Rare. $500.

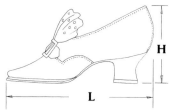

Porcelain 5-eyelet cap-toe woman's oxford in blue with scroll and lace pattern in raised turquoise enamel micro dots; unmarked; 5-1/8"L x 2-5/8"H. Royal Bayreuth, Germany. Uncommon. $275.

Porcelain pastel pink woman's evening slipper with pieced vamp ruff and in-mold buckle, both with raised white enamel micro beads; unmarked; a "right"; 5-1/4"L x 2-11/16"H. Royal Bayreuth, Germany. Rare. $500.

Porcelain pastel blue woman's evening slipper with piercing on each side of high pointed vamp trimmed in raised white enamel micro beads; unmarked; a "right"; 5-3/16"L x 2-5/8"H. Sides are dry brushed in gold to represent the wear when "she danced all night". Royal Bayreuth, Germany. Very rare. $800.

Porcelain flat-heeled evening slipper with in-mold straps and textured sock, and silver and white raised enamel micro bead design on toe; unmarked; a "left"; 5-3/16"L x 3-3/8"H. Royal Bayreuth, Germany. Very rare. $1,100.

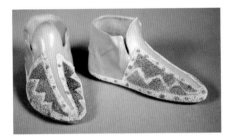

Pair of porcelain "buckskin" Indian moccasins with raised white enamel micro beads applied over a blue/green/ochre/white pattern; unmarked; each is 5"L x 2-5/8"H. Royal Bayreuth, Germany. Uncommon. $300 each.

Porcelain woman's black evening strap shoe with pieced sides; in-mold strap button and silver vamp ornament; raised white enamel micro bead patterns on toe and back of heel; inside and bottom painted a light tan; unmarked; a "right"; 5-3/16"L x 2-5/8"H. Royal Bayreuth, Germany. Very rare. $1,100.

Details in the "right" moccasin of the pair shown in the previous illustration. Note in-mold stitching detail along bottom edge. The opening separating the front from the sides was probably done with a sharp knife after casting.

View of back of woman's black evening strap shoe showing beading detail on heel.

Porcelain flat-heeled evening slipper with rim lace of raised white enamel micro beads; has barely visible remains of blue Bayreuth mark on tan-painted sole; a "right"; 5-1/4"L x 1-1/2"H. Gold crown on inside is unusual. Royal Bayreuth, Germany. Very rare. $800.

Contemporary porcelain shoes made at the Royal Bayreuth factory beginning in about the 1990s and continuing to the present. They are included here for reference. The florals are decals. The typical factory mark is on the shank and reads, "Tettau Antiquariat/*logo*/Königl. Pr. Tettau/GERMANY/*T.*/ANNO 1890". The woman's oxford is typically 5-1/4"L x 2-5/8"H; the 4 x 4 high top is typically 4-11/16"L x 3-9/16"H. They can be purchased at the factory store for about $20 each.

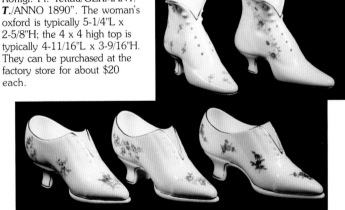

SPODE, ROYAL WORCESTER, AND COALPORT

The renowned English factories of Spode, Royal Worcester, and Coalport produced meticulously crafted porcelain shoes. They are among the more difficult to locate in the secondary market. Spode produced an inkwell in at least three patterns. Royal Worcester produced eight models of slippers, many in various décors. Coalport produced over ninety slippers, but relatively few in each model.

Porcelain slipper with applied heel and applied bow; printed blue pattern on white ground, gloss glazed; Royal Worcester model number 428; marked with blue RW logo and date code; 6-1/4"L x 3-1/4"H. Royal Worcester, England. c.1875. $350.

Porcelain *Eastern Slipper* inkwell with lid and quill containers; Saxon blue ground with pattern of a bird and leaves raised and cut up and gilded; gold sanded; sole painted ochre; pattern 4054; hand-painted in red on shank, "SPODE/4054"; 5-13/16"L x 1-9/16"H. Spode, England. c.1824. Very rare. $3,000.

Porcelain mule with applied heel; printed blue pattern on white ground, gloss glazed; Royal Worcester model number 437; marked with green RW logo and date code; 6-1/16"L x 2-5/16"H. Royal Worcester, England. c.1877. $350.

Porcelain slipper with applied heel and in-mold crossed flaps; printed blue pattern on white ground, gloss glazed; Royal Worcester model number 438; marked with blue RW logo and date code; 5-5/8"L x 2-11/16"H. Royal Worcester, England. c.1875. $350.

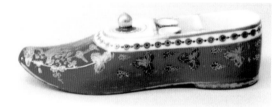

Porcelain *Eastern Slipper* inkwell with lid and quill containers; crimson ground with pattern of a bird and leaves raised and cut up and gilded; gold sanded; sole painted ochre; pattern 3993; unmarked; 5-13/16"L x 1-1/2"H. Spode, England. c.1824. Very rare. $3,000.

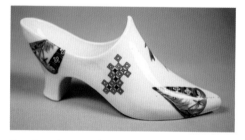

Porcelain slipper with applied heel; printed blue pattern on white ground, gloss glazed; Royal Worcester model number 439; marked with blue RW logo and date code; 7-3/8"L x 3-1/8"H. Royal Worcester, England. c.1886. $350.

Porcelain *Eastern Slipper* inkwell with lid and quill containers; *Japanese Silk* pattern; pale Nile green ground with oriental style "lantern" pattern printed in green with enamel coloring in yellow, red, and blue; solid gold gilding on upper surface and welt of slipper; sole painted ochre; hand-painted in red on shank, "SPODE"; 6-1/8"L x 1-5/8"H. Spode, England. c.1824. Very rare. $3,000.

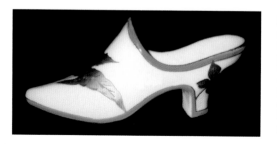

Porcelain slipper with applied heel; pattern of raised gold leaves on white ground, gloss glazed; Royal Worcester model number 439; marked with blue RW logo and date code; 7-3/8"L x 3-1/8"H. Royal Worcester, England. c.1886. Uncommon décor. $600.

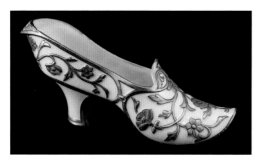

Porcelain heeled slipper with cuffed rear rim and embossed pattern of floral and foliage vines; Royal Worcester model number 700; marked with blue-green RW logo and date code; 5-5/8"L x 2-1/4"H. Royal Worcester, England. c.1879. Rare. $2,000.

Porcelain heeled slipper with applied bow and hand-pierced vamp; burnished gold ground with hand-applied gold micro beads; Royal Worcester model number 763; marked with green RW logo and date code; 5-9/16"L x 2-3/4"H. Royal Worcester, England. c.1883. Very rare. $2,600.

Bottom surface detail of Royal Worcester shoe model 763.

Porcelain high-heeled slipper with applied vamp ornament; hand-painted foliage and bird; Royal Worcester model number 899; marked with green RW logo and date code; 4-5/8"L x 4-1/2"H. Royal Worcester, England. c.1882. Uncommon. $1,500.

Porcelain Indian slipper with embossed design; Royal Worcester model number 1180; marked with purple RW logo and date code as well as purple British Registry code "R⁴N°60365" and "1180"; 6-1/2"L x 2-1/4"H. Royal Worcester, England. c.1889. Uncommon. $1,500. Not shown, the pierced version: $1,800.

The crisp detail on the front curved surface of the Indian slipper suggests multiple molds in the fabrication or retooling of the embossed pattern after casting.

Porcelain Normandy shoe, French gray ground with raised gold and jeweled vamp ornament; salmon inside; Coalport model number V1383; marked with green Coalport logo; 6"L x 2-1/2"H. Coalport, England. c.1890. Rare. $1,600.

Porcelain mule with applied open-front heel, ivory ground with raised gold and jeweled vamp ornament; blush pink inside; Coalport model number V1663; marked with green Coalport logo; 6-1/16"L x 2-1/2"H. Coalport, England. c.1890. Rare. $1,600.

Detail of hand-painted and crafted vamp ornament on Coalport shoe V1663. Note the unusual diamond shape of the pink jewel just above the crescent at the toe of the shoe as well as the raised gold micro beads, all handcrafted and applied.

Detail of heel design on Coalport shoe V1663. This type of heel is found on many Coalport shoes. It solved the problem of steam build-up in an applied heel during kiln-firing as well as providing a hanging device for use as a wall pocket; the "V" designation of Coalport shoes suggests their intended use as "Vases"

Porcelain mule with applied open-front heel in American blush pink; jewel framed, hand-tooled gold star ornament; solid burnished gold inside; Coalport model number V2349; marked with green Coalport logo; 4-3/8"L x 2"H. Coalport, England. c.1892. Rare. $1,600.

Porcelain slipper box and cover, printed crocodile pattern on green ground, sprays of foliage and raised flowers in gold; Coalport model number V4930; green Coalport logo surrounded by gold millstone within which is "BAILEY, BANKS & BIDDLE CO. PHILADELPHIA"; 5-5/8"L x 2-1/2"H, shoe only; 3"H with lid. Coalport, England. c.1895. Rare. $1,900.

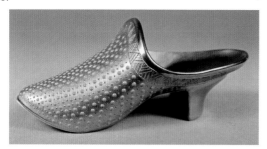

Porcelain mule with applied open-front heel with tooled geometric rim; burnished gold inside and out with turquoise-jeweled face; Coalport model number V3327; green Coalport logo; stamped in gold over Coalport logo "CHICAGO/1893/EXHIBITION"; 4-7/16"L x 1-7/8"H. Coalport, England. c.1893. Rare. $1,400.

Porcelain white-glazed mule with applied open-front heel; hand-painted gold vamp design and trim; green Coalport logo used from 1891-1915; 6"L x 2-7/16"H. Coalport, England. c.1900-1915. $450.

MEISSEN

The Meissen factory made only one shoe form, exclusively a shoe. It is the crushed heel slipper. It was made and continues to this day to be made in two sizes and in lefts and rights. Meissen's crushed heel slipper has been copied by many factories. In addition to being marked by Meissen's crossed swords, the Meissen crushed heel slippers are easy to identify because their soles are about twice the thickness of the side walls, a feature not found in the copies. The purple indish slipper shown here was measured with a micrometer caliper and showed the wall thickness to be 0.327cm (about 1/8") and the bottom to be 0.694cm (about 9/32"). The factory's "L" series of twenty-six angels doing various things includes one carrying a shoe, shown in the last of the following illustrations. Not shown here is another Meissen shoe-related form, the c.1750-1760 Flea Leg pipe tamper. It consists of a heeled shoe-shod full length left leg with a flea painted on the top of the thigh above the stocking.

The Meissen mark has been used by other factories; collectors are cautioned to be very skeptical about any shoe form carrying blue crossed swords other than the three described above. In particular, the factory adamantly refutes any claim that they ever made what is known as the hugging angels shoes, even though many of them carry a mark similar to Meissen's.

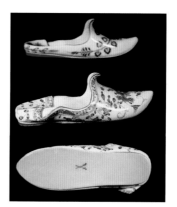

Pair of porcelain Meissen crushed heel slippers showing comparison between large and small sizes, and the typical blue crossed swords mark found on these slippers. The large slipper is described in the previous illustration. Small slipper in blue cornflower pattern is 3-3/4"L x 1-1/4"H. Meissen, Germany. Small blue cornflower pattern: $300.

Pair of porcelain large-size Meissen crushed heel slippers in HP florals and insects, each 6-1/2"L x 2-1/8"H and each with Meissen blue crossed swords. Meissen, Germany. $400 each.

Pair of porcelain large-size Meissen crushed heel slippers, each 6-1/2"L x 2-1/8"H and each marked with blue crossed swords. The "right" in purple Indian pattern (Purpur Indische Malerei, or "Purple Indish") and the "left" in blue cornflower pattern. Meissen, Germany. Large purple Indian pattern: $650. Large blue cornflower pattern: $350.

Pair of porcelain small-size Meissen crushed heel slippers in cobalt with vamp medallions, each 3-3/4"L x 1-1/4"H and each with Meissen blue crossed swords. Meissen, German. $400 each.

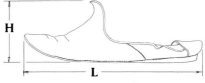

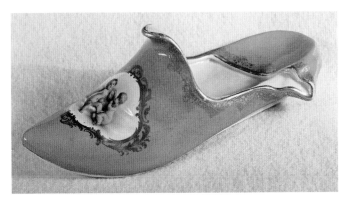

Porcelain large-size Meissen crushed heel slipper with cupids vamp medallion; Meissen blue crossed swords; 6-5/8"L x 2-1/8"H. Meissen, Germany. $450.

Porcelain angel with quiver holding shoe with ruffled rim; Meissen model number L117; Meissen blue swords mark; 6"H. One of twenty-six members of the Meissen "L" series of angels mounted on round bases doing different things. Meissen, Germany. c.1880s. Rare. $2,500.

Porcelain large-size Meissen crushed heel slipper with courting scene vamp medallion; Meissen blue crossed swords; 6-5/8"L x 2-1/8"H. Meissen, Germany. $450.

Detail of shoe in Meissen L117 figurine.

OLDER POTTERY

Shoes shown in this section generally were made from the early 1800s to the early 1900s. Included are shoes known to have been manufactured by particular companies, but the majority are unmarked and unattributed. Most were made in Europe; the scroddle and redware pottery may have been made in the United States.

Pearlware, or pearl-glaze, white pottery boot warmer; unmarked; 7-1/2"L x 6-1/4"H. prob. Scotland or England. c.1840. $375.

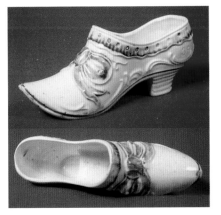

Thin pearlware (white pottery) with glaze that has blue cast where it puddles, as in edges at bottom of inside of heel; unmarked; 5-3/8"L x 2-3/16"H. Pre-1840. $85.

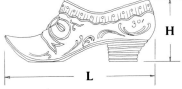

Yellow ware (pottery) slipper-inside-a-slipper pipe rest; white granular ceramic applied to outside; "A" mark of Johann Moehling; 6-3/8"L x 2-1/2"H. Johann Moehling, Bohemia. c.1860. $200.

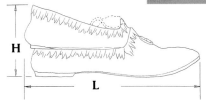

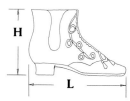

Yellow ware (pottery) ankle shoe match holder on match striker base with mottled white overglaze; unmarked, but identical shoe has been seen marked with "A.T."; 3-1/2"L x 2-1/4"H shoe on 3-7/8"L x 2-5/16"W scored base. c.1860. $150.

Yellow ware (pottery) pair of women's ankle boots with asymmetrical tassels match striker glazed gray with gold trim; impressed with Johann Moehling "A" on bottom; 3-1/8"H overall on 4-5/16"L x 4-3/4"W base. Shoes are from different molds; tassels and button plackets face different directions. Johann Moehling, Bohemia. c.1860. $200.

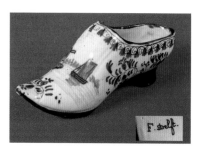

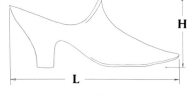

Faience (pottery) mule with applied heel HP in polychrome floral motif; red mark on shank used by Adriaen Pynacker in about 1690; 7-1/4"L x 3"H. Adriaen Pynacker was active in the late 1600s in Delft, Holland. Many Dutch marks of that era were copied in later years, leading to some skepticism about the true age of this shoe, which is clearly old. The fair value that should be placed on a piece such as this requires expertise in ceramics of the era from Holland. An initial value can be placed based on the quality of the décor. Prob. made in the Netherlands pre-1850. $500.

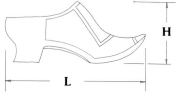

Tin-glazed faience (pottery) clog with applied heel and HP décor; underglaze on shank, "F. Delft."; 5-1/16"L x 2-1/8"H. Prob. made in the Netherlands pre-1875. $250.

Pair of pottery clog straights HP in *Rose Medallion* pattern; red mark on shank of the De Twee Scheepjees (two little ships) factory in Delft, Holland, operated by the Pennis family; each is 4"L x 1-3/8"H. Prob. made in The Netherlands in the mid-1800s, perhaps by a successor to Jan Pennis. $250 each.

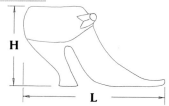

Pottery, tin-glazed HP shoe with applied high heel and bow, and elongated toe; unmarked; 5"L x 2-3/4"H. If perfect, $300.

Pair of pottery matched chip carved clog straights; hand-incised on each heel, "T P 1" and a hand signature that could not be deciphered; bottoms fully glazed with stilt marks; the one on the left, 4-11/16"L x 2-1/16"H, and the one on the right, 4-3/4"L x 2-1/8"H. Prob. made in province of Friesland, The Netherlands. c.1900. $200 each.

Pottery chip carved clog wall pocket; unmarked; 8-3/4"L x 3-3/4"H. Prob. made in the province of Friesland, The Netherlands. c.1900. $300.

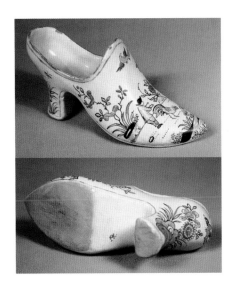

Pottery tin-glazed slipper with applied heel and HP scene; red mark on shank used by Adriaen Pynacker in about 1690; 6-1/4"L x 2-7/8"H. Adriaen Pynacker was active in the late 1600s in Delft, Holland. Many Dutch marks of that era were copied in later years, leading to some skepticism about the true age of this shoe, which is clearly old. An initial value can be placed based on the quality of the décor. Prob. made in the Netherlands, 1800s. $350.

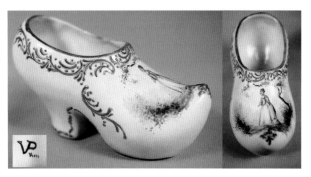

Pottery, white glazed clog with raised gold scrolls and HP woman on vamp; overglaze Veuve Perrin mark on shank; 5-3/16"L x 2-13/16"H. Skepticism should be exercised about the true age of this shoe, which appears to be old, and its origin based on the mark. A value can be placed based on the quality of the décor. Prob. European. $125.

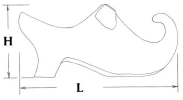

White ceramic tan glazed clog with curled toe, in-mold bow, and applied heel with large hole in its bottom surface for hanging as a wall pocket; cobalt glazed on inside and bottom with remains of stilts; black filigree and leaf pattern; hammered and tooled metallic foil rim band and vamp medallion appliqués sealed with narrow brown edge; impressed into bottom "Vieillard & Co" plus other wording that can not be deciphered; bottom also has impressed numbers and a HP "D716"; 6-3/4"L x 3"H. Vieillard, France. Mid-late 1800s. $400.

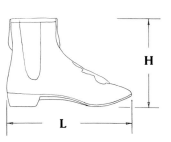

Scroddle pottery shoe bank; unmarked; 4-1/2"L x 3-1/16"H. c.1880. $90.

Red clay pottery inkwell boot with two openings for quills; black gloss glaze throughout with stilt marks on bottom; unmarked; 4-7/8"L x 2-3/8"H. Mid 1800s. $125.

Red clay pottery pipe rest slipper; bottom unglazed; 6-1/8"L x 2-3/16"H. Second half 1800s. $125.

Faience (pottery) HP clog with curled toe, in-mold bow, and applied heel; expertly HP scene on vamp; overglaze on shank, the mark of the Marseilles factory of Veuve Perrin (widow Perrin), an 18th century mark widely imitated; 7-1/4"L x 3-1/8"H. Skepticism should be exercised about the true age of this shoe, which is clearly old, and its origin based on the mark. A value can be placed based on the quality of the décor. Prob. made in France, 1800s. $300.

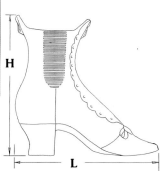

Red clay pottery woman's high-top double-buttoned shoe; unmarked; bottom unglazed; 5-3/16"L x 4-7/8"H. Second half 1800s. $125.

61

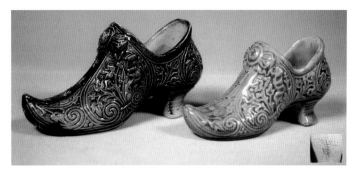

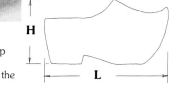

Elaborately embossed stack-heeled shoes. Left to right: salt-glazed blue and gray stoneware; unmarked except for tooled numbers impressed into sole, "193"; 4-15/16"L x 2-9/16"H; $50. Yellow pottery, mustard glazed; impressed into bottom, "HOGANAS/KP"; 4-5/16"L x 2-1/4"H. Hoganas, Sweden. $30.

Thin ceramic Dutch shoe, high-gloss glazed a mustard yellow-brown on top of which have been applied layers of dark green, blue, and brown, leaving the inside and vamp the original color; unmarked; 4-3/8"L x 2-1/4"H. Provenance suggests origin as Denmark, c.1889. $70.

Red pottery gloss glazed slipper; impressed into heel and shank, "721/ HOGANAS/KS"; 5-1/4"L x 2"H. Hoganas, Sweden. $30.

Gray white pottery gloss-glazed open vamp shoe with unusual split instep strap; unmarked except tooled numbers impressed into bottom of heel, "1051"; 5-3/4"L x 2-5/16"H. Prob. European. Uncommon. $150.

Pair of tan pottery gold-heeled shoes with in-mold bows, both unmarked; both 5-7/16"L x 2-1/2"H. Left to right: brown gloss glazed with HP vamp décor, $30; ivory crackle-glazed, HP gold trim, $30.

Buff-colored pottery slipper with applied heel and in-mold bow knot with applied bow ends; impressed into the sole, "BW/598" and additional scattered numbers; 5-3/8"L x 1-13/16"H. $70.

Tan pottery fluted rim slipper with applied Chinese man in matte maroon with black details; tooled impressed mark, "W.S.&S."; 5"L x 3-1/2"HOA. Rare, from a company in business only one year. W. Schiller & Son, Bodenbach, Bohemia, c.1885. $150.

Pottery clog with applied heel and bow; HP design; marked underglaze on shank; 6-1/4"L x 2-15/16"H. $70.

Tan pottery Eastern slipper with embossed floral and foliage design; tooled impressed mark on sole, "C.L.T.& Co/17"; 5-5/8"L x 1-1/2"H. $35.

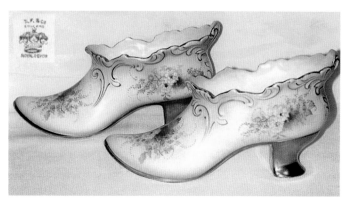

Pair of pottery Royal Devon straights in Vellum pattern X543; marked "S.F.& CO./ENGLAND/logo/ROYAL DEVON/#x543"; 8-1/2"L x 4-1/2"H. S. Fielding & Co., England; c.1902. Rare. $300 each.

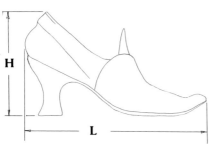

Pottery slipper with applied heel and applied shoelaces with tasseled ends; marked "Nove/*" on inside heel surface; 6-1/2"L x 3-5/8"H. The mold dates from the late 1800s, but the mark places it c.1920-1930. Barettoni, Italy. $200.

Stoneware heavily embossed drinking boot with spur; marked on shank with triangular logo and "GERZ"; a "right"; 7-1/16"L x 8"H. Gerz, Germany. c.1910. $90.

Ceramic gloss-glazed Dutch shoe with HP monotone scene on each side and HP surrounding detail; underglaze on sole, the mark shown; 4-7/8"L x 2-1/8"H. Prob. Germany or The Netherlands. $40.

ROCKINGHAM GLAZED

The color in some of the Rockingham glazed shoes shown here has been lightened to allow the in-mold detail to be seen. Boot warmers generally were made in distinguishable lefts and rights. The in-mold laces found on most of them are typically on the inside surfaces, abutting each other. They are rarely marked. Most probably were made in England or the United States in the mid 1800s.

Pottery tortoise pattern Rockingham glazed boot warmer; unmarked; a "left"; 7-3/16"L x 6-1/8"H. Bottom view illustrates a characteristic of Rockingham glaze … the color is part of the glaze. $150.

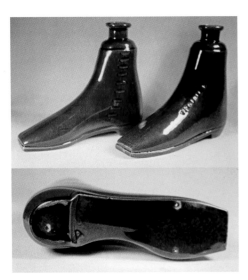

Pottery Rockingham glazed boot warmers, distinguishable left and right, with "Q VICTORIA" impressed into outside surface of each; the "left" has eleven in-mold horizontal laces, the "right" has ten; fully glazed bottom with three stilt marks; unmarked; the "right", 7-5/16"L x 6-7/16"H, and the "left", 7-7/16"L x 6-7/16"H. assumed to have been made in England. $225 each.

Pottery caramel-color Rockingham glazed boot warmer; bottom fully glazed except for three stilt marks; unmarked; a "right"; 7-3/4"L x 6-1/8"H. $150.

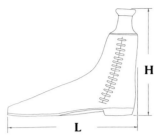

Reddish tan black-flecked pottery Rockingham glazed inkwell shoe; unmarked; 4-5/16"L x 1-3/4"H. c.1870. $75.

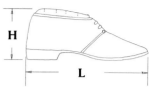

Pottery Rockingham glazed boot warmer with in-mold tie above six horizontal laces and tassel on front; incised in script into bottom, "A M^c"; a "right"; 7-5/16"L x 5-3/16"H. If perfect, $150.

Pair of pottery slippers with in-mold alligator face; unmarked. One collector has theorized that these may have been made as Florida souvenirs in the 1920s. Tan-glazed on left, 3-1/8"L x 1-7/16"H, $20. Rockingham glazed on right, 4-3/8"L x 2"H, $40.

OLDER AMERICAN POTTERY

Shown here are shoe forms representative of American potteries that could be identified with certainty.

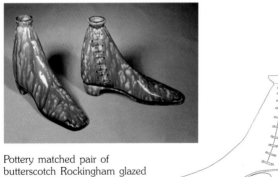

Two pottery Rockingham glazed Bennington miniature boots with handles; unmarked; typically 1-13/16"L x 1-7/8"H. Fenton, USA. Mid 1800s. $30 each.

Pottery matched pair of butterscotch Rockingham glazed Bennington boot warmers; bottoms completely glazed with stilt marks; unmarked; each is 6-1/8"L x 4-3/4"H. These boots were photographed in the Bennington Museum, Vermont, and are the only authenticated boot warmers that correctly can be called "Bennington". Prob. Fenton rather than Norton, USA. c.1850. $1,200 for the pair.

Pottery Rockingham glazed Bennington miniature boots; unmarked; larger size typically 1-1/2"L x 1-15/16"H; smaller, 3/4"L x 1"H. Fenton, USA. Mid 1800s. $30 each.

Assortment of pottery Bennington miniature slippers in various glazes; all unmarked; typically 2-3/16"L x 1"H. Fenton, USA. Mid 1800s. $25 each.

White pottery boots and shoe cast from bottom of boot mold; both boots with shank impression, "J.S.T.&CO." (J.S.Taft & Company) in black; shoe unmarked. Midnight green gloss glazed boot with souvenir gold script "Rahway, N.J."; 3-11/16"L x 4-7/16"H; $70. Reddish brown gloss glazed boot, 3-3/4"L x 4-9/16"H; $70. Midnight green gloss glazed shoe, 3-5/8"L x 1-9/16"H; $25. All from the Hampshire Pottery, USA.

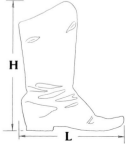

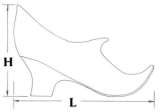

Pottery, speckled khaki gloss glazed slipper with applied heel cap; impressed into shank in a diamond shape, "C/KA/W"; 5-15/16"L x 3-13/16"H. Chelsea Keramic Art Works, USA. Rare. $300.

Pottery, speckled grayish teal gloss glazed slipper; impressed into shank in a diamond shape, "C/KA/W"; 6-7/16"L x 2-13/16"H. Chelsea Keramic Art Works, USA. Rare. $300.

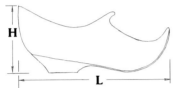

Pottery crackle glazed slipper with HP cobalt trim; marked on bottom of heel; 6"L x 3-3/4"H. The marks on the four Dedham shoes shown here are somewhat faint. This mark was taken from another piece of Dedham pottery and is similar to those found on the shoes. Dedham Pottery, USA. c.1925. Very rare. $1,500.

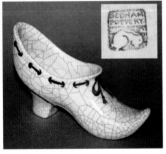

Pottery crackle glazed small boot; a "left"; marked on sole; 2-5/8"L x 2-3/16"H. Dedham Pottery, USA. c.1925. Rare. $750.

Two pottery crackle glazed boots with HP cuffs; marked; 4"L x 5"H. Dedham Pottery, USA. The pottery produced numerous patterns. The values of these boots depend on the patterns. Left: swan pattern; c. 1928; rare; $900. Right: azalea pattern; c.1938; uncommon; $675.

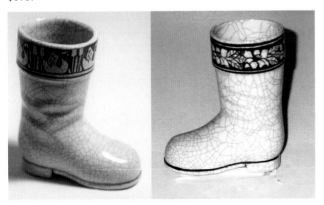

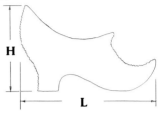

Pottery slipper with applied heel cobalt glazed; applied cylindrical-shaped granules to surface; impressed factory mark on sole; 5-3/4"L x 3-9/16"H. Cincinnati Art Pottery, USA. Pre-1891. Uncommon. $200.

Bottom view of Cincinnati Art Pottery slipper showing factory mark.

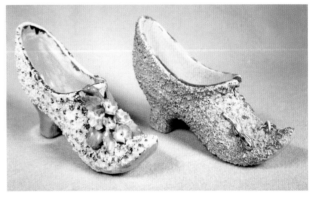

Two pottery slippers with applied heels; applied cylindrical-shaped granules to surface and appliqués. Left: unmarked, 5-7/8"L x 3-1/2"H; either Cincinnati Art Pottery or William Dell Pottery; c. 1890; Uncommon. $200. Right: impressed "WmDell/& Co/CinO"; 5-13/16"L x 3-9/16"H; William Dell & Company, USA. c.1891 or 1892. Uncommon. $200.

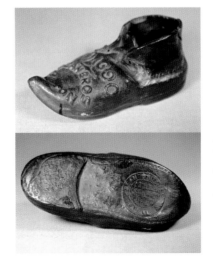

Red pottery broken down shoe with matte brown glaze; embossed on vamp "A.D.1690/DEAN BROS/ TAUNTON" and on sole "DEAN BROTHERS TAUNTON/THE SHOE MEN"; 5-3/16"L x 2-1/16"H. Prob. USA. Pos. a bicentennial souvenir, making it c.1890. $85.

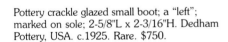

Thin pottery child's shoe with brown matte glaze; unusual post-cast tooled "stitching"; bottom completely glazed except for stilt marks; unmarked; 4-1/16"L x 2"H. $70.

Pottery sabot with airbrushed ground color and HP applied cicada; hand signed "J. Sicardo", a premier Weller artist; 6-3/4"L x 3-1/8"H. Weller, USA. Rare. $400.

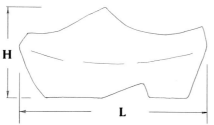

Pottery SW Indian moccasin; unmarked; 7-3/8"L x 4"H. Unattributed. $100.

MOSTLY MAJOLICA

White pottery majolica shoe with high flounce and in-mold bow; unmarked except for impressed tooled numbers in sole "6421/13"; 6-5/16"L x 5-3/8"H. Rare. $350.

Pottery majolica hiking boot with in-mold laces, buttons, and florals; unmarked except some tooled numbers impressed into the sole; 5-1/2"L x 3-5/8"H. $125.

White pottery majolica shoe with ankle ruffle; deep teal ground gloss glazed with tan and burgundy accents; unmarked; 6-1/16"L x 3-7/16"H. $250.

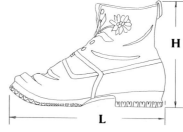

Left: pottery majolica gloss glazed slipper; Hautin and Boulanger impressed mark on sole used toward end of 19th century; 10-3/16"L x 3-3/4"H; Hautin and Boulanger, France; c.1880; uncommon; $350. Right (sketch): pottery majolica gloss glazed candlestick slipper; impressed into sole, "LE THORPE/2109"; 7-9/16"L x 2-1/2"H; uncommon; $250.

Pottery majolica low-cut heeled slipper with scalloped rim with bow and toe ornament; unmarked; 5"L x 3"H. $250.

Two red pottery Thoune majolica shoes with edelweiss motifs, both from the Thoune region of Switzerland; c.1900; unmarked; both uncommon. Left: clog with applied snail and mushroom; 5-3/4"L x 2-3/16"H; $150. Right: slipper with applied bow and sole detail including "nails"; 4"L x 1-7/8"H; $125.

Pottery majolica wall pocket slipper with ruffled rim and applied flowers and leaves; unmarked except for hand-incised "1019" in shank; 10-1/2"L x 5"H incl. ruffle. This shoe has been attributed by some to Longchamp and its designer, Robert Charbonnier, but as far as can be told, the mold for this shoe is identical to that in the previous illustration, a shoe carrying the mark of a Belgian factory. Late 1800s. $250.

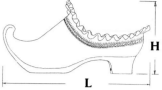

Ceramic majolica slipper held by elf on elaborate base; unmarked; 11"HOA. May be Austria. c.1880. Rare. $1,100.

Pottery majolica wall pocket slipper with straps across open vamp, stand-up ruffled rim, and applied flowers and leaves; unmarked except for hand-incised "7901" in shank; 10"L x 4-1/2"H incl. ruffle. This shoe has been attributed by some to Longchamp and its designer, Robert Charbonnier, but as far as can be told, the mold for this shoe is identical to that in the illustration of a shoe carrying the mark of a Belgian factory except for the open vamp. Late 1800s. Rare. $450.

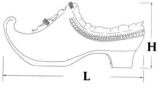

Pottery clog with applied roses and leaves; raised oval pad on shank with impressed "E.G" and raised square pad abutting it with impressed tooled numbers "46"; underglaze hand-painted in brown "22.308"; 10-1/2"L x 4-1/4"H, not incl. appliqué. Emile Gallé, France. c.1890. Rare. $800.

Pottery majolica wall pocket slipper with ruffled rim and applied flowers and leaves; circular mark on shank has a rampant lion in its center and around it "S^TE ANTONNE/DE LA FAIENCERE DE NIMY DE MONS", and below the circle, "...MOUZIN LECAT & CIE"; 10-1/2"L x 4-3/4"H incl. ruffle. Manufacture Royale et Impériale de Nimy, Belgium. Late 1800s. $250.

Pottery majolica heeled slipper with ruffled rim and applied flowers and leaves; unmarked except for embossed number that appears to be "9691", a small impressed heart, and a brown underglaze "p" or "d"; 8"L x 4-1/8"H. This specific shoe has been attributed to Longchamp, but its design features and décor are remarkably similar to the marked shoe from Manufacture Royale et Impériale de Nimy. c.1900. $250.

Pottery majolica heeled slipper with applied bow; marked on shank; 4-1/8"L x 2-1/4"H. Thomas Sargeant (also found as Sergeant, Sargent, etc.), France. Uncommon. $200.

Pottery sanded majolica pump with appliqué; unmarked; 4-3/16"L x 2"H. Prob. early 1900s. Uncommon form in this décor. $75.

Pottery majolica clog with applied flowers and leaves; unmarked; 6-3/4"L x 3-3/16"H. Prob. France. c.1900. $75.

Reddish brown pottery heeled slipper with metallic electric blue/purple high gloss glaze; marked on shank, "Grès de A. Gytère/ Rambersvillers"; 8-5/8"L x 3-3/4"H. This shoe was seen advertised in a 1920 vintage catalog. Made in Rambervillers, France. c.1920. $100.

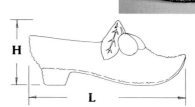

Pottery sanded majolica duck-bill toe clog with in-mold cherries and leaves; bottom completely glazed with stilt marks; unmarked; 5-9/16"L x 2-1/4"H. Assumed to have been made in France. Prob. early 1900s. $85.

Pottery sanded majolica duck-bill toe clog with in-mold cherries and leaves; bottom marked on shank as shown; 5-1/2"L x 2-1/4"H. Assumed to be somewhat later than version in previous illustration because of bottom glazing differences. France. $45.

Two pottery sanded majolica shoes with applied rose and leaves; unmarked. Left (sketch): high-top shoe whose in-mold detail is obscured by the granular surface; uncommon form in this décor; 5-3/8"L x 4-3/4"H. Prob. early 1900s. $95. Right: baby shoe; 4-5/16"L x 2-9/16"H. Prob. early 1900s. $45.

FRENCH FAIENCE

French faience refers to a particular type of pottery made in France beginning in about the 17th century. Most of the early wares reside in museums or in private collections and would not be affordable to the average collector if they could be located. What are found in today's secondary market are mainly items that were made in the late 19th and early 20th centuries. They generally have tin-glazed (white) back-grounds on which have been hand-painted the colorful décors for which each producing region is known. The Breton man and woman are common themes for the factories of Quimper. In some cases, as for Longwy products, the décor has become a signature of the factory. Technically, a case could be made for placing Longwy and some Gien products in a separate category. They are included here for simplicity and because Gien made shoes in both the Longwy mode as well as in décors that would place them with other French faience.

Five pottery sanded majolica baby shoes with flower and leaf appliqués; all unmarked; prob. early 1900s. Left to right: burgundy glazed, 4-1/2"L x 2-11/16"H, $45; mustard glazed, 4-5/8"L x 2-11/16"H, $55; green glazed, impressed "F" in sole, 4-1/2"L x 2-9/16"H, $55; white glazed, 4-1/2"L x 2-7/16"H, $65; and claret glazed, 3-7/8"L x 2-1/16"H, $55.

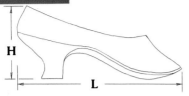

Pinkish pottery narrow slipper with applied heel and bow; HP Italian Renaissance design; origin and date signed on face of heel; 5-13/16"L x 2-1/2"H. Ulysse a Blois, France. Dated 1878. Rare. $375.

Pottery tin-glazed spade-toe slipper with applied heel; marked "GIEN" with castle logo; stilt marks on bottom; 5"L x 2-3/4"H. Gien, France. c.1875. $185.

Pinkish pottery narrow slipper with applied heel and bow; HP design; origin and date signed on face of heel and onto shank; 5-13/16"L x 2-1/2"H. Ulysse a Blois, France. Dated 1879. Rare. $375.

Pottery tin-glazed slipper with applied heel; marked "GIEN" with castle logo; stilt marks on bottom; 6-1/4"L x 3-3/16"H. c.1875. Uncommon. $250.

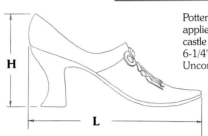

Pottery tin-glazed narrow slipper with pointed toe (portion missing); post-cast tooled design along rim; unmarked; 7-1/4"L x 2-13/16"H. France. Late 1800s. If perfect, $250.

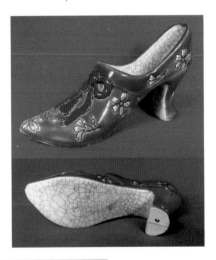

Pottery slipper cast from same mold as slipper in previous illustration; enamel glazed with enamel floral cloisons; crackle glazed inside and on the bottom, which has stilt marks; unmarked; 6-3/8"L x 3-1/4"H. Gien, France. c. 1880. Rare. $350.

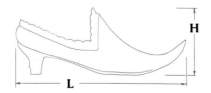

Pottery tin-glazed spade-toe slipper with applied heel; marked "GIEN" with castle logo; stilt marks on bottom; 5"L x 2-3/4"H. Gien, France. c.1875. $185.

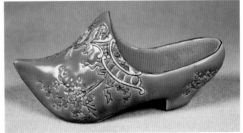

Pottery crackle glazed clog with enamel cloisons; marked on sole "LONGWY"; a "left"; 6-5/16"L x 3"H. Longwy, France. c.1900. Uncommon pattern. $275.

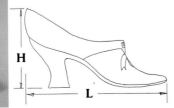

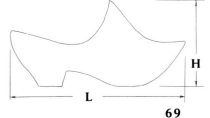

69

Pottery crackle glazed clog with enamel cloisons; marked on sole "Décor 5669" and on heel "Longwy"; a "right"; 6-5/16"L x 3"H. Longwy, France. c.1900. $175.

Pottery crackle glazed clog with enamel cloisons; marked on sole "Longwy/Made in France"; a "left"; 6-5/16"L x 3"H. Longwy, France. c.1900. $175.

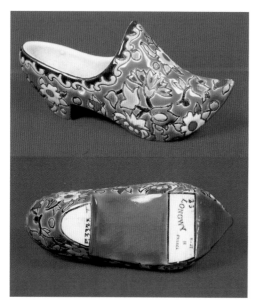

Pottery crackle glazed clog with enamel cloisons; marked on sole "Longwy/Made in France" and on heel "F.3378 T."; a "left"; 6-5/16"L x 3"H. Longwy, France. c.1900. $150.

Pottery glazed slipper with applied heel and enamel cloisons; unmarked except for tooled numbers impressed into shank, "138"; 5-9/16"L x 2"H. Prob. France. c.1890. Rare. $300.

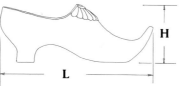

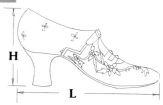

Pottery glazed heeled slipper with vamp strap and enamel cloisons; sketch shows pattern drawn on with a grease pencil after casting that acts as a barrier to prevent flow of the enamel from the cloisons, or cells; unmarked; 5-1/16"L x 2-5/8"H. Prob. France. c.1890. Rare. $300.

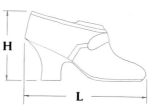

Pottery glazed heeled slipper with in-mold cross tabs and applied vamp ornament; enamel cloisons; unmarked; 4-3/8"L x 2-3/8"H. Prob. France. c.1890. $150.

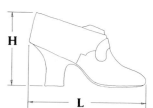

Pottery tin-glazed HP heeled slipper with in-mold cross tabs and applied vamp ornament; underglaze on shank, "RX" followed by small slashes; 4-3/16"L x 2-9/16"H. Prob. France. Late 1800s. $90.

Pottery tin-glazed HP slipper with applied heel, strap, and strap ornament; underglaze on shank, "H"; 7-7/8"L x 3-3/8"H. Mark was used by Pierre Heugue family of potters, Rouen, France, believed to have ceased operations in early 1800s, but this shoe is believed to date from the late 1800s. Rare. $300.

Pottery HP shoe with applied heel; HP on shank "Gallé í(?) Nancy/S¹ Clément"; 8-3/4"L x 4-3/8"H. France. Very rare décor. $800.

Pottery tin-glazed double salt slippers with applied ring handle; unmarked; 3-5/8"L x 1-5/8"H inc. handle. Porquier, France. c.1875-1905. $180.

Pottery, tin-glazed HP shoe with applied heel; blue overglaze mark on shank undecipherable; 8-7/8"L x 4-3/8"H. France. Prob. late 1800s. $225.

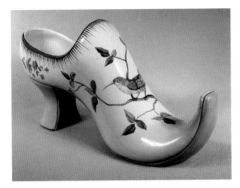

Pottery tin-glazed double salt slippers with applied ring handle; unmarked; 3-5/8"L x 1-5/8"H inc. handle. Porquier, France. c.1875-1905. $180.

Pottery tin-glazed double salt slippers with applied ring handle; un-marked; 3-5/8"L x 1-5/8"H incl. handle. Porquier, France. c.1875-1905. $180.

Pottery tin-glazed double salt slippers with applied ring handle; marked on toe of right slipper; 3-5/8"L x 1-3/4"H inc. handle. Porquier, France. c.1875-1905. Rare décor. $300.

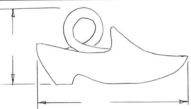

Pottery tin-glazed double salt slippers with applied ring handle; un-marked; 3-9/16"L x 1-11/16"H incl. handle. Porquier, France. c.1875-1905. $180.

Pottery tin-glazed double salt slippers with applied ring handle; marked on shank of right slipper; 3-5/8"L x 1-7/8"H incl. handle. Porquier, France. c.1875-1905. $250.

Pottery tin-glazed double salt sabots with applied ring handle; marked on shank; 3-3/8"L x 2"H inc. handle. Porquier, France. c.1875-1905. $250.

Pottery tin-glazed boot with in-mold buttons and tassel; unmarked; "SOUVENIR DE BRETAGNE"; oval base 3-7/8" x 2-5/8", and shoe 2-13/16"L x 3-1/4"H. Porquier, France. Late 1800s. $250.

Pottery tin-glazed high vamp shoe; "HB" on shank; 5-3/8"L x 2-15/16"H. Hubaudière, France. Late 1800s. $350.

Pottery tin-glazed high top shoe with in-mold buttons; unmarked; 3-3/8"L x 3-3/8"H. Porquier, France. Late 1800s. $250.

Pottery tin-glazed high vamp shoe; unmarked; 5-1/16"L x 2-7/8"H. Hubaudière, France. Late 1800s. Uncommon variation of décor. $425.

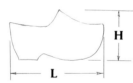

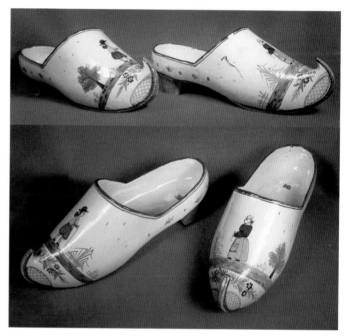

Pottery tin-glazed sabot; unmarked; 3-3/8"L x 1-3/4"H. Porquier, France. c.1900. $125.

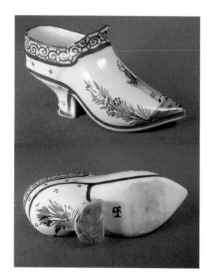

Pair of pottery matched tin-glazed life-sized clogs with applied heels; vertical heel faces with holes for use as wall pockets; marked on inside heel of each, "HB"; each is 9-11/16"L x 3-11/16"H. Hubaudière, France. Late 1800s. Rare. $2,000 for the pair.

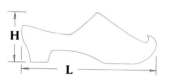

Pottery tin-glazed high vamp shoe; "HB" on shank; 5-3/8"L x 2-15/16"H. Hubaudière, France. Late 1800s. $350.

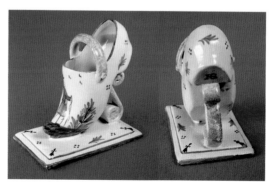

Pottery tin-glazed clog with applied strap mounted on S scroll and base; marked on bottom of heel "HB"; 2-5/16" x 3-1/2" base, 3-5/8"HOA. Hubaudière, France. Late 1800s. $225.

Pottery tin-glazed double salt slippers with applied ring handle; marked on shank of one slipper "HB"; 3-7/16"L x 1-13/16"H incl. handle. Hubaudière, France. Late 1800s. $180.

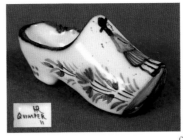

Pottery tin-glazed sabot; marked on shank "HR/Quimper/11"; 2-5/8"L x 1-3/8"H. Henriot, France. c.1904-1922. $95.

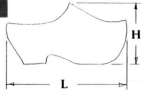

Pottery tin-glazed double salt sabots with applied ring handle; marked on shank of one sabot "HB"; 3-7/16"L x 1-13/16"H incl. handle. Hubaudière, France. Late 1800s. $250.

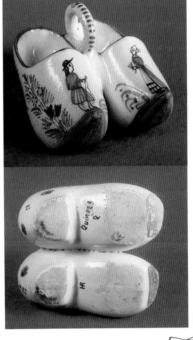

Pottery tin-glazed double salt sabots with ring handle; marked on shanks; 3-5/8"L x 1-9/16"H, shoe, 2-1/4"HOA. Henriot, France. c.1904-1922. $200.

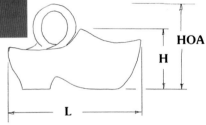

Pottery tin-glazed clog; marked on shank "HB/Quimper/xx—"; 4"L x 1-3/4"H. Hubaudière, France. 1930s. $75.

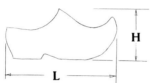

Pottery tin-glazed clog; marked on shank "HB/Quimper/France/F.414 Do.PS"; 4-1/8"L x 1-7/8"H. Hubaudière, France. 1950s. $45.

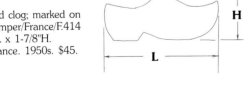

Pottery tin-glazed clog; marked on shank; 4-1/4"L x 1-7/8"H. Henriot, France. 1930s. $65.

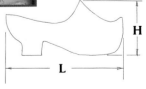

Pottery tin-glazed clog; marked on shank "Quimper/- – /France/414"; 2-13/16"L x 1-3/16"H. Hubaudière, France. Late 1930s. $35.

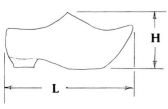

Pottery tin-glazed sabot; marked on shank; 2-3/4"L x 1-7/16"H. Henriot, France. 1930s. $50.

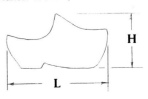

Pottery tin-glazed sabot; marked on shank; 2-11/16"L x 1-3/8"H. Henriot, France, 1930s. $50.

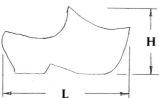

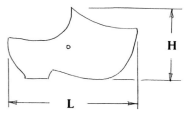

Pottery tin-glazed sabot; marked on shank; 2-3/4"L x 1-1/2"H. Henriot, France. 1950s. $45.

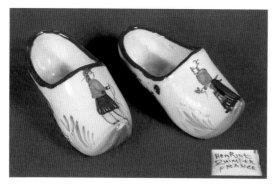

Pottery tin-glazed snuff box shoe with two holes in bottom; unmarked; 4-3/16"L x 1-9/16"H. Prob. Pouplard/Béatrix, France. c.1900. $325.

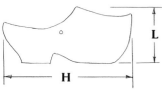

Pottery pair of matched sabots with Breton man and woman; marked on shanks; each is 3-1/2"L x 1-1/2"H. Henriot, France. 1930s. $95 for the pair.

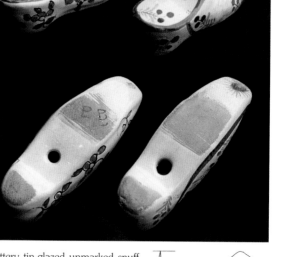

Pottery pair of matched sabots; marked on shanks; each is 3-5/8"L x 1-5/8"H. Henriot, France. 1950s. $65 for the pair.

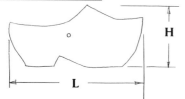

Pottery tin-glazed unmarked snuff boxes, each 4-3/16"L x 1-1/2"H, and each prob. made by Pouplard/Béatrix, France, c.1900 or early 1900s. Left, Breton woman, $325; right, sprays of cherries, $300.

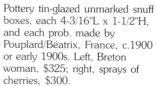

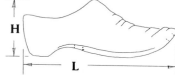

Pottery tin-glazed sabot; marked on shank; 3-7/8"L x 1-5/8"H. Henriot, France. 1950s. $45.

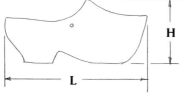

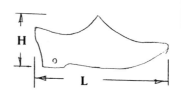

Pottery tin-glazed necklace pendant slipper; unmarked; 2"L x 13/16"H. Prob. Pouplard/Béatrix, France. c.1900. $65.

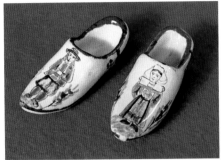

Pottery pair of matched slippers; unmarked; 2"L x 13/16"H each. Prob. Pouplard/Béatrix. c.1900. $120 for the pair.

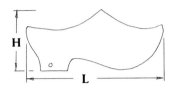

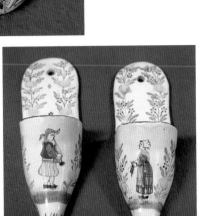

Pottery pair of matched tin-glazed wall pocket slippers; each marked on bottom; 6"L x 1-11/16"H each. Pouplard/Béatrix. c.1900. $370 for the pair.

Two pottery tin-glazed clogs with roosters and "Quand ce coq chantera mon amour finera" ("When this rooster crows my love will end."); marked on shanks; each is 3-3/4"L x 1-5/8"H. Pouplard/Béatrix, France. c. 1900. Uncommon. $125 each.

Pair of pottery tin-glazed clogs; marked on shanks; both are distinguishable "lefts"; each is 4-7/8"L x 1-5/8"H. Pouplard/Béatrix, France. c.1900. $150 each.

Pottery pair of matched tin-glazed wall pocket slippers; unmarked; 6-1/8"L x 1-11/16"H each. Prob. Pouplard/Béatrix. c.1900. $370 for the pair.

Pottery tin-glazed wall pocket slipper; unmarked; 6"L x 1-5/8"H. Prob. Pouplard/Béatrix, France. c.1900. $180.

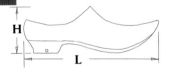

Pair of pottery tin-glazed matched clogs; note bubbles in colors, especially noticeable in woman's apron, suggesting an excessive firing temperature; unmarked; 6-3/16"L x 2-1/2"H each. Prob. Pouplard/Béatrix, France. c.1900. $190 for the pair.

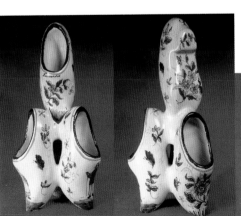

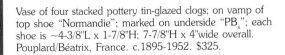

Vase of four stacked pottery tin-glazed clogs; on vamp of top shoe "Normandie"; marked on underside "PB$_x$"; each shoe is ~4-3/8"L x 1-7/8"H; 7-7/8"H x 4"wide overall. Pouplard/Béatrix, France. c.1895-1952. $325.

Pottery tin-glazed baby shoe bank with in-mold laces and tie; unmarked; 5-1/8"L x 3-1/4"H. Prob. Moreau, France. First quarter 1900s. $70.

Pair of attached pottery tin-glazed clogs with applied ties looped up and joined to form the handle of a basket; openings above vamp on each shoe form upside-down hearts; marked on shank; 13-1/2"L x 6-3/8"HOA. Jules Verlingue, France. c.1910. Rare. $400.

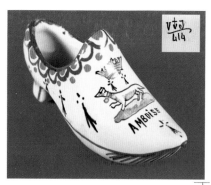

Pottery tin-glazed clog with white ermine and "Amboise" (town in France); marked on shank; 3-13/16"L x 2"H. Jules Verlingue, France. c.1903-1920. $125.

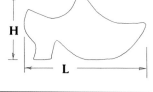

Pottery tin-glazed clog with a bee, an ant, and a butterfly on back of heel; marked on shank; 4-1/2"L x 2-1/4"H. Montagnon, France. 1880s. $110.

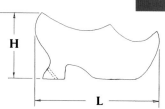

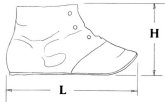

Pottery tin-glazed baby shoe with "Noirmoutier"; bottom mark includes signature of the artist, F. E. Cottard; 4"L x 2-1/16"H. Montagnon, France. 1920s. $70.

Pottery tin-glazed baby shoe with insert (for candle?); marked on bottom; 4"L x 2-1/8"H. Montagnon, France. 1920s. $90.

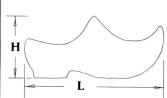

Pottery tin-glazed clog; mark on shank includes artist F.E. Cottard's initials "F.C."; 3-11/16"L x 1-5/8"H. Montagnon, France. 1920s. $60.

Pottery tin-glazed slipper with applied heel and in-mold bow; underglaze mark on shank; 8-1/8"L x 3-5/8"H. St. Clément, France. $100.

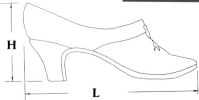

Red pottery crackle tin-glazed double salt clogs with ring handle; unmarked; 4"L x 1-3/4"H incl. handle. Alcide Chaumeil, France. First quarter 1900s. $200.

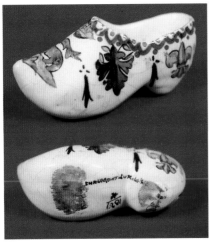

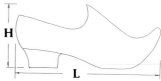

Pottery tin-glazed large clog; marked on shank; 8-7/8"L x 3-3/4"H. Fourmaintraux-Courquin, France. c.1872-1934. Uncommon. $300.

Tan pottery crackled tin-glazed sabot with décor in the style of Chaumeil Alcide, including a green fire-breathing salamander and loop & dot pattern in blue and red; marked on bottom "1027/*" and "Chaumont sur Goirz"; 3-1/2"L x 1-5/8"H. Not made by Alcide, but may have been made in Desvres, France. $20.

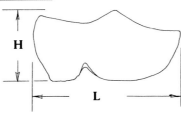

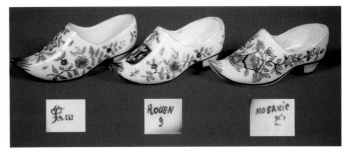

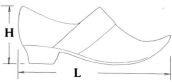

Three pink-tan pottery tin-glazed clogs from the same mold by the Fourmaintraux-Courquin factory carrying different underglaze marks on their shanks. Left: mark of Fourmaintraux-Courquin c. 1872-1934; 5-7/16"L x 2"H; $110. Middle: marked "Rouen"; 5-1/4"L x 2"H. $110. Right: mark of Mosanic, prob. pre-WWI; 5-3/8"L x 2"H; $110. All by Fourmaintraux-Courquin, France.

Pottery yellow-glazed clog; HP in black on shank "France"; 4-7/16"L x 2-1/16"H. France. $15.

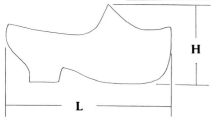

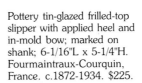

Pottery tin-glazed frilled-top slipper with applied heel and in-mold bow in Delft décor; marked on vertical face of heel; this shoe can also be found marked "Mosanic"; 6-1/4"L x 5-1/2"H. Fourmaintraux-Courquin, France. c.1872-1934. $225.

Pottery off-white glazed clog; HP in black on shank "France/K-"; 2-13/16"L x 1-3/16"H. France. $10.

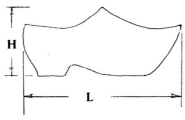

Pottery tin-glazed frilled-top slipper with applied heel and in-mold bow; marked on shank; 6-1/16"L x 5-1/4"H. Fourmaintraux-Courquin, France. c.1872-1934. $225.

Pottery tin-glazed bucket boot with applied heel, spur, and strap flap; factory mark on sole; 9"L x 9-5/8"H. Fourmaintraux-Courquin, France. c.1872-1934. Rare. $400.

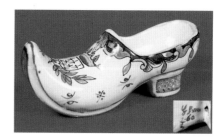

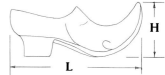

Pottery tin-glazed clog with applied heel; underglaze mark on shank; 4-5/8"L x 1-7/8"H. Gaëtan Level, Desvres, France. c.1888-1900. $150.

Pottery tin-glazed fluted top slipper with applied heel and in-mold double scalloped and buttoned front placket; underglaze black mark on shank; 5-5/16"L x 4-1/4"H. Fourmaintraux Brothers, France (Fourmaintraux Frères). c.1879-1887. Uncommon. $350.

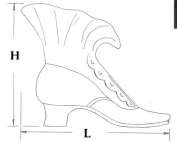

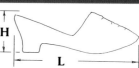

Pair of pottery tin-glazed slippers with mirror image décors on inner soles; distinguishable "left" and "right"; underglaze mark on shanks; each is 3-5/16"L x 1-1/16"H. Prob. a Desvres, France factory. Uncommon. $150 for the pair.

Pottery tin-glazed boot with ruffled top and applied heel; marked on shank; 5-1/4"L x 3-1/16"H. Fourmaintraux Brothers, France (Fourmaintraux Frères). c.1879-1887. Uncommon. $200.

Pottery tin-glazed clog with Rouen coat of arms and Rouen type décor; underglaze mark on shank and impressed "P" in heel; 3-5/8"L x 1-5/8"H. Prob. one of about five Desvres, France factories. 1930s. $40.

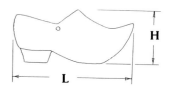

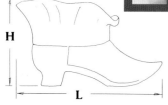

Pottery tin-glazed high ruffled top shoe with applied heel, buttoned on left; overglaze mark on shank; 7-5/8"L x 6"H. Gaëtan Level, Desvres, France. c.1888-1900. Uncommon. $350.

Pottery, tin-glazed sabot with Rouen type décor; underglaze mark on shank; 3-7/8"L x 1-7/8"H. Prob. one of about five Desvres, France factories. 1930s. $40.

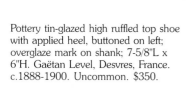

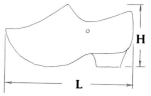

Pottery tin-glazed slipper; unmarked; 4-1/4"L x 2"H. An identical shoe was one of over eighty featured on the October 1953 *Hobbies* magazine cover. $40.

OLDER EUROPEAN PORCELAIN

Pair of porcelain boots held by angels mounted on round bases; boots and vertical surfaces of base glazed, angels and base top bisque; factory mark impressed into underside of each base; 4"diameter base x 5-3/4"HOA. Gibus & Redon, France. c.1875. Rare. $500 each.

Porcelain boot held by angel mounted on round base; HP multi-color florals on boot; top of base and pink stripe on it are matte glazed, all other surfaces gloss glazed; unmarked; 4" diameter base x 5-3/4"HOA. Gibus & Redon, France. c.1875. Rare. $600.

Porcelain (parian) shoe with cats on tasseled and corded cushion on base; inside of shoe is gloss glazed, all other surfaces except those painted gold are bisque; burnished gold; unmarked; 7-7/16" x 4-1/4" base, 6-1/2"HOA. Mid to late 1800s. Rare. $750.

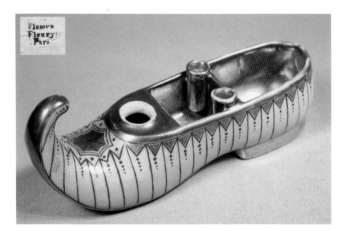

Porcelain inkwell slipper with applied well walls and quill holders; pastel peach matte ground with HP gold and red design; burnished gold on inside and toe; marked on bottom of heel; 6-1/4"L x 2-3/8"H. Fleury, France. c.1830. Rare. $1,000.

Porcelain HP slipper with applied heel on hollow base and applied strap; unmarked; 3-1/2"L x 3"H. Possibly by A. Hachez & Pépin Lehalleur Frères, Vierzon, France. Late 1800s. $175.

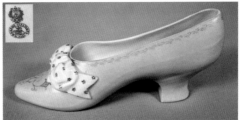

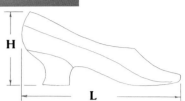

Thin but heavy porcelain slipper with applied heel; matte pink ground with gloss glazed applied bow; marked on shank; 6-3/4"L x 3-1/16"H. Kusnetzoff, Russia. Uncommon. $150.

Porcelain HP slipper with applied heel on hollow base; unmarked; 3-7/8"L x 2-7/8"H. Possibly by A. Hachez & Pépin Lehalleur Frères, Vierzon, France. Late 1800s. $150.

Thin porcelain semi-matte glazed wing tip slipper with ruffled rim; unmarked; 6-1/4"L x 2-5/8"H. An example has been seen with stamped bottom mark "GERMANY/crown & shield logo with RW/RUDOLSTADT". Royal Rudolstadt, Germany. Late 1800s. Uncommon. $200.

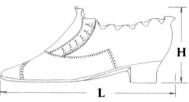

Porcelain trinket box on top of which is mounted a central vessel with hollow top and attached pair of Eastern slippers; unmarked, but a small rectangular section of glazing on the bottom has been scratched off; 4-1/2"L x 1-5/8"H slipper; 5-1/4" x 4-1/16" base, 6-5/16"HOA. Possibly Germany. Late 1800s. Uncommon. $200.

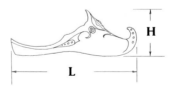

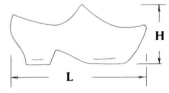

Porcelain cobalt glazed clog with gold heraldic coat of arms of Louis XII; marked on shank; 3-5/8"L x 1-9/16"H. Jagetet Pinon, Tours, France. $45.

Porcelain inkwell slipper with quill holders; unmarked; 4-5/8"L x 1-5/16"H. Prob.1800s. $50.

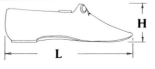

Two porcelain cobalt glazed shoes with gold heraldic symbols, both probably from France, early 1900s. Left: clog marked in script on shank "G. ASCH" and on heel "DEPOSE"; 4-3/8"L x 1-7/8"H; $45. Right: slipper with applied heel; marked on shank with hand painted gold axe and "S82"; 5-3/8"L x 2-3/16"H. A larger version of this mold has been seen marked from Tours, France. $60.

Porcelain cobalt glazed clog; raised and cut up gold leaves and vine framing color transfer medallion with hand-detailing; unmarked; 4-7/16"L x 1-3/4"H. c. 1900. $75.

Porcelain pair of attached Hessian boots with rococo tops; gold paste fruit and foliage design; match striker base; unmarked; 3-1/4" x 2-1/8" base, 5"HOA. Late 1800s. Uncommon. $125.

MADE IN FRANCE

Porcelain wall pocket slipper, HP florals and gold filigree; marked on bottom; 6"L x 2-1/16"H. France. $45.

Porcelain, thick soled, match striker slipper with protruding man whose hat, head, and body are hollow to hold matches; unmarked; 5-7/16"L x 2-9/16"H. Uncommon to find this piece with its décor intact. Late 1800s. $175.

Porcelain pastel yellow luster high top boot with applied tassel and in-mold cross ties; unmarked; 3-1/4" x 1-7/8" base, 4-5/16"HOA. $60.

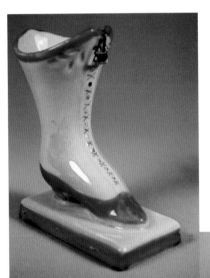

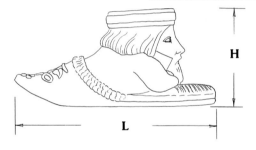

Porcelain flat heeled slipper with applied flat flower shouldered by attached man on match striker base; impressed on underside of hollow base, numbers that may be "1383"; 2-3/4" x 1-7/8" base, 4-7/8"HOA. Pos. Germany. Prob. second half of 1800s. Uncommon. $225.

Heavy porcelain cobalt glazed shoe with in-mold white glazed "knitted" sock held up by in-mold buckled garter; appliqués of roses, lily-of-the-valley, and leaves; unmarked; 4-9/16"L x 3-13/16"H. Late 1800s. Uncommon. $150.

Three thin porcelain slippers with pierced vamp medallions; unmarked except for embossed arch-type device on soles. Prob. late 1800s. Left: 7"L x 2-1/2"H; $45. Middle and right: 5-1/2"L x 2-1/8"H. $40 each.

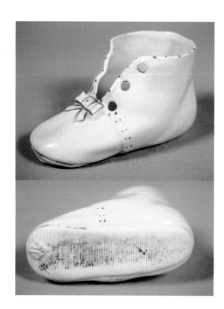

Thin porcelain baby shoe with match striker bottom that has unusual raised pad with embossed "R"; 3-15/16"L x 2-1/4"H. Late 1800s. $55.

Porcelain glazed slipper whistle; hollow; unmarked; 2-11/16"L x 1"H. Possibly Germany. c.1880-1910. $175.

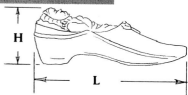

Porcelain glazed shoe box with brass collar and fittings; HP; bottom mark is similar to one c.1875 used by Samson & Co., Paris, France. $300.

Thin porcelain stacked heel matte black ankle boot with in-mold crack being eyeballed by a pair of applied heads on long necks; marked on bottom "Rᵈ Nº 403915", a British Registry number assigned in the year 1903; 4-3/16"L x 2-9/16"H. A British Registry search revealed that the registration was granted to Max Emanuel and Company whose address was given as 41-42 Shoe Lane, London. The factory of origin is unknown; the chalky white porcelain looks German suggesting that it may have been made in Emanuel's own factory in Mitterteich. c.1903. $45.

Porcelain hanging hat pin holder with Masonic logo; airbrushed ground with HP details and color transfer; stamped "Germany" on bottom; 6-3/4"L x 2-3/16"H. Germany, prob. c.1900. Uncommon. $500.

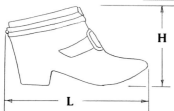

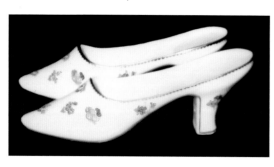

Pair of porcelain Minton straights, model # 3591; HP; 6"L. (Smaller size of 4-1/2"L, not shown, is also Minton model # 3591.) Minton, England. c.1891-1902. Rare. $400 each.

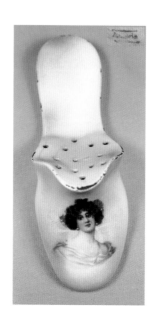

Porcelain hanging hat pin holder airbrushed and matte glazed with vamp transfer; hand-incised "9876" in shank; 3/8"L stamp "Austria" between two parallel lines; 6-3/8"L x 2"H. Austria, c.1900. $250.

Porcelain glazed hanging hat pin holder with floral transfers; hand-incised "9876" in shank; 3/8"L stamp "Austria" between two parallel lines; 6-3/16"L x 1-15/16"H. Austria, c.1900. $125.

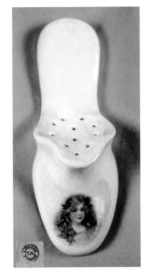

Ceramic pearl luster glazed hanging hat pin holder; decal or transfer on vamp; 9/16"OD millstone mark "Limoges/T.H./France"; 5-15/16"L x 1-7/8"H. France. $80.

Porcelain wing tip ankle shoes with in-mold cats. Left: dip glazed brown with "Germany/4965" impressed into left face of heel; 3-1/2"L x 1-3/4"H; Germany, c.1900. $15. Middle: blue glazed, outside only; "326" impressed on left face of heel; 4-1/4"L x 2-7/16"H; prob. Germany or Austria, c.1900. $25. Right: brown glazed inside and out; "961" impressed on left face of heel; 3-13/16"L x 2-3/16"H; prob. Germany or Austria, c.1900. $35.

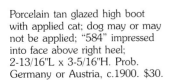

Back side of left shoe in previous photo showing location and type of incised country of origin and model number.

Porcelain tan glazed high boot with applied cat; dog may or may not be applied; "584" impressed into face above right heel; 2-13/16"L x 3-5/16"H. Prob. Germany or Austria, c.1900. $30.

Ceramic glazed ankle shoe with in-mold cat; partially glazed down inside; unmarked; 4"L x 2-3/4"H. Prob. Germany or Austria. $20.

Ceramic ankle boot with in-mold edelweiss; green colored glaze; hand incised "7761" on shank; 3-3/4"L x 2-3/8"H. Prob. Germany or Austria, c.1900. $20.

Ceramic shoes; pos. Germany or Austria. Left: tan glazed Turkish type slipper with applied pompom; unmarked; 4-1/2"L x 1-13/16"H; $35. Right: green glazed Normandy shoe with in-mold cord rim and tie; unmarked; 4-13/16"L x 2-1/4"H; prob. c.1900; $30.

Thin porcelain 3-eyelet ankle shoe with vamp transfer; inside glazed white, with pastel blue glaze applied outside and about 1/2" down inside (dip glazed over the white); unmarked; 3-1/16"L x 1-9/16"H. A similar shoe was manufactured by Schmidt Victoria, but the toe section of this is shorter. Prob. Germany or Austria, c.1900. $20.

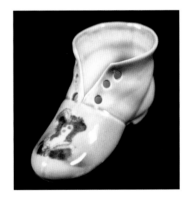

Thin porcelain glazed clog with Porsgrund pattern # 0943 *Farmer's Rose* and "Hilsen fra Arendal" ("Greetings from Arendal" … a seaport city in Norway) on vamp; underglaze in green on vamp, an anchor with a "P" on each side of the shank; 5-5/8"L x 1-3/4"H. This is the only shoe model known to have been made by Porsgrund. Porsgrund, Norway. c.1920. $30.

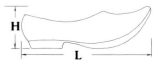

OLDER GERMAN PORCELAIN

Many of the shoes in this section are unmarked in any way but are included in this group because various characteristics led to the speculation that they may be German. Unless otherwise noted, all of these are HP.

Porcelain glazed boot applied to skate blade and draw-string case all mounted on oval match striker base; boot was once painted gold; unmarked; 4"L x 3"H. Prob. Germany. c.1880s, $125.

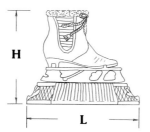

Porcelain gloss black slipper with scored match striker heel and trunk match holder on triangular-shaped base; unmarked; 2-13/16"L x 1-11/16"H. Prob. Germany. c. 1880s. $75.

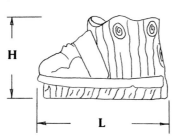

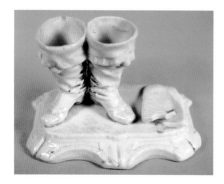

Pair of porcelain ruffle cuffed boots and match striker bootjack mounted on base; unmarked; 4-7/8" x 3-1/2" base, 3"HOA. Prob. Germany, late 1800s. If perfect, $85.

Porcelain pair of cuffed boots, scored bootjack match striker, ladies slipper, and two cats mounted on a base; unmarked; 4-7/16" x 3-1/2" base, 3-1/4"HOA. Germany, late 1800s. Uncommon. $275.

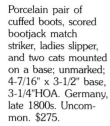

Porcelain beetle fly match striker bases with applied match striker wings and a shoe on each; embossed on front of base of each, "DON'T BODDERME"; unmarked; 4-1/4" x 2-11/16" base. Germany, late 1800s. Left: 2-7/8"HOA; $125. Right: 2-3/8"HOA; $125.

Porcelain pair of match striker bases, each with a pair of bucket boots; unmarked except for embossed, backwards (mirror image) "1007" on underside of base of each. Germany, late 1800s. Left, marbleized: 3" x 2-7/16" base, 3"HOA; $60. Right, boots once painted gold: 2-7/8" x 2-7/16" base, 3"HOA; $60.

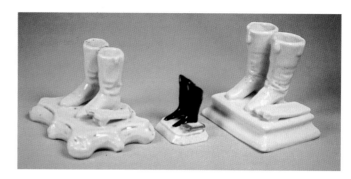

Porcelain pairs of boots with bootjack match strikers on bases, all unmarked; Germany, late 1800s. Left: 3-1/16" x 2-3/8" base, 2"HOA; $55. Middle: 1-5/16" x 1-1/16" base, 1-1/2"HOA; $35. Right: 2-5/8" x 1-15/16" base, 2-3/8"HOA; $65.

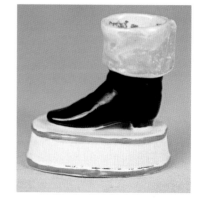

Porcelain cuffed boot on oval match striker base; unmarked; 2-11/16" x 1-3/4" base, 2-5/8"HOA. Germany, late 1800s. $40.

Thin porcelain pincushion HP slipper with in-mold bow; unmarked; 3-1/8"L x 15/16"H. Germany, late 1800s. Uncommon. $65.

Porcelain glazed Normandy shoe with in-mold ruching and vamp flower; unmarked; 3-5/16"L x 1-1/2"H. Germany, late 1800s. $25.

Porcelain HP shoe with duck bill toe; unmarked; 3-11/16"L x 1-1/4"H. Prob. Germany. Late 1800s. $40.

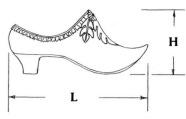

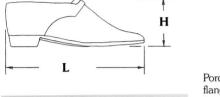

Porcelain slipper inkwell with flanged cylindrical insert in front for pen; in-mold bow; a "left"; bottom painted tan; unmarked; 3-5/16"L x 1-1/8"H. Prob. Germany. Late 1800s. Uncommon. $100.

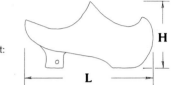

Porcelain pair of glazed clog wall pockets; unmarked; 4-9/16"L x 2-5/16"H each; Germany, late 1800s. Left: HP florals, uncommon, $95. Right: appliqué of rose and curled leaves, uncommon, $95.

Porcelain pair of attached slippers with applied bows and elaborate applied vamp ornaments; unmarked; 4-1/16"L x 1-9/16"H. Germany, late 1800s. $85.

Porcelain glazed scalloped rim slipper with applied heel and vamp appliqué; unmarked; 5-7/8"L x 2-5/8"H. Germany, late 1800s. $40.

Porcelain glazed clog with in-mold vamp ornament and applied cat; unmarked; 4-7/16"L x 2-5/16"H. Germany, late 1800s. $35.

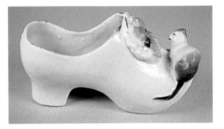

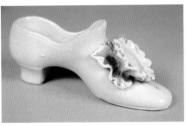

Porcelain glazed slipper with sunflower and leaves appliqué; unmarked; 3-7/8"L x 1-9/16"H. Germany, late 1800s. $30.

Porcelain clog with duck bill toe; applied vamp flower and leaves; applied cookie cutter flowers on rim and a garland of them encircling the lower part of the clog; unmarked; 3-5/16"L x 1-1/4"H. Germany, late 1800s. $55.

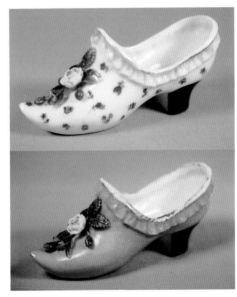

Two porcelain Normandy shoes with in-mold ruching from the same mold; rose, buds, and leaves vamp appliqués; unmarked; 4-1/4"L x 1-15/16"H each; Germany, late 1800s. Top: HP overall tiny florals, $65. Bottom: blue ground, $60.

Porcelain bisque Normandy shoes with in-mold pin flower and oak leaves (at top of vamp, obscured by appliqués) and narrow ruching; appliqués; unmarked; Germany, c. late 1800s. Left: singleton; 4-7/16"L x 2-1/8"H; $65. Right: held by kneeling, applied glazed girl; 4-1/16"LOA x 3"HOA; $75.

Porcelain ivory glazed Normandy shoe with in-mold ruching and vamp appliqué of carnation (unusual), leaves and forget-me-nots; unmarked; 5-5/16"L x 2-9/16"H. Germany, late 1800s. $65.

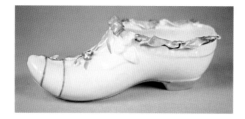

Porcelain shoe with in-mold ruching and bow as well as an applied bow and applied vamp flowers; rim appliqué of twisted "ribbon" and small flowers; unmarked; 5-3/4"L x 2-1/8"H. Germany, late 1800s. $55.

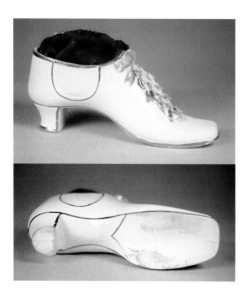

Porcelain, ivory glazed slipper with gusset sides and in-mold bow; appliqué of forget-me-nots and variegated green leaves; unmarked; 4-5/8"L x 2"H. Prob. Germany. Late 1800s. Uncommon. $85.

Porcelain matte pink slipper with applied vamp and back-of-heel ornaments; heel on tasseled pillow; Small underglaze blue cross on underside of pillow; 4-1/8"L x 2-5/8"H. Germany, late 1800s. $85.

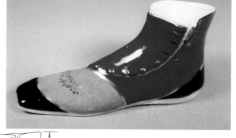

Porcelain side-buttoned, squared-toed, ankle shoe with flat heel; a "left"; unmarked; 5"L x 2-3/8"H. Prob. Germany; Late 1800s. Uncommon. $125.

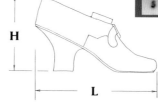

Porcelain heeled slipper with in-mold crossed flaps and buckle; blue underglaze mark on shank; 4-5/16"L x 2-5/8"H. Prob. Germany. Late 1800s. $75.

Porcelain trinket box of trunk whose lid has a child holding rabbit inside buckled shoe on draped blanket; unmarked; 4"L x 4-7/16"HOA. Prob. Germany or England. Late 1800s. $125.

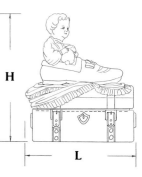

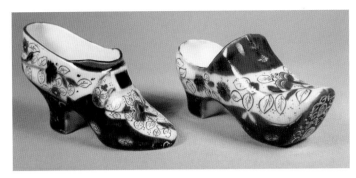

Two porcelain shoes whose cobalt, reds, and gold décor suggests that they were made by the same company; the glaze puddles blue in heel wells; unmarked; prob. Germany, late 1800s. Left: heeled slipper with in-mold crossed flaps and buckle; 4-5/8"L x 2-3/4"H; $75. Right: clog, 4-13/16"L x 2-7/16"H, $60.

Ceramic cuffed drinking boot with applied spur; on vertical face of heel "C. Auvera/1876"; 11"LOA x 6-3/4"H. Same design as Mettlach (Villeroy & Boch) drinking boot, but not so marked. Germany. c.1876. Rare. $350.

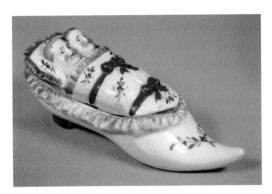

Porcelain triple boot, shoe, and slipper match striker; underside of slipper scored; raised pad mark on shank of boot; impressed into boot heel "1874" with a small "59" at right angles to the "4"; 5-3/4"L x 4-3/4"H. Royal Rudolstadt, Germany. Late 1800s. Rare. $350.

Porcelain twin babies-in-a-blanket shoe box; both lid and shoe are molded, rather than cast; 4-15/16"L x 2-1/16"H. Prob. Germany. Late 1800s. Uncommon. $175.

Porcelain bucket boot with applied and gilded beads on pale pink ground; marked in green on sole; 4-9/16"L x 4-3/4"H. Royal Rudolstadt, Germany. c. 1900. Uncommon. $125.

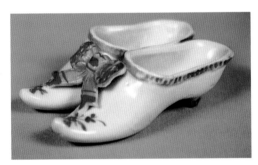

Porcelain pair of attached slippers with applied bow; unmarked; 3-3/4"L x 1-3/16"H. Prob. Germany. Late 1800s. $70.

Porcelain scalloped vamp mule with applied heel; ivory ground with arabesque HP décor; marked on toe; also has incised "87/P/S" on bottom of heel; 6-3/4"L x 2-3/4"H. Royal Porcelain Manufactory, Germany. Late 1800s. Very rare. $1,000.

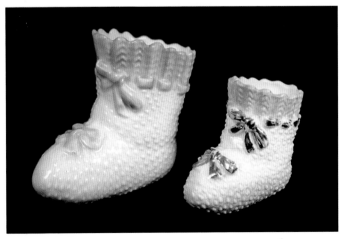

Two porcelain "knitted" baby socks with in-mold ribbon, bows, and rice pattern below cuffs; unmarked; prob. Germany, late 1800s. Left: 3-1/8"L x 2-3/4"H, $40. Right: 2-1/2"L x 2-1/16"H, $35.

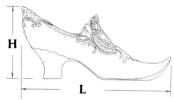

Porcelain glazed slipper with scattered floral transfers; marked on sole; 6-7/16"L x 3"H. Porcelain Factory Stadtlengsfeld, Germany. c.1894-1904. Uncommon. $90.

Porcelain mix of matte, luster, and gloss glazed clown shoes with applied heads; unmarked; Germany, prob. late 1800s. A size between these two probably exists. Left: large, 5-15/16"L x 4-1/2"H, uncommon, $250. Right: small, 4"L x 3-1/16"H, uncommon, $200.

Porcelain glazed high top shoe with double 10-button rows of in-mold buttons on each side of ruffled front panel; gold dry brush on rim; marked on sole; 4-3/4"L x 4-15/16"H. Porcelain Factory Stadtlengsfeld, Germany. c.1894-1904. Uncommon. $90.

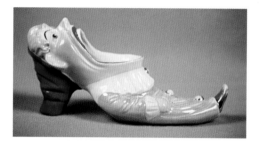

Thin porcelain glazed big mouth pierrot shoe; unmarked; 7-1/4"L x 3-1/2"H. Conta & Boehme and Schafer & Vater are among those known to have made similar pieces. Germany. c.1900. Very rare. $375.

Blue tinted porcelain bisque with white porcelain overlays of sole, scalloped rim, lacing placket, and perf strip; unmarked; 4-1/2"L x 2-1/8"H. Prob. Germany, late 1800s. Rare. $125.

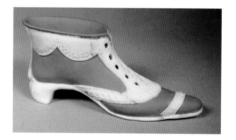

Two porcelain bisque slippers with in-mold ruching and florals; prob. Germany, c. 1900. The larger shoe is one of those on the cover of *Hobbies* magazine, Oct. 1953. Left: 4-3/16"L x 2"H, $35. Right: 5-1/16"L x 2-9/16"H, $40.

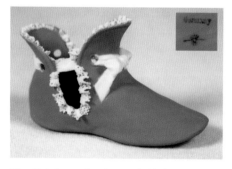

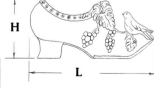

Porcelain shoe with in-mold bird, leaves, and grapes; unmarked; 4-9/16"L x 2-1/16"H. Germany. Late 1800s. $50.

Blue tinted porcelain bisque baby bootee with applied ribbon, bow and lace; four drilled holes to provide illusion that the porcelain ribbon is threaded through them; marked on sole; 4-5/16"L x 2-5/8"H. This shoe was on pg. 26 of the *Montgomery Ward* catalog, Fall/Winter 1901-1902, where it was advertised as a toothpick holder. Oldest Volkstedt Porcelain Factory, Germany. $75.

Green tinted porcelain bisque slipper with in-mold pattern enhanced by applied slip; impressed into sole, tooled numbers "2858"; 5-3/8"L x 2-1/4"H. Appears to be missing a lid. Prob. Germany, late 1800s. As is, $25.

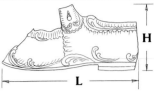

Porcelain Mary Janes in three sizes, the largest HP along the in-mold details, the others with florals. Germany, late 1800s. Left: 5-3/4"L x 2-3/4"H, uncommon size and décor, $60. Middle two: 4-5/8"L x 2-3/16"H, $35 each. Right: 3-11/16"L x 1-11/16"H, $35.

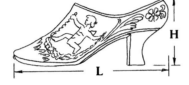

Blue tinted porcelain bisque shoes with in-mold pattern slip-enhanced; blue color is significantly darker than shown; Germany. Left (sketch): unmarked, 3-5/16"L x 1-3/8"H, $75. Right: matched pair, distinguishable "left" and "right"; stamped on each in black both "Germany" and undecipherable logo containing "??DECCO"; the "right" impressed with "5149A", 2-1/2"L x 1"H; the "left" impressed with "5149B", 2-9/16"L x 1-1/16"H; $50 each.

Porcelain Mary Jane with gold left side, color transfer; white glazed right side has "Souvenir Johnstown, Pa."; brown mark on heel; 4-5/8"L x 2-1/4"H. Germany. c.1900. $35.

Porcelain blue glazed boot with in-mold side straps and spur; applied vine with leaves and granular berries; gold dry brush on rim; on back in gold "A Present from Minehead"; unmarked; 4-1/8"L x 4-3/8"H. Germany. Late 1800s. $45.

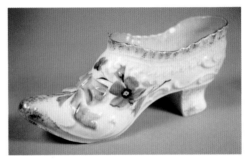

Porcelain glazed slipper with rim ruffle and in-mold bow; unmarked; 6-3/4"L x 3"H. Germany. Late 1800s. $55.

Porcelain bisque stacked heel slipper with in-mold bow; unmarked; 4-13/16"L x 2"H. Germany. Late 1800s. $35.

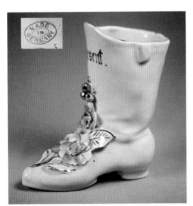

Porcelain glazed boot with in-mold side straps; appliqués of flowers and gold-veined leaves; a "right"; marked on sole; 4-1/2"L x 4-3/4"H. Germany. c.1900. $45.

Porcelain blue glazed stacked heel slipper with scalloped ruching and in-mold bow; unmarked; 4-13/16"L x 2"H. Germany. Late 1800s. $35.

Porcelain Aladdin slipper with in-mold vamp leaf pattern; pierced and curled toe; unmarked; 5-1/4"L x 2-3/16"H. Prob. Germany, early 1900s. $40.

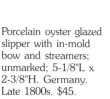

Porcelain oyster glazed slipper with in-mold bow and streamers; unmarked; 5-1/8"L x 2-3/8"H. Germany. Late 1800s. $45.

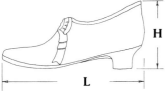

Porcelain dark camel glazed 4 x 4 cap toe ankle shoe with vertical back strap; factory logo under which is "Made in Germany"; 5-1/2"L x 2-7/8"H, shoe only; 3-7/16"HOA. Heber & Co., Germany. c.1900-1922. $50.

Porcelain slipper with in-mold bow and streamers; unmarked; 5-3/8"L x 2-7/16"H. Germany. c.1900. $45.

Porcelain gray glazed 3 x 5 cap toe ankle shoe; unmarked; 5-1/2"L x 3-1/16"H. Prob. Germany, c.1900. $35.

Porcelain cobalt glazed slipper with applied granular gold rim; unmarked; 6-1/16"L x 2-11/16"H. Prob. Germany, c.1900. $50.

Porcelain matched pair of Dutch shoes; landscape continues on back sides; marked on soles; 4-7/8"L x 2-3/8"H each. Swaine & Co., Germany. c. 1920. $90 for the pair.

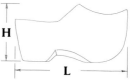

Porcelain variegated olive green glazed slipper with in-mold pattern of clovers painted gold; unmarked except for tooled numbers impressed into left shank "882"; 5-7/8"L x 2-3/4"H. Germany. c.1900. Uncommon. $55.

Porcelain Dutch shoe; landscape continues on back side; unmarked; 5-7/8"L x 2-3/4"H. Swaine & Co., Germany. c.1920. $45.

Porcelain Dutch shoe with HP scenes on both sides and art deco motif on heel; marked underglaze on shank; 5"L x 2-3/8"H. Swaine & Co., Germany. c.1920. $45.

Porcelain bisque slipper with in-mold roses and leaves; impressed into shank "GERMANY"; 2-13/16"L x 1-3/16"H. Early 1900s. $20.

Blue tinted porcelain bisque slipper with in-mold bow and streamers; impressed into shank "GERMANY"; 2-11/16"L x 1-1/16"H. Early 1900s. $15.

Porcelain Dutch shoe with HP florals on both sides and art deco motif on heel; marked underglaze on shank; 4-1/8"L x 2"H. Swaine & Co., Germany. c.1920. $35.

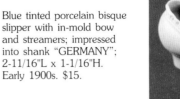

Ceramic two-tone green clog; undecipherable mark; 4"L x 1-1/2"H. Prob. Germany, early 1900s. $25.

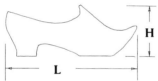

Thin porcelain bisque ankle shoe with in-mold mother and three babies; cold-painted; unmarked; Prob. Germany, c. 1900. $30.

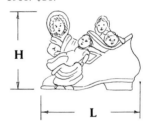

Thin porcelain glazed baby shoe with in-mold bow; dry brush gold trim; unmarked; 2-7/8"L x 1-5/8"H. Germany. c.1900. $20.

Two porcelain pairs of connected (opening between them) slippers; applied angel head and wings; impressed into left shank "Germany"; impressed into right shank "5536"; 2-1/4"L x 1-1/16"H each set. Left: pearl luster glazed, $18. Right: yellow matte, cold painted gold, cut-out straps; $15.

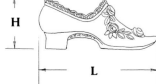

Porcelain bisque slipper with in-mold roses and leaves; impressed into shank "GERMANY"; 2-13/16"L x 1-3/16"H. Early 1900s. $15.

Thin porcelain attached slippers with applied flower and bird; unmarked; 1-7/8"L x 5/8"H, slippers only. Prob. Germany, late 1800s. Rare detailed miniature. $45.

Porcelain miniature slippers, all unmarked; Germany. Left: applied bird; 1-7/8"L x 13/16"H; $15. Middle: attached pair; 1-3/8"L x 7/8"H; $10. Right: singleton; 1-3/8"L x 7/8"H; $7.

Porcelain bisque slipper with in-mold ribbed pattern, in-mold sock, and appliqué of rose and beaded leaves; unmarked except "Depose"; 4-7/8"L x 2-3/4"H. Germany. c.1900. $50.

GERMAN PORCELAIN:
Stem Rose and Offshoots

Most of the shoes in this section may have come from the same factory, as yet unidentified, or they may not have. Their arrangement here may illustrate what caused the first speculation.

Porcelain glazed side buttoned high top wing tip shoe with elaborate appliqué of rose, leaves, and stem that is brought under the shoe and connected there; unmarked; 5"L x 4-1/2"H. Germany. Late 1800s. $75.

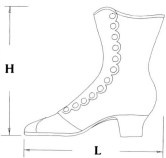

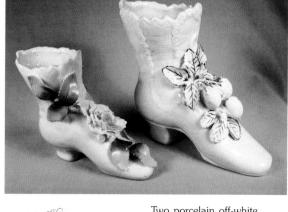

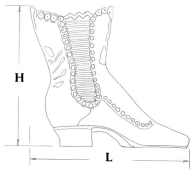

Two porcelain off-white glazed high top shoes with gusset sides; unmarked; Germany, late 1800s. Left: appliqué of stem with rose and leaves; 4-1/2"L x 3-7/8"H; $65. Right: appliqué of stem with berries and gold-trimmed leaves; 5-5/8"L x 4-7/8"H; $65.

Porcelain bisque and semi gloss glazed high top with gusset sides; beaded grape and leaf appliqués; unmarked; 6-1/2"L x 6"H. Germany. Late 1800s. Uncommon. $90.

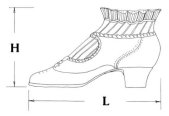

Three porcelain shoes from same mold incorporating a loomed or knitted sock illustrating granular and glazed surface treatments and uniqueness of the hand made appliqués, all of which include stems brought under the shoe and connected there. All are approximately 4-3/4"L x 2-3/4"H. Germany, late 1800s. $70 each.

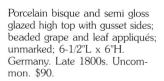

Porcelain off-white glazed scalloped rim shoe with applied strap and stem with rose, leaves, and forget-me-nots; unmarked; 4-1/8"L x 2-5/16"H, shoe only; 2-9/16"HOA. Germany. Late 1800s. $60.

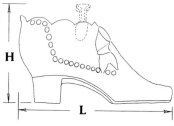

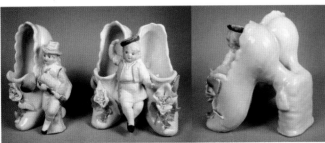

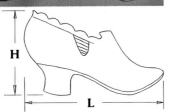

Two porcelain figurine and shoe sets with shoe appliqués of rose, leaves, and forget-me-nots; unmarked; Germany, late 1800s. Left: boy with bagpipe; 3-5/8"L x 2-3/16"H, shoe only; $75. Right: dancer; 3-5/8"L x 2-3/16"H, each shoe only; $85.

Porcelain double salt with applied ring handle and in-mold pin flower and leaves; green glazed with applied gray-green granules, gold dry brushed; unmarked; 4-11/16"L x 1-9/16"H, clog only, 2-5/16"HOA. Identical mold to larger pair in previous photo. Germany, prob. c.1900. $40.

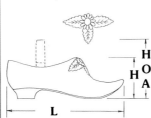

Porcelain pair of attached ivory glazed clogs with applied ring handle; in-mold pin flower and leaves; appliqué of blossoms, raspberries, and gold trimmed leaves; marked on sole; 4-1/16"L x 1-5/16"H, clog only, 1-15/16"HOA. Germany, late 1800s. $65.

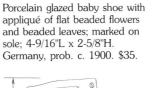

Porcelain glazed baby shoe with appliqué of flat beaded flowers and beaded leaves; marked on sole; 4-9/16"L x 2-5/8"H. Germany, prob. c. 1900. $35.

Porcelain ivory glazed baby shoe with appliqué of stem with granular flat flowers, buds, and leaves; unmarked; 4-1/2"L x 2-5/8"H. Germany. Late 1800s. $50.

Porcelain pair of attached glazed clogs with applied ring handle; in-mold pin flower and leaves; appliqué of pussy willows and beaded leaves; unmarked; 4-1/8"L x 1-3/8"H, clog only, 2"HOA. Germany, late 1800s. $55.

Porcelain bisque baby shoe with in-mold ribbed pattern and cording rim; stem with rose and leaves appliqué; unmarked; 3-5/8"L x 2-3/16"H. Germany, prob. late 1800s. $35.

Two pairs of porcelain double salts with applied ring handles and in-mold pin flower and leaves; Germany, prob. c.1900. Left: marked on sole, 4-1/8"L x 1-7/16"H, clog only, 2-1/16"HOA, $65. Right: larger version, bird-on-a-branch décor, unmarked, 4-11/16"L x 1-9/16"H, clog only, 2-1/4"HOA, $75.

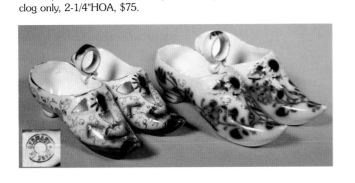

Porcelain glazed baby shoe with in-mold ribbed pattern and cording trim; tiny floral appliqués; unmarked; 3-1/2"L x 2-3/16"H. Germany, prob. late 1800s. $45.

Porcelain baby snow shoe with in-mold cording trim; ribbed pattern of two previous shoes barely visible beneath the granular porcelain surface; floral appliqué; unmarked; 3-5/8"L x 2-1/8"H. Germany, prob. late 1800s. $45.

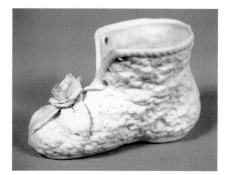

Porcelain baby shoe with in-mold textured surface and cording rim; floral appliqué; unmarked; 3-11/16"L x 2-3/16"H. Germany, prob. late 1800s. $40.

Porcelain pair of attached boots and match striker bootjack on base; bootjack scored horizontally and diagonally; marked under base; small size boots, 2-1/4"H; 3-9/16" x 2-9/16" base, 2-5/8"HOA. Germany. Late 1800s. $125.

Pale blue tinted porcelain pair of attached boots and match striker bootjack on base; bootjack scored horizontally and diagonally; floral appliqué; unmarked; medium size boots with triple vertical mold lines on outsides, 2-11/16"H; 3-1/2" x 2-1/2" base, 3-1/4"HOA. Germany. $100.

Two porcelain cuffed boots, both unmarked; Germany, prob. late 1800s. Both of these have characteristics of other shoes in this section, but they were not cast from the same mold. Left: bisque, airbrushed peach ground, appliqué of beaded raspberries and leaves; 2-7/8"L x 2-5/8"H; $45. Right: glazed, floral appliqué; 2-3/4"L x 2-13/16"H; $40.

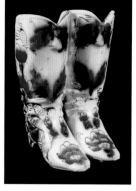

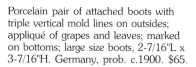

Porcelain pair of attached boots with triple vertical mold lines on outsides; marked with millstone typical for this group; large size boots, 2-7/16"L x 3-1/2"H. Germany, prob. c.1900. $75.

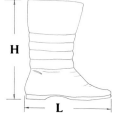

Three porcelain boots cast from the same mold, all approximately 3-3/4"L x 4-1/8"H; Germany. Left: glazed with floral appliqué; unmarked; prob. late 1800s; $50. Middle: gold face with hand-tinted transfer of "MACHIN-ERY BUILDING. WORLDS FAIR ST. LOUIS MO. 1904"; marked on sole; $90. Right: glazed with appliqué of leaves and flat speckled flowers; marked on sole; prob. c.1900; $45.

Porcelain pair of attached boots with triple vertical mold lines on outsides; appliqué of grapes and leaves; marked on bottoms; large size boots, 2-7/16"L x 3-7/16"H. Germany, prob. c.1900. $65.

GERMAN PORCELAIN
with FIGURINES

Not all the German porcelain shoes with figurines are in this section … just those that did not drop into some other category. All of these are HP unless otherwise noted.

Porcelain girl carrying huge applied shoe; unmarked; 10-7/8"H. Note overturned stool that provides three contact points to base for stability. Germany, late 1800s. Very rare. $750.

Detail of meticulously HP florals.

Porcelain boy carrying huge applied shoe; unmarked; 11-1/4"H. Note overturned chair that provides three contact points to base for stability. Germany, late 1800s. Very rare. $750.

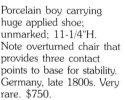

Illustration showing relative proportions of the small and large sizes of the children paddling clogs series. They came in pairs, in three sizes known to this author. Shown in the following illustrations is one child in each of the three sizes. On those rare occasions when this piece can be found, some damage can be expected. It is rare to find the top of the paddle intact, and even more infrequent to find the fragile, but exquisitely crafted florals undamaged. Values given for this group of figurals allow for small imperfections.

Porcelain small size clog with appliqués of roses, leaves, and girl child paddling; unmarked; 6-1/4"L x 2-5/8"H, clog only; 4-1/4"HOA. Germany. Late 1800s. Rare. $350.

Porcelain medium size clog with appliqués of roses, leaves, and boy child paddling; unmarked; 8-1/8"L x 3-1/8"H, clog only; 5-1/8"HOA. Germany. Late 1800s. Rare. $375.

Porcelain large size clog with appliqués of roses, leaves, and girl child paddling; unmarked; 10-1/4"L x 4"H, clog only; 6-7/8"HOA. Germany. Late 1800s. Rare. $400.

Porcelain clog being scrubbed by child; appliqué of rose and leaves; unmarked; 5-3/4"LOA x 4-7/8"HOA. There may be a female version of this piece. Germany. Late 1800s. Uncommon. $225.

Porcelain slipper with applied heel on wheeled vehicle drawn by angel with garlands of applied flowers; underglaze factory mark; 7" x 3-3/8" base, 5-1/8"HOA. Well over a dozen molds were required to create the pieces for this assembly. This is one of a mirror image pair. Kister, Germany. Late 1800s. Rare. $500.

Large 6-3/4"L porcelain shoe with in-mold protrusion from underside of toe allowing it to stand at angle held by attached, fully formed, standing Dutch girl; unmarked except for impressed "4646" on protrusion; 7-1/4"HOA. Featured prominently on Oct. 1953 *Hobbies* magazine cover. Prob. Germany, late 1800s. Uncommon. $200.

Porcelain scalloped bucket boot with spur, with attached boy; unmarked except "3296" impressed on heel of boot; 4-3/16"L x 4-3/8"H, boot only. Germany, late 1800s. Uncommon. $225.

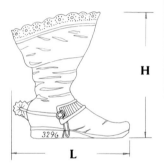

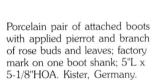

Porcelain pair of attached boots with applied pierrot and branch of rose buds and leaves; factory mark on one boot shank; 5"L x 5-1/8"HOA. Kister, Germany. Late 1800s, Rare. $325.

Thin porcelain shoe mounted on pair of applied wheels; lady with lyre partially applied – the lower drape of her gown is incorporated into the mold of the shoe; impressed "S" in rectangle in shank and "9279" or "2279"; 8-1/2"L x 6-1/4"HOA. Kister, Germany. c.1880. Rare. $275.

Porcelain scalloped bucket boot with partially in-mold cavalier cabinet piece; unmarked except for "3270" or "3210" on back of base; 4-1/2"L x 4-7/8"HOA. There is a female mate to this. There are Japanese copies of both. Prob. Germany. $75.

Porcelain pink matte slipper with applied heel held up by attached cat all mounted on bulbous base; unmarked; 2-5/8" wide base x 5"H. Prob. Germany, late 1800s. Rare. $350.

Porcelain pair of bisque shoes each with an applied glazed figurine; shoes are from different molds, the boy sits on a "right", and the girl on a "left"; unmarked; boy and shoe: 3-11/16"L x 3-1/2"HOA; girl and shoe: 3-7/8"L x 3"HOA. Prob. Germany, late 1800s. Uncommon. $150 for the pair.

Porcelain left-facing semi-matte glazed ankle shoe with butterscotch airbrushed ground and applied cupid; color transfer in medallion; unmarked; 5"L x 4"H. Prob. Germany, late 1800s. Uncommon. $150.

Porcelain slipper with in-mold stocking vase held up by attached boy; blue "R" in diamond frame stamped on base underside, and impressed "J?376"; 3-5/8" x 3-1/4" base, 7"HOA. Prob. Germany, late 1800s. $125.

Porcelain pearl luster riding boot with in-mold spur, florals, and medallion with horse head; applied puck-like figurine; unmarked; 4-1/8"L x 4-3/4"H. Germany. c.1900. $75.

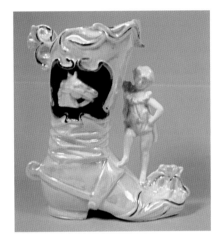

Pair of tinted green bisque porcelain side-buttoned shoes with painted medallion and slip enhanced in-mold details, each with applied bisque cherub; unmarked except for tooled numbers "51" impressed into bottom of heel of right-facing shoe; left facing shoe (on left): 5-1/16"L x 4"H; right facing shoe: 5"L x 3-15/16"H. Prob. Germany, late 1800s. Uncommon. $175 each.

Two porcelain heeled boots with applied figurines; unmarked; Germany; c.1900. Left: pearl luster; 3-9/16"L x 3-1/8"H; $40. Right: blue glazed; 3-9/16"L x 3-1/8"H; $40.

Porcelain wing tip ankle shoe with in-mold florals and applied angel; unmarked; 4-1/4"L x 2-3/16"H. Prob. Germany, c.1900. $85.

Porcelain glazed cuffed side-buttoned boot being cleaned by in-mold young girl; factory logo, "DEP", model number "14082", and "Germany" impressed into back of base; 3-15/16"L x 3-3/4"H. Unger, Schneider; Germany. Early 1900s. $70.

Porcelain glazed slipper with in-mold bow held by attached angel on base; right arm of angel, holding heel of shoe, is incorporated into the shoe mold; unmarked; 4-1/8" x 2-3/16" oval base, 4-13/16"HOA. Prob. Germany, late 1800s. Uncommon. $200.

Porcelain bisque pastel blue woven ribbon slipper with in-mold bow and appliqué spray of flowers held by in-mold girl connected at bottom to slipper by in-mold flowers; cold painted; factory logo, "DEP", and model number "9305" impressed into base; 4-5/8"L x 5-7/16"H. Unger, Schneider; Germany. Early 1900s. $70.

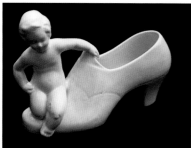

Ceramic off-white semi-glaze woman's shoe with cherub sitting on vamp; cherub is slipped onto a projection from the vamp; stamped in black on sole "Germany"; impressed into shank "7974"; 4-15/16"L x 2-1/4"H, shoe only; 3-9/16"HOA. c.1900. $35.

Porcelain bisque broken down shoe with pair of in-mold baby birds emerging from broken eggs; wings applied; factory logo, "DEP", and model number "9375" impressed into base; 4-7/8"L x 4-11/16"H. Unger, Schneider; Germany. Early 1900s. $75.

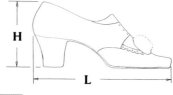

Fine-grained ceramic glazed man's oxford with applied cherub holding open book; a "left"; tooled "88" stamped into sole; 4-3/8"L x 1-5/8"H, shoe only; 2-5/8"HOA. Pos. Germany, c.1900. $35.

Porcelain shoemaker boy with applied oversized shoes; factory logo impressed into base; 6-1/2" x 3-13/16" oval base, 7-5/8"HOA. Unger, Schneider; Germany. c.1890. $50.

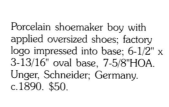

Porcelain bisque shoe being cleaned by applied young boy; cold painted gold; factory logo and model number impressed into bottom of toe; 5-3/4"LOA x 5-1/4"HOA. Unger, Schneider; Germany. Early 1900s. $75.

Porcelain low heeled slipper with in-mold bow held by applied girl; unmarked; 5"HOA. Germany, late 1800s. $55.

Porcelain bisque seated girl with applied toe container to slipper she is holding, the heel portion of which is part of the casting of the girl; unmarked; 3"L x 4-3/4"H. Germany, late 1800s. $60.

Porcelain slipper with applied child in nightshirt; unmarked; shoe: 3"L x 1-5/16"H; 3-1/8"L x 3-1/16"HOA. Germany, late 1800s. $75.

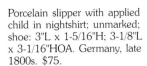

Porcelain bisque bow shoe with in-mold sock vase held up by applied boy whose lower arms are part of the sock mold; unmarked except "5348⁶/2" impressed into back of base; 3-9/16"L x 4-3/4"HOA. Germany, late 1800s. $60.

Porcelain low heeled side-buttoned shoe with applied dapper young boy missing his pants, shoes, and socks; the reason for memorializing such a state of undress has apparently been lost during the intervening century; unmarked; shoe: 4-15/16"L x 1-9/16"H; 4-7/16"HOA. Germany, late 1800s. $85.

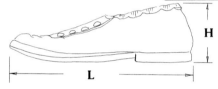

Porcelain ruffle-topped boot with partially applied young woman; left arm and part of torso are part of boot mold; unmarked in any way; 3-7/8"LOA x 5"HOA. Reminiscent of Weiss, Kühnert. Germany. c. 1900. $75.

Porcelain bucket boot held by child on base that is a part of its mold; underside of base is stamped with a blue "R" inside a diamond frame and over it "N104" is impressed; boot: 3-3/8"H; 2-5/8" diameter base x 6-1/2"HOA. Germany, late 1800s. $90

Porcelain bisque ankle shoe with in-mold dog and partially in-mold girl (legs and skirt); arms and upper part of girl applied; very faint red stamp on bottom that may or may not say "Germany"; 4-15/16"L x 3-3/16"H, shoe only; 4-1/4"HOA. Reminiscent of Weiss, Kühnert and similar to Heinz & Co. model 5397. Germany. c.1900. $85.

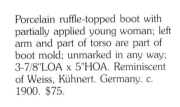

Porcelain taupe luster glaze and black semi-gloss glaze high shoe with applied farm boy playing a flute; unmarked; 6-1/2"L x 4-5/8"H; shoe only; 5-1/8"HOA. Germany, c.1900. $50.

Porcelain good luck shoe on applied good luck 4-leaf clover wheels driven by an angel postman and carrying a bag of good wishes in a bag impressed "1000/M" including a gold wedding band; unmarked; 2-7/16"L (not inc. ring) x 2-1/2"H. Germany, c.1900. Rare miniature. $95.

Porcelain boot with tassel and applied boy mounted on oval base; unmarked; boot: 1-7/8"L x 2-9/16"H; 2-1/4" x 2-3/16" oval base, 3-3/16"HOA. Germany. $45.

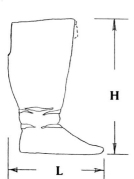

Thin porcelain single mold "snow babies" shoe house with elf and robin; impressed into back side, "1634"; 2-1/16"L x 2-3/16"HOA. Germany, first quarter 1900s. Very rare. $200.

Porcelain boot with tassel and attached boy mounted on circular base; unmarked; boot: 1-3/8"L x 1-13/16"H; 1-3/8" diameter base, 2-1/16"HOA. Germany. $35.

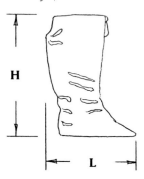

Porcelain glazed woman's oxford with in-mold tie and applied bisque dapper man wearing spats and holding a work boot; unmarked; shoe: 4-11/16"L x 2-7/16"H; 3-1/4"HOA. Advertises the shoe stores of O. Aeschbach. Prob. Germany, early 1900s. Uncommon. $90.

Porcelain ladies cap toe oxford being held by perplexed monkey mounted on an octagonal advertising ashtray; factory logo on underside of base; 6-1/2" wide base x 5"HOA. Fraureuth, Germany. c.1900. $50.

Porcelain bisque bow slipper held by attached angel; unmarked except for incised numbers on back of angel that may be "836"; shoe: 1-7/8"L x 3/4"H. Germany. c.1900. $35.

GERMAN PORCELAIN including von Schierholz and Hugging Angels

The theme that connects many of the shoes in this section is the appliqué of cookie-cutter tiny yellow-centered flowers with dots of turquoise enamel on each of the five petals. As a collector, the existence of this décor was a helpful beginning toward categorization by factory, even when that factory remained unidentified. Additional hugging angels can be found in the Conta & Boehme section.

Porcelain glazed crushed heel slipper wall pocket with applied roses, leaves, and angel; factory mark on bottom and impressed model number "469"; 9-3/8"L x 3-1/2"H. Von Schierholz, Germany. c. 1870-1894. Rare. $450.

Porcelain glazed crushed heel slipper with applied flowers and leaves held by attached angel; factory mark underglaze and impressed model number "240"; 9-3/4"HOA. One of a matched pair. Von Schierholz, Germany. c.1870-1894. $375.

Porcelain glazed crushed heel slipper with applied flowers and leaves held by attached angel; factory mark underglaze and impressed model number "240"; 9-3/4"HOA. The other of the matched pair. Von Schierholz, Germany. c.1870-1894. $375.

Porcelain glazed clog with applied roses, leaves, and three ducklings; underglaze factory mark and impressed model number "420"; 7-1/2"L x 3-7/8"HOA. Von Schierholz, Germany. c.1870-1894. Rare. $450.

Hugging angels shoes can be found with a pair of embracing angels as shown on the shoe to the right in this photo, or with the much less common angel holding a baby, as shown in the shoe on the left. The shoe on the left, without the applied floral décor, has been seen with a c.1902 von Schierholz mark. The shoe portion of the piece on the right is clearly from the same set of molds. The speculation is that if a shoe with these mold characteristics does not carry a von Schierholz mark, it is a von Schierholz blank that either failed to be marked at the factory or was sold to a decorator shop. At least two other factories made these shoes, as will be seen in photos following the von Schierholz models and in the section on Conta & Boehme.

Porcelain glazed matched pair of crushed heel slippers with applied flowers and leaves held by attached painted angels; decorator's mark on underside of bases; 9-3/8"HOA. Assumed to be von Schierholz factory blanks. Mark of Josef Rieber, Germany. c.1910-1915. $850 for the pair.

Porcelain glazed bow slipper with applied heel on tasseled quilted pillow with angel holding a baby; applied florals; impressed into underside of cushion "DEPOSE", a hand-incised script letter that may be a "G", and the hand painted initials "HR."; 6-1/4"L x 5-1/2"HOA. Von Schierholz blank, Germany. Rare with applied décor. $350.

Two porcelain glazed hugging angels bow slippers with applied heels on tasseled pillows; unmarked except for a hand-incised script letter that appears to be an "L"; 6-1/2"L x 5-3/4"HOA. Appear to be von Schierholz blanks. Germany. $150 each.

Two sizes of heavy porcelain hugging angels bow slippers with applied black matte heels; unmarked; Germany. Large peach luster: 5-11/16"L x 3-3/16"H, shoe only, 3-3/16"HOA, $70. Small white: 3-1/4"L x 1-7/8"H, shoe only, 2-1/8"HOA, $65.

Porcelain glazed hugging angels bow slipper with applied heel on tasseled pillow; fake Meissen mark; 6-13/16"L x 5-3/8"H. A 9"L version has been seen with an embossed VB mark, pos. by Vion-Baury, France. Note that toe is longer than von Schierholz model. Careful examination will show other differences. Prob. Germany or France. $200.

Porcelain glazed ruffle-rim slipper with applied heel held up by attached kneeling angel with dropped lantern, all mounted on a tasseled quilted pillow; unmarked; 5-1/4" x 3-3/4" oval base, 7-1/2"HOA. Germany, late 1800s. Rare. $350.

Two identical hugging angels bow slippers with applied heels on tasseled pillows; pink is unmarked; blue has an underglaze green anchor on underside of pillow; each is 3-15/16"L x 3-1/8"HOA. Figurines with this anchor mark have been seen attributed to Charles Baury, France. These are the very uncommon small size. Prob. Germany or France. $200 each.

Porcelain hugging angels bow slipper with applied heel on tasseled pillow; fake Meissen mark on underside of pillow; 4"L x 3-3/16"H. This mark has been seen attributed to Dornheim, Koch & Fischer, Germany. Uncommon small size from identical molds as blue trimmed shoe in previous photo with the green anchor mark. Prob. Germany or France. Uncommon HP interior décor. $250.

Porcelain glazed Thomas à Becket shoe with applied florals; unmarked; 5-7/16"L x 1-11/16"H. Germany, late 1800s. $65.

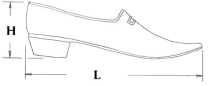

Porcelain low heeled slipper with appliqué of berries, buds, and leaves; decorator mark underglaze on shank; 5-3/8"L x 1-7/8"H. Josef Rieber, Germany. Prob. early 1900s. $75.

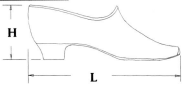

Thin porcelain ivory-glazed crushed heel slipper wall pocket with floral appliqué; bottom glazed except for three stilt marks; 6-3/16"L x 2"H. Germany. Late 1800s. $75.

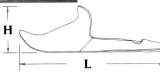

Thick porcelain glazed crushed heel slipper wall pocket with appliqués of blackberries and leaves; underglaze decorator mark on shank; 7-7/16"L x 1-5/8"H. Josef Rieber, Germany. Prob. early 1900s. $65.

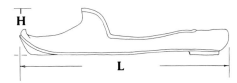

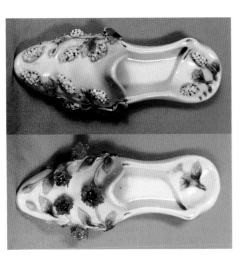

Two thick porcelain glazed crushed heel slippers with appliqués; impressed rectangular mark with letters that may be STM or SPM, or something else; bottoms totally flat, i.e., no heel of any kind; Germany, prob. early 1900s. Top: molded raspberry appliqués: 6-1/8"L x 2-1/16"H, $45. Bottom: bachelor buttons and pink bell flowers appliqués; 6-1/8"L x 2"H, $55.

Two porcelain glazed slippers with in-mold ruching and cat (it is part of the shoe mold), peering at an insect that is painted on the innersole; Germany, c.1900. Left: applied flat flowers with turquoise enamel drops; unmarked; 5-5/8"LOA x 2-3/16"H; $85. Right: appliqués of bachelor buttons and pink bell flowers; impressed rectangular mark with letters that may be STM or SPM; 5-9/16"L x 2-1/4"H; $85.

Two porcelain glazed left-side buttoned roller skates with tassels on bases; unmarked; Germany, late 1800s. Left: delicate floral appliqué; 3-7/8" x 2-3/8" base, 4-5/8"HOA; uncommon; $165. Right: floral garland appliqué; painted base; 3-3/4" x 2-1/4" base, 4-1/4"HOA; uncommon; $175.

Porcelain glazed wing tip square toe boot with ruffled rim, in-mold vine of berries and leaves, and applied bow with in-mold streamers; unmarked; 5-1/2"L x 4-1/16"H. Germany, prob. late 1800s. $130.

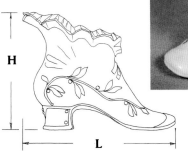

Porcelain glazed wing tip square toe boot with ruffled rim, in-mold vine of berries and leaves, and applied bow with in-mold streamers; applied green eyed cat; mounted on base with in-mold florals; unmarked; 5-1/4" x 3-3/8" base, 4-1/2"HOA. Germany, prob. late 1800s. Uncommon. $225.

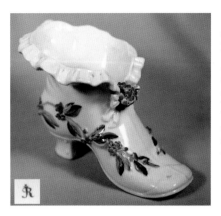

Porcelain glazed wing tip square toe boot with ruffled rim, in-mold vine of berries and leaves, and applied bow with in-mold streamers; groups of applied flat flowers with turquoise drops over berries and bow; decorator's mark on shank; 5-1/2"L x 4-1/16"H. Josef Rieber, Germany. $140.

Same as previous shoe only mounted on full base; decorator's mark on underside of base; shoe same dimensions as previous examples; 5-3/8" x 3-5/8" base, 1-1/8"H base. Josef Rieber, Germany. $165.

Porcelain glazed wing tip square toe boot with ruffled rim, in-mold vine of berries and leaves, and in-mold (note this) bow with streamers; flowers and leaves applied over in-mold detail; cat bent over compared to earlier example; underglaze blue mark; 6-1/8"L x 4"H, shoe only. Mark is suspicious. It is apparently meant to imitate that of the Royal Porcelain Manufactory Berlin. However, that mark has a branch in the talons, whereas this has an arrow. There are also differences in the shape of the bird. Origin and age unknown. Value based on quality of décor. $75.

Same description and remarks as for previous shoe. Origin and age unknown. Value based on quality of décor. $55.

GERMAN PORCELAIN including Ernst Bohne

A group of shoes toward the end of this section may not have been made by Ernst Bohne. However, Bohne's uniquely sized and shaped tooled numbers found on a small slipper with an unusual spade shaped sole led to the inclusion of a group that could be tentatively connected using this design characteristic.

Thick porcelain glazed Ernst Bohne, Germany baby shoes with ruffled rims, all c.1880. Left: large size with in-mold bow in ivory matte glaze with HP florals; blue factory logo and impressed model number "2179"; 5-1/8"L x 2-3/4"H; $35. Middle: large size with in-mold bow; impressed into sole "EBS" and model number "2179"; 5-1/4"L x 2-13/16"H; $25. Right: medium size with floral appliqué; factory logo on heel; "EBS" and model number "2180" impressed into heel; 4-1/8"L x 2-1/8"H; $35.

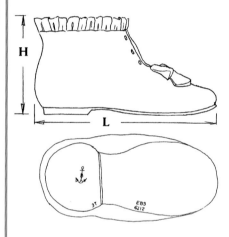

Sketch of large Ernst Bohne shoe showing typical location and relative size of model number. Anchor factory logo is often missing or undecipherable.

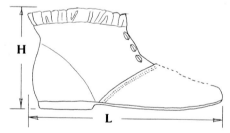

Sketch of medium Ernst Bohne shoe.

Porcelain glazed Ernst Bohne, Germany small size baby shoes with in-mold bows and ruffled rims; c. 1880. Left: pair of attached pink shoes; model number "2181" impressed into one heel; 2-11/16"L x 1-3/8"H; $20 if perfect. Right: white singleton; unmarked; 2-3/4"L x 1-7/16"H; $10.

Porcelain baby shoe with ruffled rim and in-mold bow; in-mold textured surface painted to resemble animal skin; factory logo and "GESCHUTZT" (patented) on bottom; 4"L x 2"H. Ernst Bohne, Germany, late 1800s. $45.

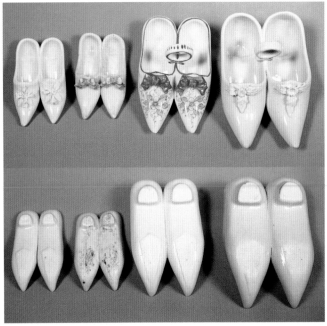

Four pairs of porcelain glazed attached clogs with spade shaped soles; Germany, late 1800s. There may be a size between the smallest and the next size up shown, explaining the choices in the following descriptions. Left to right: (a) mini-size with floral appliqués; impressed into heel of

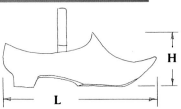

left shoe, ~3/32"H tooled numbers "2237" (same size and type numbers as Bohne shoes); 2-3/4"L x 7/8"H; $35. (b) mini-size with applied bows; unmarked; 2-11/16"L x 13/16"H; $20. (c) medium size with applied ring handle and bows (see sketch); HP; unmarked; 3-11/16"L x 1-1/4"H, clogs only; 1-13/16"HOA; $65. (d) large size with applied ring handle, pin flower and leaves; unmarked; 4-3/16"L x 1-9/16"H, clogs only; 1-15/16"HOA; $40.

Porcelain washer woman shoes; Ernst Bohne, Germany, late 1800s. Left: medium size; model number "2180" impressed into heel (same number as medium size baby shoe); 4-11/16"L x 2-1/16"H; uncommon; $45. Right: small size; blue factory logo on shank and "2181" impressed into heel (same number as small baby shoe); 3-7/8"L x 1-5/8"H; uncommon; $40 if perfect.

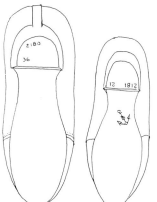

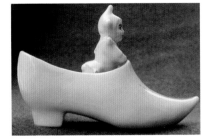

Porcelain glazed spade shaped sole clog with full body jester inserted; unmarked; 4-3/8"L x 1-11/16"H, clog only; 2-15/16"HOA. Germany, late 1800s. $50.

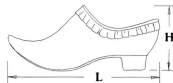

Four porcelain glazed baby shoes that may have come from the same factory; all unmarked; Germany, prob. late 1800s. Left to right: (a) attached pair with floral appliqués; 2-3/4"L x 1-7/8"H; $35. (b) singleton from same mold as (a) with original pincushion; 2-13/16"L x 1-15/16"H, shoe only; $30. (c) open vee (see sketch) with inserted full body jester; 3-1/4"L x 2-1/16"H, shoe only; $50. (d) open vee with inserted full body pierrot; 4-1/16"L x 2-5/8"H, shoe only; 3-3/4"HOA; $75.

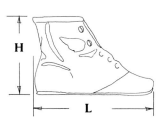

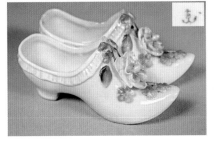

Porcelain pair of attached glazed clogs with in-mold ruching and floral appliqué; underglaze factory logo and impressed "2178" or "2173" in one sole; 4-1/16"L x 1-11/16"H. $65.

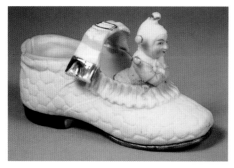

Porcelain bisque shoe with spade shaped sole, in-mold ruching, and applied strap; full body jester inserted; unmarked; 4-5/16"L x 1-5/8"H, body of shoe only; 2-3/16"H inc. strap; 2-5/8"HOA. Germany, prob. late 1800s. Uncommon. $125.

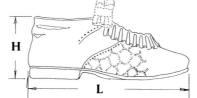

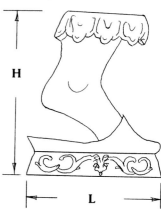

Porcelain glazed sock-in-slipper with applied bow on rococo base; #1068 (that and "315" incised in underside of base); 2-3/8"L x 1-7/16" base, 2-13/16"HOA. Conta & Boehme, Germany. Late 1800s. $60.

GERMAN PORCELAIN including
Conta & Boehme

Shoes were only a small portion of the enormous variety of Conta & Boehme products, but some of their shoes were produced in great quantity. As a result, many collectors have shoes from this factory in their collections but are unaware of this because so few of them were marked with a factory identification. Most C & B shoes, however, carry an important clue about their origin … a three or four digit incised mark of hand-scrawled numbers. It is those scrawled numbers that are referred to as model numbers. All the C & B pieces are HP.

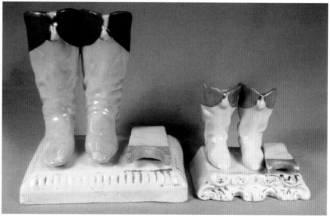

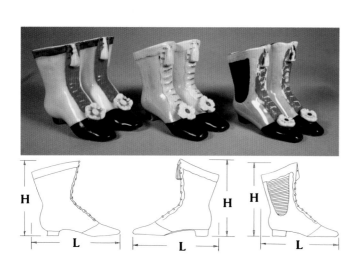

Three porcelain pairs of attached boots match strikers (front plackets) from Conta & Boehme, Germany; applied vamp ornaments; all from different molds and all unmarked except for an incised number; late 1800s. Left: #1007 (incised in sole), applied tassel; 3-13/16"L x 3-1/8"H; $40. Middle: no incised number; in-mold tassel; 3-11/16"L x 3-3/16"H; $40. Right: #44 (found incised on other pairs), in-mold tassel; 3-3/8"L x 3-1/16"H; $40.

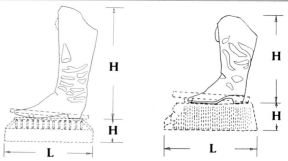

Two porcelain glazed pairs of attached boots and boot jack match strikers on bases; Conta & Boehme, Germany, late 1800s. Left: #579 (incised under base) size II; 3-5/16"H boots; 3-15/16"L x 2-11/16" wide x 11/16"H base, 4"HOA; $90. Right: #579 (incised under base) size III; 1-13/16"H boots; 2-11/16"L x 2" wide x 9/16"H base, 2-3/8"HOA; $35.

Porcelain glazed pair of attached boots and boot jack match striker on base; #579 (impressed into underside of base) size II; 3-5/16"H boots; 3-13/16" x 2-3/4" base, 4"HOA. Conta & Boehme, Germany. Rare HP décor. $175.

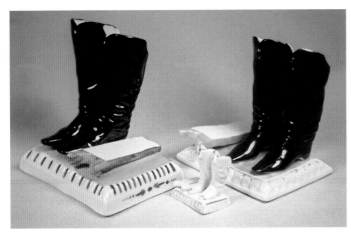

Three porcelain glazed pairs of attached boots and boot jack match strikers on bases; Conta & Boehme, Germany; late 1800s. The two large sets are #579 size I; 3-3/4"H boots; $125 each. The miniature has unreadable incised numbers; 1-1/2" x 1" base, 1-1/2"HOA; $40.

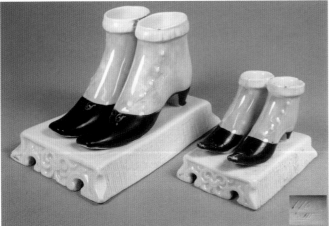

Two porcelain glazed pairs attached cuffed and side buttoned boots on rococo match striker bases; Conta & Boehme, Germany; late 1800s. Left: #1762 size I; 4-1/2"L x 3-1/8" wide base, 2-7/8"HOA; $90. Right: #1762 size III (see inset mark); 2-7/8"L x 2-1/8" wide base, 2"HOA; $60.

Porcelain glazed boot maker with "leather" apron, top hat open at top, applied boots to hold matches, and striker plate applied to left side, mounted on a rococo base; # 1781 (incised under base); 2-3/8" diameter base, 5-3/4"HOA. Conta & Boehme, Germany. Late 1800s. $300.

Porcelain medium size hugging angels bow slipper; embossed "2424/XXX" on sole; 5-13/16"L x 2-7/8"H. Conta & Boehme, Germany. Late 1800s. $150.

Porcelain glazed medium size hugging angels bow slipper; unmarked; 5-5/8"L x 2-13/16"H. Conta & Boehme, Germany. Late 1800s. If perfect, $150.

Porcelain glazed medium size hugging angels bow slipper; floral appliqués on toe and inside back of heel; incised into sole "2445"; 5-11/16"L x 3"H. Conta & Boehme, Germany. Late 1800s. If perfect, $175.

Porcelain glazed large size hugging angels bow slipper watch holder (hook missing) with applied heel on tasseled cushion; #2734 (incised into sole); 6-1/2"L x 4-3/4"H. Conta & Boehme, Germany. Late 1800s. If perfect, $275.

Porcelain glazed pair of ruffle-rimmed pumps with applied medallions and heels; appear to have been made from same mold but carry consecutive incised numbers, one "2431" and the other "2432", suggesting they were intended to be sold in pairs; 6-9/16"L x 3-13/16"H each. Conta & Boehme, Germany. Late 1800s. Rare. $175 each.

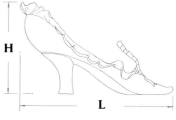

107

Pair of green tinted porcelain spade toe pumps with inserted green eyed cats; shoes are straights, but asymmetrical mirror image floral sprays were applied to create mates; impressed into heel of each the factory shield logo and tooled numbers "2439"; each is about 4-13/16"L x 2-5/8"H. Conta & Boehme, Germany. Late 1800s. $80 each.

Pair of porcelain glazed spade toe pumps with inserted green eyed cats; shoes are straights, but asymmetrical mirror image floral sprays were applied to create mates; shoe on right has hand-incised "2439" on sole and other is unmarked; each is about 4-13/16"L x 2-5/8"H. Conta & Boehme, Germany. Late 1800s. $130 each.

Heavy gauge porcelain glazed high top shoe with applied heel on pillow; applied bows; applied angel with quiver of arrows in right hand and bow in left; on the underside of hollow pillow, raised shield factory logo and "1222"; 5-3/8"L x 6-7/8"H. Conta & Boehme, Germany. Late 1800s. Rare. $275.

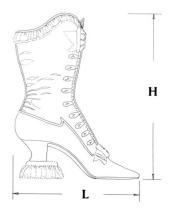

Porcelain glazed boots and basket mounted on match striker base; incised into base, "2465"; 4-1/4" x 3" base, 2-7/8"HOA. Conta & Boehme, Germany. Late 1800s. $50.

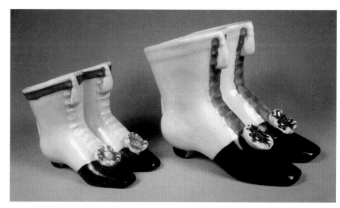

Two pairs porcelain glazed attached boots with applied match striker plate in back, vamp ornaments, and tassels; Conta & Boehme, Germany, model # 3103; late 1800s. Left: size II; 2-13/16"L x 2-3/8"H; $60. Right: size I; 3-3/4"L x 3-3/16"H; $65.

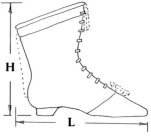

Porcelain trinket box with miniaturization of hugging angels bow shoe; base, lid, and mirror are molded rather than cast; handles on base are prob. cast and applied; "2986" hand incised on underside of cover; 4-1/8"LOA x 3-1/8" deep x 3-3/4"HOA. Conta & Boehme, Germany. Late 1800s. $150.

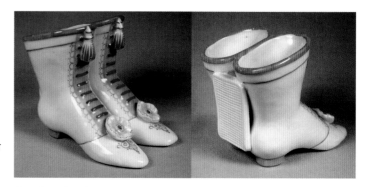

Porcelain glazed pair of boots with applied tassels, vamp ornaments, and match striker plate; hand incised into sole of left boot "3303"; 3-3/4"L x 3-3/16"H. Conta & Boehme, Germany. Late 1800s. Uncommon décor. $90.

Porcelain bisque shoe with applied bow and florals containing a pair of Edwardian children; bottom of heel impressed with factory shield logo and "5035"; 5-9/16"L x 3-7/8"H, shoe only; 5"HOA. Conta & Boehme, Germany. c. 1900. $200.

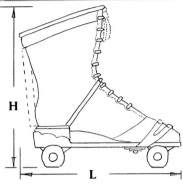

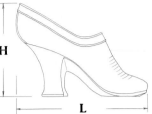

Porcelain glazed attached roller skates with applied tassels, match striker plate, and wheel assemblies; bottom view shows that the skates themselves are a "left" and "right", with toe straps lapped over in opposite directions; factory shield logo and "II" impressed into bottom of each; 2-7/8"L x 2-13/16"HOA. Conta & Boehme, Germany. Late 1800s. Rare. $200.

Porcelain glazed young boy trying on his Dad's boots, match striker; raised pad with factory shield logo on underside of base and impressed "3186"; 2-3/8"H boots only; 3-1/4" x 2-3/8" base, 6"HOA. Conta & Boehme, Germany. Late 1800s. Uncommon décor. $300.

Porcelain glazed two-piece box; "5187" impressed into shank; 3-3/4"L x 3-1/8"H assembled. Conta & Boehme, Germany, early 1900s. $125.

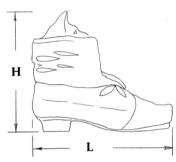

Porcelain piano baby holding Mary Jane; blue stamp of factory shield logo and "Germany" on bottom; 7-1/2"H. Shown in a c.1912-1917 C & B catalog as one of a pair, the other holding a rattle, and both given the model number "8180". Conta & Boehme, Germany. $250.

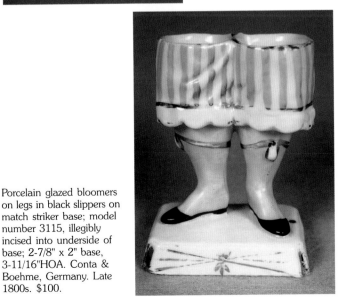

Porcelain glazed bloomers on legs in black slippers on match striker base; model number 3115, illegibly incised into underside of base; 2-7/8" x 2" base, 3-11/16"HOA. Conta & Boehme, Germany. Late 1800s. $100.

Porcelain pair of cuffed boots with spurs and boot jack match striker on base; embossed hand formed numbers on underside, "2315"; 3-11/16" x 2-5/8" base, 2-15/16"HOA. Pos. Conta & Boehme, Germany. Late 1800s. $125.

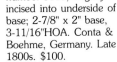

Porcelain cuffed boot with spur on scored base; incised hand scrawled underside of base, "1048"; 2-9/16" x 1-7/16" oval base, 2-3/8"HOA. Pos. Conta & Boehme, Germany. Late 1800s. $20.

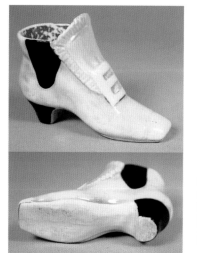

Porcelain ankle shoe with side gussets, buckled ruff and tan painted bottom; unmarked; 4"L x 2-15/16"H. Pos. Conta & Boehme, Germany. Late 1800s. $40.

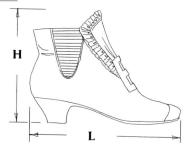

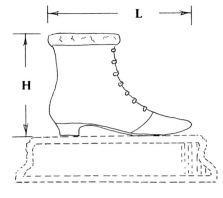

Porcelain glazed pair of attached boots with applied bows on scored match striker base; hand scrawled "247" on underside of base; 2-7/16"L x 1-5/8"H, boot only; 3-5/16" x 2-7/16" base, 2-3/8"HOA. Pos. Conta & Boehme, Germany. Late 1800s. $65.

GERMAN PORCELAIN:
Fantasy Shoes

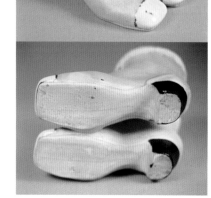

Porcelain pair of attached boots with tan painted bottoms; unmarked; 3-15/16"L x 2-11/16"H. Pos. Conta & Boehme, Germany. Late 1800s. $75.

Pair of porcelain bisque matched large size fantasy shoes, each with two applied angels, florals, and beading; unmarked; 9"L x 5-3/16"H, shoe only. The large angel on the right facing shoe always carries a bow; that on the left facing, a small shoe. Germany. c.1900. $200 each.

Comparison of large angels on left-facing large size fantasy shoes. In this photo, the angel on the left is representative of what is commonly found on these shoes. The angel on the right is applied to a shoe from the same mold except that its heel is applied, and this angel has different hair than what is commonly found. The flyaway locks are more subject to damage during the fabrication process and the head mold may have been retooled for what may be the later models.

Pair of porcelain glazed medium size fantasy shoes, each with one applied angel; applied and HP florals; unmarked; right facing, 6-5/8"L x 4-1/4"H, shoe only, bow in-mold; left facing, 6-1/4"L x 4-1/8"H, shoe only. The angel on the right facing shoe always carries a bow; that on the left facing, a small shoe. Germany. c.1900. $150 each.

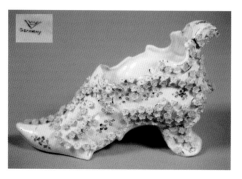

Porcelain glazed medium size fantasy shoe covered on left face with applied florettes and HP florals in manner of Conta & Boehme; blue factory logo (unidentified) and "Germany" on toe; 6-1/2"L x 4-3/16"H. This unidentified mark has been seen on a number of pieces with this type décor whose basic mold could be traced back to Conta & Boehme. But there is no current evidence that these pieces came from the C & B factory. Germany, c.1900. $85.

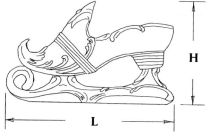

Porcelain glazed slipper mounted on double skate blades; in-mold yellow strap; applied florettes and bow; HP flowers; unmarked; 3-5/8"L x 2-1/8"H. Germany, c.1900. Uncommon. $150.

Porcelain glazed slipper with tie strap; applied florettes; HP flowers; unmarked; 4-1/4"L x 1-13/16"H, shoe only. Germany, c.1900. Uncommon. $100.

Porcelain bisque mule with applied heel, angel, large fluted vamp flower, and smaller flowers and leaves; unmarked; 9-1/4"L x 4-1/2"H, shoe only; 5-1/8"HOA. Thin pad at top of vamp once held a small cherub; Germany, c.1900; uncommon form; as shown, $150. If perfect, $250. This model is known in left- and right-facing mates. It is also known in a smaller size with a single cherub sitting on the heel; 6-1/4"L x 3-1/8"H, shoe only; 4-1/2"HOA; $200. There may be a third, intermediate size.

Porcelain glazed slipper with applied flat heel held by angel, on oval base; applied large roses, buds, leaves, and florettes; unmarked; slipper is 6-5/8" to 6-3/4"L; base without florettes: 4-1/2" x 2-9/16"; 6-13/16"HOA. Germany. c.1900. Rare. $350.

Porcelain large size fantasy shoe with two applied angels, one with a butterfly box and butterfly; applied curl on heel back; "8131" impressed into bottom; unmarked; 9-1/8"L x 5-13/16"H, shoe only; 7"HOA. Prob. Germany, c.1900. Rare. $350.

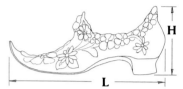

Two sizes in thin porcelain glazed low-cut crackows; unmarked; Germany, late 1800s. Larger with HP in-mold design: 6-13/16"L x 2-7/8"H; $65. Smaller: 4-3/8"L x 2-7/8"H; $20.

GERMAN PORCELAIN:
Crackows

First introduced in Krakow, Poland, shoes with long pointed toes worn in the late 13th century became known as crackows. While some shoes in this section may not qualify, the name is a convenient designation for reference purposes.

Thin porcelain glazed crackow ankle boots; note small open loop near toe; unmarked; Germany, late 1800s. Left to right: (a) 4-3/8"L x 2-5/8"H; HP in-mold design; $60. (b) 5-1/2"L x 3-3/8"H; $35. (c) 6-13/16"L x 4-1/16"H; HP in-mold design; $65. (d) 6-7/8"L x 4-1/16"H; $45.

Two sizes in porcelain glazed strap crackows with elaborate in-mold designs and transfer medallions; unmarked; Germany, late 1800s. Smaller: 5-1/4"L x 2-1/16"H; $35. Larger: 6-3/8"L x 2-1/2"H; $50.

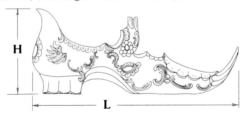

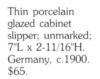

Thin porcelain glazed cabinet slipper; unmarked; 7"L x 2-11/16"H. Germany, c.1900. $65.

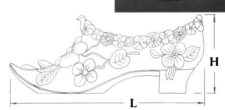

Two sizes in thin porcelain glazed crackows with three pairs open eyelets and three pairs in-mold grommets aside open vee; unmarked; Germany, late 1800s. Larger: 6-11/16"L x 3-1/2"H; $45. Smaller with HP in-mold design: 5-1/4"L x 2-11/16"H; $60.

Porcelain glazed medallion crackow ankle boot; color transfer; unmarked; 6-1/2"L x 4-3/16"H. Known in other sizes. Germany, late 1800s. $50.

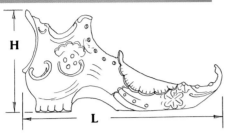

Two sizes in thin porcelain glazed lace-up medallion crackows; color transfers; unmarked; Germany, late 1800s. Larger: 5-5/16"L x 2-5/8"H; $50. Smaller, a Napoleon portrait (Hortense) shoe: 4-3/8"L x 2-3/16"H. $65.

Other cabinet-side versions of the porcelain needlenose shoe; Germany, c.1900. Left to right: (a) large size, heavily embossed and indented double flowers; 7-3/4"L x 3-1/2"H; $75. (b) large size, heavily embossed and indented double flowers; marked "GERMANY"; 7-5/8"L x 3-1/2"H; $75. (c) small size, souvenir of "The Royal Exchange, Glasgow"; 5-5/16"L x 2-1/2"H; $35. (d) mini size, heavily embossed and indented single flower; 4-1/8"L x 1-7/8"H; $45.

GERMAN PORCELAIN: CABINET SHOES including Needle-noses, Snowdrops, and Related

The factories of origin of these shoes have yet to be identified. Among collectors of a figural for which there are thousands of unmarked examples, attaching a moniker, however irreverent it may seem, provides a convenient way to quickly reference a category of shoe.

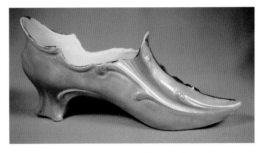

Back side of large shoe; all needlenose shoes have this in-mold pattern on their back sides.

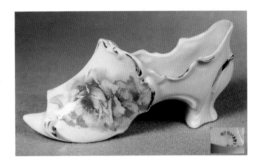

Four sizes of porcelain glazed needlenose Napoleon portrait shoes; transfer portraits with some hand tinting; generally unmarked, but occasionally with a Germany mark; Germany, c.1900. Left to right: (a) large size, Queen Louise portrait, turquoise airbrushed ground; 7-1/2"L x 3-3/8"H; uncommon size, $125. (b) medium size, Queen Louise portrait; 6-9/16"L x 3"H; $75. (c) small size, Josephine portrait; 5-1/2"L x 2-11/16"H; $65. (d) mini size, Hortense portrait; 4-1/8"L x 1-7/8"H; $60.

Porcelain needlenose shoe with mold modification of cabinet side; color transfer; marked on bottom of heel "GERMANY"; 5-7/16"L x 2-5/8"H. Germany, c.1900. $75.

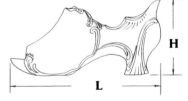

Two porcelain glazed boots with identical rim and sole in-mold design detail; unmarked; Germany, c.1900. Left: in-mold snowdrop on vamp (prob. original design); 4"L x 4-9/16"H; $45. Right: in-mold beading framed medallion, HP floral (prob. a modified mold); 3-3/4"L x 4-3/16"H; $65.

Back side of large Queen Louise shoe; all needlenose shoes have this in-mold pattern on their back sides.

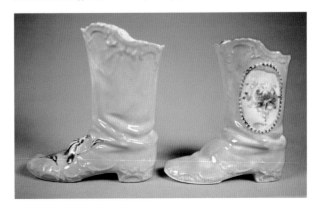

Porcelain glazed boot with HP floral; unmarked; 3-3/4"L x 4-3/16"H. This boot has been seen with a Queen Louise portrait within the beaded medallion. Germany, c.1900. $65.

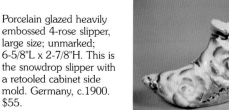

Four versions of the snowdrop cabinet slipper; three unmarked in any way; Germany, c.1900 (smallest is dated). Left to right: (a) large size; 6-5/8"L x 2-7/8"H; rare HP décor, $100. (b) medium size; 5-3/4"L x 2-1/2"H; $45. (c) small size; 5"L x 2-1/8"H; $30. (d) mini size, HP "Souvenir St. Louis 1904"; 4-3/16"L x 1-13/16"H; $50.

Porcelain glazed in-mold snowdrop small size boot with straps; in-mold patches and "holes" (do not go through) on each ankle; Germany millstone mark on sole; 3-3/16"L x 3-15/16"H. Germany, c.1900. $40.

Porcelain glazed heavily embossed 4-rose slipper, large size; unmarked; 6-5/8"L x 2-7/8"H. This is the snowdrop slipper with a retooled cabinet side mold. Germany, c.1900. $55.

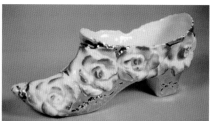

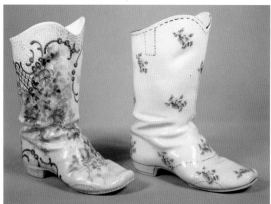

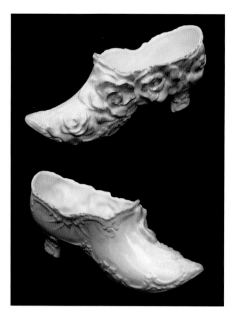

Porcelain glazed heavily embossed 4-rose slipper, medium size; unmarked; 5-15/16"L x 2-7/16"H. This is the snowdrop slipper with a retooled cabinet side mold. Germany, c.1900. $45.

Two porcelain boots with in-mold patches and "holes" (do not go through) on each ankle; unmarked; c.1900. Left: 4-5/16"L x 5-3/16"H; uncommon HP décor; $90. Right: HP florals and stitching detail; 4-1/2"L x 5-5/16"H; $75. This boot mold has been seen marked "Carlsbad/*shield logo*/China/Austria", a mark that may have been used by the Charles Ahrenfeldt decorating shop in Altrohlau or by Bawo & Dotter.

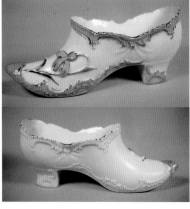

In-mold details of the snowdrop cabinet slipper.

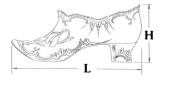

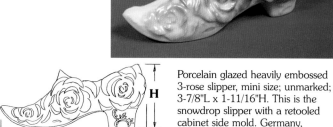

Porcelain glazed heavily embossed 3-rose slipper, mini size; unmarked; 3-7/8"L x 1-11/16"H. This is the snowdrop slipper with a retooled cabinet side mold. Germany, c.1900. $35.

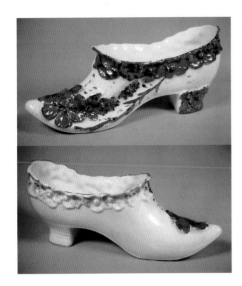

In-mold details of the floral garland slipper.

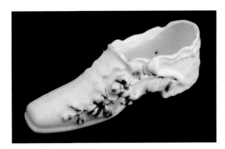

Small size porcelain wing tip oxford with scalloped rim and heavily embossed floral spray on left side; orange millstone mark on bottom "MADE IN GERMANY"; on back side "New London"; 5-1/16"L x 1-5/8"H. Germany, c.1900. Excessive wear of gold. $25.

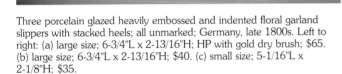

Three porcelain glazed heavily embossed and indented floral garland slippers with stacked heels; all unmarked; Germany, late 1800s. Left to right: (a) large size; 6-3/4"L x 2-13/16"H; HP with gold dry brush; $65. (b) large size; 6-3/4"L x 2-13/16"H; $40. (c) small size; 5-1/16"L x 2-1/8"H; $35.

Porcelain wing tip oxfords with scalloped rims and heavily embossed floral sprays on left side; unmarked; Germany, late 1800s. Left: large size (sketch); 7"L x 2-7/16"H; $75. Right: medium size; unmarked; 6-1/8"L x 2-3/16"H. $65.

Thin porcelain baby bootee airbrushed and HP; unmarked; 3-15/16"L x 3"H. Germany, late 1800s. Uncommon lack of décor wear. $70.

Detail of right side of wing tip oxford with embossed floral spray.

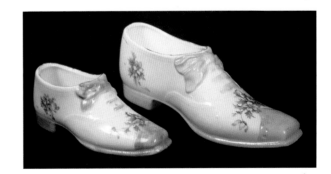

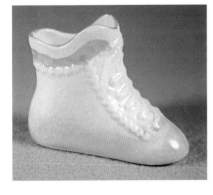

Thin porcelain baby bootee; unmarked; 2-3/4"L x 2-3/16"H. Germany, late 1800s. $15.

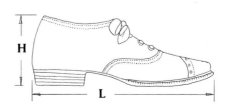

Thin porcelain low-heeled wing tip oxfords with in-mold bow; color transfers of florals; unmarked; Germany, late 1800s. Left: small size; 4-3/8"L x 1-5/8"H; $45. Right: large size; 6"L x 2-1/8"H; $55.

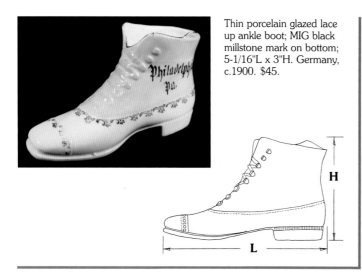

Thin porcelain glazed lace up ankle boot; MIG black millstone mark on bottom; 5-1/16"L x 3"H. Germany, c.1900. $45.

Thin porcelain glazed cobalt wash Dutch shoe with in-mold young woman on vamp; "*Delft*" impressed into back face of shoe, then over painted; 3-1/4"L x 3-1/8"H. Prob. Germany, c.1900. $35.

GERMAN PORCELAIN: BLUES

There are a number of porcelain shoes marked only "Delft" that are decorated in the Delft blues for which The Netherlands is renown. The ones shown here are believed to have been made in Germany. Several other shoes are included here that are not marked in this way but are usually found in a blue and white décor.

Porcelain glazed cobalt wash platform shoe with two in-mold women and cart; impressed into back face of heel "Germany 6725"; 3-5/8"L x 3-3/16"H. Not shown is the two-man mate facing in the opposite direction. Germany, c.1900. $25.

Thin porcelain glazed cobalt wash Dutch shoes with in-mold basket weave pattern; HP scenes on both sides; both marked underglaze "*Delft*"; Germany, c.1900. These are not marked with a country of origin, but another has been seen with a gray-green millstone mark "MADE IN GERMANY". Left: small size, "601" or "109" impressed into shank side; 4"L x 2-1/16"H; $40. Right: large size, 7"L x 3-1/4"H. $50.

Thin porcelain glazed cuffed low cut HP shoe with in-mold pompom and partially open vee; unmarked; 4"L x 1-11/16"H. Prob. Germany, c.1900. Uncommon. $65.

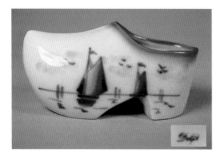

Porcelain glazed Dutch shoe with HP scene; marked underglaze on shank; 4-3/8"L x 2-3/16"H. Prob. Germany, c.1900. $25.

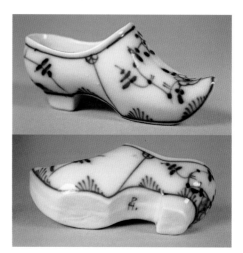

Ceramic clog with Dutch mother and daughter scenic; "*Delft IV*" underglaze and "1089" impressed on shank; 6-3/16"L x 2-3/8"H. Pos. Germany, c.1900. $35.

Porcelain glazed clog with HP cobalt *Straw Flower* pattern; 4-13/16"L x 2-1/8"H. The pattern in this shoe is a match to Royal Bayreuth's *Old Tettau Blue* pattern, but the mark is not. Other factories that made patterns that appear to match this shoe include the Poessneck Porcelain Factory, precursor to Conta & Boehme, but again, the mark is not known to be one from this factory. Germany, 1800s. $90.

Thin porcelain glazed Normandy shoe with sailing scene; 5"L x 2-5/16"H. Prob. Germany, late 1800s. $50.

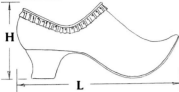

Porcelain glazed shoe with open sides and stacked heel; 3-9/16"L x 1-11/16"H. Pos. Germany. $15.

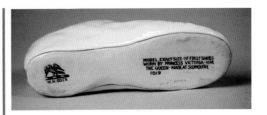

Bottom view of Princess Victoria's shoe for versions made late 1880s – c.1901.

Two thin porcelain Goss Boulogne wooden shoes with applied heels; bottom description includes "R^DN^O 539421", British Registry number assigned in early 1909; both approx. 4-3/4"L x 1-1/2"H; c.1909-pre-1929; Goss, England. Left: matching crest "Boulogne Sur Mer"; $155. Right: crest of "Herne Bay" (non matching); $65.

Bottom view of Boulogne wooden shoe.

GOSS CRESTED CHINA

The W. H. Goss company of Stoke-on-Trent, England originated heraldic porcelain in the 1880s. Queen Victoria had introduced bank holidays for workers in 1871. With time, growing financial resources, a network of rail lines spreading across the countryside, and the popularity of seaside and resort trips, Victorian Great Britain was on the move and Goss had the idea of producing small porcelain souvenirs with the local town's coat of arms for tourists to take back to their homes as mementos. They were based on famous landmarks or famous objects found in museums throughout the country. If decorated with the crest of the town in which the object was found, the crest is said to be "matching", and is more valuable. The thin-walled, high quality Goss products were produced until 1934 when the firm went into receivership. Although introduced earlier, some shoes continued to be produced well into the 1930s; an agent's ordering card used between 1929 and 1934 showed Queen Elizabeth's riding shoe, the Norwegian wooden shoe, and Queen Victoria's baby shoe still available. Goss products are the top of the line in crested china. They are superbly crafted of the finest porcelain, developed after hundreds of experiments by Goss. The crests, whose black outlines were applied using transfers, were hand-colored to exacting standards by highly trained paintresses. Values are driven by the British market where crested china is highly collectible and where there are several dealers who specialize in it.

Three thin porcelain Goss Dinant wooden shoes with in-mold leaf design; all approx. 2-7/8"L x 1-5/8"H; made beginning 1914; Goss, England. Left: crest of "Arms of Hertford" (non matching); c. 1914-c.1930; $55. Middle: crest of "Semper Fidelis/City and County of the /City of Exeter"; prob. made by a Goss successor company; c.1930-1939; $30. Right: color transfer on vamp, "Souvenir/from/Canada" on back of heel; made by a Goss successor company; $20.

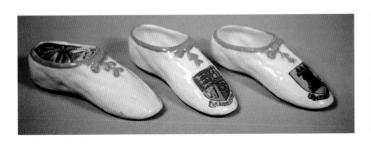

Three very thin porcelain Goss Princess Victoria baby shoes with in-mold laces and bow, all with factory logo and description on tan-painted bottoms; all approx. 4-1/16"L x 1-5/16"H; Goss, England. Left: no crest; professionally made pin cushion, but not known if it came with the shoe; printed description on bottom does not include "LATE QUEEN –(WHO DIED JAN.22nd 1901)", making this an uncommon version; late 1880s-c.1901; $85. Middle: matching crest "H. M. Queen Victoria"; bottom description includes "LATE QUEEN …"; c.1901-1934. $65. Right: crest of "Isle of Wight Ancient" (non-matching); bottom description includes "LATE QUEEN …"; c. 1901-1934; $45.

Two thin porcelain Goss Norwegian wooden shoes with in-mold rim pattern; both 4-3/16"L x 1-1/8"H; c.1914-1934; Goss, England. Left: matching crest of "Norge" (Norway); $135. Right: crest of "A Deo et Regie/ Richmond (Surrey)" (non matching); $55.

Two thin porcelain Goss Lancashire clogs with in-mold straps and buckle; both approx. 3-3/4"L x 2-1/8"H; Goss, England. Left: crest of "Bacup" (non matching); c. 1916-pre 1929; $85. Right: crest of "British Empire Exhibition/Wembley 1924"; c.1924; $130.

Bottom view of Lancashire clog.

Two thin porcelain Goss Dutch sabots; both 3-1/4"L x 1-1/2"H; c.1916-pre 1929; Goss, England. Left: matching crest of "Antwerpen"; $70. Right: crest of "Falmouth" (non matching); $45.

Thin porcelain Goss Queen Elizabeth's riding shoe; crest of "Walton-on-the-Maze" (non matching); 4-3/16"L x 1-5/8"H. Goss, England. c.1921-1934. Rare. $215.

Thin porcelain Goss slipper wall pocket; crest of "Bruxelles"; Goss hawk and "W. H. GOSS" on bottom; 3-7/8"L x 1-1/16"H. Goss, England. Prob. 1920s. $35.

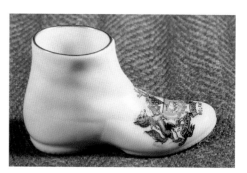

Thin porcelain ankle shoe; crest of "Belfast"; Goss hawk and "W. H. GOSS/ENGLAND" on bottom; 2-7/8"L x 1-5/8"H. Designed and made by a Goss successor company. c.1930-1939. $25.

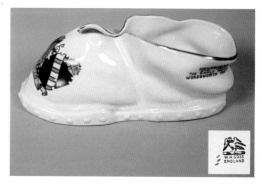

Thin porcelain John Waterson's clog (reputedly a mole catcher who had the largest feet in England); crest of "Hawkshead"; on left rear quarter "HAWKSHEAD/ THE EARLY HOME OF/WORDSWORTH THE POET"; impressed into bottom "719"; Goss logo on bottom; 4-1/8"L x 1-5/8"H. Arcadian factory model. Arcadian, England. c.1930-1939. $85.

OTHER CRESTED CHINA,
mostly English

 Carlton was probably the first of the major Goss competitors to make heraldic china, beginning about 1902. They soon were joined by seven other major, and a few lesser, companies in the making of crested china. Shelley, Grafton and Carlton were among the producers of high quality items. Unlike Goss, whose miniatures were authentic historic objects, the competitors branched out into any items of marketability. Production of crested china declined after WWI, and had waned by the 1930s. Typically, the coat of arms was applied as a line transfer that was then filled in with color by hand. The shoes are glazed and usually have a thin gold trim line on the rim. Crests are a study in themselves, and books can be obtained that are devoted to the subject. Rare crests in high demand will increase the value of a piece. Values are driven by the British market where the demand is highest for crested china.

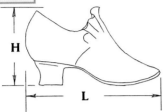

Thin porcelain ruffled vamp slipper with crest of "London 1908/ Franco British Exhibition"; factory logo on bottom; 3-3/16"L x 1-13/16"H. Max Emanuel, Germany/England. c.1908. $45.

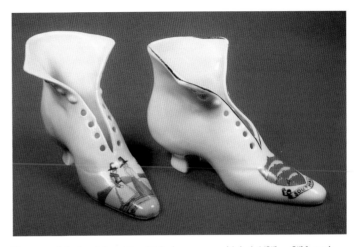

Two porcelain 4 x 4 flared top high shoes; unmarked; 4-1/8"L x 3"H; prob. Saxony, Germany, early 1900s. Often misidentified as Royal Bayreuth. Uncommon form. Left: Welsh ladies scenic; $70. Right: crest of "Southall"; $60.

Four thin porcelain ruffled vamp slippers with different marks that would lead one to expect them to have come from that many factories. The three on the left have a barely visible string tie near the top of the ruffled vamp, and all came from Taylor & Kent, from the same mold design. Left to right: (a) crest of "Wick"; 3-1/2"L x 1-7/8"H; Atlas China, England; $20. (b) crest of "Wrexham"; 3-1/2"L x 1-15/16"H; "J. R. & Co" was a wholesaler who purchased items from several factories including Taylor & Kent; Victoria China, England; c.1910-1924; $20. (c) crest of "North Berwick"; 3-3/8"L x 1-7/8"H; Keltic, England; $20. (d) crest of "Darlington"; 3-7/16"L x 1-7/8"H; H. M. Williams & Sons, England; $20.

Two porcelain lace up shoes; unmarked; prob. Saxony, Germany, early 1900s. Left: crest of "Littlehampton"; a "left"; 3-1/8"L x 1-5/16"H; $40. Right: crest of "Folkestone"; 3-1/16"L x 3-1/4"H; $40.

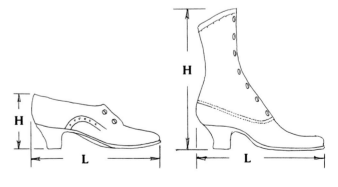

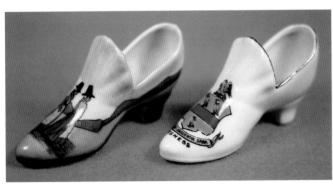

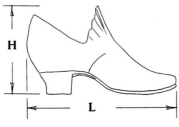

Two thin porcelain ruffled vamp slippers from the same mold; 3-3/16"L x 1-13/16"H; unmarked; prob. Germany, early 1900s. Left: Welsh ladies scenic; $40. Right: crest of "Skegness"; $20.

Thin porcelain scalloped shoe with vamp placket triple-buttoned on both sides; crest of "Shrewsbury"; 4"L x 2-1/16"H. Tuscan, England. $35.

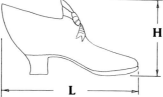

Porcelain slipper with in-mold bow on high pointed vamp; crest of "Wallingford"; unmarked; 4-3/16"L x 2-1/4"H. Pos. Willow or S. Hancock (Dutchess China trademark), England. $35.

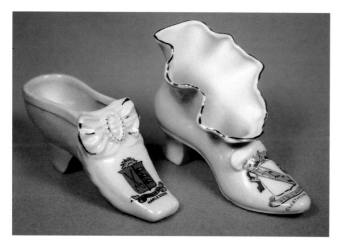

Left: heavy ceramic in-mold bow and trailing streamers slipper with color transfer crest of "Harlesden"; unmarked; 4-1/4"L x 1-13/16"H; prob. Germany, early 1900s; $15. Right: thin porcelain slipper with flounced rim and in-mold bow; HP black line transfer crest of "Cleethorpes"; unmarked; pos. Saxony, Germany, early 1900s; $45.

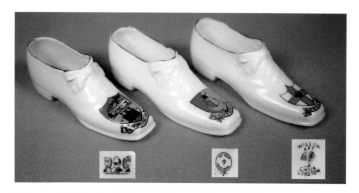

Thin porcelain low heeled shoes with in-mold bows. Left: crest of "Bidford-on-Avon"; 4-3/8"L x 1-3/8"H; Fenton, England; $25, Middle: crest of "Southsea"; 4-1/2"L x 1-7/16"H; Wy Knot? China, England; $25. Right: crest of "Cowes"; 4-1/2"L x 1-7/16"H; Willow Art, England; $25.

Thin porcelain moccasin with in-mold bow and a great amount of in-mold detail that does not photograph well; crest of "Herne Bay"; 3-7/8"L x 1-3/4"H. Cyclone, England. $55.

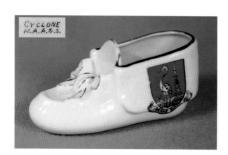

Porcelain John Waterson's clog; crest of "Blandford-Forum"; 4-1/8"L x 1-5/8"H. Carlton, England. Uncommon. $85.

Porcelain hollow baby-in-a-quilted bootee; crest of "City of Bristol"; 3-1/8"L x 3"H. Mark is found on products that probably came from the Corona and Florentine factories, England. $30.

Thin porcelain hollow puppy-in-slipper; crest of "Dymchurch"; 3-11/16"L x 1-9/16"H. Carlton, England. Uncommon. $140. Not shown: this piece with crest of "British Empire Exhibition Wembley 1924" sold in Nov. 1999 in England for $310.

Porcelain in-mold cat-on-shoe with blue neck ribbons; each 3-5/8"L x 2-11/16"H; Willow Art, England. Left: crest of "Great Yarmouth"; $45. Right: crest of "British Empire Exhibition 1924 Wembley"; $75.

Thin porcelain hollow black cat in boot; "REG^D N^O 708645" (registered in 1924); crest of "New Haven/Sussex"; 2-7/16"L x 2-3/8"H. Part of the highly collected black cat series by this company. Arcadian, England. $145.

Porcelain hollow pair of riding boots with rabbit and cat; crest of "Birmingham"; unmarked; 1-7/8"L x 3-5/16"H. England or Germany, early 1900s. Uncommon. $70.

Thin porcelain work boot and three smaller tramp shoes. Left to right: (a) crest of "Dunfermline"; 3-5/16"L x 2"H; Porcelle, England; $25. (b) crest of "Wakefield"; 2-13/16"L x 1-5/8"H; Carlton, England; $20. (c) crest of "Margate"; 2-7/16"L x 1-7/16"H; Ivora, England; $20. (d) crest of "Leith"; 2-7/16"L x 1-7/16"H; Nautilus, Scotland; $20.

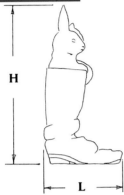

Thin porcelain ankle boot; crest of "Elstree"; Arcadian logo on sole; 3"L x 1-11/16"H. Sketch illustrates in-mold detail found in many of the small crested china shoes. Arcadian, England. $20.

Thin porcelain hollow roller skate with four applied wheels; "RᴰNᵒ 565604 (registered in 1910); crest of "Thetford Crest"; 4-9/16"L x 1-7/8"H. Carlton, England. Uncommon; $120.

Thin porcelain Thomas Á Becket shoe; crest of "Bournemouth"; 4-1/8"L x 1-7/16"H. Carlton, England. Uncommon. $110.

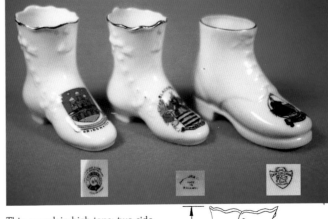

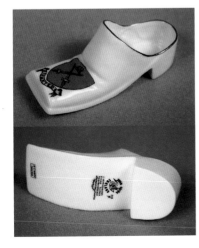

Thin porcelain Queen Elizabeth's riding shoe; crest of "Thaxted"; 4-1/16"L x 1-5/8"H. Swan China, England. Rare. $200.

Thin porcelain high tops: two side button and bow tassel shoes (sketch) and a work boot; left and center shoes from same mold (Hancock, Sampson & Sons). Left to right: (a) crest of "Bridgwater"; 2-15/16"L x 2-11/16"H; Corona, England; $40. (b) crest of "Blackpool"; 2-7/8"L x 2-5/8"H; Alexandra, England; $40. (c) crest of "Knutsford"; mark used c.1915-1933; 3-1/4"L x 2-3/8"H; Grafton, England; $35.

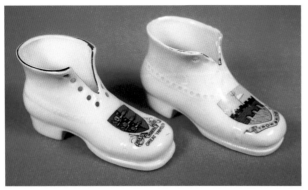

Two porcelain lace up ankle shoes, both unmarked and not from the same mold; prob. Germany, early 1900s. Left (sketch): crest of "Great Yarmouth"; 4-1/16"L x 2-3/8"H; $25. Right: crest of "Trowbridge"; 4-1/8"L x 2-7/16"H; $20.

Left: porcelain shoe with in-mold buckle; crest of "Birmingham"; unmarked; 4-3/8"L x 2-3/8"H; prob. Germany, early 1900s; $20. Middle: porcelain strap shoe; crest of "Borough of Hastings"; unmarked; 3-1/4"L x 1-3/4"H; prob. Germany, early 1900s; $20. Right: porcelain boot; crest of "Tonbridge"; brown stamp "Made in Austria"; 2-3/16"L x 1-7/8"H; early 1900s; $15.

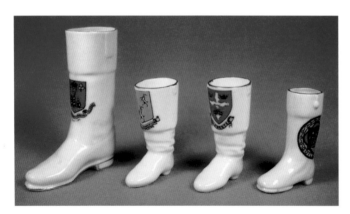

Porcelain boots, all bottom marked. Left to right: (a) crest of "Queenstown"; Swan China logo; 3-1/16"L x 4-1/8"H; uncommon; $70. (b) crest of "Merionethshire"; marked "The Foley China/England/"Ivory""; 1-3/4"L x 2-3/4"H; Foley China, England; $40. (c) crest of "Colchester"; marked "Late Foley/Shelley/England"; 1-7/8"L x 2-13/16"H; Shelley, England; $40. (d) crest of "Guildford"; Carlton logo; 1-13/16"L x 2-9/16"H; Carlton, England; $35.

Porcelain riding boot; crest of "Rochester"; Arcadian logo; 2-3/4"L x 3-5/8"H. Arcadian, England. $55.

Left: porcelain boot with sterling rim impressed with "A.B.&C." and hallmarks, one of which is the English hallmark for 1909; porcelain unmarked; crest of "City of London"; 1-7/8"L x 3-1/16"H; $100. Middle: porcelain Dutch shoe scent bottle with sterling top impressed with "A.B.&C." and three hallmarks; porcelain unmarked; crest of "City of London"; 2-3/8"L x 1-11/16"H (with cap); $80. Right: porcelain boot with puttee; crest of "City of Manchester"; Grafton logo for c.1915-1933; 1-15/16"L x 3"H; Grafton, England; $50. Not shown: Boot with puttee, color transfer of Canadian Pavilion and "Light O' Wembley/Souvenir Wembley Exhibition 1925"; sold in Nov. 2000 for $95.

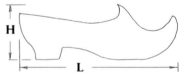

Thin porcelain large Grafton clog (comes in three sizes) with upturned toe; crest of "Isle of Wight"; factory logo for c.1900-1915; 4-1/4"L x 1-7/16"H. Grafton, England. $25.

Thin porcelain small Grafton clog (comes in three sizes) with upturned toe; crest of "Bordeaux"; factory logo for c.1915-1933; 3-3/16"L x 1-1/8"H. Grafton, England. $20.

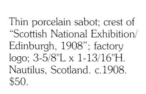

Thin porcelain sabot; crest of "Scottish National Exhibition/Edinburgh, 1908"; factory logo; 3-5/8"L x 1-13/16"H. Nautilus, Scotland. c.1908. $50.

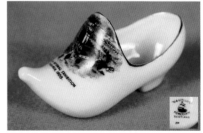

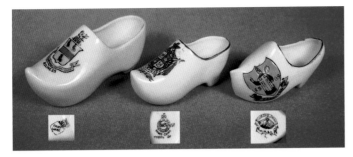

Porcelain clogs. Left: crest of "Skegness"; factory logo; 3-1/2"L x 1-3/4"H; Fairy Ware (Schmidt Victoria), Austria; $20. Middle: crest of "St. Ives"; factory logo; 2-7/8"L x 1-7/16"H; Savoy, England; $20. Right: crest of "Crediton"; factory logo; 2-3/4"L x 1-7/16"H; Clifton, England; $20.

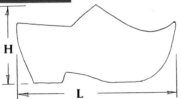

Porcelain sabot; crest of "Ventnor"; factory logo; 3-7/16"L x 1-5/8"H. Foley, England. $20.

Porcelain wall pocket slippers with in-mold bows. Left to right: (a) crest of "Upstreet"; factory logo; 4-1/16"L x 1-3/4"H; Carlton, England; $40. (b) crest of "Port Leven"; factory logo; 4-1/16"L x 1-3/4"H; Arcadian, England; $40. (c) crest of "King's Lynn"; factory logo; 4-1/8"L x 1-3/4"H; Clifton, England; $40. (d) crest of "Windsor"; factory logo; 5-15/16"L x 2-1/2"H; Willow Art, England; uncommon size; $75.

Thin porcelain Lancashire clogs with in-mold straps, buckles, and bottom cleats, all with factory logo marks. Left to right: (a) crest of "Rolvenden"; verse on back (see following photo); 4-7/16"L x 2-7/8"H; Carlton, England; $35. (b) crest of "Stalybridge"; verse on back (see following photo); 3-7/8"L x 2"H; Carlton, England; $25. (c) crest of "Kingston Upon Thames"; 3-5/8"L x 2-1/16"H; Shelley, England; $25. (d) crest of "Willesden"; 3-9/16"L x 1-15/16"H; Arcadian, England; $25.

Verse on Carlton Lancashire clogs, found on side or back.

Two thin porcelain Lancashire clogs cast from same mold design, both with factory logos. Left: crest of "Pembroke Dock"; 3-7/16"L x 1-7/8"H; Milton, England; $20. Right: crest of "British Empire Exhibition/1924/Wembley"; 3-3/8"L x 1-13/16"H; Willow Art, England; $45.

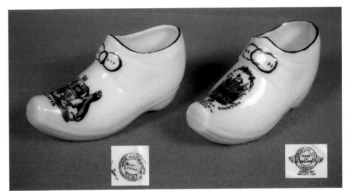

Two thin porcelain Lancashire clogs cast from same mold design, both with factory logos; 3-7/16"L x 1-7/8"H each. Left: crest of "Ballater"; Albion China, England; $20. Right: crest of "British Empire Exhibition/Wembley 1925"; Florentine, England; $45.

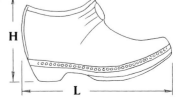

Porcelain Lancashire clog; crest of "Bradford"; unmarked; 4-1/16"L x 2-3/16"H. Pos. Germany. $20.

Porcelain Lancashire clog with "Lucky White Heather"; impressed into bottom sole "3587 foreign"; 5"L x 2-7/8"H. Germany, post WWI. $35.

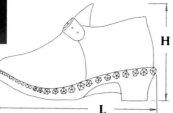

Porcelain "Lucky White Heather" slipper with in-mold star flowers and "Germany/ 3322"; stamped on bottom in orange "FOREIGN"; 4-7/8"L x 2-1/16"H. Design adapted from Galluba & Hofmann 1926A series. Germany, post WWI. $40.

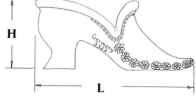

SOUVENIR CHINA, mostly German

Most souvenir china is German and most of it is porcelain. There are many cross collectors who specialize in certain kinds of views, so the value of a shoe will depend not only on its shape but in particular on the view it carries. Other qualities that affect the value are the overall décor and color. The mantra with some souvenir china dealers is "form, scene, and location", not necessarily in that order, as the trio for establishing value. Cobalt is highly collected. Plum, green, and brown are uncommon colors. Most souvenir china was made between about 1890 and 1915, though some was made into about the 1920s. Many additional souvenir shoes are shown in sections following this, but those could be grouped with other shoes known or believed to have been made by specific manufacturers. On most German pieces, the view was an outline transfer then hand-painted by local craftspeople. Souvenir china comprises an inadvertent record of the way we looked as a nation a century ago.

Porcelain cobalt glazed molded flat men's work boots pipe rests; Germany, c.1900; uncommon forms. Left: view of "The Square, Cahir"; unmarked; 5-1/4"L x 4-1/4"H; $90. Right: view of "State Capitol, Indianapolis, Ind."; orange "Germany" in rectangle; 4-3/8"L x 3-3/8"H; $80.

Bottom view of molded pipe rest showing bottom ridges like those found on molded saucers. Note barely visible mark in center.

Porcelain cobalt glazed 8-eyelet large cap toe man's work boot with view of "Memorial Hall, Rutland, Vt."; unmarked; a "right"; 5"L x 3-7/16"H. Believed to be a Royal Bayreuth blank with a mold modification of the vee to distinguish it from the factory's own versions of this form. Note indentations across cap toe that would serve as guides to a painter if being decorated in the RB mode. Germany, c.1900. Uncommon souvenir form. $135.

Porcelain green glazed 8-eyelet large cap toe man's work boot with view of "Welsh Costumes."; unmarked; a "right"; 5"L x 3-7/16"H. Believed to be a Royal Bayreuth blank with a mold modification of the vee to distinguish it from the factory's own versions of this form. Note indentations across cap toe that would serve as guides to a painter if being decorated in the RB mode. Germany, c.1900. Uncommon souvenir form. $125.

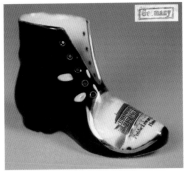

Porcelain cobalt glazed 5-eyelet medium man's cap toe work boot with view of "Public Library, Boston, Mass."; marked in orange rectangle "Germany"; a "right"; 4-1/8"L x 2-13/16"H. May be a Royal Bayreuth blank in a medium size eyelet-modified form-off not found with factory décor in this size. There are indentations across cap toe that would serve as guides to a painter if being decorated in the RB mode. Germany, c.1900. $70.

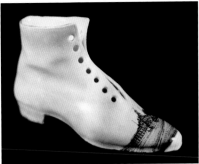

Porcelain pearl luster glazed 7-eyelet cap toe ankle shoe; view of "?emony Square, Claremont, N. Y."; impressed into shank "325" or "329"; a "right"; unmarked; 4-1/2"L x 2-11/16"H. May be a Royal Bayreuth blank. Germany, c.1900. Uncommon souvenir form. $65.

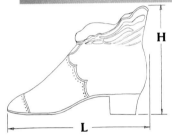

Porcelain ankle boots with asymmetrical rim flounce; Germany, c.1900. Left: cobalt; view of "The Old Bridge, Trenton, N.J."; unmarked; 5-1/8"L x 3-3/4"H; $70. Right: green; view of "State Capitol, Albany, N. Y."; marked in orange rectangle "Germany"; 5-1/4"L x 3-3/4"H; $50.

Porcelain cobalt glazed large Dutch shoe; view of "Residence of Jessie Murphy, Spaulding, Nebr."; unmarked; 6-1/4"L x 2-9/16"H. Germany, c.1900. Collectible scene. $70.

Porcelain ankle boots with asymmetrical rim flounce; unmarked; Germany, c.1900. Left: large; view of "Passenger Depot, Cheyenne, Wyo."; 5-1/16"L x 3-3/4"H; collectible scene; $60. Right: small; crest of Cleethorpes"; 3-5/8"L x 2-5/8"H; $20.

Porcelain cobalt glazed low-cut shoe with shirt collar rim; view of "Parish Hall & All Saints Church/ Hagersville, Ont."; 5-15/16"L x 2-1/2"H. Germany, c.1900. Uncommon form. $75.

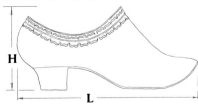

Porcelain large Normandy shoes with in-mold lace ruching; Germany, c.1900. Left: uncommon dark teal green glazed; "Willamette Falls/Souvenir of Oregon City"; marked with personalized stamp typical of much c.1900 German souvenir china; 6-1/2"L x 3-1/16"H; common scene. $60. Middle: airbrushed and matte glazed; view of "Gannet Rock, Grand Manan, N. B."; orange "Germany" stamp; 6-3/16"L x 2-13/16"H; uncommon ground; $70. Right: cobalt glazed; view of "Souvenir of Coaticook" (town in Canada); unmarked; 6-1/2"L x 3"H; $70.

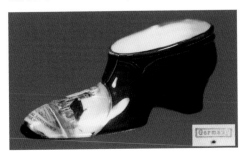

Thin porcelain cobalt glazed small Normandy shoe with in-mold lace ruching; view of "Main Street, Lost Nation, Iowa"; orange "Germany" stamp; 3-3/8"L x 1-11/16"H. Germany, c.1900. $45.

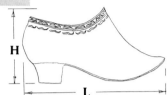

Porcelain glazed Dutch shoes; Germany, c. 1900. Left: white; view of "Court House/Morgan County, Ala."; Wheelock/Germany/Dresden mark; 3-13/16"L x 1-15/16"H; collectible scene; $40. Middle: cobalt; view of "The Garfield Monument, Cleveland, Ohio"; orange "Germany" in rectangle mark; 3-9/16"L x 1-7/8"H; $35. Right: cobalt; view of "New High School Bldg., Tomah, Wis."; orange "Germany" in rectangle mark; 3-1/8"L x 1-5/8"H; common scene; $35.

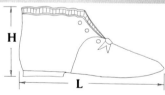

Porcelain cobalt slippers with in-mold ribbed rims; Germany, c.1900. Left: large size: view of "Weymouth Beach Looking West"; MIG mark; 5-1/4"L x 2-3/8"H; $75. Right: small size: view of "Whitaker's Dock Theatre/Clear Lake, Iowa"; unmarked; 3-5/8"L x 1-3/4"H; collectible scene; $110.

Porcelain small size slippers with in-mold ribbed rims; unmarked; Germany, c.1900. Left: view of "High School, Bolivar, N. Y."; 3-9/16"L x 1-3/4"H; $25. Right: crest of "Ramsgate"; 3-9/16"L x 1-3/4"H; $20.

Porcelain cobalt glazed medium size slipper with in-mold ribbed rim and appliqués of flowers, berries, and leaves; unmarked; 4-1/4"L x 2-1/8"H. Uncommon décor on this model that is normally found as a souvenir. Germany, c.1900. $70.

Porcelain cobalt glazed Juliet type slipper with view of "Gruss aus Bremen/Rathaus"; unmarked; 6"L x 3-3/8"H. Germany, c. 1900. Uncommon form. $75.

Porcelain unmarked glazed slippers with in-mold ruching; uncommon molds; Germany, c.1900. Mold of slipper on left was retooled for adaptation to views, as in slipper on right. Left: transfer portrait of young woman; 4-1/8"L (not incl. back protrusion) x 1-1/2"H; $40. Right: cobalt, view of "High School, Gardiner, Mass."; 4-1/8"L x 1-1/2"H; $45.

Porcelain unmarked high vamp glazed clogs with narrow in-mold ruching; Germany, c.1900. Left: white, view of "Nebhonoc Power Plant, West Salem, Wis."; 4-3/8"L x 2-1/4"H; $40. Right: cobalt, view of "Bridge Over East Branch of Black River/Elyria, Ohio"; 4-7/16"L x 2-1/4"H; $45.

Porcelain slipper, white gloss glazed inside, matte glazed variegated green ground; impressed into right face of heel "1060"; view of "The Treaty Stone, Limerick"; unmarked; 6-1/16"L x 3"H. Color lightened to show mold detail. Germany, c.1900. Uncommon color. $55.

Porcelain Sultan's slipper with view of "Court House, Hurley, Wis.", which is printed in tooled script on bottom; unmarked; 5-1/4"L x 2-3/4"H. Germany, c.1900. Uncommon form. $65.

Porcelain tilted tramp shoes; unmarked; Germany, c.1900. Left: all over pattern of purple flowers; 4-1/2"L x 2-1/2"H; $40. Right: crest of "Dornoch"; 4-1/2"L x 2-3/8"H; $35.

Porcelain glazed lace up high shoe; view of "Richmond, Va./ Virginia State Capitol"; unmarked; 5-7/8"L x 4-1/4"H. Prob. Germany, c.1900. Uncommon form. $75.

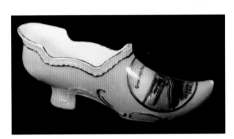

Porcelain luster glazed slipper with view of "Greetings from Plymouth/Plymouth Bathing Cove, The Hole"; unmarked; 5-7/8"L x 2-5/16"H. Germany, c.1900. $50.

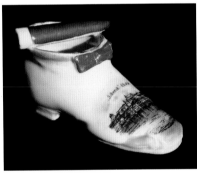

Porcelain ladies cap toe oxford, view of "Memorial Library, Winsted, Conn."; stamp on sole; 5-7/16"L x 2-7/16"H. Germany, c.1900. Collectible scene. $40.

Thin porcelain tramp ankle shoe with in-mold bow and applied cigar; view of " Sibeniĺ '-Obala.' " (seaport city in former Yugoslavia); unmarked; 4"L x 1-13/16"H. Prob. Germany, c.1900. $50.

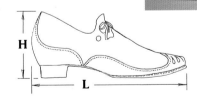

Thin porcelain glazed sport shoe with in-mold bow; view of "White Street, Waikerie" (Australia); orange stamp "Made in Czechoslovakia * "; 4-3/4"L x 2"H. Czechoslovakia, c.1920s. $30.

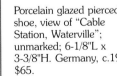

Porcelain glazed pierced shoe, view of "Cable Station, Waterville"; unmarked; 6-1/8"L x 3-3/8"H. Germany, c.1900. $65.

Porcelain tilted tramp shoes, unmarked; both 4-1/2"L x 2-1/2"H; Germany, c.1900. Left: HP detailing; $55. Right: view of "New Municipal and County Buildings, Toronto"; $40.

Left: porcelain glazed ski boot on ski, view of "Ricordo di Fai"; unmarked; 4-5/8"L ski x 1-7/8"HOA. Pos. Germany. c.1900. Uncommon form. $75. Right: ceramic black glazed boot on yellow ski; unmarked; 5-15/16"L x 2"H. $40.

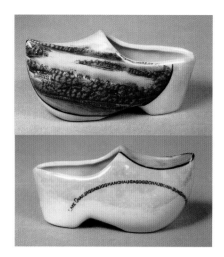

Porcelain luster glazed sabot with view of lake with longest name in world; bottom marked with Jonroth palette, including name of merchant in Webster, MA and "Hand-painted Germany"; 3-1/2"L x 1-5/8"H. Germany, c.1900. $35.

Porcelain glazed pierced vamp HP slipper; decorator's mark overglaze on shank; 6-1/16"L x 2-7/8"H. This shape shoe is known to have been made by Bawo & Dotter, and probably by Schmidt Victoria and at least one other factory; it is not clear what factory was the source of the blank. Franziska Hirsch, Germany. Late 1800s. $250.

Porcelain glazed HP slipper; decorator's mark overglaze on shank; 5-7/8"L x 2-15/16"H. Same mold as previous shoe but without the piercing; vamp design is free hand and does not follow in-mold design. Franziska Hirsch, Germany. c.1900. $200.

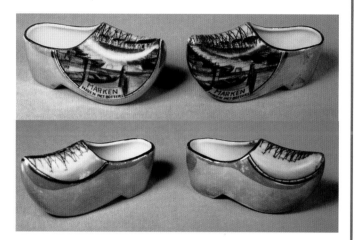

Pair of porcelain glazed sabots with uncommon and novel application of color transfers to create the illusion of a mirror imaged pair, when careful examination will reveal that the views are identical; view of "Markem Haven Met Botters"; unmarked; 2-7/8"L x 1-5/16"H each. $25 for the pair.

Porcelain glazed HP slipper with high ruffled rim and in-mold bow; decorator's mark stamped on unglazed sole; 6-5/8"L x 5"H. Franziska Hirsch, Germany. c.1900. $250.

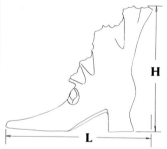

GERMAN PORCELAIN: DECORATORS

Companies often purchased what are referred to as "blanks" from factories and then provided those pieces with the décor. This eliminates for the decorating shop the factory processes of casting and the initial very high temperature kiln firing, both of which require specialized equipment, space, and craftsmanship. Subsequent firings after the initial one require much lower temperatures to set the various categories of décor. Among the few decorating shops important to shoe collectors is Josef Rieber. His work is included in the von Schierholz sections for its similarity of décor to some work by that factory. This section illustrates the work of a few others who made shoes of interest to collectors. They are sought for their superior hand-painted décor.

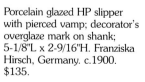

Back view of previous slipper showing meticulous HP detail typical of the Hirsch shop.

Porcelain glazed HP slipper with pierced vamp; decorator's overglaze mark on shank; 5-1/8"L x 2-9/16"H. Franziska Hirsch, Germany. c.1900. $135.

Porcelain glazed cap toe 7-eyelet HP ankle shoe; impressed into shank "325"; decorator's mark stamped on yellow/tan-painted bottom; a "right"; 4-5/8"L x 2-5/8"H. Rare décor on a Royal Bayreuth blank. Franziska Hirsch, Germany, c.1900. $400.

Porcelain glazed slipper with pierced vamp; decorator's mark on unglazed sole; 4-5/8"L x 2-3/8"H. This may be a form-off of the previous shoe mold. If so, the differences in the sketches for these two shoes represent the limitations imposed in attempting to decipher mold details using the finished products. Charles Ahrenfeldt, Bohemia. c.1886-1910. $80.

Porcelain crushed heel cobalt slipper with HP raised gold medallion frame; bottom completely glazed with barely visible stilt marks; decorator's mark overglaze on heel; 6-1/2"L x 2"H. Décor is of equivalent quality to correspondingly decorated Meissen slippers. Unlike Meissen crushed heel slippers, this one has the same wall thickness throughout (about 1/8"). A. Lamm, Germany. c.1887-1890. $350.

GERMAN PORCELAIN including R. S. and E. S.

Thin porcelain glazed wing tip T-strap pierced sandal shoe, in-mold buttoned on left; factory logo on unglazed sole; 4-5/8"L x 1-3/4"H. Reinhold Schlegelmilch, Germany. c.1905-1910. $275.

Bottom view of RS Germany T-strap sandal shoe showing mark.

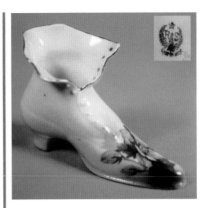

Thin porcelain glazed partially open right-side buttoned shoe; airbrushed ground, color transfers; factory logo stamped on unglazed sole; 4-1/2"L x 3-3/16"H. Reinhold Schlegelmilch, Germany. Early 1900s. $325.

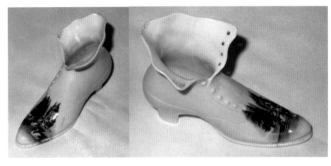

Thin porcelain glazed partially open right-side buttoned shoe; swans on pine bordered lake; unmarked; 4-1/4"L x 3-1/4"H. Reinhold Schlegelmilch, Germany. Early 1900s. Rare pattern. $800.

Thin porcelain glazed partially open right-side buttoned shoe; gold stamped and color transfer florals; Hapsburg shield (often referred to as a beehive) mark widely used in many variations by many companies to imitate marks used by the Imperial and Royal Porcelain factory of Vienna that closed in 1864; 3-3/4"L x 2-5/8"H. RS Germany form-off blank, may have been finished by a decorator shop. Germany, prob. early 1900s. $140.

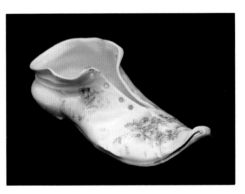

Thin porcelain tramp shoe; unmarked; 4-3/4"L x 1-1/2"H. Often reported to be an RS Germany shoe, it has been widely copied including by the California company Heirlooms of Tomorrow. If authenticated, value is in range of $200.

Porcelain wall pocket slipper with scalloped toe rim; unmarked; 6-7/8"L x 1-1/2"H. Reinhold Schlegelmilch, Germany. c.1890. $300.

Pair of porcelain glazed straights with different courting scenes; stamped gold background pattern, color transfers; factory logo on unglazed sole; 4-15/16"L x 2-1/4"H each. Erdmann Schlegelmilch, Germany. c.1900. Uncommon. $230 each.

Porcelain glazed slipper with applied heel, reticulated vamp apron, and bow; factory logo on bottom of unglazed heel; 8-1/2"L x 5-1/2"H. Erdmann Schlegelmilch, Germany. c.1900. Rare. $375.

Porcelain glazed slipper with in-mold vamp ornament and rear quarter lattice work; applied bow; decorator's logo on unglazed sole; 7-7/8"L x 5-3/16"H. This shoe can be found with a wide range of finishes by various decorators. (It can also be found with the mold retooled to eliminate in-mold design; the origin of these is not known.) The factory that furnished the blanks is unknown. Similarities in design features to the shoe in the previous illustration suggest ES Germany as a possibility. Charles Ahrenfeld, Germany. c.1886-1910. $175.

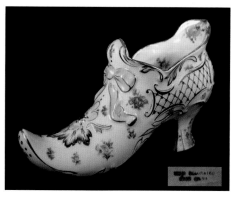

Heavy porcelain slipper with in-mold bow, vamp ornament, and rear quarter lattice work; smeared bottom stamp that may read "HAND DECO-RATED/FINE CHINA"; 7-15/16"L x 4-7/8"H. Contemporary version of the old German shoe, this one was probably made in the last quarter of the 1900s, perhaps in Taiwan. It is well painted, but its only value is decorative.

GERMAN PORCELAIN: FACTORY X

There are so many unidentified factories that made porcelain shoes about a hundred years ago that there could be an alphabet soup series of sections dedicated to them. This was resisted except in one case, and that factory was designated "X" after the best-known variable in mathematics associated with unknowns. Factory X mass produced porcelain shoes, souvenir china, and other smalls. What else they may have produced is not currently known by this author. The factory maintained a high degree of quality control while still experimenting with imaginative décors, glazes, and appliqués. Their souvenir china in all forms is among the most highly collectible for the quality of its views, all hand tinted after the outline was applied with a transfer. This factory is also the source of much of the prized plum, green, and brown souvenir china as well as great amounts of cobalt blue glazed pieces. Their millstone Germany mark is unique. It is unusually small and has a * between the last and first words. They also made the series of smalls with Dutch scenes bottom-marked with the outline of a sabot inside which was "Holland". With no other marking, collectors are often misled about the country of origin of these pieces. A starting point in the identification of Factory X would be the elimination of Bauer, Rosenthal & Co. (1897-1903), which became Philip Rosenthal & Co. (1903-present), and Carl Thieme as contenders.

Porcelain cobalt glazed large buttons and bows boots with rickrack rims and in-mold tassels; Factory X, Germany, c.1900. Left to right: (a) mold modified; in-mold HP floral and leaf design; unmarked; 5-1/4"L x 5"H; $75; (b) original mold; view of "The New Elms/Excelsior Springs, Mo."; Wheelock/Germany logo; 5-3/8"L x 4-15/16"H; $75; (c) mold modified; in-mold HP branch of fruit; unmarked; 5-5/16"L x 4-7/8"H; $75.

Pair of matched porcelain cobalt glazed large buttons and bows boots with rickrack rims and in-mold tassels; facing transfer portraits; unmarked; both 5-3/8"L x 4-15/16"H. Factory X, Germany. c.1900. Uncommon. $250 for the pair.

Porcelain ankle snow shoes with appliqués; in-mold lace up front topped with string tie visible from inside; unmarked; Factory X, Germany, c.1900. Left: white: 4-7/16"L x 2-5/8"H; $60. Right: granular applied porcelain over-brushed with tan luster; 4-3/8"L x 2-9/16"H; $60.

Porcelain ivory glazed large buttons and bows boot with rickrack rim and in-mold tassel; floral and granular appliqués; unmarked; 5-5/16"L x 4-7/8"H. Factory X, Germany. c.1900. Uncommon décor. $100.

Porcelain cobalt glazed large low clog with two bands of in-mold scrolls; view of "Mt. Hood, Ore."; Factory X millstone; 6-3/16"L x 2-1/2"H. Factory X, Germany, c.1900. $60.

Porcelain tortoise shell glazed large buttons and bows boot with rickrack rim and in-mold tassel; floral appliqué; unmarked; 5-1/8"L x 4-13/16"H. Factory X, Germany. $65.

Porcelain cobalt glazed large low clogs; all 6-3/16"L x 2-3/8"H; Factory X, Germany; c.1900. Left to right: (a) Dutch mother and daughter; "Holland" in sabot mark; $70. (b) Dutch girl with dog; "Holland" in sabot mark; $70. (c) view of "Multnoman Falls/Oregon"; impressed into sole "3295"; $60.

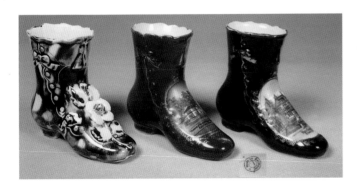

Porcelain small buttons and bows boots with scalloped rims and in-mold tassels; Factory X, Germany; c.1900. Left to right: (a) tortoise shell glazed with appliqués; unmarked; 3-1/2"L x 3"H; $50. (b) plum matte, view of "Museum of Natural History and Art/Pittsfield, Mass."; Factory X millstone; collectible scene; 3-1/2"L x 3"H; $90. (c) cobalt glazed, view of "State Capitol/Albany, N.Y."; Factory X millstone; 3-9/16"L x 3-1/16"H; common scene; $40.

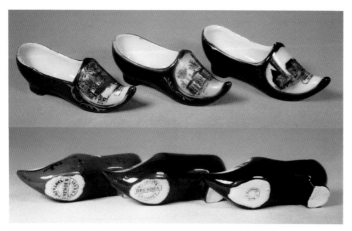

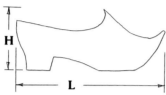

Porcelain glazed small low clogs; Factory X, Germany, c.1900. Left to right: (a) green; view of "Bienville Square/Mobile, Ala."; Wheelock/Dresden/Germany logo; 3-15/16"L x 1-1/2"H; collectible scene; $65. (b) cobalt; view of "City Hall, Lewiston, Me."; Wheelock/Dresden/Germany logo; $35. (c) brown; view of "Union Station/ St. Louis"; Factory X millstone; 4-1/8"L x 1-5/8"H; $40.

Porcelain cobalt glazed small low clog with hand tinted transfer; unmarked; 3-7/8"L x 1-1/2"H. Factory X, Germany. c.1900. $45.

Porcelain glazed HP mold-modified Factory X small low clogs; unmarked; all 4-1/16"L x 1-1/2"H; Factory X, Germany, c.1900. Left to right: (a) cobalt with fall leaves; $35. (b) green with flower and leaves; $35. (c) dragonfly and drip; $35.

Porcelain snow shoes with HP orange berry and cobalt leaf appliqués; unmarked; Factory X, Germany, c.1900. Left: large Normandy shoe; 6-1/4"L x 2-11/16"H; $75. Middle: medium high clog; uncommon form; 4-7/16"L x 2"H; $60. Right: small low clog; 4-1/16"L x 1-1/2"H; $40.

Porcelain large Normandy shoes; unmarked; Factory X, Germany, c.1900. Left: tortoise shell glazed with appliqués; 6-1/4"L x 2-3/4"H; $50. Right: ivory matte with HP brown glazed beaded vamp design; 6-1/8"L x 2-11/16"H; $60.

Porcelain large Normandy shoes; Factory X, Germany, c.1900. Left: snow shoe with vamp transfer; unmarked; 6-3/16"L x 2-3/4"H; $55. Right: cobalt glazed; view of "Guadalupe Church/1549 A.D./Juarez, Mexico"; MIG bottom mark found on Factory X pieces; 6-3/16"L x 2-11/16"H; $60.

Porcelain small low snow clog with appliqués; unmarked; 4-1/16"L x 1-1/2"H. Factory X, Germany; c.1900. $40.

Porcelain large Normandy shoe; unmarked; 6-1/4"L x 2-3/4"H. Factory X, Germany, c.1900. Uncommon décor. $60.

Porcelain small Normandy shoes with in-mold pin flower, two leaves, and ruching; unmarked; Factory X, Germany; c.1900. Left: bisque with appliqués; 4-3/8"L x 2-1/8"H; $60. Middle: glazed with appliqués; 4-1/4"L x 2-1/8"H; $40. Right: snow shoe with HP, gold-outlined florals; 4-7/16"L x 2-3/16"H; $75.

Porcelain cobalt glazed small Normandy shoes; unmarked; Factory X, Germany; c, 1900. Left: in-mold pin flower, two leaves and ruching; rose and stick-leaf appliqués; 4-9/16"L x 2-1/4"H; $40. Right (sketch): in-mold ruching; beaded vamp frame of hand tinted sepia transfer; 4-9/16"L x 2-3/16"H; uncommon décor; $50.

Porcelain small Normandy shoes with in-mold pin flower, two leaves, and ruching; Factory X, Germany, c.1900. Left: plum matte; view of "High School/'Eau Claire, Wis."; Factory X millstone; 4-5/8"L x 2-1/4"H; $45. Right: cobalt glazed; view of "The North Union Station/Boston, Mass."; Factory X rectangular logo with merchant; common scene; $35.

Porcelain small Normandy shoes with in-mold ruching; unmarked; Factory X, Germany; c.1900. Left: snow shoe in original mold with appliqués; 4-5/8"L x 2-5/16"H; $50. Middle: mold-modified, with in-mold HP florals; 4-9/16"L x 2-5/16"H; $45. Right: same as middle shoe, but in cobalt; $45.

Porcelain small Normandy shoe with in-mold pin flower, two leaves, and ruching; cobalt glazed with airbrushed front panel ground and dog transfer; unmarked; 4-3/4"L x 2-3/8"H. Factory X, Germany. c.1900. Uncommon décor. $50.

Porcelain small Normandy shoe with in-mold ruching; HP vamp design; unmarked; 4-5/16"L x 2-1/8"H. Prob. Factory X, Germany. c.1900. $50.

Porcelain small Normandy shoe with in-mold pin flower, two leaves, and ruching; tortoise shell glazed with appliqués; unmarked; 4-9/16"L x 2-1/4"H excluding bird. Factory X, Germany. c.1900. $55.

Porcelain Normandy shoes with in-mold ruching; cobalt glazed with snow faces and HP appliqués; unmarked; Factory X, Germany. c.1900. Left (sketch): medium Normandy; 5-1/8"L x 2-1/4"H; $80. Right: small Normandy with in-mold pin flower, two leaves, and ruching; 4-3/8"L x 2-1/8"H; $65.

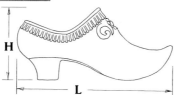

Porcelain bisque Normandy shoe with in-mold pin flower, curls, and ruching; cold-painted appliqués; unmarked; 4-13/16"L x 2-1/8"H. Factory X, Germany. c.1900. $55.

Porcelain cobalt glazed Normandy shoe with in-mold pin flower, curls, and ruching; flat floral appliqués; unmarked; 4-13/16"L x 2-3/16"H. Factory X, Germany. c.1900. $55.

Porcelain Normandy snow shoe with in-mold pin flower, curls, and ruching; unmarked; 4-13/16"L x 2-1/8"H. Factory X, Germany. c.1900. $45.

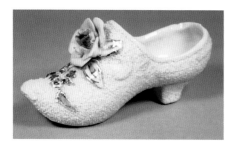

Porcelain Normandy snow shoe with in-mold pin flower, curls, and ruching; HP appliqués; unmarked; 5"L x 2-1/4"H. Factory X, Germany. c.1900. $60.

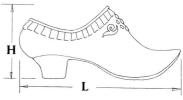

Porcelain glazed small Normandy shoes with in-mold pin flower, tendrils, and ruching; tortoise shell glazed; unmarked; Factory X, Germany; c.1900. Left: with appliqués and bird; 4-5/16"L x 1-15/16"H not inc. bird; $45. Right: with appliqués; 4-3/16"L x 1-7/8"H; $45.

Porcelain bisque small Normandy shoe with in-mold pin flower, tendrils, and ruching; HP vamp design; unmarked; 4-5/16"L x 1-15/16"H. Factory X, Germany. c.1900. $40.

Porcelain small Normandy shoes with in-mold pin flower, tendrils, and ruching; 4-1/8"L x 1-7/8"H each; unmarked; Factory X, Germany, c.1900. Left: glazed; pansy and leaves appliqué; $60. Right: bisque; berries and flat leaves appliqué; $50.

Porcelain small Normandy snow shoe with in-mold pin flower, tendrils, and ruching; appliqués; unmarked; 4-5/16"L x 1-15/16"H. Factory X, Germany. $60.

Porcelain cobalt glazed small Normandy shoes with in-mold pin flower, tendrils, and ruching; both bottom marked with "Holland" inside the shape of a sabot (part of mark missing); 4-1/4"L x 1-15/16"H each; Factory X, Germany, c.1900. Left: Dutch woman and dog scene; $45. Right: Dutch father and son, both smoking pipes; $45.

Porcelain mini Normandy shoes with in-mold ruching; unmarked; c.1900. Left: snow shoe with appliqués; 2-5/8"L x 1-1/4"H, shoe only; Factory X, Germany; uncommon miniature; $40. Right: glazed with appliqués, adhered to velvet oval pad; 2-3/8"L x 3/4"H; pos. Factory X, Germany; uncommon miniature; $40.

Porcelain cobalt glazed small Normandy shoes with in-mold ruching; unmarked; Factory X, Germany, c.1900. Left: in-mold pin flower and tendrils; mold modified to include in-mold moth and flowers, HP; 4-1/4"L x 1-15/16"H; $45. Right: mold modified, in-mold dragonfly and drip; 4-5/16"L x 2"H; $45.

Porcelain mini Normandy snow shoe with appliqués; unmarked; 2-5/8"L x 1-1/4"H. Factory X, Germany. c.1900. Uncommon miniature. $40.

Porcelain small Normandy shoes with in-mold ruching; unmarked; Factory X, Germany, c.1900. Left: cobalt glazed with in-mold HP hexagonal medallion; 4-1/4"L x 2"H; $45. Right: Blue-gray matte ground painted around in-mold ladies to imitate Wedgwood jasperware; 4-1/4"L x 2"H; $45.

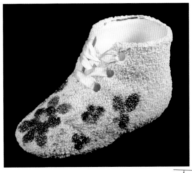

Porcelain 3-eyelet baby snow shoe with HP gold-outlined florals; unmarked; bottom incised for striking matches; 4-1/4"L x 2-5/16"H. Factory X, Germany. c.1900. $75.

Porcelain 3-eyelet baby shoes with ruffled rims and vee edges; in-mold bows at vee bottoms; unmarked; Factory X, Germany; c.1900. Left: small with appliqués; 3-1/4"L x 1-11/16"H, shoe only; if perfect (angel missing wings), $50. Right: medium with appliqués; 4-1/16"L x 2-1/8"H; $45.

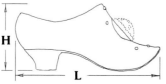

Porcelain tortoise shell glazed small Normandy shoe with in-mold mounting for applied hemispherical vamp ornament; unmarked; 4-3/8"L x 2"H. Factory X, Germany. c.1900. $45.

Dutch sabots; c.1900. Left: porcelain cobalt glazed with view of "Norman Williams Public Library/Woodstock, Vt."; Factory X millstone; 4"L x 1-15/16"H; Factory X, Germany; $40. Right: ceramic green matte with seashore motif appliqués; impressed into sole "2/94"; same décor has been seen on a Factory X small low clog; 3-3/4"L x 1-15/16"H; prob. Factory X; $35.

Porcelain cobalt glazed Dutch sabots with Dutch scenes; marked "Holland" inside sabot shape; Factory X, Germany, c.1900. Left: Dutch woman and dog; 3-7/8"L x 1-15/16"H; $30. Right: Dutch man handing fish to boy; 3-3/4"L x 1-15/16"H; $30.

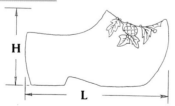

Porcelain cobalt glazed Dutch sabot with in-mold décor; unmarked; 3-7/8"L x 2"H. Prob. Factory X, Germany. c.1900. $35.

those that mimic other factories, including one form that almost certainly came from Galluba & Hofmann. This latter is such an anomaly, one is tempted to say, "escaped to" G&H. To further confuse matters, a set of boots from this group has been seen with a red mark used in black by Arnstadt. Nothing about this group, however, meshes with what is known to date about G&H or Arnstadt footwear shapes and décors. The factory, then, currently remains unidentified. For footwear used as souvenir china, the most easily identified feature is the device used for the name of the view. It is typically enclosed in a long scroll whose curled end is visible on the left side. It has not escaped notice that a unique bottom mark was used by Arnstadt that included a curved scroll. In addition, Williams showed two engravings with the scroll device in the possession of the Paul Seiler porcelain decorating shop in Kahla, Germany in 1965 (formerly Julius Lange decorating shop, c.1863-1940).

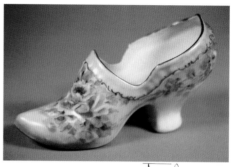

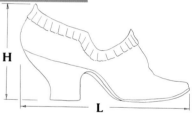

Porcelain HP large high-instep slipper with in-mold ruching; matte outside, gloss glazed inside; unmarked; 6-3/16"L x 3-3/8"H. Germany, c.1900. $95.

Porcelain large high-instep slipper with in-mold ruching; airbrushed outside and in; view of "Memorial Library Westbrook, Me." in scroll device; personalized logo on sole; 6-3/8"L x 3-7/16"H. Germany, c.1900. $125.

GERMAN PORCELAIN: HIGH INSTEP, THE ENIGMA VARIATIONS

Several shoe and boot forms of c.1900 are distinguished by designs that would have been appropriate for a foot with a high arch. These figurals may or may not have been originated at the same factory by the same designer, but it is useful to group them together. The difficulty with this grouping is that there are wide variations in their décor, from high quality finish to poor, from décors that are unique to

Porcelain medium high-instep slipper with in-mold ruching; airbrushed with floral transfer; green stamp on heel bottom "THREE CROWN CHINA/logo/GERMANY"; 5-1/16"L x 2-7/8"H. Germany, c.1900. $30.

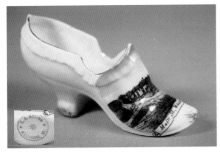

Porcelain small high-instep slipper with in-mold ruching; view of "Main St., Masardis, Me." in scroll device (note curled end of scroll on left side); personalized orange logo on sole; 4-1/4"L x 2-3/8"H. Germany, c.1900. $65.

Porcelain high-instep slippers with in-mold ruching; all have applied vamp décors as well as hand tinted floral transfers that can be found on Galluba and Hofmann shoes; none is marked in any way except shoe on left, with a millstone mark; medallion on left shoe reads "Love the giver"; all are approx. 6"L x 3-1/4"H. Germany, c.1900. $45 each.

Porcelain glazed high-instep slipper with in-mold ruching and applied floral spray; "Think/of Me" hand scripted on vamp; 5/8"OD MIG millstone; 5-13/16"L x 3-1/4"H. Germany, c.1900. $45.

Porcelain high-instep slippers with in-mold ruching; in-mold star flowers framing vamp, typical of Galluba & Hofmann; both with impressed "6078A" on left shank, typical of G&H; both unmarked in any other way. Left: gray luster with view of "Worlds Fair St. Louis Mo./Machinery Building/1904", line-framed in manner of G&H souvenir china; 5-13/16"L x 3-3/16"H; $75. Right: pink glazed with floral transfer; 5-11/16"L x 3-1/8"H; $15. Both of these almost certainly were made in the G&H factory.

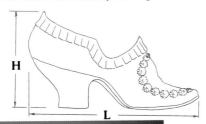

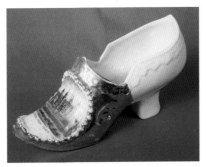

Porcelain high-instep gold face slipper with in-mold details shown in sketch; view of "The Tower of London, from Tower Hill"; unmarked; 5-7/16"L x 2-13/16"H. Germany, c.1900. $30.

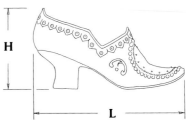

Porcelain high-instep slipper with rim pleat; in-mold beading; floral appliqué; unmarked; 4-1/16"L x 2-7/16"H. Germany, c.1900. $35.

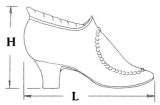

Porcelain high-instep slipper with rim pleat and in-mold gussets; applied beading over in-mold narrow beading; hand-tinted floral transfer; unmarked; 4"L x 2-5/16"H. Germany, c.1900. If gold not worn, $35.

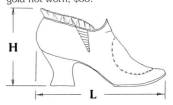

Porcelain boot with applied beading; hand tinted vamp transfer, "Pan American/Buffalo 1901"; four tooled numbers impressed into sole "2(?)711"; 3-7/8"L x 3-15/16"H. Pos. an early Galluba & Hofmann. Germany. $40.

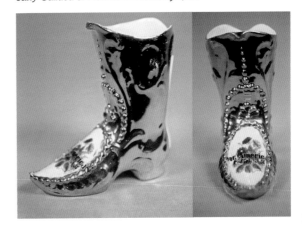

Porcelain Dutch sabot; view of "Hair pin turn on the Mohawk Trail, Mass." (North Adams, Massachusetts); note curl on left side of scroll device; Jonroth logo on bottom; 4"L x 1-15/16"H. Germany, c.1900. $35.

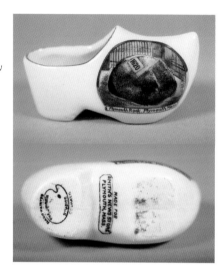

Porcelain Dutch sabot; view of "Plymouth Rock, Plymouth , Mass."; note curl on left side of scroll device; Jonroth logo on bottom; 4-3/16"L x 2"H. Germany, c.1900. Common view. $20.

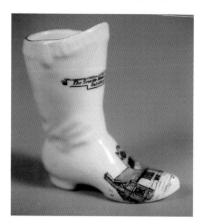

Porcelain small high-instep boot with in-mold ruching; view of "The Scoville Memorial Library,/Salisbury, Conn." in scroll device; stamped in red on bottom "Wheelock/Made in Germany/for/ .... (smeared)"; 3-1/4"L x 3-5/8"H. Germany, c.1900. $65.

Porcelain high-instep boots with in-mold ruching; hand tinted sepia transfers; all unmarked; Germany. Left: small with view of "Lewis & Clark Centennial Portland Oregon 1905/Festival Hall"; 3-5/16"L x 3-9/16"H; $125. Middle: small with view of "World's Fair St. Louis Mo. 1904/Palace of Electricity/Souvenir"; 3-3/16"L x 3-1/2"H; $125. Right: large with view of "World's Fair St. Louis Mo. 1904/United States Government Building/Souvenir"; 4-5/8"L x 4-7/8"H; $150.

Porcelain medium high-instep boot with in-mold ruching; airbrushed ground; view of "Main Street, Great Barrington, Mass."; personalized Germany logo on sole; 3-3/4"L x 4-1/4"H. Collectible scene. Germany, c.1900. $90.

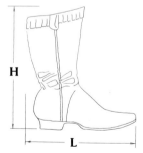

Porcelain loops and tassels side-buttoned high-top straights with location of in-mold buttons creating a "left" and a "right"; extruded slip applied over in-mold lower sets of loops and frames containing "Forget me not" on one, and "Love the giver" on the other; unmarked; both approx, 6"L x 5-1/8"H. Germany, c.1900. $50 each.

Porcelain medium high-instep boot with in-mold ruching; airbrushed ground with transfer florals; sole marked "ROYAL ROSE/logo with WHEELOCK/GERMANY"; 3-7/8"L x 4-1/4"H. Germany, c.1900. $35.

Porcelain loops and tassels side-buttoned straight; applied beading framing floral transfer and "Atlantic City"; millstone mark on heel; 5-7/8"L x 5-1/16"H. Germany, c.1900. $45.

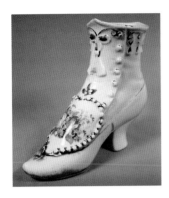

Porcelain loops and tassels side-buttoned straight with in-mold beaded heart framing color transfer; unmarked; impressed into shank, tooled "1410"; 6"L x 5-3/16"H. Germany, c.1900. $45.

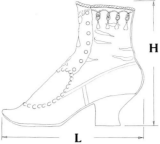

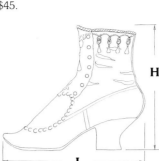

Porcelain loops and tassels side-buttoned straight with turned up toe; view of "Hastings Castle"; unmarked; 5-11/16"L x 4-7/8"H. Germany, c.1900. $45.

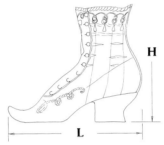

Back detail of women holding sabots with frogs.

Porcelain glazed sabot catboat with in-mold bow and applied sail and Dutch sailor; impressed "4512" and factory logo; 5-1/8"L x 6-3/8"HOA. There may be a female mate to this piece. Schafer & Vater, Germany. c.1900. Rare. $300.

GERMAN PORCELAIN
including Schafer & Vater

Schafer & Vater is known for its thin porcelain, imaginative table wares, and exquisitely sculpted models, often with an offbeat sense of humor. They also made tinted porcelain with applied slip intended to mimic Wedgwood. Occasionally their wares were cold painted; their condition today can show extreme loss of the original color, which will affect their value. Their factory mark, usually lightly impressed and extremely difficult to decipher, is a crown beneath which is a nine-pointed star within which is a script R.

Back view of the sailor on the sabot catboat and the barely visible mark on its bottom.

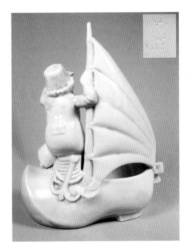

Porcelain glazed sabots being held by attached women; applied frogs whose limbs appear to be partially in-mold; impressed with factory logo; Schafer & Vater, Germany, c.1900. Left: small; impressed "4544"; 4-7/8"L x 4-1/8"H; $175. Right: large; 5-3/4"L x 5-3/8"H; $200. Not shown: there are mates to the women, where the men are holding sabots with applied lobsters; values similar.

Porcelain glazed Dutch sabot with in-mold Dutch man on vamp; impressed factory logo; 3-3/4"L x 3-3/16"H. There may be a female mate to this piece. Schafer & Vater, Germany. c.1900. $125.

Porcelain bisque cap-toe ankle shoe with textured upper; in-mold triple-tie bow and branch of cherries; has been found both unmarked and with factory logo impressed; 3-15/16"L x 3-1/16"HOA. Schafer and Vater, Germany. c.1900. Uncommon. $200.

Porcelain glazed wall pocket slipper with molded and applied roses and back of heel; impressed factory logo and what may be "8399" (it would make more sense if it were 4399); 8-1/8"L x 3-1/4"H. Schafer & Vater, Germany. c.1900. $150.

Tinted porcelain basket slipper with in-mold roses, twig handle, and bow; impressed factory logo; evidence of cold painted roses; has been seen with impressed # "6296"; 7"LOA x 5-1/4"HOA. Schafer & Vater, Germany. c.1900. Uncommon. $300.

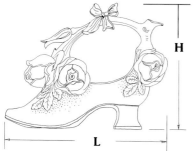

Porcelain bisque young woman holding pair of attached slippers on cold painted base; impressed factory logo and what may be "7764"; 2-15/16"OD base x 4-1/8"HOA. Schafer & Vater, Germany. c.1900. $85.

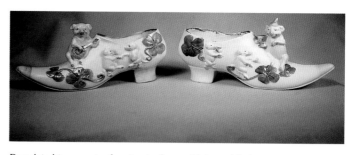

Porcelain bisque pair of party pig shoes with in-mold pigs on vamps; Schafer & Vater, Germany, c.1900. Left-facing, with banjo playing pig: impressed into shank "4100A"; 6-5/16"L x 3-1/8"HOA; $125. Right-facing, with drinking pig: impressed into shank "4100B"; 6-7/16"L x 3-1/2"HOA; $125.

Porcelain stack heel slipper with in-mold branch of roses; cold painted; 5-15/16"L x 3-3/8"HOA. Schafer & Vater, Germany. c.1900. Uncommon. If painting intact, $150.

Porcelain glazed double slipper wall pocket with molded and applied roses and backs of heels; impressed "4400" and factory logo; "Made in Germany" blue stamp on bottom; 6-3/8"L x 6-1/8"wide. Schafer & Vater, Germany. c.1900. $175.

Tinted porcelain bisque ankle slipper with HP in-mold angel medallion; slip-enhanced rococo in-mold detail; barely visible impressed number that may be "6641"; unmarked; 5"L x 3-1/2"H. Prob. Schafer & Vater, Germany. c.1900. $85.

Porcelain bisque and matte glazed shoe box; unmarked; applied head and arms, and prob. beard and cigar; 4-11/16"L x 1-3/8"H, shoe only; 5-7/8"HOA. Pos. Schafer & Vater, Germany. c.1900. Rare. $350.

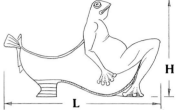

Porcelain bisque stack heel slipper with in-mold frog; bow partially in-mold; unmarked; 4-1/4"L x 2-1/2"H. Prob. Schafer & Vater, Germany. c.1900. Uncommon. $85.

Box with cover removed.

GERMAN PORCELAIN including Heubach

In addition to the well-known baby-in-a-tramp shoe, Heubach made baby shoes and elaborately painted snow shoes. Many of their shoes are made of a white material that may or may not be porcelain. They are seldom marked. Occasionally a unique hand-incised scrawled letter that may be a "G" is found.

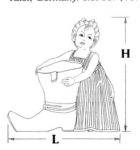

Porcelain bisque canted boot held by girl in nightclothes; arms in-mold with boot; unmarked; 3-15/16"L x 3-15/16"HOA. Pos. Schafer & Vater, Germany. c.1900. $75.

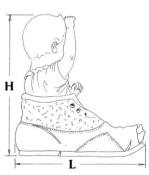

Matte glazed baby-in-a-tramp shoe; applied arms, head, and prob. a portion of the toes; factory logo; 4-11/16"L x 4-7/8"HOA. Heubach, Germany. Early 1900s. $600. Not shown: this was made in several sizes, the smallest and most accessible of which was 3-1/2"L, valued at $350. The values of the larger sizes increase substantially with an increase in size. Those in the range from about 6-1/2"L to about 12"L have been seen selling on Internet auctions for prices from about $1,000 at the shorter length to about $3,000 at the longer. The largest sizes have open eyelets. The opening through the hand in the raised arm may have been for a shoelace on these larger models.

Back view of canted boot.

Ceramic 3-eyelet open vee snow baby shoe; HP, gold-outlined florals; unmarked except for hand incised script G; 4-3/16"L x 2-3/16"H. Heubach, Germany. Early 1900s. $180.

Ceramic pierced baby bootees with in-mold knitted texture comparing the piece with and without the application of ground ceramic; both with in-mold factory logo and DEP; Heubach, Germany; early 1900s. Left: glazed; 3-7/16"L x 2-1/2"H; $35. Right: snow bootee with HP, gold-outlined florals; 3-11/16"L x 2-5/8"H; $180.

Comparison of glazed and snow Heubach baby shoes, showing in-mold detail. Left: glazed with HP detail; bottom partially scored for striking matches; factory logo on sole; 4-1/16"L x 2-1/4"H. Heubach, Germany. Early 1900s. $40.

Detail in Heubach pierced snow bootee.

Bottom view of glazed Heubach baby shoe showing factory logo.

Ceramic snow slipper with HP, gold-outlined florals; unmarked except for hand-incised script G; 4-3/16"L x 2-7/16"H. Heubach, Germany. Early 1900s. $150.

Comparison of ceramic and porcelain versions of baby shoe showing asymmetrical in-mold bow; narrow HP band outlining sole. Left: marked Heubach, ceramic. Right: thin porcelain version, unmarked.

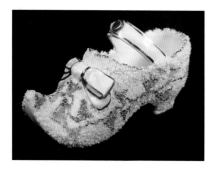

Ceramic strap shoe with applied bow; HP, gold-outlined florals; inside and bottom glaze crackled; unmarked; 4-1/2"L x 2-1/2"H. Heubach, Germany. Early 1900s. Rare. $275.

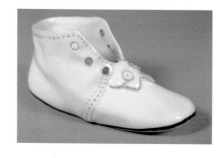

Porcelain glazed baby shoe with in-mold asymmetrical bow and HP raised enamel stitching detail; bottom part scored for striking matches; unmarked; 4-3/8"L x 2-1/16"H. Prob. Heubach, Germany. Early 1900s. $40.

Ceramic semi gloss glazed baby shoe with in-mold asymmetrical bow; HP narrow band outlining sole; bottom partially scored for striking matches; unmarked; 4-1/8"L x 2-3/16"L. Heubach, Germany. Early 1900s. $30.

Ceramic HP clog; factory logo; 8"L. Heubach, Germany. Early 1900s. $125.

Detail of hand painting on Heubach clog.

Thin porcelain in-mold pebble-textured shoes with elaborately decorated bands HP with garnet enamel and gold floral motif; unmarked except that both have a hand incised script G like that found on some Heubach shoes; pos. Heubach, Germany, early 1900s. Left: baby shoe with partially scored bottom for striking matches; 4-5/16"L x 2-3/16"H; uncommon; $140. Right (sketch): clog with applied heel; 6-1/2"L x 2-3/16"H; uncommon; $170.

GERMAN PORCELAIN: PIKED TOES, CRUSHED

Shoes like those shown in this section were made by several factories, among them Weiss, Kühnert. These, however, may possibly have been early Galluba & Hofmann shoes; they do not match the known Weiss, Kühnert mold models 1472 and 1488 which look similar but have beads edging the side rims.

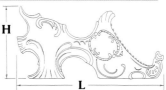

Porcelain large piked toe slippers, both unmarked but both with tooled numbers "1617" impressed into the edge of the sole in the same location; pos. Galluba & Hofmann, Germany; c.1900. Left: applied beads down center; hand-tinted floral transfers; 6-1/2"L x 3-1/16"H; $60. Right: mold-modified vamp; HP details; 6-3/8"L x 3-1/16"H; $60.

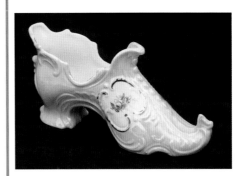

Porcelain small piked toe slipper; unmarked; 5-1/2"L x 2-1/2"H. pos. Galluba & Hofmann, Germany. c.1900. $45.

Porcelain large piked toe slipper with applied beading framing hand tinted transfer; mold-modified vamp; tooled number impressed into edge of sole "1617"; unmarked; 6-5/16"L x 3-1/16"H. Pos. Galluba & Hofmann, Germany. c.1900. $60.

Porcelain large piked toe slipper with applied beading framing hand tinted transfer and script "Till Minne (sic)"; mold-modified vamp; tooled number impressed into left edge of shank "1617", a Galluba & Hofmann characteristic; unmarked; 6-5/16"L x 3-1/16"H. Pos. Galluba & Hofmann, Germany. c.1900. $60.

Vamp detail of gold piked toe slipper.

Porcelain small slipper with applied beads framing an applied flower; mold-modified to eliminate piked toe; other mold details are similar to 1617 shoes; tooled number impressed into edge of sole that may be "1685"; unmarked; 5-3/8"L x 2-11/16"H. Pos. Galluba & Hofmann, Germany. c.1900. $50.

Porcelain small slipper with extruded slip and ornamental appliqués; mold-modified to eliminate piked toe; unmarked; 5-3/8"L x 2-5/8"H. Pos. Galluba & Hofmann, Germany. c.1900. $50.

GERMAN PORCELAIN including Galluba & Hofmann

The Ilmenau, Germany factory of Galluba & Hofmann mass produced porcelain shoes of high quality, often with elaborate extruded hand appliqués resembling the decorations on wedding cakes. They may have begun to produce them as early as 1891 when the factory's ownership came under Galluba & Hofmann. The factory closed in the early 1930s, but it is doubtful that many of their shoes were produced much after WWI. There is a great deal of evidence to suggest that the bulk of them were manufactured before the start of WWI. Examination of the sketches will show that the mold designs are among the most elegant, beautifully proportioned shoes ever created. This is probably why four of them have been the most copied of all shoes.

G&H shoes and boots typically carry a 4-digit tooled number, nearly always impressed into one side of the shank. Most models were made in three sizes. Each successively smaller size (assumed to have been formed off larger sizes) generally carries the next highest number. The addition of the letter A means that the factory modified the mold (perhaps for Abanderung, meaning "modification"). There are occasional aberrations in this system. There are so many numbers that the author gave the various designs names that she could remember. All are high quality porcelain, and always fully glazed inside. The factory name has been shortened to G&H. All are believed to have been made between the late 1800s and approx. 1915 unless otherwise noted, so dates generally are not noted in the descriptions.

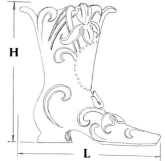

Medium tulip boots 1687; in-mold beading though neither boot has an impressed A; color transfers; uncommon mold; G&H, Germany.
Left: 4-3/16"L x 4-3/16"H; $60.
Right: 4-3/8"L x 4-1/4"H; $60.

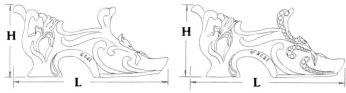

Large tulip slipper 1717; G&H, Germany. Left: original tulip slipper 1717; HP; 6-9/16"L x 3"H; $80. Middle: original tulip slipper 1717; appliqués; 6-5/8"L x 2-15/16"H; $100. Right: mold-modified, in-mold beading tulip slipper 1717A; 6-1/2"L x 2-7/8"H; $30.

Medium 1718 and small 1719 original tulip slippers, all with appliqués; numbers impressed into soles; G&H, Germany. Left: tulip slipper 1718; 9/16"dia. millstone mark; 5-7/16"L x 2-7/16"H; $90. Middle: tulip slipper 1718; HP details; 5-7/16"L x 2-7/16"H; $80. Right: tulip slipper 1719; 4-7/16"L x 2-1/16"H; $60.

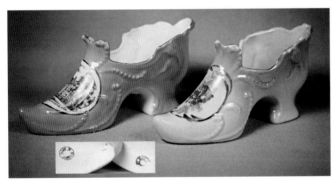

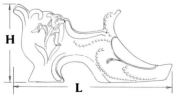

Large modified tulip slippers without impressed numbers; both with smeared 9/16"dia. MIG millstone marks as on a previous G&H slipper; both 6-3/4"L x 3-1/4"H; prob. G&H before numbering system established (would be 1717A, otherwise). Left: view of "Memorial Library, Winsted, Conn."; $50. Right: floral transfer; $25.

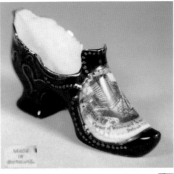

Modified cobalt glazed tulip slipper with in-mold beading; view of "Corner of Woodward Avenue and Michigan Avenue/ Detroit, Mich."; proportions, décor, and in-mold detail suggest that this may not have been made by G&H; 5-3/4"L x 3"H. Common view. $40.

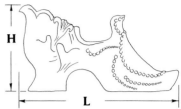

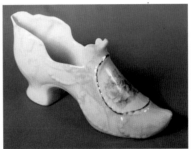

Modified tulip slipper with in-mold beading; floral transfer; small orange MIG millstone mark; proportions suggest that this may not have been made by G&H; 5-13/16"L x 2-13/16"H. $25.

Modified tulip shoe with in-mold vamp flower; inside only partially glazed; unmarked; 6-9/16"L x 2-15/16"H. Almost certainly not G&H; note angle of tulip on rear quarter compared to sketch of original tulip shoe. Prob. early 1900s. $35.

Medium and small rim ruffle and scrolls slippers (factory numbering system apparently still not fully established); uncommon mold; unmarked; G&H, Germany. Left: 1698 impressed into sole; applied beading and ornament framing medallion with hand tinted florals; HP details; 5-3/8"L x 2-3/8"H; $100. Right: 1727A impressed into shank; in-mold vamp beading; vamp floral transfer; inside gold glazed; 4-5/16"L x 1-3/4"H; $70.

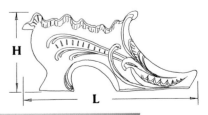

Medium rim ruffle and scrolls gold face slipper; in-mold beading framing angel vamp transfer; 1698A impressed into sole; uncommon mold; unmarked; 5-1/4"L x 2-3/8"H. G&H, Germany. $35.

Large 1797 and small 1799 scrolls and pleats slippers; unmarked; G&H, Germany. Left: large with applied flowers framing vamp transfer; 6-3/4"L x 2-3/4"H; $45. Middle: small with applied florals; 4-3/8"L x 1-13/16"H; $50. Right: small gold face with vamp transfer; 4-1/2"L x 1-7/8"H; $25.

Large daisy boot 1784 (impressed into edge of sole); "Souvenir of Toronto"; unmarked; 5-3/16"L x 5"H. G&H, Germany. Uncommon size in this mold. $50.

Large bleeding heart slipper 1808; appliqués; unmarked; 6-11/16"L x 2-13/16"H. G&H, Germany. $70.

Modified medium daisy boot 1785A; in-mold beading; color transfer; unmarked; 4-3/8"L x 4-1/16"H. G&H, Germany. $40.

Medium and small bleeding heart slippers; unmarked; G&H, Germany. Left: medium 1809; vamp color transfer; 5-1/2"L x 2-1/4"H; $35. Middle: medium mold-modified 1809A; in-mold beading framing vamp transfer; 5-7/16"L x 2-1/4"H; $25. Right: small mold-modified 1810A with orig. pincushion; 4-3/8"L x 1-7/8"H; $25.

Modified small daisy boot 1786A; in-mold beading framing vamp transfer; unmarked; 3-1/2"L x 3-3/8"H. G&H, Germany. Uncommon size in this mold. $40.

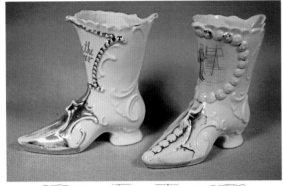

Small plantain lily boot 1886; applied star flowers; vamp transfer; unmarked; 3-9/16"L x 3-7/16"H. G&H, Germany. $45.

Large modified-mold scrolls boots 1830A; G&H, Germany. These boots have different mold modifications but are numbered the same, although on different sides of the shank. Left: in-mold beading framing "Love the Giver"; smudged black MIG millstone mark on heel; 5-1/16"L x 4-7/8"H; c.1903; $35. This boot was advertised in the Spring 1903 Butler Brothers catalog, pg. 223, "1/3 doz. in pkg." for $2.00. Right: in-mold star flowers framing transfer of "Royal Navy" sailor; unmarked; 5-5/16"L x 4-7/8"H; $35.

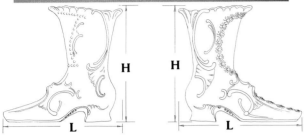

Medium mold-modified plantain lily boots 1885A; in-mold star flowers; unmarked; G&H, Germany. Although carrying the same numerical designations, these are different mold modifications; one has nine star flowers on each side of the heart frame, the other eleven. Left: white with vamp transfer; 4-1/4"L x 4-3/16"H; $30. Right: pink; 4-3/8"L x 4-5/16"H; $25.

Small and mini scalloped scrolls slippers; unmarked; G&H, Germany. Left: small 1879; 3-3/4"L x 1-3/8"H; $25. Middle: small mold-modified 1879A; in-mold beading framing vamp transfer; 3-3/4"L x 1-3/8"H; $20. Right (sketch): mini mold-modified, bearing unclear numbers impressed into shank that may be "?412A", where they should be "1880A"; 3-3/8"L x 1-1/8"H; $20.

Large geranium slipper 1923; applied star flowers and narrow cording over gold stamped yellow luster with cobalt wash, HP details; unmarked; 6-3/8"L x 3-1/4"H. G&H, Germany. $70.

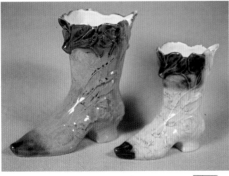

Large and medium plantain lily boots; unmarked; G&H, Germany. Left: large 1884; gold-stamped design over pink and cobalt wash; 5-1/4"L x 5-3/16"H; $70. Right: medium 1885; gold stamped design over yellow luster and cobalt wash; 4-1/4"L x 4-1/4"H; $60.

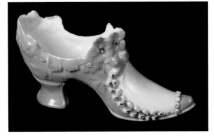

Medium geranium slipper 1924; appliqués framing vamp that once had gold script; unmarked; 5-1/2"L x 2-5/8"H. G&H, Germany. $35.

Three sizes of geranium slipper; all unmarked; G&H, Germany. Left: large 1923 with applied and granulated shells framing vamp transfer; 6-1/2"L x 3-5/16"H; $50. Middle: medium mold-modified 1924A with view of "Iowa State Capitol Des Moines IA."; 5-9/16"L x 2-5/8"H; $40. Right: small mold-modified 1925A with view of "The Regina Mercedes, Spanish Warship/Portsmouth Navy Yard, N.H."; 4-3/8"L x 2-1/8"H; $60.

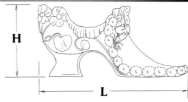

Mold-modified geranium slippers; in-mold star flowers framing vamp; all unmarked; G&H, Germany. Left to right: (a) medium 1924A; view of "Court House, Lima, Ohio"; 5-1/2"L x 2-5/8"H; $50.
(b) medium 1924A; view of "Hoosac Tunnel-A.A. Hughes/North Adams Mass."; 5-5/16"L x 2-5/8"H; $85. (c) medium 1924A; view of "World's Fair St. Louis 1904/Palace of Electricity/Souvenir of St. Louis"; 5-3/8"L x 2-5/8"H; $125. (d) small 1925A; view of "Palace of Education/Souvenir of St. Louis"; apparently no room for the "World's Fair St. Louis 1904" line, but this is from that WF; 4-1/2"L x 2-1/8"H; $100.

Mold-modified medium geranium slipper 1924A with simple script souvenir location; unmarked; 5-1/2"L x 2-5/8"H. G&H, Germany. $20

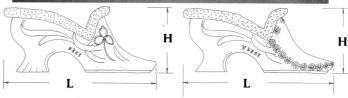

Large clover and swirls slippers; both unmarked; G&H, Germany. Left: large 1926 with applied star flowers; 6-1/2"L x 2-3/4"H; $50. Right: large mold-modified 1926A with in-mold star flowers framing vamp; applied row of star flowers down center of vamp; 6-7/16"L x 2-11/16"H; $40.

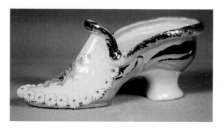

Medium clover and swirls slipper 1927; applied star flowers framing vamp transfer; unmarked; 5-7/16"L x 2-3/16"H. G&H, Germany. $45.

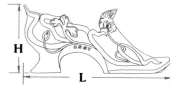

Violet and ribbon slippers; unmarked; uncommon mold; G&H, Germany. Left: medium 1950; applied vamp florals; 5-1/4"L x 2-3/8"H; $70. Right: small mold-modified 1951A; in-mold star flowers; vamp transfer; 4-5/16"L x 1-13/16"H; $35.

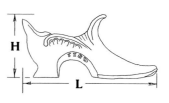

Left: Mini scalloped scroll pair of attached slippers 6210; made by using two 1880As; vamp transfers; unmarked; 3-3/8"L x 1-1/8"H not inc. ring holder; G&H, Germany; $35. Right (sketch): mini border shell slipper 6311; stamped gold flowers; unmarked; 3-9/16"L x 1-5/8"H; prob. G&H, Germany; $15.

Medium mold-modified sweet pea boot 6505A; in-mold star flowers; view of "United States Government Building. Syracuse, N.Y."; unmarked; 4-5/8"L x 4-5/16"H. G&H, Germany. $30.

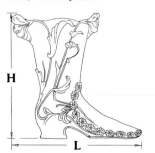

Daisy slippers with extruded appliqués; unmarked; G&H, Germany. Left: large 6495 with applied shirring and star flowers; 6-9/16"L x 3-3/16"H; uncommon size; $50. Middle: medium 6496 with applied shirring and star flowers; 5-7/16"L x 2-5/8"H; $40. Right: small 6497 with granulated vamp florals; 4-9/16"L x 2-3/16"H; uncommon; $70.

Medium daisy slipper 6496 with small applied gold flowers; unmarked; 5-5/16"L x 2-5/8"H. G&H, Germany. Uncommon décor. $70.

Sweet pea boots; all unmarked; G&H, Germany. Left: medium 6505 with applied shirring and star flowers; 4-1/2"L x 4-3/16"H; if perfect (yellow luster worn), $60. Middle: medium mold-modified 6505A; in-mold star flowers; view of "The Old State House, Boston, Mass."; 4-3/8"L x 4-3/16"H; $30. Right: small 6506; appliqués and granular outlining; 3-11/16"L x 3-5/8"H; uncommon size; $70.

Poppy slippers; all unmarked; uncommon mold; G&H, Germany. Left: large 6498 with applied granulated shells framing vamp transfer; 6-3/8"L x 3-3/8"H; $90. Middle: medium mold-modified C6499; in-mold 5-petaled flowers framing vamp transfer; 5-1/2"L x 2-3/4"H; $50. Right: small 6500 with applied shirring; 4-7/16"L x 2-1/4"H; $70.

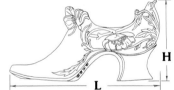

Medium sweet pea boot 6505; applied shirring and star flowers; unmarked; 4-1/2"L x 4-1/4"H. G&H, Germany. $60.

Peony boots in three sizes; G&H, Germany. Left: large 6854; applied shirring and HP sponge pattern; unmarked; 4-7/8"L x 4-15/16"H; $50. Middle: medium 6855; appliqués inc. gold nesting birds in granulated branches; factory logo on sole; 4-1/8"L x 4-3/16"H; $50. Right: small 6856; appliqués including granulated pods; factory logo on sole; 3-5/8"L x 3-1/2"H; $40.

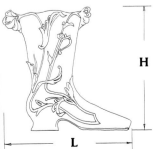

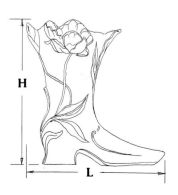

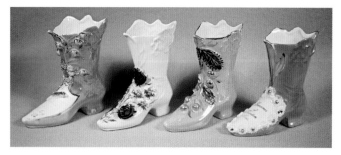

Medium (the most common size in this mold pattern) peony boots 6855; factory logo on sole of each; G&H, Germany. Left to right: (a) applied granular flower and gold buds; "Souvenir of Wheeling, W. Va."; 4-1/8"L x 4-1/4"H; $35. (b) applied flowers and outlining of cobalt leaves; 4-1/8"L x 4-3/16"H; $40. (c) applied cherries and outlining of cobalt leaves; 4-1/4"L x 4-3/8"H; $40. (d) applied star flowers framing vamp with "Souvenir of Taunton, Mass."; 4-3/16"L x 4-1/4"H; $35.

Souvenir china peony boots; all unmarked; G&H, Germany. Left: large 6854 with applied star flowers framing view of "The Reversing Falls/St. John N.B."; 5-3/16"L x 4-15/16"H; $40. Middle: medium 6855 with applied star flowers framing view of "Old Town Mill Built 1650/New London, Conn."; 4-7/16"L x 4-1/4"H; $45. Right: medium 6855 with applied star flowers framing view of "Blufe Point Lake Keuka, N.Y./Steamer Yates en roote (sic)"; 4-1/8"L x 4-3/16"H; $70.

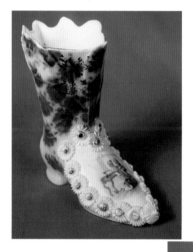

Medium peony boot 6855; sponge pattern and gold stamped ground; star flower appliqués framing vamp transfer; unmarked; 4-1/2"L (incl. appliqué at toe) x 4-1/4"H. G&H, Germany. $40.

Medium peony boot variation 6855; in-mold curled vine with buds on front panel; "Souvenir/of/ North Adams/Mass."; unmarked; 4-1/4"L x 4-3/16"H. G&H, Germany. $35.

Medium peony boot 6855; appliqués and HP details; factory logo on sole; 4-3/16"L x 4-1/4"H. G&H, Germany. $40.

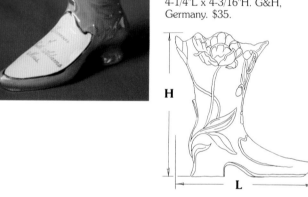

Small peony boot 6856; color transfer and applied beading; factory logo on sole; 3-7/16"L x 3-9/16"H. G&H, Germany. Uncommon size in this mold pattern. $60.

Textured and standard peony boots; all unmarked; G&H, Germany. Left: large textured peony boot 7224; texture achieved in-mold; HP scene; 5"L x 4-15/16"H; uncommon; $100. Middle: medium peony boot 6855; HP scene; 4-3/16"L x 4-1/8"H; $70. Right: small peony boot 6856; HP scene; 3-9/16"L x 3-7/16"H; $60.

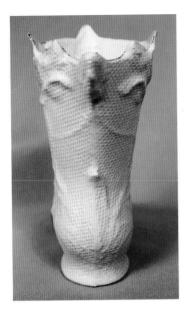

Detail of back seam of textured G&H peony boot. The tip off that the texture of this boot was achieved in-mold not in-kiln can be seen along the back seam, especially down toward the heel area; use of a tool to remove excess material where the two mold halves came together while the piece was being cast also removed some of the texture resulting from the casting process. In Royal Bayreuth tapestry shoes, the texture is achieved in-kiln **after** the casting process.

Rear quarter view of the three sizes of bear claw slippers showing the characteristic identifying embossed marks that resemble the marks of a triple bear claw. This view also shows the deeply sculpted pointed back heel line.

Souvenir china large bear claw slippers 6857; all unmarked; G&H, Germany. Left: view of "Pilgrim Monument, Provincetown, Mass."; collectible scene; 6-5/8"L x 3-1/8"H; $75. Middle: applied shells framing view of "Bank of Montreal"; 6-1/2"L x 3-1/16"H; $40. Right: applied star flowers framing view of "Wells Fargo Building/Portland, Oregon"; 6-9/16"L x 3-1/16"H; $40.

Textured peony boots; unmarked; both uncommon; G&H, Germany. Left: medium textured peony boot 7225; HP scene; 4-3/16"L x 4-3/16"H; $90. Right: small textured peony boot 7226; HP; 3-9/16"L x 3-1/2"H; $80.

Medium bear claw slippers 6858; G&H; Germany. Left: vamp transfer; 5-1/2"L x 2-11/16"H; factory logo on sole; $40. Middle: appliqués; HP gold details; 5-1/2"L x 2-3/4"H; $40. Right: rare micro-beaded vamp (prob. in-mold) framed with applied shells; unmarked; 5-3/8"L x 2-5/8"H; $50.

Medium bear claw slipper 6858 with appliqués; millstone mark on heel; 5-1/2"L x 2-11/16"H. G&H, Germany. $45.

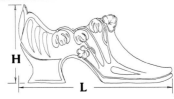

Three sizes of bear claw slippers; G&H, Germany. Left: large 6857; appliqués; factory logo on sole; 6-7/16"L x 3-1/16"H; $60. Middle: medium 6858; granulated appliqués; unmarked; 5-5/16"L x 2-5/8"H; $50. Right: small 6859; applied star flowers and beading; unmarked; 4-1/2"L x 2-3/16"H; $40.

Large bear claw slipper 6857; applied shells framing vamp transfer; unmarked; 6-1/2"L x 3-1/4"H. G&H, Germany. $60.

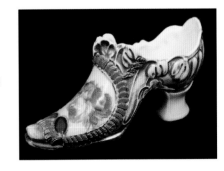

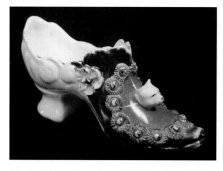

Medium bear claw slipper 6858 with applied star flowers framing vamp with applied cat's head (rare); factory logo on sole; 5-1/2"L x 2-3/4"H. G&H, Germany, $75.

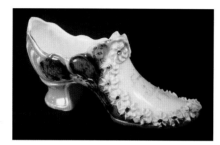

Medium bear claw slipper 6858 with applied flowers framing vamp with "Souvenir/of/Watertown/N.Y."; unmarked; 5-3/8"L x 2-3/4"H. G&H, Germany. $30.

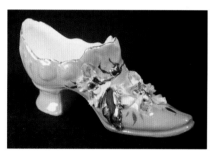

Small bear claw slipper 6859 with appliqués and HP details; factory logo on sole; 4-9/16"L x 2-3/16"H. G&H, Germany. $40.

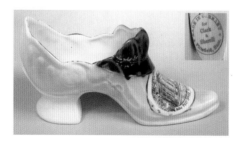

Small bear claw slipper 6859 with view of "New Post Office, Pittsfield, Mass." (was built in 1910); personalized "Made in Germany" logo on sole; 4-9/16"L x 2-1/4"H. G&H, Germany. Collectible scene. $80.

Large bear claw slipper 6857 with applied molded swan under which are extruded hand-applied granulated reeds; factory logo on sole; 6-1/2"L x 3-1/8"H. G&H, Germany. Rare. $130.

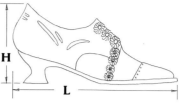

Ladies cap toe oxford 7405 with applied star flowers, three pairs pierced eyelets; "Souvenir/of/Newburgh/N.Y."; factory logo on sole; 5-7/8"L x 2-13/16"H. Sketch shows the appliqués because all versions of this shoe seen have had them. G&H, Germany. $30.

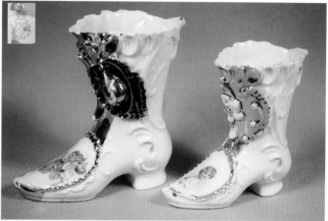

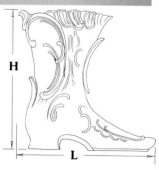

Scrolls and border shells boots; factory logo on soles; G&H, Germany. Left: large 7370 (impressed along edge between sole and shank); piped-on vine with molded and applied fruits; applied border framing vamp transfer; 4-15/16"L x 4-13/16"H; $40. Right: medium 7416 with applied flower framed by applied border; applied border framing vamp transfer portrait; 4-1/16"L x 4-1/16"H; $35.

Large floral and medallion cuff boot 8232 with floral appliqués and HP details; factory logo; 4-7/8"Hx5"L. G&H, Germany. $50.

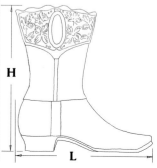

GERMAN PORCELAIN including
Ilmenau Porcelain Factory

A few shoes have been found with marks attributed to the Ilmenau Porcelain Factory. These very few shoes also often have an unusual rectangular bottom stamp with "Made in Germany" either in mixed upper and lower case, or all in caps. A very large group of shoes can be tied together primarily by similar mold designs and various décors. Because this latter large group also often have these same rectangular marks, the leap across the bottomless chasm has been made and the two groups have been assumed to be from the same factory. The fragile connection is marginally supported by two observations. The large group that may have come from the Ilmenau Porcelain Factory often have applied decorations that were created using extruded slip, in much the same manner as the other major shoe producer of wedding cake shoes, Galluba and Hofmann, a factory in the same city of Ilmenau. Special skills are required to manufacture the volumes of wedding cake shoes produced with so much hand craftsmanship. Workers moving between the two factories may have exchanged the knowledge needed to successfully apply the décors. The second observation is that Hugo Galluba was an executive with the Ilmenau Porcelain Factory for a decade before becoming a partner in 1891 in the firm that then became Galluba & Hofmann. If the techniques of using extruded slip for decorating were actually developed first at the IPF, it is possible that Galluba, though an executive, took that knowledge with him when he moved to G&H.

All of the shoes in this section are porcelain, fully glazed inside. The porcelain is high quality and generally thin. Ilmenau Porcelain Factory has been shortened to IPF. The IPF mark found on only two shoe forms consists of a pair of triangles, one inverted and superimposed on top of the other, with either the letters IPF or JPF in the center. This mark was used c.1903. It is assumed that all of the shoes shown in this section were manufactured between the late 1800s and WWI, or perhaps into the 1920s, and no further attempts at dating are made within the individual descriptions in this section, with one exception.

Bottom view of IPF man's cap toe oxford showing three important marks: the green factory logo, the 3/4" x 1/2" black rectangle with "Made in Germany" in mixed upper and lower case letters, and the partially visible numeric factory stamp beginning with a "7".

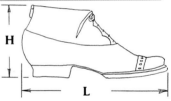

Men's cap toe oxfords; IPF, Germany. Left: large; a "left"; unmarked; 6-1/4"L x 2-13/16"H; $50. Right: small (sketch); a "left"; unmarked; 3-1/2"L x 1-11/16"H; $25.

Three sizes of cherries slipper. The cherries and leaves are part of the mold. Note the unusual heel formed of cherries. None of the shoes photographed has the IPF mark, but other versions of this shoe have been seen with the IPF mark.

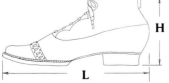

Man's cap toe oxford; factory logo in underglaze green; a "left"; 6-5/16"L x 2-7/8"H. The gold on the lower part of this shoe has worn away over time, revealing the fact that the pink was applied first, kiln fired to set it, and then the gold applied, which requires a lower temperature to affix it. Because of the worn gold, this shoe has little value except for its marks, shown in the bottom view of the shoe. IPF, Germany. $10.

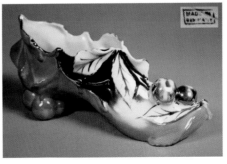

Large cherries slipper; 1/2" x 1/4" black rectangle with MADE IN GERMANY; 6-7/8"L x 3-1/4"H. Occasionally, a barely readable "2307" can be found on the left face above the sole. This is a known IPF shoe. Note that the caption in the rectangle is all in capital letters. IPF, Germany. $50.

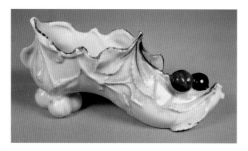

Medium cherries slipper; impressed into right face near sole "2308"; unmarked; 5-3/4"L x 2-3/4"H. IPF, Germany. $45.

Small cherries slipper; impressed into right face near sole "2309"; importer's logo on sole; 4-13/16"L x 2-5/16"H. IPF, Germany. $40.

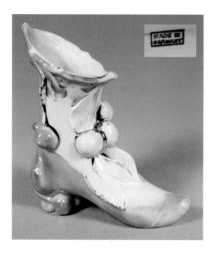

Cherries boot; in-mold cherries and heavily embossed leaves; 4-digit number impressed into right face above sole – first two undecipherable, last two "11"; 1/2" x 1/4" black rectangle with MIG; 4-1/16"L x 1-1/2"H. IPF, Germany. $45.

High shank piked toe slipper with applied columbine, leaf outlines, and tiny florettes; MIG logo; 6-3/8"L x 3-1/8"H. Tentatively attributed to IPF, Germany. $75.

High shank piked toe slipper with applied columbine, leaves, and double bands of beads; unmarked; 6-3/8"L x 3-1/4"H. Tentatively attributed to IPF, Germany. $75.

High shank piked toe slipper with applied leaf outlines and vamp design; unmarked; 6-1/2"L x 3-1/4"H. Tentatively attributed to IPF, Germany. $50.

High shank piked toe slipper with view of "Missouri State Building. World's Fair, St. Louis. Mo. 1904."; MIG millstone; 6-3/8"L x 3-1/4"H. Tentatively attributed to IPF, Germany. $125.

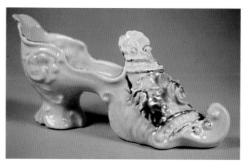

High shank piked toe slipper with applied columbine and leaves; unusual in-mold design; unmarked; 6-7/16"L x 3-1/8"H. Tentatively attributed to IPF, Germany. $65.

Slipper with fluted heel; applied cherries, cherry blossom, stem, and leaves; unmarked; 5-7/8"L x 3"H. Tentatively attributed to IPF, Germany. Uncommon mold. $85.

Boots with fluted heels; applied granulated flower and other vamp appliqués; unmarked; both 3-11/16"L x 4"H. Tentatively attributed to IPF, Germany; $60 each.

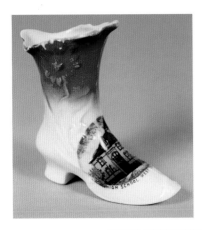

Boot with view of "High School. West Concord, Minn.";
unmarked; 3-3/4"L x 3-7/8"H.
Tentatively attributed to IPF,
Germany. $40.

Boot with applied slip and beads
framing applied vamp ornament;
unmarked; 4-1/2"L x 4-3/4"H.
Tentatively attributed to IPF,
Germany. $55.

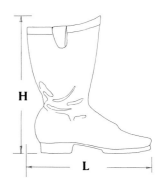

Low heeled slipper with applied vamp shirring and
beading framing granulated ornament; unmarked;
4-3/4"L x 2-1/4"H. Tentatively attributed to IPF,
Germany. $60.

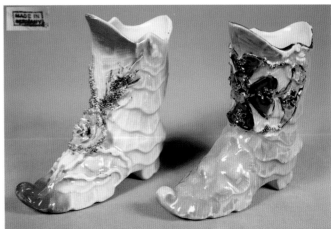

Shell boots with vamp appliqués;
MIG rectangular logo; 3-7/8"L x 3-
7/8"H. Tentatively attributed to IPF,
Germany. $65 each.

Slender yellow luster evening slipper with cobalt toe
and applied vamp flower; extruded and applied
5-petaled flowers; MIG rectangle mark; 4-7/16"L
x 2-5/16"H. Tentatively attributed to IPF, Germany.
$70.

Pair of slender boots with applied granular ornaments and slip outlined
leaves; MIG rectangular mark, "handpainted", and importer's logo on
each; 3-3/8"L x 4"H each. Importer's mark is Montgomery Ward.
Tentatively attributed to IPF, Germany. $45 each.

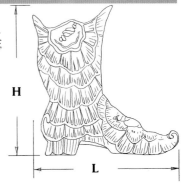

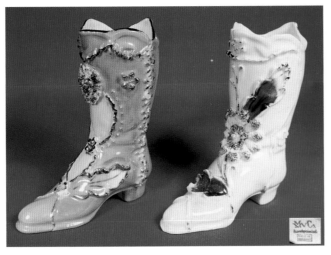

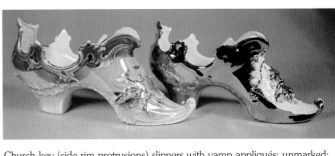

Church key (side rim protrusions) slippers with vamp appliqués; unmarked;
tentatively attributed to IPF, Germany. Left: granulated slip outlining HP
florals; 6-3/8"L x 3-1/8"H; $65. Right: extruded and applied shells on upper
vamp and applied vamp ornament; 6-1/4"L x 2-15/16"H; $65.

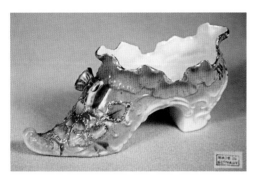

Slipper with dentil ruching, applied bow, and applied granulated slip outlining HP vamp floral design; HP "Washington/D.C." on back of heel; MIG rectangular logo; 6-5/8"L x 3-1/8"H. Tentatively attributed to IPF, Germany. $65.

Slippers with dentil ruching; all unmarked; all 6-1/2"L x 3-1/8"H; tentatively attributed to IPF, Germany. Left: fuchsia ruching; $35. Middle: cobalt ruching and applied bow; HP vamp design; $55. Right: slip outlined leaves flanking slip outlined vamp flower with granulated center; applied beading along upper vamp; $65.

Slippers with dentil ruching; tentatively attributed to IPF, Germany. Left: cobalt glazed with view of "School House, Hadley, Minn."; MIG rectangular logo; 6-1/2"L x 3"H; $85. Right: green glazed with view of "New Bridge, Fort Fairfield, Me."; 6-3/8"L x 3-1/16"H; $65.

Cobalt glazed boots with in-mold loops; tentatively attributed to IPF, Germany. Left: view of "Souvenir of Alvinston"; MIG rectangular logo; 4-3/8"L x 4-7/8"H; $40. Right (sketch): view of "A Ludington Car Ferry, Ludington, Mich."; personalized stamp "Made in Germany/for/Joseph Sahlmark/Ludington/Mich."; $75.

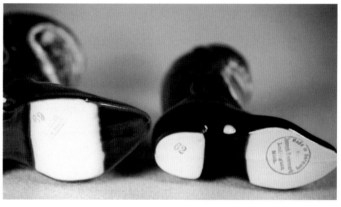

Bottom views of cobalt boots. Note large tooled numbers typical of shoes that may be from the IPF.

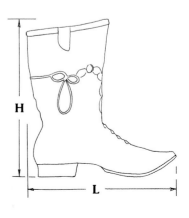

Boots with in-mold loops; tentatively attributed to IPF, Germany. Left: worn gold glazing; 4-1/4"L x 4-13/16"H; $15. Middle: applied granular gold starburst framing view of "Hotel Weirs, Weirs, N.H."; personalized stamp "Made in Germany /for/F. E. Nelson/Laconia/N.H."; 4-1/2"L x 4-7/8"H; $65. Right: gray/green luster with stamped designs and HP cobalt details; unmarked; 4-1/8"L x 4-11/16"H; uncommon décor; $75.

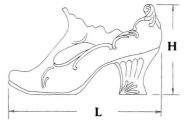

Scalloped rim slipper with open sides; thirteen applied white beads on vamp and two rows applied extrusions along front half of rim; underglaze blue cross that may or may not be a factory mark; 6-1/2"L x 3-1/8"H. Tentatively attributed to IPF, Germany. $50.

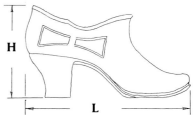

Slipper with in-mold side gussets; applied extrusions and slip work on vamp; barely visible impressed "867A" on left shank; 5-1/16"L x 2-3/4"H. Tentatively attributed to IPF, Germany, but has some characteristics of a Galluba & Hofmann product. $40.

Scalloped rim slipper with open sides; applied ornament on toe; 6-1/4"L x 3-3/16"H. Photo shows in-mold detail on front of rim that could not be deciphered for sketch of previous shoe because of the appliqués on that shoe. Tentatively attributed to IPF, Germany. $30.

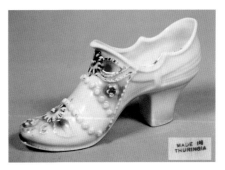

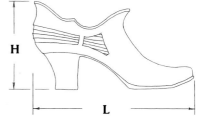

Slipper with in-mold side and back gussets; applied rows of beads across vamp, slip outlined leaves and flowers; 5-1/16"L x 2-9/16"H. Tentatively attributed to IPF, Germany. $40.

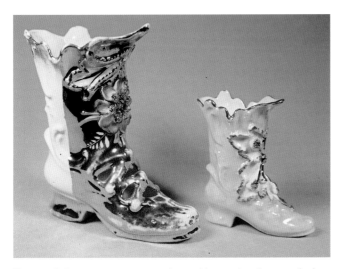

Boots with front rim projections and in-mold vamp beads; unmarked; tentatively attributed to IPF, Germany. Left: large pierced vamp gold face with applied flower and leaf outlines; 4-5/16"L x 4-11/16"H; $50. Right: small yellow luster with applied leaf outlines and central design; 2-11/16"L x 3-3/16"H; $25.

Three sizes of slipper with in-mold side and back gussets; tentatively attributed to IPF, Germany. Left: small with applied slip work; "A Present from/Ireland"; 9/16"dia. green millstone MIG mark; 4-3/16"L x 2-1/4"H; $25. Middle: elaborate slip work appliqués on vamp; black rectangular MIG mark; 5"L x 2-1/2"H; $55. Right: large with in-mold vamp and heel designs; 7-3/4"L x 3-7/8"H; $40.

Crimped sole slipper with applied flower and applied slip and extruded vamp design; MIG rectangular bottom stamp; 4-9/16"L x 2-3/16"H. Tentatively attributed to IPF, Germany. $55.

Crimped sole slipper with extruded vamp appliqués; unmarked; 6-1/2"L x 3-1/8"H. Tentatively attributed to IPF, Germany. $55.

Crimped sole boot with applied extrusions partitioning surface into painting areas; unmarked; 4-3/16"L x 4-13/16"H. Tentatively attributed to IPF, Germany. $45.

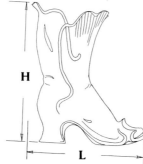

Slipper with turned up toe and applied extruded ribbon slip forming outline of vamp flower; applied slip outlining leaves; 6-13/16"L x 3"H. Tentatively attributed to IPF, Germany. $45.

Boot with turned up toe and applied slip outlining central medallion and leaves; applied flower; piped on tiny flowers; orange MIG rectangle mark; 5-15/16"L x 5-13/16"H. Tentatively attributed to IPF, Germany. $50.

Ruffled rim strap shoes with in-mold vamp heart; each with an elaborate applied flower flanked by applied slip bordered leaves with HP details; both "lefts"; both unmarked; 5-5/8"L x 3"H each. Both of these were wedding favors, probably filled with candies, at the wedding reception of the current owner's grandparents in 1910. Tentatively attributed to IPF, Germany. $65 each.

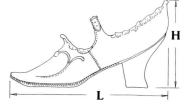

Ruffled rim strap shoes with in-mold vamp heart; all are "lefts"; tentatively attributed to IPF, Germany. Left: applied beading and vamp transfer; unmarked; 5-11/16"L x 3-3/16"H; $55. Middle: applied beading with vamp transfer; unmarked; 5-11/16"L x 3"H; $55, Right: cobalt glazed with view of "Wilson Boulder, Farmington" (N.H.); personalized bottom mark; 5-9/16"L x 3"H; $60.

Bottom view of cobalt ruffled rim strap shoe showing relative sizes of bottom stamped marks. Large size of tooled number 52 is typical of many shoes believed to have been made by the IPF.

Retooled mold of a ruffled rim strap shoe eliminating strap buckle and incorporating beading in-mold; variegated green with inserted pink pig; unmarked; 5-11/16"L x 3-3/8"H. Tentatively attributed to IPF, Germany. $80.

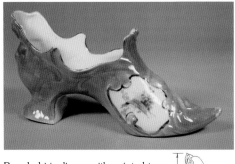

Bearded iris slipper with pointed toe; unmarked; 6-5/16"L x 3-1/16"H. Tentatively attributed to IPF, Germany. $25.

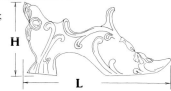

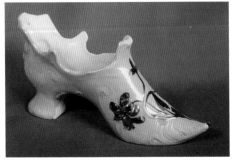

T-strap shoe with in-mold 4-petaled flowers; unmarked; 6"L x 3-1/4"H. Tentatively attributed to IPF, Germany. $30.

Tulip and swirl straight top boot; view of "Court House & City Hall, Rochester, N.Y." framed by in-mold beading; orange MIG millstone mark; 4-3/4"L x 5"H. Tentatively attributed to IPF, Germany. $35.

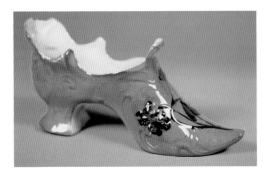

Slipper with pointed toe and in-mold floral and swirl design; unmarked; 5-3/8"L x 2-1/2"H. This and the following two slippers inspired the designs of shoes made by Hobé and Vee Jackson in the 1940s and 1950s. Tentatively attributed to IPF, Germany. $25.

Slipper with pierced ruff and in-mold buckle; unmarked, but has been seen with black MIG millstone mark; 5-1/16"L x 2-9/16"H. This shoe is a copy of a Royal Bayreuth slipper. Tentatively attributed to IPF, Germany. $30.

Slipper with pointed toe and in-mold floral and swirl design; unmarked; 6-1/4"L x 3-1/16"H. Tentatively attributed to IPF, Germany. $25.

GERMAN PORCELAIN including Martinroda and Scheidig

Many of the shoes in this short section appear to provide answers to the disposition of some molds after Galluba and Hofmann closed in the early 1930s and raise questions about the origin of a boot well known to collectors. The Porzellanfabrik Martinroda Friedrich Eger & Co. in Martinroda, Thuringia, Germany (1900–present), is only a few miles north of the Ilmenau factories of Galluba & Hofmann and the Ilmenau Porcelain Factory, making those factories accessible for the purchase of discarded molds. The Martinroda factory produces today some shoes that are known to have originated at G&H. The boot in question may have begun its life at the IPF, but it is currently produced at Martinroda.

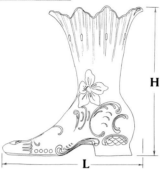

Porcelain fluted top boots with keyhole mold impressions and in-mold floral, scale, and scrolls design. Left: pink; unmarked; inside glazed down about one inch; 5"L x 5-1/4"H; reminiscent of décor and designs of some shoes that may have been made by the Ilmenau Porcelain Factory; it is, of course, possible that the design was originated at the Martinroda factory; unknown factory, Germany, c.1900; $45. Right: white with color transfers; bottom marked with crown logo and "Elfinware/Germany"; 2-7/8"L x 3"H; prob. Martinroda; $20.

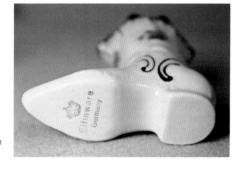

Bottom view of small white fluted top boot showing mark with "Elfinware" typically found. It is possible that this boot was commissioned by Breslauer-Underberg of New York sometime between their incorporation in January 1940 and the entry of the United States into WWII, although they did not trademark the name Elfinware until 1947. The type of color transfers or decals found on this boot are typical of Breslauer-Underberg wares manufactured in New Jersey when they could no longer obtain them from Germany during WWII.

Three versions of the porcelain fluted top boot produced by Martinroda post WWII. Left: view of "Niagara Falls, Canada"; gold stamped "Made in/East Germany"; 4-3/16"L x 4-1/2"H; $15. Middle: floral decals and applied buckle; paper label with "Made/in German/Democratic/Republic"; 4-1/8"L x 4-1/2"H; $20. Right: floral decals and applied buckle; gold stamped factory logo and "Made/in/German Democratic Republic"; 4-3/16"L x 4-1/2"H; $20.

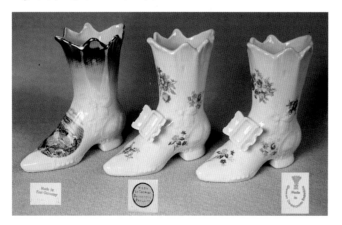

Porcelain slippers and factory plaque purchased new at the Martinroda factory in 1997, the slippers for under $15 each. The print under the "M" in the factory logo reads "Thüringer Handarbeit". Left: the tulip slipper originated by the Galluba & Hofmann factory; decals and HP gold details; factory logo as in plaque; 4-1/2"L x 2-1/4"H. Right: the bear claw slipper originated by the Galluba & Hofmann factory; decals and HP gold details; factory logo as in plaque; 4-9/16"L x 2-3/16"H.

Porcelain slippers purchased new at the Martinroda factory in 1997 for under $15 each. Both have factory logo shown on plaque in previous photo. Left: decals and HP gold details; 5-3/4"L x 3"H. Right: barely visible in-mold floral and swirl design identical to that on slippers at end of previous section tentatively attributed to the Ilmenau Porcelain Factory; 3-3/4"L x 1-7/8"H.

Porcelain 3 x 3 (3 pairs in-mold grommets, 3 pairs open eyelets) Victor shoes with looped back strap, both with "3586" impressed into right face of heel. Left: white glazed; unmarked; 5-1/8"L x 3"HOA; Carl Scheidig, Germany, early 1900s; $30. Right: brown high-gloss glazed; underglaze shank mark of Porzellanfiguren Gräfenthal GmbH, a successor of Carl Scheidig; purchased at the factory store in 1998 in Germany for about $10 with comment from manager that this was the last one in the outlet store and that they were breaking the mold and the shoe would never be made again; 5-3/8"L x 3-1/4"H.

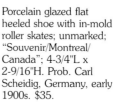

Porcelain glazed flat heeled shoe with in-mold roller skates; unmarked; "Souvenir/Montreal/Canada"; 4-3/4"L x 2-9/16"H. Prob. Carl Scheidig, Germany, early 1900s. $35.

GERMAN PORCELAIN including Mardorf & Bandorf, the Arnstadt Shoes

The factory of Mardorf & Bandorf in the city of Arnstadt, Germany produced variegated green wares, often with members of the animal kingdom in featured roles. Careful examination of the four shoes and other products in the four catalog pages that have survived and are housed in the museum in Arnstadt along with study of the design characteristics of the shoes known to have been made at the Arnstadt factory have led the author to conclude that most if not all of the shoes shown in this section were made there. (See Mardorf & Bandorf in manufacturers' section for additional detail.) The Arnstadt shoes comprise a group of original designs and color combinations. Since no other porcelain factory existed in the city when Mardorf and Bandorf were in operation, the shoes are usually referred to herein as the Arnstadt shoes. The variegated greens and blues favored by the company probably were achieved by airbrush.

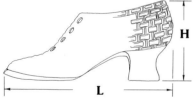

Porcelain variegated green glazed basket weave woman's oxford with attached dog; unmarked, but it is the unique shoe illustrated on one of the four catalog pages of Mardorf and Bandorf wares possessed by the museum in Arnstadt; 6"L x 2-3/4"H, shoe only. Arnstadt, Germany. c.1910. Uncommon shoe. $175.

Back view of the basket weave woman's oxford showing the variation in color and the typical orange contrast used by Arnstadt with their variegated green wares.

Bottom view of the basket weave woman's oxford showing the dark smudge typically remaining where the glaze was wiped off to prevent the piece from sticking to the kiln shelf during firing.

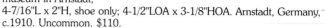

Porcelain variegated green glazed woman's cap toe oxford with in-mold dog body and applied dog head; unmarked, but this is one of the shoes illustrated in the four catalog pages of Mardorf and Bandorf wares possessed by the museum in Arnstadt; 4-7/16"L x 2"H, shoe only; 4-1/2"LOA x 3-1/8"HOA. Arnstadt, Germany, c.1910. Uncommon. $110.

Bottom view of the woman's cap toe oxford with dog showing the dark smudge typically remaining where the glaze was wiped off to prevent the piece from sticking to the kiln shelf during firing.

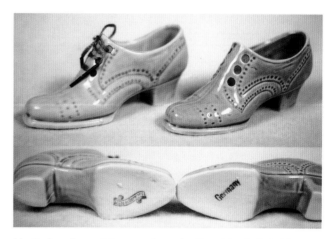

Identical small porcelain women's cap toe 3-eyelet oxford straights with different bottom marks; 3-3/4"L x 1-3/4"H each; Arnstadt, Germany; c.1910; $15 each. Left: "Made in Germany" in a curved scroll, the bottom portion of a mark unique to Arnstadt. Right: one of several marks used by Arnstadt that appear generic but which the practiced eye recognizes as potentially Arnstadt.

Small porcelain women's cap toe 3-eyelet oxford straights comparing the blue known to be an Arnstadt shoe with the solid green that is identical in all measurements and mold detail except for the perf pattern on the cap toe; green is believed to be Arnstadt, Germany; $15.

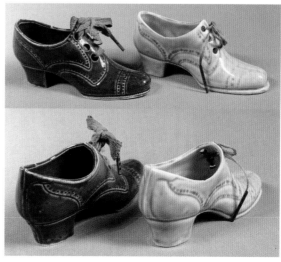

161

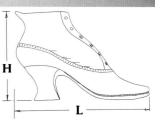

Porcelain women's 2 x 4 heeled ankle shoes with perf detail; all are 4-7/8"L x 3-1/4"H; all unmarked; Arnstadt, Germany, early 1900s. Left: variegated green with rare original orange fabric shoelace with metal aglets; $65. Middle: variegated blue; $45. Right: variegated green with attached pug, uncommon; $65.

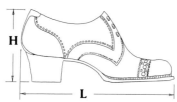

Identical large porcelain women's cap toe 3-eyelet oxford straights with different bottom marks; 5-1/2"L x 2-1/2"H each; Arnstadt, Germany; c.1910; $25 each. Left: script "Germany". Right: the Arnstadt millstone mark.

Porcelain mottled green glazed cap toe 4-eyelet man's ankle shoe with original dark orange braided fabric shoelace with metal aglets; full Arnstadt bottom mark; 4-5/8"L x 2-3/8"H. Arnstadt, Germany. Early 1900s. $55.

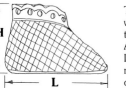

Two sizes of porcelain quilted baby bootees with ten drilled holes, one of which illustrates that the full Arnstadt mark often washes off; Arnstadt, Germany, early 1900s. $15 each. Left to right: (a) small blue; full Arnstadt mark; 2-3/4"L x 1-13/16"H. (b) medium size olive green; full Arnstadt mark almost completely lost during mild washing; 3-3/16"L x 2-1/16"H. (c) medium white glazed with crest of "Weston Super Mare"; Arnstadt MIG scroll mark; 3-3/16"L x 2"H. (d) medium size dark khaki green; "Germany" stamp; 3-3/16"L x 2-1/16"H.

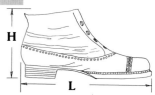

Bottom view of mottled green man's ankle shoe showing full Arnstadt bottom mark.

Large porcelain quilted baby bootees in variegated green and variegated pastel blue with original fabric cords and pompoms; unmarked; 3-13/16"L x 2-7/16"H each. Arnstadt, Germany, early 1900s. Rare with original cords and pompoms. $110 each.

Porcelain variegated green man's ankle shoe with applied roller skate; orig. lace; unmarked; 4-5/8"L x 2-3/8"H, shoe only; 4-3/4"LOA x 3-9/16"HOA. Arnstadt, Germany. Early 1900s. Uncommon. $150.

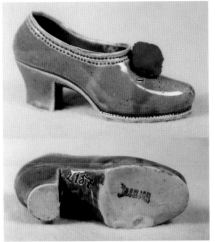

Typical metallic/fabric cord with metal aglets found on the more heavily produced Arnstadt shoes.

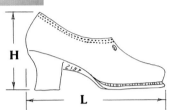

Porcelain olive drab glazed pump with pair of pierced holes near rim through which are threaded a faded red cord whose ends are red pompoms; "2157" impressed into shank; "Germany" stamp; 3-5/16"L x 1-13/16"H. Arnstadt, Germany, early 1900s. $40.

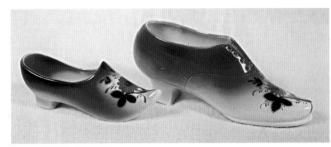

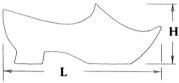

Porcelain variegated royal blue glazed shoes with HP orange daisy and cobalt leaf design with gold accents; unmarked; rare décor; Arnstadt, Germany, early 1900s. Left (sketch): clog; 4-1/4"L x 1-9/16"H; $50. Right: large wing tip woman's 4-eyelet oxford; impressed into right face of heel what may be "7124"; 5-7/16"L x 2-1/4"H; $70.

Porcelain variegated green pumps with pair of locations for piercing to accommodate fabric lace; Arnstadt, Germany, early 1900s. Left: inserted cat with orange bow; indentations not pierced; unmarked; 5-3/8"L x 2-3/4"H, shoe only; uncommon; $75. Middle (sketch): in-mold tail with applied mouse; pierced indentations; Arnstadt millstone mark; 5-1/2"L x 2-7/8"H, shoe only; $50. Right: pierced indentations; Arnstadt script "Germany"; 5-1/2"L x 2-13/16"H; $35.

Porcelain large variegated green glazed 4-eyelet cap toe woman's oxford; original orange fabric shoelace with metal aglets; Arnstadt millstone mark; 5-1/4"L x 2-5/8"H. Arnstadt, Germany, early 1900s. $40.

Porcelain wing tip women's 4-eyelet oxfords; Arnstadt, Germany, early 1900s. Left: large variegated green with inserted fully formed terrier; unmarked; 5-5/8"L x 2-5/16"H; uncommon; $65. Middle: large variegated green with Arnstadt millstone mark; "Cottage City" across vamp; 5-5/16"L x 2-1/4"H; common; $25. Right: medium variegated blue with applied bear; unmarked; appears to be an impressed "7291" on right rear quarter; 4-3/4"L x 1-7/8"H; uncommon; $55.

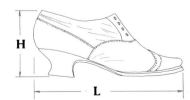

Porcelain variegated green glazed 4-eyelet cap toe women's oxfords; all unmarked; Arnstadt, Germany, early 1900s. Left: medium size with attached person in a rooster costume; 4-1/4"L x 2"H, shoe only; 3-3/4"HOA; rare; $125. Middle: medium size with attached dog; 4-3/8"L x 2-1/8"H, shoe only; 2-9/16"HOA; $45. Right: large size; 5-1/4"L x 2-5/8"H; $30.

Porcelain medium size variegated green glazed 4-eyelet cap toe woman's oxford with attached child in dimpled blouse over orange shorts; in-mold texture on child's clothing similar to texture on other Arnstadt pieces in extant catalog pages; unmarked; 4-1/2"L x 2-1/4"H, shoe only; 3-5/8"HOA. Arnstadt, Germany. Early 1900s. Uncommon. $90.

Porcelain 2-tone gray bisque and matte glazed cuffed boot with attached large size pink pig wearing dust cap tied below neck; unmarked; 2-3/4"L x 2-7/8"H, boot only. This piece is pictured on the 1953 *Hobbies* magazine cover. Arnstadt, Germany. Early 1900s. Uncommon. $150.

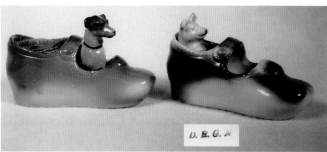

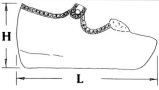

Porcelain variegated green glazed Mary Janes with in-mold button on strap and in-mold pompom on vamp; each is 3-13/16"L x 1-11/16"H, shoe only; Arnstadt, Germany, early 1900s. Left: inserted terrier (airbrush got away from the operator) and threadbare silk velvet pincushion, which may be original; unmarked; uncommon insert; $65. Right: inserted pink pig; stamped on bottom "D.R.G.M." (*Deutsches Reich Gebrauchs Muster*, the German patent law that became effective in 1891); $75.

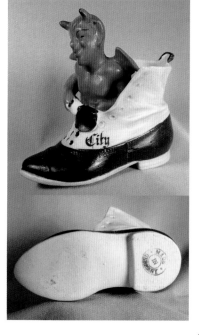

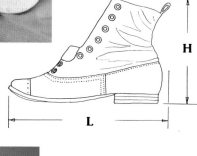

Porcelain man's high top shoe with inserted red devil brushing tongue; brown glazed lower and tan bisque upper; Arnstadt millstone mark; 4-7/8"L x 3-1/8"H, shoe only; 4-3/8"HOA. Arnstadt, Germany, early 1900s. Uncommon. $175.

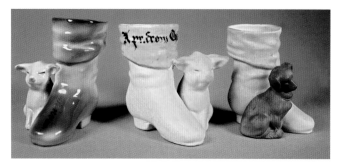

Porcelain cuffed boots; Arnstadt, Germany, early 1900s. Left: Variegated green glazed with attached small size (1-3/4"H) glazed sitting pig; gold script on vamp "Denver"; Arnstadt millstone mark; 2-7/8"L x 3"H, boot only; $75. Middle: peach bisque with camel bisque cuff with "A pr. From The Forth Bridge" (Scotland); attached medium size (2-3/16"H) sitting pig; unmarked; 2-7/8"L x 3"H, boot only; $75. Right: peach bisque with attached bisque dog; unmarked; 2-13/16"L x 2-15/16"H; uncommon animal; $65.

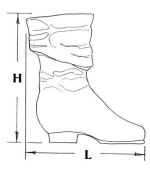

Bottom view of variegated green cuffed boot showing Arnstadt millstone mark.

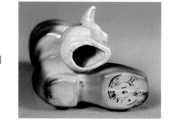

Porcelain man's high top shoe with inserted full body bisque pierrot with orange matte cap and neck ruffle; brown glazed lower and tan bisque upper; unmarked; 4-13/16"L x 3"H, shoe only; 4-1/4"HOA. Arnstadt, Germany, early 1900s. Uncommon. $175.

Porcelain man's high top shoe with two pink pigs; brown glazed lower and tan bisque upper; unmarked; 4-7/8"L x 3"H, shoe only. Arnstadt, Germany, early 1900s. Uncommon. $175.

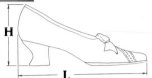

Porcelain medium heeled variegated green wing-tip pump with in-mold orange and yellow bow; unmarked; 7"L x 3-1/8"H. Arnstadt, Germany, early 1900s. $50.

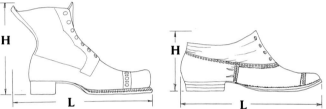

Porcelain variegated green men's shoes; Arnstadt, Germany, early 1900s. Left: 4x3 high-top cap-toe work boot with square toe; unmarked; 6"L x 3-7/8"H; uncommon; $70. Right: 4-eyelet cap-toe low-cut shoe; Arnstadt millstone mark; 5-1/8"L x 2-1/8"H; common; $20.

Porcelain variegated green tramp shoes; unmarked; Arnstadt, Germany, early 1900s. Left: large with inserted full-body black & white cats, larger of which has an orange mouth; 7-1/4"L x 2-3/8"H; $150. Right: small with inserted pink pig; impressed into shank "0 572 KC"; 5-1/8"L x 1-11/16"H; $90.

Porcelain tramp shoes; may have been pipe or cigar holders; unmarked; Arnstadt, Germany, early 1900s. Left: large variegated green with applied full body fox and hound; 7-3/16"L x 2-7/16"H; $150. Right: medium size glazed; impressed into shank "0 572/I"; 6-1/8"L x 2-1/8"H; $30.

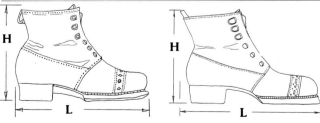

Porcelain 3 x 3 men's cap toe work boots (note mold differences between small and large); Arnstadt, Germany, early 1900s. Left: small variegated green; Arnstadt script "Germany" stamp; 3-9/16"L x 2-1/2"H; $35. Middle: large variegated blue; Arnstadt millstone mark; 5"L x 3-5/16"H; $45. Right: large variegated green; unmarked; 5"L x 3-1/4"H; $45.

Porcelain white glazed ankle shoe with in-mold bow tipped to one side; palest blue airbrushed details; unmarked; 4"L x 2-5/16"H. Arnstadt, Germany, early 1900s. $40.

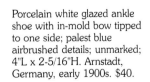

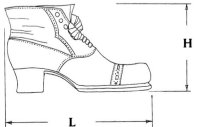

Porcelain white glazed shoes with palest blue airbrushed details; unmarked; prob. Arnstadt, Germany, early 1900s. Left: man's 4-eyelet cap toe ankle shoe; 5-3/8"L x 2-13/16"H; $25. Right: woman's lace-up high top; 5"L x 3-7/8"H; $50.

Porcelain women's cap toe oxfords. Left: 3-eyelet with pale gray-blue areas showing on both inside and outside; unmarked; 5-3/8"L x 2-5/8"H; unknown factory; $35. Right: in-mold matte black bow and wide laces; palest blue airbrushed details; orange matte glazed inside; hand-written "1600" impressed into shank; "Germany" stamped on sole; 5-1/4"L x 2-9/16"H; pos. Arnstadt, Germany; early 1900s; uncommon; $60.

GERMAN PORCELAIN including
Weiss, Kühnert & Company

Weiss, Kühnert is the source of the well crafted, mated animal shoes and a number of mated shoes with figures. Copies of seven pages from two undated WK catalogs have confirmed the source of these shoes, except as noted. WK products usually had bright gold work and for the bird and figurine shoes were expertly hand-painted. The company began operations in 1891. The shoes illustrated in this section were probably made beginning at some point shortly thereafter. Their production probably went into the 1920s. No further dating is done by individual shoe within this section except as noted.

Porcelain glazed Normandy shoe with in-mold ribbon ruching, grapes and leaves; WK model # "2112" impressed into left face of heel; 7/16"L red "Germany" mark on sole; 6-7/16"L x 2-5/8"H. Weiss, Kühnert, Germany. $35.

Porcelain glazed paneled-top boot with in-mold cherries and leaves; vamp transfer; WK model # 2596; impressed into right face just above shank "Germany"; 3-7/8"L x 4-1/8"H. Weiss, Kühnert, Germany. $45.

Porcelain glazed high top shoe with in-mold laces; WK model # "2864" impressed into shank; 4-3/16"L x 3-1/8"H. Weiss, Kühnert, Germany. $30.

Porcelain bisque and matte glazed boy and girl clowns applied to tramp shoes with in-mold dogs; one leg of each clown is in-mold; WK model # 2621; unmarked in any way; both shown on cover of 1953 *Hobbies* magazine; Weiss, Kühnert, Germany. Left: 5-1/8"L x 4-1/16"H; $75. Right: 5-1/4"L x 3-15/16"H; $75.

Porcelain matched pair of gray bisque large Dutch shoes with in-mold glazed grapes and leaves held by separately molded and attached Dutch boy and girl; each has impressed "3216" on back face of shoe; Weiss, Kühnert, Germany. None of the Dutch shoes illustrated herein were pictured in the seven catalog pages possessed by the author. However, those with the attached Dutch figurines often are found, including one of those pictured here, with a Weiss, Kühnert factory logo bottom stamp. Left: brunette girl with pink cap; 7-9/16"LOA x 5"HOA; $185. Right: brunette boy with pink cap; 7-1/8"LOA x 5"HOA; $185.

Porcelain gray bisque large Dutch shoe with in-mold glazed grapes and leaves held by separately molded and attached blond Dutch girl with blue cap; impressed "3216" on back face of shoe; 7-1/2"LOA x 5"HOA. The pairs with attached figurines are known with both brunettes in pink caps and blonds in blue caps. Weiss, Kühnert, Germany. $185.

Comparison of three sizes of Dutch shoes with grapes held by Dutch figures. Left: small, in-mold figure, # 11141. Middle: medium, applied figure, # 3217. Right: large, applied figure, # 3216.

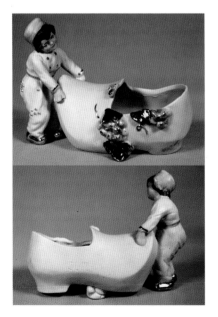

Porcelain gray bisque medium Dutch shoe with in-mold glazed grapes and leaves held by separately molded and attached brunette Dutch boy with pink cap; impressed "3217" on back face of shoe; factory logo stamped on bottom; 6"LOA x 4-1/4"HOA. Weiss, Kühnert, Germany. $175.

Bottom view of medium Dutch shoe and boy showing barely visible Weiss, Kühnert factory logo above the letters "LEIA". The logo consists of the letters "WKC" below which is a large "X" that separates "Graefen" and "thal", Gräfenthal, being the location of the factory. Note that the bottoms of the boy's shoes are closed; the figurines on these pieces are fully formed dolls.

Porcelain glazed pair of small Dutch shoes with in-mold figures, grapes, and leaves; impressed on back face of each "11141/Germany"; HP in mode of similar Weiss, Kühnert pieces; attributed to Weiss, Kühnert, Germany. Left: girl; 4-3/8"LOA x 2-1/4"HOA; $65. Right: boy; 4-1/4"LOA x 2-5/16"HOA; $65.

Back view of small Dutch shoe with in-mold figure showing location of impressed model number and country of origin, "11141/Germany".

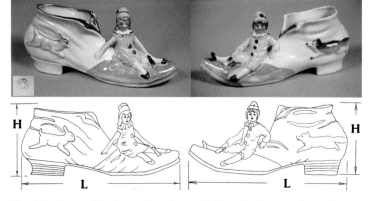

Porcelain glazed pair of large clown shoes with in-mold pierrots and animals; insides glazed only part way down; WK model # 3406; Weiss, Kühnert, Germany. Left: girl pierrot with rabbit; impressed on back face just above sole "3406"; orange WK circle stamp "Germany *"; 5-11/16"L x 2.5"H; $135. Right: boy pierrot with fox; impressed on back face just above sole "Germany 3406"; 5-11/16"L x 2-1/2"H; $135.

Porcelain glazed medium clown shoe with in-mold boy pierrot and fox; WK model # 3407; impressed on back face above heel and shank "Germany 3407"; 4-11/16"L x 2-1/8"H; Weiss, Kühnert, Germany. $115.

Porcelain glazed left and right facing women's lace-up cap toe oxfords with pairs of in-mold cockatiels and an in-mold bird in flight on the outside rear quarter; HP on outside face of each "A Present from/Brighton"; WK model # 5492; impressed into each heel back face "5492"; left-facing has 7/16"L red "Germany" stamp on sole; 5-3/8"L x 2-1/4"H each. Weiss, Kühnert, Germany. $115 each.

Porcelain glazed right and left facing women's oxfords with in-mold pairs of roosters and an in-mold chick on the outside rear quarter; in-mold laces and buckle; WK model # 3542; impressed into back face of each heel "Germany/3542"; 6-5/8"L x 2-3/4"H. Weiss, Kühnert, Germany. $150 each.

Two sizes of porcelain glazed women's tie shoes with pairs of in-mold cats playing with a ball and pairs of in-mold mice on outside rear quarter; WK model #s 3408 (large) and 3409 (medium); Weiss, Kühnert, Germany. Left and middle: fully-glazed-inside right facing, only partly glazed inside left facing; right facing is 5-5/8"L x 2-3/16"H, orange "Germany" stamp on sole, no impressed model number visible, $150; left facing is 5-3/4"L x 2-5/16"H with "Germany 3408" impressed on inside face just above sole; $150. Right: medium left facing with "A Present from/Blackpool"; "3409" impressed on back face above sole; 4-3/4"L x 2"H; orange "Foreign" stamp suggests this dates to just after WWI; $130.

Porcelain glazed left and right facing women's side-buttoned cap toe shoes with in-mold pairs of geese and an in-mold gosling on the outside rear quarter; WK model # 3544; impressed into back face of each heel "Germany/3544"; Weiss, Kühnert, Germany. Left: 6-1/2"L x 2-3/4"H; inside glazed only part way down; $150. Right: 6-7/16"L x 2-5/8"H; inside fully glazed; $150.

Pair of matched porcelain glazed ankle shoes each with a mirror image in-mold cat; WK model # 3683; impressed into back heel face of each "3683; each bottom stamped with orange "Germany"; 2-3/4"L x 1-3/8"H each. These have been copied by a Japanese factory and have been seen in the same color combination marked "Japan". Weiss, Kühnert, Germany. $50 for the pair.

Comparison between two sizes of women's lace-up oxfords with pairs of in-mold cockatiels described in more detail in following illustrations.

Pair of porcelain glazed right and left facing strap pumps with in-mold 4-leaf clovers; inside soles not glazed; right facing bottom stamped "Germany", left facing bottom stamped with WK tiny circle stamp "Germany *"; no impressed model numbers; these are either WK models 4122 or 5481; 4-3/8"L x 2-3/8"H each. Weiss, Kühnert, Germany. $70 each.

Porcelain glazed right facing (left face is toward camera) lace-up cap toe woman's oxford with pair of in-mold cockatiels and bird in flight on outside rear quarter; glazed only part way down inside; impressed into back face of heel "Germany"; 6-3/4"L x 3"H. WK catalog pages show "3472" and "3495" as potential model numbers for this shoe. No number was visible on it. Weiss, Kühnert, Germany. $135.

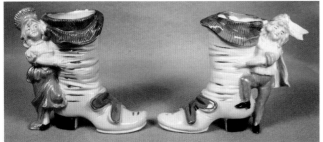

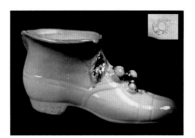

Porcelain variegated green glazed ankle shoe with in-mold bow, leaves, and berries; "7322" impressed into right heel face; orange MIG millstone mark; 3-13/16"L x 1-7/8"H. Pos. Weiss, Kühnert, Germany. $35.

Pair of porcelain glazed matched right and left facing boots with in-mold figures; she has "5492" impressed into back of her boot; no other marks on either; she is 4-3/8"L x 3-7/8"H, he is 4-5/8"L x 4"H. Pos. Weiss, Kühnert, Germany. $150 for the pair.

Porcelain boot with in-mold grapes and leaves; unmarked; 4-3/16"L x 4"H. Pos. Weiss, Kühnert, Germany. $30.

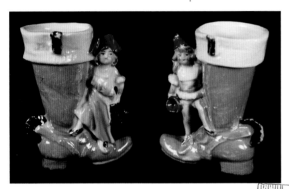

Pair of small porcelain glazed matched right and left facing boots with in-mold spurs and figures; each has impressed Germany" and "6221" on back face; she is 2-1/4"L x 3"H, he is 2-3/8"L x 3"H. Pos. Weiss, Kühnert, Germany. $80 for the pair.

Porcelain glazed left facing woman's shoe with in-mold dog on vamp and in-mold dog on rear quarter; unmarked except orange "Foreign" stamp, suggesting it was made just after WWI; 6-3/8"L x 3-1/4"H. A 4"L version marked "Germany" has been reported. A 3"L version of this copied and marked "Japan" has been seen. Pos. Weiss, Kühnert, Germany. $75.

Pair of porcelain baby bootees with in-mold figures and bugs; "Germany/3160" impressed on back face of each; Pos. Weiss, Kühnert, Germany. Left: girl, glazed; 2-3/4"L x 3-1/16"H; $45. Right: boy, cold painted; 2-7/8"L x 3-1/8"H; $35.

Medium porcelain glazed left facing boot with in-mold spur and boy with horn; "Germany" and "5049" impressed into back face; 2-7/8"L x 3-3/4"H. Pos. Weiss, Kühnert, Germany. $50.

Porcelain woman's cap toe oxford with in-mold laces; may be WK model # 3718; unmarked; 4-1/2"L x 2-1/4"H. Pos. Weiss, Kühnert, Germany. If perfect (without gold wear), $35.

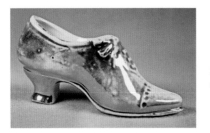

Back view of baby bootee with boy, showing location of data.

169

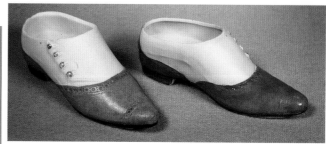

Porcelain bisque, matte glazed, and cold painted side-button women's shoes with in-mold animals; appear to have been inspired by Weiss, Kühnert shoes, but HP is poorly done. A shoe similar to these has been seen with in-mold roosters, also poorly HP; it had impressed marks "Geschutzi Depose/5146.H", and was clearly not from the known WK mold. Left: frogs; impressed into left edge of shank "Depose 5198/Germany"; 6-5/8"L x 2-3/4"H; manufacturer unknown; $25. Right: birds; impressed into left side just above heel line what may be "Germany 5146" and additional undecipherable info. 6-7/16"L x 2-13/16"H; unknown manufacturer; $25.

Pair of porcelain matte glazed right side-buttoned and left side-buttoned low-cut men's spats; unmarked; 5-1/4"L x 1-7/8"H each. A curved horizontal line is often found on these; it is not clear whether this was intentional or a consequence of the molding process. $55 each.

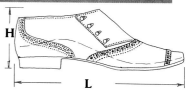

GERMAN PORCELAIN: GANGSTER SHOES

This small group of shoes is often misidentified as Royal Bayreuth. The author has never seen any of them marked in any way. They have been assumed to have been made as RB competitors by a German factory c.1900. The quality of the hand-painted finishes varies widely, affecting value. Values herein are for shoes as illustrated.

Pair of attached porcelain matte glazed side buttoned low-cut men's spats; unmarked; 5-1/4"L x 1-7/8"H. $85.

Pair of attached porcelain matte glazed lace-up men's cap toe low-cut shoes; unmarked; 5-1/8"L x 1-3/4"H. $85.

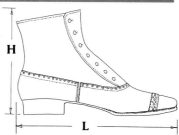

Porcelain matte glazed right side-buttoned and left side-buttoned men's spats; unmarked; 5"L x 3-1/8"H each. $75 each.

Porcelain matte glazed lace-up woman's high top shoe; unmarked; 4-1/2"L x 3-3/16"H. $85

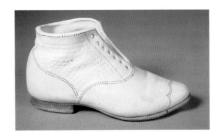

Porcelain tramp shoes, both unmarked, that may have come from the same factory as the gangster shoes. Left: bisque with vee spread open in green ware stage to accommodate separately cast child in paper hat; 4-3/4"L x 2-3/4"HOA; hand incised lines in bottom for striking matches; uncommon; $80. Right (sketch): matte glazed; 4-13/16"L x 1-5/8"H; $30.

GERMAN PORCELAIN: DGCWs

There was a German factory, yet to be identified, that glazed its shoes such that they appear to have been dipped upside down in the glaze, then uprighted for completion. The remainder of the insides and most of the bottoms are left unglazed. When cleaned, the porcelain in these unglazed parts feels and looks like chalk—thus the designation Dip Glazed Chalk Whites. As best as can be determined, the glaze itself was colored. The factory experimented with colors and textures in glazes. Several models are so often misidentified as Royal Bayreuth that the dip glazed characteristic is an easy marker for which to look.

Porcelain bisque tramp shoe with seated child, at least part of which was separately cast and inserted in the green ware stage; unmarked; 4-3/4"L x 2-13/16"HOA. $60.

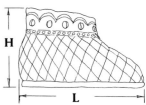

Porcelain dip glazed quilted baby bootees with ten pierced eyelets; 3-3/8"L x 2-1/16"H each; Germany. Left: cobalt glazed; 15/16"L black stamp "Germany"; $15. Right: butterscotch glazed; unmarked; $15.

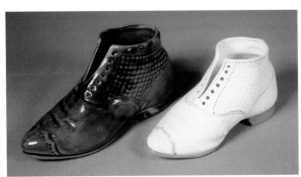

Two sizes of porcelain men's 7-eyelet ankle shoes with in-mold texture in uppers; both unmarked. This is a mold that in its various décors has been misidentified as Royal Bayreuth. Left: green gloss glazed version, a finish not known in RB shoes; barely a "left"; 5-1/2"L x 2-11/16"H; hand written on bottom, "Grace from Dad 1910", where the 1910 is written over "1903"; $15. Right: white bisque; orange sole edges and bottom; a "right"; 4-7/8"L x 2-3/8"H; $60.

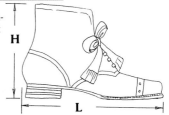

Porcelain dip glazed ankle shoes with in-mold tilted bows; Germany. Left: cobalt glazed; 3-3/4"L x 2-7/16"H; unmarked; $25. Right: butterscotch glazed; 3-13/16"L x 2-3/8"H; remains of black "Germany" stamp; $25.

Pair of porcelain green dip glazed large men's 4- eyelet cap toe oxfords; a "right" and a "left"; unmarked; Germany. Left: the "right", 6-3/16"L x 2-7/16"H; $35. Right: the "left", 6-1/8"L x 2-3/8"H; $35. Add $10 for an original fabric shoelace with metal aglets in good condition.

Porcelain dip glazed 4-eyelet cap toe ankle shoes with flared tops in various glazes; approx. 5-1/2"L x 2-7/8"H each; usual bottom stamp, a black "Germany". Germany. $30 each; add $10 for an original fabric shoelace with metal aglets in good condition.

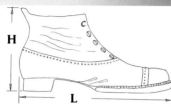

Typical bottom marks on dip glazed shoes; these are on the dark brown and milk chocolate glazed ankle shoes in previous illustration. The mark on the left is 11/16"L, and that on the right is 13/16"L.

Pair of porcelain dip glazed large men's 4-eyelet cap toe oxfords; unmarked; Germany. Left: brown glaze thinned at edges; a "right"; 6-1/4"L x 2-1/2"H; $35. Right: butterscotch glazed; a "left"; 6-1/8"L x 2-3/16"H; with original shoelace with metal aglets, $45.

Porcelain dip glazed 1 x 3 ankle shoe with in-mold texture; iridescent blue/purple glaze; unmarked; 5-7/16"L x 2-13/16"H. Germany. Uncommon form and glaze. $85.

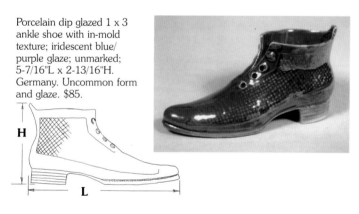

Porcelain dip glazed large men's 4-eyelet cap toe oxford; white glaze on inside goes down only about 1" from rim; ivory matte glaze outside; unmarked; Germany. With original shoelace with metal aglet and HP stitching detail, $50.

Pair of porcelain black dip glazed large men's 4-eyelet cap toe oxfords; a "right" and a "left"; 11/16"L "Germany" stamp; Germany. This model shoe was made in numerous glazes in large and small sizes, and in lefts and rights. There may be additional in-mold details not shown in the sketch, but the glaze on all in the author's possession is so heavy that it would obscure them. The soles of these oxfords have in-mold "stitching". Left: the "right" is 6-1/4"L x 2-3/8"H; $35. Right: the "left" is 6-1/16"L x 2-1/4"H; $35.

Pair of matched porcelain milk chocolate dip glazed small men's 4-eyelet cap toe oxfords; a "right" and a "left"; unmarked; 5-3/16"L x 2"H each. Germany. Shoelaces not original (plastic aglets). $70 for the pair.

Porcelain dip glazed small men's 4-eyelet cap toe oxfords in various glazes; left and right shoes stamped "Germany", the others are unmarked; all are approx. 5"L x 1-15/16"H; Germany. Left to right: (a) speckled khaki glaze; a "right"; original shoelace with metal aglet; $45. (b) milk chocolate glaze; a "right"; original shoelace is decomposed and adds no value; $35. (c) khaki drip glaze; a "left"; $35. (d) green glaze; a "right"; gold heel, sole edge, and stitching detail; original shoelace with metal aglets; $50.

Small and large porcelain dip glazed men's 4-eyelet cap toe oxfords with HP boat scenes; the small is a "right", has a souvenir bottom mark, and is 5-1/16"L x 2"H; the large is a "left", unmarked, and is 6-1/8"L x 2-5/16"H. Germany. $65 each.

Bottom mark of small man's cap toe oxford with HP boat scenes: "Kaiserhof/Hotel-Restaurant/Chicago".

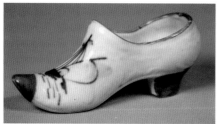

Porcelain dip glazed stack-heeled Normandy shoe with in-mold ruching; HP boat scene; unmarked; 5-1/8"L x 2-1/8"H. Germany. $65.

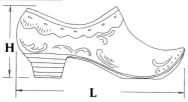

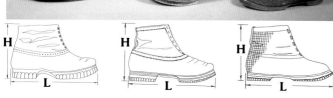

Porcelain dip glazed work boots. Left: 6-eyelet green; black stamp "Germany" on sole; 6-1/4"L x 3-3/4"H; $40. Middle: 7-eyelet brown; impressed underglaze on shank "Germany/3846"; 4-5/8"L x 3"H; may not be from same factory as others – porcelain is fine grained and hard; $30. Right: 5-eyelet cobalt wash with in-mold texture; unmarked; 3-3/4"L x 2-5/16"H; $15.

GERMAN PORCELAIN: PGGPs

Unlike the dip glazed shoes whose insides are generally glazed to a regular line circumnavigating the inside of the shoe, there is another group of shoes whose partially glazed insides form ragged edges, and are of the conventional clear glaze. In addition, the porcelain from which these shoes are made is often granular, or gritty to the feel. Because the factory that manufactured them has yet to be identified, these shoes have been designated the Part Glazed Granular (or Gritty, if you like) Porcelains. Souvenir china collectors will recognize the color palette employed in the hand-painted views on forms other than shoes as being from this factory. All of these were made in Germany, c.1900 (i.e., from the late 1800s, possibly, to the early 1900s).

Porcelain souvenir shoes with uncommon décor consisting of pale butter yellow graduated to orange with HP white dots over which are black arrow heads; 13/32"OD small black "MIG*" millstone mark is one of the two common marks found on these shoes; other two unmarked; Germany. Left: fan rim ankle shoe with view of "New Post Office, Chicago"; 6-3/4"L x 3-3/4"H; $65. Middle: hooked vamp slipper with view of "Winne Kennie Castle, Haverhill, Mass."; 5-3/4"L x 2-7/8"H; $60. Right: C-scrolls and lattice slipper with view of "Pergola on the Paseo, Kansas City, Mo."; 5-5/8"L x 2-11/16"H; $60.

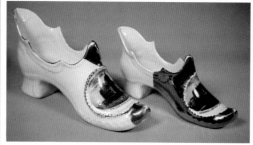

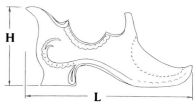

Porcelain hooked vamp slippers; unmarked; Germany. Left: white with view of "New Court House, Wilkes-Barre, Pa."; 6-7/8"L x 3-5/16"H; $35. Right: gold face with view of "Memorial Library, Adams, Mass."; 5-13/16"L x 2-13/16"H; collectible view; $45.

Porcelain C-scrolls and lattice slippers with in-mold bow; Germany. 9/16"OD MIG black millstone mark is one of two common marks found on these shoes. Left: gold glazed with view of "Springbank, London, Canada"; unmarked; 6-3/4"L x 3-3/8"H; $40. Middle: yellow luster glazed with view of "Wissahickon Creek at P. & R. RY. Bridge/Fairmount Park, Philadelphia, Pa."; MIG millstone mark; 5-5/8"L x 2-13/16"H; $35. Right: gold face with view of "Boardwalk and Sanatorium, Asbury Park, N.J."; MIG millstone mark; 5-1/2"L x 2-13/16"H; $35.

Bottom view of green luster diamond lattice and beaded heel slipper showing gritty porcelain. Note tiny nodules over entire sole.

Porcelain scalloped rim slipper with view of "Court House, Spokane, Washington"; 13/32"OD MIG* millstone; 5-13/16"L x 3-1/8"H. Germany. Uncommon form. $50.

Porcelain gold face fish scale (in-mold on sides of vamp) slipper with vamp transfer; 9/16"OD MIG millstone mark on heel; 6-15/16"L x 3-9/16"H. Germany. $35.

Three sizes of porcelain daisy and beaded vamp slippers; Germany. Left: white glazed, view of "City Hall, Fall River, Mass."; 13/32"OD MIG* millstone mark; 6-11/16"L x 3-9/16"H; $35. Middle: pink glazed, view of "Slater Memorial, Norwich, Conn."; 13/32"OD MIG* millstone mark; 5-5/8"L x 2-15/16"H; $35. Right: pastel green luster glazed, vamp transfer; 9/16"OD MIG millstone mark; 4-5/8"L x 2-1/2"H; $30.

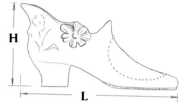

Porcelain fish scale (in-mold on sides of vamp) slippers; Germany. Left: Yellow luster with HP vamp leaf; 9/16"OD MIG millstone mark on sole; 6-7/8"L x 3-5/8"H; $55. Middle: white with view of "Keokuk & Hamilton Water Power, Keokuk/Iowa"; 13/32"OD MIG* millstone mark; 5-13/16"L x 3"H; $45. Right: gray luster with view of "Old Mill, Newport Beach"; 13/32"OD MIG* millstone mark; 5-11/16"L x 3"H; $35.

Bottom views of pink and green luster daisy and beaded vamp slippers showing the comparative sizes of the two common millstone marks found on PGGP shoes.

Porcelain reticulated diamond lattice and beaded heel slipper; vamp transfer; 9/16"OD MIG millstone mark on sole; 7"L x 3-5/8"H. Germany. Piercing uncommon. $55.

Three sizes of porcelain diamond lattice and beaded heel slippers; Germany. left to right: (a) white glazed with HP details, "A Present/ from/Ballinamore"; unusual orange MIG stamp; 6-3/4"L x 3-1/2"H; $20. (b) green luster with vamp transfer; 9/16"OD MIG millstone mark; 5-15/16"L x 3-1/8"H; $35. (c) pastel yellow matte with HP details and view of "Weymouth/Pavilion and Pier"; unmarked; 5-7/8"L x 3"H; uncommon décor; $50. (d) pink glazed, view of "New County Court House, Portland, Me."; 13/32"OD MIG* millstone mark; 5-1/16"L x 2-3/4"H; $30.

Three sizes of porcelain daisy and beaded vamp boots; Germany. Left to right: (a) gold glazed, view of "??ce Viger, C.P.R. Hotel and Station, Montreal"; 13/32"OD MIG* millstone stamp; 5"L x 4-3/4"H; $35. (b) pink glazed, view of "Excursion Steamer, Christopher Columbus" (used to run between Chicago and Milwaukee); 13/32"OD MIG* millstone; 4-3/16"L x 4"H; $50. (c) pastel green luster, view of "?.C.R.R. Depot, Skowhegan, Me."; 13/32"OD MIG* millstone; 3-5/8"L x 3-7/16"H; $45. (d) white glazed, vamp transfer; 9/16"OD MIG millstone; 3-1/2"L x 3-1/4"H; $30.

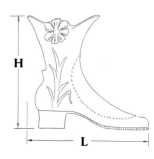

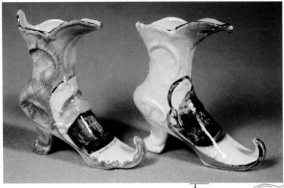

Porcelain curled toe high top rococo boots; Germany. Left: mottled pink glazed, view of "Buchtel College, Arkon (sic), O."; unmarked; 3-13/16"L x 3-3/4"H; $45. Right: white glazed, view of "The Common, Greenfield, Mass."; personalized Germany mark; 3-7/8"L x 3-15/16"H; $45.

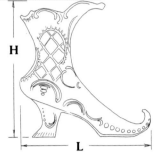

Bottom view of mark on white curled toe rococo boot (above). Note gritty porcelain.

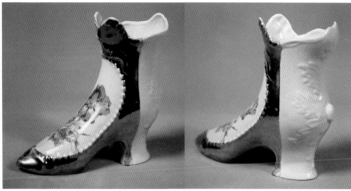

Porcelain boot with gold face and in-mold beaded framed vamp transfer; 9/16"OD MIG millstone; 4-5/8"L x 4-1/4"H. Germany. $35.

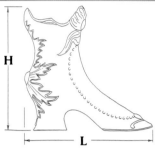

Porcelain lattice top, beaded rim boots with in-mold bow; Germany. Left: reticulated, view of "Pergola on the Paseo, Kansas City, Mo."; 13/32"OD MIG* millstone; 4-7/8"L x 5-1/8"H; if perfect (back rim missing), $75. Middle: gold glazed, view of "Post Office, Sherbrooke, P.Q."; 13/32"OD MIG* millstone; 4-7/8"L x 5-1/16"H; $45. Right: pink glazed, vamp transfer; 13/32"OD MIG* millstone; 4"L x 4-1/8"H; $40.

Porcelain fan rim boots; Germany. Two variations of the rim front are shown, one extended, as in the larger left boot, and without the extension, as in the two smaller boots. Left: gold face, view of "Portals of the Past, Golden Gate Park/San Francisco, Ca."; 13/32"OD MIG* millstone; 4-1/8"L x 3-11/16"H; $35. Middle: pastel green glazed, vamp transfer; 9/16"OD MIG millstone; 3-1/4"L x 3-3/16"H; $35. Right: gold face, view of "Souvenir Kingsbury, P.Q."; 9/16"OD MIG millstone; 3-3/8"L x 3-1/4"H; $30.

Porcelain slippers; Germany. Left: applied beading framing vamp transfer and "A present from Southend-on-Sea"; 9/16"OD red MIG millstone; 5-5/16"L x 3-1/16"H; $30. Right: gold glazed, view of "Mayflower Grove from Easton Lake, Bryantville, Mass."; red personalized MIG mark; 5-1/4"L x 2-7/8"H; $45.

Bottom marks on soles of two slippers in previous illustration.

Porcelain gold glazed man's lace-up field boot; a "left"; unmarked; very gritty porcelain; "View from Foxhill, Rockville, Conn."; 5-1/16"L x 4-5/8"H. Germany. Uncommon form and scene. $90.

Porcelain heart and leaf spray boots; both unmarked; Germany. Left: cherub transfer; 3-15/16"L x 4-1/8"H; $25. Right: floral transfer; 2-3/4"L x 2-3/4"H; $20.

Porcelain boots and slipper with in-mold grapes and leaves; Germany. Left: pink with in-mold bird and bell flowers on sides; unmarked; 5"L x 4-3/4"H; $30. Middle: white glazed with "A present from Ireland"; 9/16"OD MIG millstone mark; 4-15/16"L x 4-3/4"H; $25. Right: orange glazed with "A present from Dublin"; 3/4"L oval stamp on bottom within which is "Thuringia"; 5-1/2"L x 3-1/8"H; $25.

Porcelain boots; Germany. Left: gold face, in-mold beaded vamp frame with floral transfer; unmarked; 4"L x 4-1/16"H; $20. Middle: gold face with hooked front rim; crest of "Montreal"; unmarked; 3-15/16"L x 3-15/16"H; $20. Right: view of "Summit House, Mt. Tom, Mass."; personalized bottom mark (shown in next illustration); 4-1/8"L x 4-3/16"H; $35.

Bottom view of Mt. Tom boot showing two marks. The black rectangular mark is the personalized mark. The gold mark reads, "Hand Painted/The Jonroth/Studios/Germany".

GERMAN PORCELAIN: ELFINWARE

This category takes its name from a German bottom stamp occasionally found on a piece that includes the word "Elfinware". The most valuable pieces are those that have been covered with liquid slip extruded through a sieve that has been applied to the surface and painted green to resemble moss. Typical floral appliqués are a central rose flanked by lilacs, moss bordered by phlox, and a rim edged in tiny forget-me-nots. On some pieces, a very tiny bud or two can be found within the moss. Some shoes were produced without the applied moss. Where they were found, they have been shown with their moss encrusted counterparts so that collectors can see what is under the moss. The moss covered shoes are valued at twice or more than their mossless versions.

Porcelain pumps with pointed toes in three sizes; Germany. Left to right: (a) large with moss and floral appliqués; remains of red illegible bottom stamp; 3-11/16"LOA x 2-9/16"HOA; uncommon size; $110. (b) medium with moss and floral appliqués; unmarked; 3-1/16"LOA x 2-3/16"HOA; $85. (c) small with moss and floral appliqués; red millstone mark; 2-1/2"LOA x 1-13/16"HOA; $70. (d) pink tinted with floral appliqués and floral transfers; red "Germany" stamp; 2-5/16"L x 1-3/4"H; $30.

Porcelain high vamp slippers; Germany. Left: attached pair with moss and floral appliqués; red "Germany" in caps on sole; 2-3/4"LOA x 1-7/16"HOA; $70. Middle: pearl luster glazed attached pair with rim and vamp appliqués; red "Germany" on sole; 2-3/8"L x 1-9/16"HOA; $45. Right: single with moss and floral appliqués; illegible red mark; 2-3/8"LOA x 1-3/8"HOA; $40.

Bottom view of left and middle shoes in previous illustration showing the uncommon "Germany" in caps bottom mark and the common mark on these shoes, found in both red and black.

Porcelain attached pairs of high vamp slippers; all approx. 2-1/8"L x 1-1/4"H; all stamped "Germany". Left to right: (a) pearl luster with spray of forget-me-nots; $35. (b) blue sponge on white with spray of forget-me-nots; $35. (c) pink tinted with floral appliqué and transfers; $30. (d) pink tinted with poppy and leaves appliqué; $30.

Porcelain work boots; moss covered is 3-1/8"LOA x 2-1/16"HOA, the other three are 2-7/8"L x 1-15/16"L; Germany. Left to right: (a) moss and floral appliqués; $70. (b) pearl luster with spray of forget-me-nots; $30. (c) pink tinted with appliqués and transfers; $25. (d) blue tinted with appliqués and transfers; $25.

Three porcelain moss covered shoes with floral appliqués; Germany. Left: man's medium ankle shoe; bottom mark found on some Elfinware items consists of "GERMANY" below which are three dots; 4-5/8"LOA x 2-1/4"HOA; $85. Middle: woman's ankle shoe; unmarked; 4"L x 1-3/4"H; $75. Right: man's small ankle shoe; smudged blue mark on heel that could be "S."; 3-3/8" LOA x 1-9/16" HOA; $70.

Porcelain medium baby bootee with moss and floral appliqués; millstone mark; 3-1/2"LOA x 2-1/16"HOA. Germany. $90.

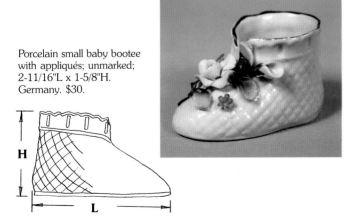

Porcelain small baby bootee with appliqués; unmarked; 2-11/16"L x 1-5/8"H. Germany. $30.

Porcelain large Dutch shoe with moss and floral appliqués; unmarked; 4-3/4"L x 2-1/8"H. Germany. $75.

Porcelain clogs; Germany. Left to right: (a) large with moss and floral appliqués; unmarked; 5-1/4"LOA x 2-1/8"HOA; $90. (b) small clog with moss and floral appliqués; 7/16"OD black circle MIG mark; 3-3/4"LOA x 1-5/8"HOA; $70. (c) small clog with floral appliqués; 3/8"L black "Germany"; 3-1/2"L x 1-7/16"H; $35. (d) small textured with spray of forget-me-nots; 7/16"L black "Germany"; 3-5/8"L x 1-1/2"H; $40.

Porcelain low heeled strap shoes; Germany. Left: moss and floral appliqués; red stamped in caps on bottom "ELFINWARE/GERMANY"; 3-7/16"LOA x 1-1/4"HOA; $70. Right: tinted with poppy and leaves appliqué; unmarked; 3"L x 1-1/16"H; $25.

Bottom mark of moss covered low-heeled strap shoe that gives these items their moniker.

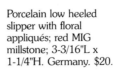

Porcelain low heeled strap shoe with floral appliqués and transfers; stamp on sole "ELFINWARE/GERMANY"; 2-15/16"L x 1-1/16"H. Germany. $30.

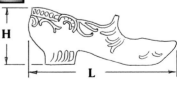

Porcelain low heeled slipper with floral appliqués; red MIG millstone; 3-3/16"L x 1-1/4"H. Germany. $20.

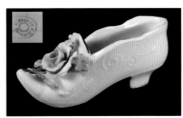

Porcelain crushed heel slippers; Germany. Left: moss and floral appliqués; unmarked; 4"LOA x 1-1/2"HOA, $70. Right: vamp and rim appliqués, and floral transfers; red "Germany" stamp and what is apparently an importer's mark (see bottom view); 3-11/16"L x 1-7/16"H; $40.

Bottom marks on crushed heels slipper without moss consisting of a smudged "Germany" stamp and "SICO/??USE FOR NOVELTIES".

Porcelain flared high top women's shoes; Germany. Left: white glazed with vamp appliqué; 3/8"L black "Germany"; 2-1/4"L x 2"H; $15. Middle: gray luster glazed with applied spray of lilies of the valley; unmarked; 4-9/16"L x 3"H; $45. Right: (same mold as middle shoe) two tone glazed with rim and sole appliqués; unmarked; 4-1/2"L x 3"H; $35.

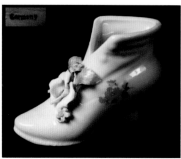

Pink tinted porcelain high top woman's shoe with appliqués and transfers; "Germany" stamp; 2-3/4"L x 1-7/8"H. Germany. $25.

Two porcelain women's oxfords from same mold; each has two pairs of open eyelets at top of vamp; Germany. Left: green luster with applied bow and ribbon with forget-me-nots; 3/4"L "GERMANY" mark; 3-13/16"L x 1-5/8"H; $35. Right: gray lavender luster with yellow luster inside; appliqués; 1/2"L "Germany" mark; 3-7/8"L x 1-5/8"H; $45.

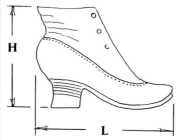

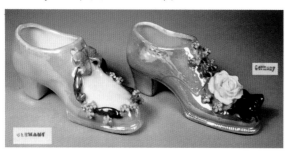

Porcelain pearl luster double tongue woman's shoe with appliqué; 3/4"L red "GERMANY" mark; a "left"; 3-13/16"L x 1-5/8"H. Germany. $40.

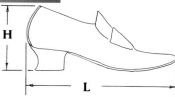

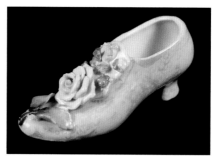

Porcelain pearl luster double tongue woman's shoe with appliqué 1/2"L red "Germany" mark; a "left"; 4"L x 1-11/16"H. Germany. $40.

Blue tinted porcelain small double tongue woman's shoe; appliqués and transfers; 1/2"L red "Germany" mark; a "left"; 3"L x 1-3/8"H. Germany. $25.

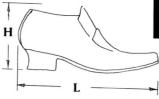

Porcelain gray luster woman's shoe with appliqués including strips of bocage; "Foreign" stamp, suggesting it was made immediately after WWI; 3-3/16"L x 1-9/16"H. Germany. $45.

Blue tinted porcelain high top shoe with appliqués and transfers; MIG millstone; 2-11/16"L x 1-13/16"H. Germany. $25.

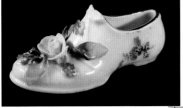

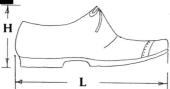

Porcelain low cut shoe with in-mold tie; appliqués and transfers; a "left"; unmarked; 2-15/16"L x 1-1/8"H. Germany. $25.

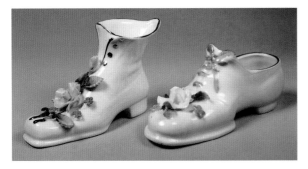

White glazed porcelain shoes; Germany. Left: square toe high top work boot with applied spray of carnations and forget-me-nots; 3/8"L black "Germany" mark; 4-7/16"L x 2-3/4"H; $45. Right: cap toe man's oxford with in-mold shoelace and appliqués; unmarked; a "right"; 4-7/16"L x 2-3/4"H; $40.

Thin porcelain baby shoe airbrushed from pastel pink to pastel yellow with HP gold florals; "Made in Austria" millstone mark; 4"L x 2"H. B. F. Hunt, Austria. Uncommon décor. $70.

Thin porcelain baby shoes, two with HP florals; 4"L x 2"H each; B. F. Hunt, Austria. Left: blue with gold bow; unmarked; $60. Middle: white; unmarked; $60. Right: solid blue; "Made in Austria" millstone mark; $30.

Thin porcelain baby shoe; HP and dated; 4"L x 2"H. B. F. Hunt, Austria. c.1903. Uncommon décor. $70.

AUSTRIAN PORCELAIN

Included in this section is a high quality baby shoe easy for the collector to identify because its characteristic pair of open eyelets at the bottom of the right side is unusually close together. Souvenir versions of this shoe can be found with the mark of Benjamin F. Hunt and Sons. They were an American firm that bought into the Carl Speck porcelain factory in Elbogen, Bohemia (now Loket, Czechia) in 1893. They sold the factory in 1902 to Adolf Persch who operated it until it closed in 1937. The "Washington Exposition 1891" souvenir shoe predates the B.F. Hunt ownership and is assumed to have been made by Speck. Some of the hand-decorated baby shoes may also predate Hunt. For convenience, however, baby shoes made from this mold are referred to as the B. F. Hunt baby shoes.

Thin porcelain baby shoe; HP florals; unmarked; 4"L x 2"H. B. F. Hunt, Austria. $60.

Porcelain baby shoe with HP gold details; toe marked "Rochester, N. Y./ 1900" and with interlocking rings containing "F", ""L", and "T" believed to stand for "Friendship, Love, and Truth" used by the Fraternal Order of Odd Fellows; not same mold as B. F. Hunt baby shoes; 4"L x 2"H. Austria. c.1900. $40.

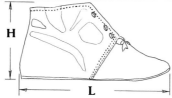

Thin porcelain baby shoes; both 4"L x 2"H; both collectible views; B.F. Hunt, Austria. Left: view of "Western Washington/ Exposition-1891"; $85. Right: view of "Memorial Building/ Westerly" (Rhode Island); $85.

Porcelain curled toe slipper with in-mold tassel in back and in-mold vamp detail; factory logo on sole; 4-5/8"L x 2-3/8"H. Bawo & Dotter, Bohemia. c.1891-c.1914. $65.

Two sizes of porcelain glazed shoes with in-mold 4-leaf clovers held by in-mold gnomes; both with impressed "Austria" on back face of shoe; both with unglazed insides; Austria. Left: large; "965" impressed on left thigh; 3-13/16"L x 2-3/4"H; $50. Right: small; "2067" impressed on left thigh; 3"L x 2-3/16"H; $40.

Back view of small gnome holding shoe showing location of country of origin and model number.

Porcelain double side 6-buttoned shoe with in-mold "love" birds; dip glazed; impressed on right side with "Austria" and "6262"; 3-3/4"L x 1-1/8"H. This and the two following shoes have slightly different mold characteristics but appear to have come from the same factory. Austria. $55.

Porcelain glazed double side-buttoned shoes with in-mold "love" birds; Austria. Left: 6-button tan; impressed "28" on heel face; 3-3/4"L x 2-1/4"H; $55. Right: 7-button blue; impressed "555" on heel face; partially glazed inside; 3-9/16"L x 2-3/16"H; $55.

AUSTRIAN PORCELAIN
including Schmidt Victoria

The Charles Schmidt Porcelain Factory, also known as the Victoria Porcelain Factory, made a wide range of shoes. There is no consistent design or décor to their shoes. Further, they often are unmarked. It has required finding a marked version to assemble the examples of their shoes shown in this section.

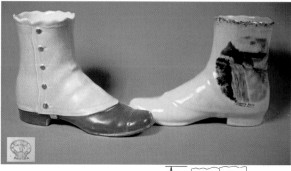

Porcelain rickrack rimmed spat with in-mold side buttons; 5-3/16"L x 3-3/4"H each; Schmidt Victoria, Austria; c.1900. Left: ivory and camel matte glazed; blue Victoria/Carlsbad/Austria mark on sole; $50. Right: white glazed; view of "Niagara Falls/ Prospect Point"; unmarked; common scene; $25.

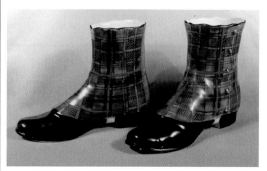

Matched pair of porcelain rickrack rimmed spats, in-mold left and right side-buttoned; HP black transfer plaid spat pattern; both with blue Victoria/Carlsbad/Austria mark; 5-1/8"L x 3-13/16"H each. Schmidt Victoria, Austria. c.1900. Uncommon décor. $135 for the pair.

Porcelain matte black and plaid woman's high top; HP black transfer plaid pattern; double 3-button vamp and scalloped ruching obscured by black glaze; unmarked; 4-7/8"L x 4-13/16"H. Prob. Schmidt Victoria, Austria. c.1900. Uncommon form and décor. $60.

Porcelain men's 3-eyelet low cut shoes; 3-5/8"L x 1-7/16"H each; Schmidt Victoria, Austria; early 1900s. Left: airbrushed ground with HP florals; unmarked; $40. Right: crest of "Westmoreland"; underglaze green "Gemma"; $25.

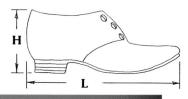

Porcelain 5-eyelet men's small high tops; 3-5/8"L x 2-1/2"H each; Schmidt Victoria, Austria; early 1900s. Left: black gloss and camel matte glazed; unmarked; often misidentified as Royal Bayreuth; $35 (add $10 for an original shoelace with metal aglets). Right: white glazed, crest of "City of London"; underglaze Gemma mark on shank; uncommon crested china form; $45.

Porcelain 6-eyelet man's large high top straight; personalized factory logo on shank "A Present from Southport/ Made in Bohemia"; HP stitching; 5"L x 3-5/8"H. Schmidt Victoria, Austria. Late 1800s. $50 (add $10 for an original shoelace with metal aglets).

Porcelain gloss and matte glazed black 6-eyelet man's large high top straight; blue Victoria/ Carlsbad/Austria mark; 4-7/8"L x 3-1/2"H.Schmidt Victoria, Austria. c.1900. $50.

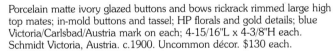

Porcelain matte ivory glazed buttons and bows rickrack rimmed large high top mates; in-mold buttons and tassel; HP florals and gold details; blue Victoria/Carlsbad/Austria mark on each; 4-15/16"L x 4-3/8"H each. Schmidt Victoria, Austria. c.1900. Uncommon décor. $130 each.

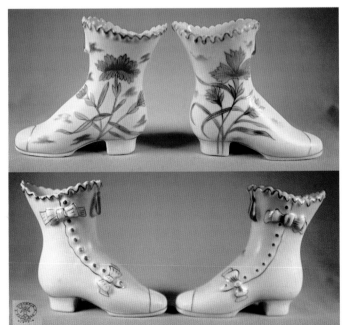

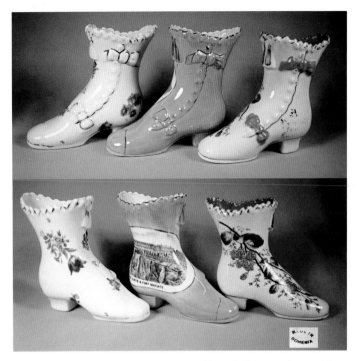

Porcelain buttons and bows rickrack rimmed large high tops with in-mold buttons and tassels; Schmidt Victoria, Austria; c.1900. Left: white glazed with transfers; unmarked; 4-3/4"L x 4-3/8"H; $40. Middle: pink glazed, view of "The Cliffs & Fort Margate"; unmarked; uncommon souvenir china form; 4-7/8"L x 4-1/2"H; $45. Right: white glazed with blue bows; hand tinted dark brown transfer; "Made in Bohemia" stamp on sole; 4-15/16"L x 4-3/8"H; $50.

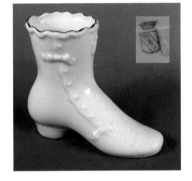

Porcelain buttons and bows rickrack rimmed small high top with in-mold buttons and tassel; Gemma stamp on sole; 3-9/16"L x 3"H. Schmidt Victoria, Austria. Early 1900s. $35.

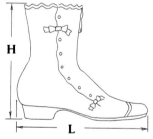

Another view of previous shoe showing crest of "Cheltenham" on left side.

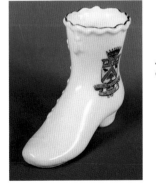

Porcelain buttons and bows rickrack rimmed small high top with in-mold buttons and tassel; hand tinted sepia transfer of pansies; Victoria/ Carlsbad/Austria blue mark; 3-7/16"L x 2-15/16"H. Schmidt Victoria, Austria. c.1900. $45.

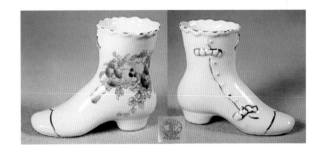

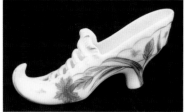

Porcelain matte glazed pierced vamp HP slipper with in-mold tassel at back; upturned toe; unmarked, but this shape has been seen marked "Carlsbad China/Austria"; 6-1/4"L x 2-7/8"H. Prob. Schmidt Victoria, Austria. c.1900. $100.

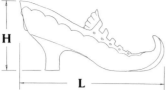

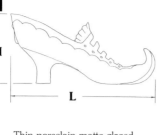

Thin porcelain matte glazed pierced vamp HP slipper with in-mold tassel in back; burnished gold trim; unmarked; 5-7/8"L x 3"H. Pos. Schmidt Victoria, Austria. c.1900. $95.

Porcelain pierced vamp slipper with in-mold tassel at back; burnished gold ground with hand tooled diamond pattern filled with graduated turquoise enamel jewels; in-mold pattern outlined with hand applied gold micro beads; unmarked; 4-13/16"L x 2-3/8"H. Appears to be from same mold as following white slipper with orange trim. Pos. Schmidt Victoria, Austria. c.1900. Uncommon. $450.

Thin porcelain white glazed slipper with speckled orange trim; in-mold vamp pattern often found pierced; un-marked; 4-3/4"L x 2-3/8"H. Pos. Schmidt Victoria, Austria. c.1900. $45.

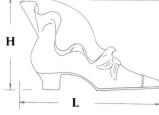

Pair of matched porcelain glazed cap-toe slippers with asymmetrical flounced tops; gold stamped trim and floral transfers; unmarked; pos. Schmidt Victoria, Austria; c.1900; $75 for the pair. On left: 5-1/16"L x 3-1/4"H; on right: 4-13/16"L x 3-3/8"H.

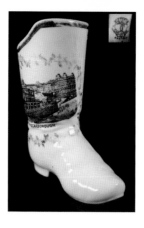

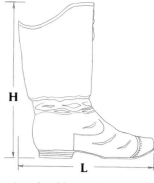

Porcelain glazed boot with in-mold tassel at front; view of "The Spa Scarborough"; blue Victoria/Carlsbad/Austria mark underglaze on shank; 4-13/16"L x 5-3/8"H. Schmidt Victoria, Austria. c.1900. Uncommon form. $45.

Porcelain glazed slipper with looped back rococo toe and heel loop; crest of "Guernsey"; unmarked; 6-7/16"L x 3-5/8"H. Schmidt Victoria, Austria. Uncommon form, and one of the largest of crested china shoes. $75. Not shown: same shoe but with view of "Palace of Electricity/St. Louis Exposition 1904"; blue Victoria/Carlsbad/Austria mark; Schmidt Victoria, Austria; $250.

Porcelain narrow ruffle rimmed ankle slippers; both with Gemma marks; Schmidt Victoria, Austria; early 1900s. Left: turned up toe; view of "French Opera House"; 3-1/4"L x 1-7/8"H; $35. Right: tapered toe; crest of "Robin Hood's Bay"; 3-3/8"L x 2"H; $15.

Porcelain narrow ruffle rimmed ankle slippers with tapered toes; all approx. 3-3/8"L x 2"H; Schmidt Victoria, Austria. Left: view of "Education Building/St. Louis Exposition 1904"; blue Victoria/Carlsbad/Austria mark; $90. Middle: HP ground, view of Castle of the McLellans, Kirkcudbright"; green Gemma mark; $20. Right: view of "Palace of Liberal Arts/St. Louis Exposition 1904"; green stamp "AUSTRIA"; $90.

Porcelain spiked heel, hooked vamp small slippers; all 3-3/16"L x 2-5/16"H; Schmidt Victoria, Austria. Left: crest of "Great Yarmouth"; Gemma/Czecho-Slovakia mark (part missing); $15. Middle: HP transfer, "Lucky/White Heather/From Colwyn Bay"; Gemma/Czecho-Slovakia mark; $25. Right: floral decals; crown logo/Victoria/Czechoslovakia/HU mark (c.1918-1939) underglaze on shank; $12.

Porcelain glazed spiked heel, hooked vamp large slipper with crest of "Brighton"; unmarked, but has been seen with factory logo; 5-15/16"L x 4-1/16"H. Schmidt Victoria, Austria. c.1900. One of the largest of crested china shoes. $45.

Porcelain spike heeled hooked vamp large slipper; color transfer of rooster scene on airbrushed ground; unmarked; 5-13/16"L x 3-15/16"H. Often misidentified as Royal Bayreuth. Schmidt Victoria, Austria. c.1900. $75.

Thin porcelain low heeled, hooked vamp strap slipper with view of "Palace of Manufactures/St. Louis Exposition 1904"; blue Victoria/Carlsbad/Austria mark; 6-1/2"L x 3"H. Schmidt Victoria, Austria. $150. Not shown: same shoe with black transfer view of "Glasgow International Exhibition 1901/Kelvingrove Park, Glasgow."(Scotland); $150.

Porcelain glazed clog with crest of "City of London"; Gemma mark underglaze on shank; 3-7/16"L x 1-3/8"H. Schmidt Victoria, Austria. Early 1900s. Uncommon décor for crested china shoe. $40.

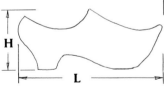

Porcelain 3-eyelet ankle shoe; HP transfer of ribbons and wreath garland; Empire factory trade name; 3-1/4"L x 1-5/8"H. Schmidt Victoria, Austria. c.1900. $25.

Porcelain 3-eyelet ankle shoe with crest of "Manchester"; unmarked; 3-3/8"L x 1-5/8"H. Pos. Schmidt Victoria, Austria. c.1900. $10.

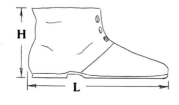

Porcelain 3 x 3 cap toe Victor shoes with looped back strap; both "lefts"; Gemma/Czecho-Slovakia mark on each; Schmidt Victoria, Austria, early 1900s. Left: crest of "Clent"; 5-3/8"L x 3-3/8"H inc. strap; $20. Right: HP transfer of "Lucky/White Heather/From Torquay"; 5-1/4"L x 3-1/4"H; $25.

Porcelain Lancashire clog with in-mold buckle and crest of "Great Yarmouth"; factory logo; 5"L x 3"H. Schmidt Victoria, Austria. $30.

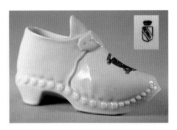

AUSTRIAN AND CZECHOSLOVAKIAN CERAMICS

Porcelain woman's high top shoe with in-mold lace up front; airbrushed shades of yellow; floral transfers; HP gold details; stamped "Austria" on sole; 7-1/16"L x 4-3/4"H. Austria. Early 1900s. $85.

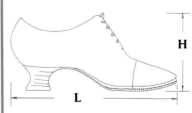

Ceramic woman's cap toe oxford with in-mold lace up front; airbrushed ground; floral transfers; HP gold details; bottom stamp "KONIGIN/crown logo/LUISE"; 7-1/8"L x 3-1/4"H. Mark has similarities, but is not a match, to marks known to have been used by H. Wehinger & Co., Horn (1905-1945), Bohemia (now Hory, Czechia), and to Jaeger & Co. (1898-present), Marktredwitz, Bavaria, Germany, the latter company being in the wrong country for this series of shoes. Austria. Early 1900s. $50.

Porcelain stacked heel woman's oxford with in-mold lace up front and branch of fruit; airbrushed color; HP gold details; "Austria" stamped on sole; 7"L x 3-1/8"H. Austria. Early 1900s. Uncommon. $90.

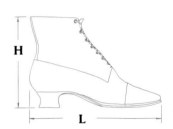

Ceramic pearl luster woman's cap toe oxford with in-mold lace up front; stamped "Made in/Czecho-/Slovakia"; 6-1/4"L x 2-11/16"H. Czechoslovakia. Post WWI. $25.

Ceramic pearl luster man's low cut shoe; stamped "Made in / Czecho-/Slovakia"; 5-1/4"L x 2-1/8"H. Czechoslovakia. Post WWI. $25.

Porcelain matte glazed man's low cut shoe; unmarked; 5-1/4"L x 2-1/8"H. Austria, prob. early 1900s. $45.

Ceramic heeled clogs. Left: airbrushed ground with color transfer; in-mold C-scrolls; unmarked; 7"L x 2-7/8"H; a plate decorated in similar manner has been found with factory mark of Franz Anton Mehlem, Germany, which may only mean that two companies were using transfers from the same supplier; prob. Austria, early 1900s; $40. Middle: yellow luster glazed; stamped "Trade Mark/crown logo/Coronet/Czechoslovakia Registered", an importer's mark used by Borgfeldt Co., N.Y., which imported pottery from several factories; 6-5/16"L x 2-1/2"H; Czechoslovakia, post WWI; $20. Right: airbrushed ground with color transfer; same mold as yellow clog in middle; unmarked, but this shoe with this décor often found stamped "Austria"; 6-5/16"L x 2-1/2"H; Austria; early 1900s; $40.

Ceramic shoes with airbrushed grounds and floral transfers; both unmarked; prob. Austria, early 1900s. Left: clog with in-mold C-scrolls; undecipherable incised numbers; 6-1/2"L x 2-9/16"H; $40. Right (sketch): slipper with in-mold lace rim and low sock; hand incised "12089" on bottom; hand written on bottom "From Patton to Grace, Dec. 25, 09"; 6-3/8"L x 2-3/8"H; uncommon form; $70.

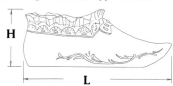

ASIAN CERAMICS
including Nippon Porcelain

The only authentic Nippon shoes seen by this author are in the shape of Dutch shoes. All are expertly hand-painted and carry the M in a green wreath logo and "Nippon" used by the Morimura Brothers factory, Nippon Toki Kaisha Ltd., in Noritake, Japan. On the typical shoe, the left side has the more detailed hand painting, although the motif is carried through to the right side. Thus, most are intended to be displayed with the left side out, as cabinet pieces. Numerous patterns can be found.

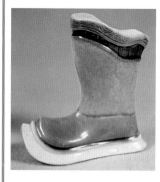

Stoneware warrior's boot; unmarked; 3-7/8"L x 4"H. China. Pos. 1800s. $125.

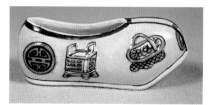

Porcelain Chinese slipper with embossed symbols, HP; unmarked; 3-15/16"L x 1-1/2"H. China, prob. first half of 1900s. $20.

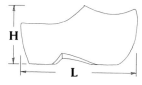

Porcelain Dutch shoes, or sabots, each HP and marked with the green M in a wreath *Nippon* mark found on these shoes; Morimura, Japan, c.1911-1921. Left (sketch): large size, cut down rim; border of foliage vines outlined in raised gold paste; 4-3/16"L x 2-1/16"H; $125. Middle (sketch): large size, cut down rim; pink blossom scenic; narrow brown rim edged with applied raised micro beads; 4-1/8"L x 2"H; $125. Right: small size, sloped rim; raised gold vine with florals; 3-7/16"L x 1-3/4"H; $70.

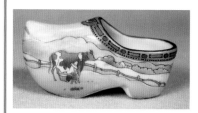

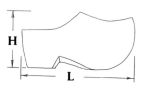

Porcelain small sabot with cut down rim; HP scene with farmer milking cow; raised micro beads and pattern outlining rim border; green M in wreath factory logo; 3-7/16"L x 1-11/16"H. Morimura, Japan. c.1911-1921. $200.

Porcelain matte glazed small sabots; HP scenics with palm trees; green M in wreath factory logo; Morimura, Japan; c.1911-1921. Left: cut down rim with narrow brown band edged with applied micro beads; moriage foliage; 3-7/16"L x 1-11/16"H; $150. Right (sketch): sloped rim; 3-7/16"L x 1-13/16"H; $100.

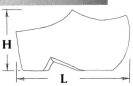

Porcelain HP semi gloss glazed small sabots; green M in wreath factory logo; Morimura, Japan; c.1911-1921. Left: sloped rim with poppies motif; 3-1/2"L x 1-3/4"H; $85. Right: cut down rim with hydrangea motif; 3-7/16"L x 1-11/16"H; $85.

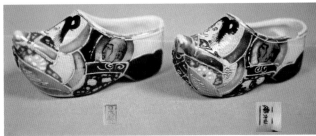

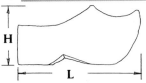

Porcelain Satsuma sabots with HP Samaria/geisha motif; 3"L x 1-3/8"H each. Note differences in painting of the two. Japan, prob. first half of 1900s. $40 each.

Back view of Satsuma sabot showing the cross within a circle symbolic of the Province or family of Satsuma (Province is now State of Kagoshima-ken, Japan).

Pottery Satsuma 5-eyelet woman's oxford with HP décor; red and gold factory logo; 4-13/16"L x 2-9/16"H. Asymmetrically flounced-top slippers with in-mold bows across the vamps, made c.1900, with décor similar to this shoe have been reported to have been reproduced with the same décor and bottom marks in the 1980s using the old molds. It is not known whether this shoe, also, was reproduced. Satsuma, Japan. $50.

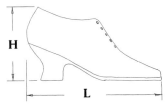

Bottom view of Satsuma woman's oxford. The underglaze bottom logo translates to "crafted by Gyoku-shu/made in Satsuma/Empire of Japan".

THE GAINSBOROUGH COLLECTION

Figural shoes often have been designed from their real life counterparts. The shoes in this section provide context because they are authentic bone china representations of shoes actually worn at various historical times. All of them were researched, designed, and sculpted by Wendy Lankester, whose original idea it was to create porcelain shoes that replicated historical shoe fashions. Lankester also produced the shoes, using the casting and firing facilities of existing English factories. Hand painting was done using her color guides by master painters who have worked for renown English porcelain firms. The first of the shoes was produced by Lankester in February 1984. Each was packed in a maroon miniature shoe box with an enclosure describing the shoe model. Most of the ten editions limited to two hundred each are in private collections. Because no values have yet been established in the secondary market, the values shown for each are the issue prices.

Porcelain ivory matte glazed T-strap low shoe with applied heel and gathered "ribbon" rose vamp ornament; fully marked on shank; 7-1/8"L x 3-3/8"HOA. Haute couture model A002, Early Stuart Rose Shoe 1613, first issued in September 1985, limited to 200. Gainsborough Collection, England. $395.

Bottom view of Early Stuart Rose Shoe showing fully painted bottom typical of Gainsborough shoes and the typical bottom marks. This one reads "JF (initials of painter)/hat logo/Gainsborough/fine bone china/Made in England/Early Stuart Rose Shoe 1613 (historical date of shoe design)/number 77 of 200"

Porcelain matte and gloss glazed "crewel embroidered" shoe with applied buckle and "leather" heel; fully bottom marked; 5-5/8"L x 4"H. Haute couture model A003, French Regency Shoe 1775, first issued in March 1986, limited to 200. Gainsborough Collection, England. $395.

Porcelain matte glazed strap crackow with applied back lacing, silver strap button and silver beads; bottom was sculpted with imprint of a foot and toes; fully bottom marked; 7-1/4"L x 2-1/4"H. Haute couture model A004, Medieval Rose Window Shoe 1380, first issued in August 1986, limited to 200. Gainsborough Collection, England. $395.

Porcelain matte and semi gloss glazed double buttoned high top with applied buttons; fully bottom marked; 4-1/2"L x 4-1/4"H. Miniature model B001, Victorian Ladies Bootee 1890s style, first issued in February 1984, limited to 200. Gainsborough Collection, England. $195.

Porcelain glazed strap shoe with applied strap button; fully bottom marked; 4-3/4"L x 1-15/16"H. Miniature model B002, Satin Bar Shoe 1920s style, first issued in February 1984, limited to 200. Gainsborough Collection, England. $195.

Porcelain glazed woman's oxford with applied laces and bow; fully bottom marked; 4-7/16"L x 2-7/16"H. Miniature model B004, Gibson Shoe 1900s style, first issued in May 1986, limited to 200. Gainsborough Collection, England. $195.

Bottom view of Gibson Shoe showing typical marks on Miniature Shoe models. This one reads "JF (painter's initials)/hat logo/Gainsborough/fine bone china/Made in England/1900's style/number 161 of 200"

Porcelain glazed mule with applied heel and shank assembly and applied vamp ornament; fully bottom marked; 3-7/8"L x 2-5/16"H. Miniature model B005, Stiletto Mule 1950s style, first issued in October 1986, limited to 200. Gainsborough Collection, England. $195.

Porcelain glazed slipper with in-mold strap and applied buckle; fully bottom marked; 4-7/16"L x 2-3/8"H. Period Fashion model M001, Sophie – 1740s style, first issued in July 1994, unlimited edition. Gainsborough Collection, England. $125.

Porcelain glazed slipper with in-mold strap and applied buckle; fully bottom marked; 4-5/16"L x 2-5/16"H. Period Fashion model M002, Marie– 1740s style, first issued in July 1994, unlimited edition. Gainsborough Collection, England. $125.

Porcelain matte glazed flat heeled slipper with shadow painted corded rim; fully bottom marked; 5"L x 1-9/16"H. Period Fashion model M003, Frederica– 1791s style, first issued in April 1995, unlimited edition. Gainsborough Collection, England. $125.

Porcelain slipper with in-mold ruching and embossed pattern; fully bottom marked; 4-1/2"L x 2-5/8"H. Period Fashion model M004, Nell– 1665s style, first issued in April 1995, unlimited edition. Gainsborough Collection, England. $115.

Porcelain glazed high-heeled shoe with small side openings and applied bow; fully bottom marked; 4-1/8"L x 3-1/16"H. Period Fashion model M005, Carmen– 1680s style, first issued in April 1995, unlimited edition. Gainsborough Collection, England. $135.

Porcelain matte glazed triple strap evening shoe with raised gold micro beads; fully bottom marked; 4-1/4"L x 1-15/16"H. Period Fashion model M009, Georgina– 1912s style, first issued in July 1998, unlimited edition. Gainsborough Collection, England. $135.

Porcelain large cowboy boot with in-mold over and under layered "stitched" pieces and applied side straps; fully bottom marked; 5-3/4"L x 6-1/4"H. Limited edition of 50 for Thomas Goode & Co., London. Issued in October 1987. Gainsborough Collection, England. $495.

Bottom view of cowboy boot showing HP "wear" pattern and location of marks. Bottom marked "Goode elephant logo/Gainsborough hat logo/Gainsborough/fine bone china/Made in England/DS (painter's initials)".

Porcelain matte glazed high heeled slipper with small side openings and applied buckle; fully bottom marked; 4-3/8"L x 2-3/8"H. Queen Charlotte's shoe of 1761, Millennium project for the City of Charlotte, limited to 2,000. Issued October 1999. Gainsborough Collection, England. $179.

Part III

Manufacturers, Designers, Decorators, and Importers

In this section are listed in alphabetical order facts about the companies, designers, decorators, and importers who were responsible for the shoes shown in this book whose origins have been identified. Where there is reference material readily available, the information presented here generally consists only of the name, location, years of operation, and a few facts. Additional information is provided where the references are obscure, out of print, or in some other way normally inaccessible to the general reader and shoe collector. Most of the entities listed have complex histories and intriguing stories related to them that are too lengthy for the briefs below and the interested reader is encouraged to seek out books devoted to the particular subject. If a producer is cited in the illustrated shoe section of this book but there is no corresponding entry below, it is because the author was unable to locate reliable information on the firm.

Abbreviations and Translations

AG: abb. for Aktiengesellschaft, or "joint stock company" (German)

Cie: abb. for company (German and French)

Gebr.: abb. for Gebrüder, or "brothers" (German)

GmbH: abb. for Gesellschaft mit beschränkter Haftung, or "limited liability company" (German)

KG: abb. for Kommanditgesellschaft, or "limited partnership" (German)

söhn/söhne: son/sons (German)

steingut: earthenware (German)

strasse: street (German)

VEB: abb. for Volkseigener Betrieb, "People's Own Enterprise." VEB was used in the German Democratic Republic for nationalized or nationally owned companies from the conclusion of WWII in 1945 until the reunification of Germany in 1990.

Ahrenfeldt, Charles. Charles Ahrenfeldt & Son, New York, pre 1880–1910. Charles Ahrenfeldt (b. 1807, d. 1894) was a U. S. entrepreneur who exported porcelain from Limoges, France and Altrohlau, Bohemia to Germany, England, and the United States. Although primarily in the import/export business, he and his son, Charles Jr. (b. 1857, d. 1934), owned a factory in Limoges and a porcelain decorating shop in Altrohlau. The Altrohlau shop was in operation until 1910 under the name Charles Ahrenfeldt & Son. The beginning of their decorating shop has been given variously as 1886 and 1894. While Ahrenfeldt actually produced porcelain in Limoges, his Bohemian operation was strictly a decorating shop that used blanks from local factories in the vicinity of Karlsbad. The finished products carried an Ahrenfeldt mark rather than the mark of the factory that produced the blank. The New York firm not only imported porcelain from its two operations in France and Bohemia, but also from the von Schierholz Porcelain Factory in Germany. In 1910, the Ahrenfeldt company in New York was taken over by Hermann C. Kupper of New York. At that time, the Altrohlau decorating shop closed.

Albion China (T.C.&P.). See Taylor and Kent.

Alexandra China. Alexandra China was a trademark used by an unknown wholesaler who purchased models from several major manufacturers of crested china, notably Sampson Hancock (*Corona,*

common trademark) and Hewitt & Leadbeater (*Willow,* common trademark).

Arcadian. See Arkinstall & Sons.

Arkinstall & Sons. Arkinstall & Sons Ltd. (became a branch of J. A. Robinson in 1912), Arcadian Works, Stoke-on-Trent, Staffordshire, England, 1903–c.1932. Arkinstall & Sons was started in 1903 by Harold Taylor Robinson and was probably the only factory specifically created to produce crested china. The company was the largest British manufacturer of crested china over the longest period. Robinson's interest was in acquiring as many companies as he could, and he built an empire of china companies by means of buyouts and mergers. In 1910, Robinson acquired a number of factories, whereupon he formed a new company, J. A. Robinson and Sons (J. A. Robinson was his father's name). The Charles Ford factory was one of the firms acquired in 1910 (trademark *Swan China),* becoming a branch of J. A. Robinson. Once they were moved to the Arcadian Works, the original Charles Ford *Swan* models became difficult to distinguish from *Arcadian* models. Either form could be marked with the other's trademark, and some items have been found with both marks.

Arkinstall became a branch of J. A. Robinson in 1912. Another branch of J. A. Robinson, Cauldon Ltd., used the unregistered trademark *Clifton,* though the items made by this branch were more commonly marked with the *Arcadian* trademark because they were made in the Arcadian Works at the same time as Arcadian and Swan models. The *Clifton* mark is believed not to have been used after about 1920.

Harold Taylor Robinson had to deal with a series of financial disasters culminating in the Great Depression of 1929. By 1932, he was in bankruptcy proceedings. Arkinstall was folded into other companies over the years, but its most common trademark, *Arcadian,* has been found on wares made through the late 1930s.

Arnstadt. See Mardorf & Bandorf.

Atlas Heraldic China. This trademark of Taylor and Kent was used for a wholesaler in Scotland. See Taylor and Kent.

Barettoni. Barettoni già Antonibon, Nove, VI, Italy, 17th century–present. Current production includes table accessories and gift items that often draw inspiration from nature and sea themes. The factory is one of Italy's oldest. It was founded in 1685 by the Antonibons, who were part of the Italian nobility. The Antonibons were granted privileges by the Venetian Republic to protect the ceramics business that gave prestige to the Republic. The current owner is Lodovico Barettoni.

Bawo & Dotter. Bawo & Dotter, Fischern, Bohemia (now Rybare, Czechia), c.1884–c.1924. Bawo & Dotter were an American importing firm located in New York City that owned a porcelain factory and decorating shop in Fischern, Bohemia. They specialized in dolls, doll heads, coffee and tea sets, and decorative objects. Authorities disagree on the actual dates of operation as well as the extent of the operations of this firm, which apparently were extensive..

Bennington. Bennington is the name of a town in Vermont. The term *Bennington* is incorrectly used to name just about anything that looks like the mottled brown pottery once made in the town of

Bennington. *Bennington* is also used incorrectly to refer to anything that looks remotely like a Rockingham glazed piece, whether or not it is a Rockingham glazed piece made by a factory in the town of Bennington, or whether or not it has a glaze of metallic salts. The factories in Bennington, Vermont made only a few shoe forms. In this text they, and only they, are referred to as *Bennington*.

Two important potteries were located in the town of Bennington, Vermont in approximately the 19th century: the Norton Potteries and the Fenton Potteries (United States Pottery). Capt. John Norton established the first pottery in Bennington in 1793, making red earthenware products. He began making salt-glazed stoneware in a separate kiln as early as 1800. His two sons and his grandson, Julius, continued the business in various partnership arrangements until 30 June 1844, when Julius formed a partnership with his brother-in-law, Christopher Webber Fenton. They produced wares together until 1 January 1845, a brief time during which the Norton factory made Rockingham glazed wares. The partnership was dissolved on 25 June 1847, and Fenton immediately began his own pottery in Bennington. Julius continued the Norton Potteries, which passed through several other Nortons until the factory closed in 1894 when the last of the Norton potters, Edward Lincoln Norton, died at age 29.

Christopher Webber Fenton began his own pottery in Bennington in June 1847. He was an experimenter who produced not only the redware and stoneware he had made with Norton, but also graniteware, flint enamel, scroddled ware, and an enormous amount of Rockingham glazed wares. His products were ranked among the country's finest achievements in ceramics. It has been estimated, however, that the Fenton factory marked only twenty percent of its products, leading many to make erroneous assumptions about unmarked wares that resemble those made by Fenton. Unfortunately, Fenton was not a good businessman and his United States Pottery closed on 15 May 1858.

Barret pictured a parian pair of cuffed boots on a rectangular base as being from a Bennington factory. That assessment has since been reversed and the piece is now designated non-Bennington. The only shoe shapes authenticated as having been made in Bennington are a pair of uniquely shaped boot warmers, a tiny heeled shoe, and several styles of tiny boots, all in Rockingham glazes. The tiny boots and shoe were designed by William Leake while he worked at the Fenton factory. (*See also, Leake, William*)

Figure M1. Products of the 1800s Bennington factories.

Birks, Rawlins and Co. Birks, Rawlins and Co. Ltd., Vine Pottery, Stoke, Staffordshire, England, 1900–1933. Birks, Rawlins began manufacturing crested china about 1910. On these pieces they

used their trade name *Savoy China*. This range of their products has a granular texture to the slip used in the castings. The company merged with Wiltshaw and Robinson Ltd. (*Carlton China*) in 1932. Wiltshaw and Robinson continued to use the *Savoy* trademark for a short time.

Blois. Blois is a town in France. It is also the name used for a particular factory there. *See Ulysse à Blois.*

Bohne, Ernst. Ernst Bohne Söhne, Rudolstadt, Thuringia, Germany, 1854–c.1920. Ernst Bohne established a porcelain decorating shop in 1848. By about 1850, he had started a porcelain production facility. In about 1856, his sons joined him in the business of producing figurines, coffee and tea sets, and decorative porcelain. One of the décors used by the company was the "Copenhagen Style", characterized by a great deal of blue painting. In about 1920, the company became a branch of the Brothers Heubach, who in turn sold it to Albert Stahl & Co. in 1937. The company was nationalized in 1974. In 1990, the company was privatized as the Albert Stahl & Co. formerly Ernst Bohne Sons, under which name it continues today. The Bohne mark most commonly found on shoes is an anchor with "EB" on its main shaft (1878–c.1920) or the impressed initials "E.B.S." (1887–1896).

Figure M2. Products of the Ernst Bohne & Sons factory, c.1890.

British Manufacture. The inscription "BRITISH MANUFAC-TURE", which may or may not be enclosed in a rectangular frame, is found as the sole bottom mark of porcelain models believed to have been made by both Taylor and Kent, and Sampson Hancock & Sons.

BT Co. Burley and Tyrrell Company, Chicago, Illinois, c.1862–1919. Anthony Burley and John Tyrrell formed an early American importing business. The earliest reference found for them is an 1862 court settlement where Benjamin Jones and Perry Smith, doing business as B. Jones & Co., were ordered to pay off a note in the amount of $252.33 plus costs of $21.73 to Anthony Burley and John Tyrrell, doing business as Burley and Tyrrell of Chicago. A mark attributed to Burley and Tyrrell is occasionally found on a porcelain shoe. It consists of a crown beneath which is a shield separated into three portions, with "B", "T", and "Co" in the partitions.

Butler Brothers. Butler Brothers, New York, NY, 1877 – ?; importers, wholesalers, factory agents, and jobbers. They are best known to researchers for their voluminous, illustrated wholesale catalogs. Although original catalogs still can be found for purchase, this author found it most efficient to access Butler Brothers product lines through a local university that had most of their publications on microfiche retrievable through an interlibrary loan. The firm was founded in 1877 by the three brothers Charles H., Edward B., and George Butler. Butler Brothers had branches in the American cities of Boston, Chicago, Dallas, Minneapolis, San Francisco, and St. Louis, and in the German city of Sonneberg, where they were the most important customer for the Dressel Doll Factory.

Carlton China. *See Wiltshaw and Robinson.*

Chaumeil, Alcide. Alcide Chaumeil faïence works, Paris, France, mid 1880s–mid 1920s. The identity of the intertwined letters "CA" on the bottom of certain French faience pieces had eluded experts for decades. One of the sleuths on the trail was Millicent Mali, who wrote in 1986 in *French Faïence* of her extensive efforts in France and with Canadian sources to track down the mysterious maker of the CA products. When the author first visited Mali in 1997, Mali was certain that she had finally pinned down CA. Mali published her research in 2000 in her book, *CA, a French Faïence Breakthrough,* where she presented a conclusive case that CA was Alcide Chaumeil (It was common in the era to reverse the order of initials, i.e., last initial first).

The Chaumeil factory used a deep red clay for its products, to which was applied a grayish crackle glaze. CA made exquisite busts of royalty and famous people, figurines, figural items, table accessories, and souvenirs. The most common design elements found on CA shoes are a blue loop and red dot rim design; a two-toned orange and yellow fleur-de-lys; a stylized black ermine tails (symbol of Anne de Bretagne); and a green, fire breathing-salamander (symbol of François I) or a swan pierced through the heart (symbol for both Claude de France and her mother-in-law, Louise de Savoie). The symbols are emblems of the Loire Valley in France. Numbers on pieces indicate mold numbers; the lower the number, the earlier the mold.

When Alcide died in 1919, his son Henri inherited the factory. Henri may have continued the souvenir production in the design elements created by his father for as long as five years after his father's death. But his entrance into the prestigious reproductions of old French faience and the creation of prize-winning serious art works would become the legacy the family would remember, one carried on by his gold-medal-winning son, Paul. Not until Mali tracked down numerous family members and acquaintances and found the key connecting piece was it recognized that Alcide's colorful souvenirs and the artistic works of his son and grandson came from one and the same small factory.

Figure M3. Products of the CA, or Alcide Chaumeil, factory.

Chelsea Keramic Art Works. Chelsea, Massachusetts, c.1872–1889. *See also, Dedham Pottery.* Soon after James Robertson arrived from Scotland in 1853, he began the Plympton and Robertson Pottery with Nathaniel Plympton in East Boston, Massachusetts. Robertson's two sons, Alexander and Hugh, had their own pottery in

Chelsea. Alexander began it in 1866 and was joined by Hugh in 1868. Their father left Plympton in 1872 and joined his sons in Chelsea. In an 1878 competition where they won first place, they were listed as James Robertson and Sons with the firm listed as Chelsea Keramic Art Works. After his father died in 1880 and his brother left for California, Hugh discovered the process for making crackleware, which would become famous when the pottery eventually would be moved to Dedham, Massachusetts. Early Chelsea clay was red; by the late 1870s, they were using a light yellow clay. Early products were not marked. From 1875 to 1889, their wares carried easily identifiable impressed marks.

In 1889, Hugh was forced to close the pottery because there was no market for the products that in this day are valuable art pottery. One of his two great achievements, a blood red glazed stoneware, was so expensive to produce that too few could afford it; breakeven for a typical vase was $300 in the dollar value of that era. He reopened the pottery in 1891 as the Chelsea Pottery US and specialized in the crackleware, his other great achievement. Chelsea, adjacent to Boston, proved too damp to make crackleware. The pottery was moved to East Dedham, Massachusetts in 1895 and began production in 1896 as the Dedham Pottery.

Cincinnati Art Pottery. *See Dell, William.*

Clifton. *See Arkinstall & Sons.*

Coalport. Coalport Company, Shropshire, England, c.1750–present. In its long history, the factory has produced some of the most exquisite ware ever made in porcelain. For shoe collectors, the over ninety shoes, slippers, and shoe boxes the company made beginning about 1890 and continuing to about 1900 are among the most treasured, when and if they can be located. A jeweler named Mr. Lardy was employed at the factory during the 1890s. He supervised all the jeweled ornamentation. This was a highly skilled craft that at the time was being used on the more highly decorative pieces. Meticulously crafted, hand-painted, and often jeweled with enamel beads and sometimes featuring miniature landscapes by well-known artists, these shoes are among those at the epitome of the craft. The technique of creating enamel "jewels" on china involves the fusing of small drops of colored enamel over a thin layer of gold, silver, or other chemically and thermally agreeable ground. The intended result is to imitate precious gems such as rubies, sapphires, emeralds, and pearls. The desired effect was also produced on backgrounds of cobalt blue, turquoise, and deep maroon. Each drop of enamel must be applied by hand in the pattern dictated by the piece. Often, the beads of enamel are graduated in size. One misapplication in position or proportion will ruin the piece. Coalport did not originate jewelling. Indeed, some of the finest examples of the technique were done at Royal Worcester in about 1865, a quarter century before Coalport began producing the elaborate jeweled ware for which it became famous. Although Coalport made a large variety of shoes, it did not make great numbers of any model; they were labor-intensive pieces. This makes it difficult to find them. Further, when they do become available, they often end up in private collections before ever going on the market because people seeking them often have a network of antique dealers who contact these preferred buyers before placing the object for general sale. This is also true of Royal Worcester and certain Royal Bayreuth shoes.

The specific value of a Coalport shoe depends largely on its décor. Those with jewelling and miniature landscapes are among the most desirable. The shoes made with tops to serve as small boxes are also very valuable. Coalport shoes are well marked. Their age can be approximated by knowing how the factory positioned the various elements of the mark. From 1880 to 1891, the mark was usually green and consisted of a crown beneath which was a curved "COALPORT" and beneath it on a straight line "A.D.1750", the latter the claimed date of the factory's establishment. From 1891 to 1915, the word "ENGLAND" was added above the crown on a curved line; the mark continued usually to be green. From 1915 to 1949, the mark had "MADE IN" added to "ENGLAND" above the crown. This mark can be found in such colors as green, black, and gold. From 1949 to 1958, the order of the wording was reversed, and "COALPORT" was now above the crown while the country of origin and factory establishment date were below. With this mark and those that followed was also added "BONE CHINA".

Coalport's pattern books are now housed in the Wedgwood museum archives and are generally inaccessible to the public. Original sketches of twelve Coalport shoes photocopied directly from Coalport pattern books are shown in Figure M4. Each page of the pattern books typically had on it patterns for several products, although only the shoes are shown here. The photocopies were scanned into a computer, cropped to the image of the shoe, and the twelve sketches presented here as a collage. Wherever parts of the shoe sketch or notes accompanying it have been cut off, it is the way in which the pattern book page was copied and received by the author.

Before the pattern books became inaccessible, Wendy Lankester of England made a hand-written list of the shoes made from about 1890 to 1900 that were found in those books with the pattern number assigned to each. The pattern number should also be found on the actual shoe, hand-painted near the Coalport mark. A "V" preceding the number indicates the intention of Coalport that the piece be used as a vase, though V-numbers can be found on boxes, bells, and other items not remotely useful as vases. Coalport made slippers and shoes in both a mule style and with full backs, in both high and low heels, and with completely enclosed heels and those whose front vertical surface was open. This latter feature can be seen in this book where Coalport shoes are pictured. The heels were always applied. Coalport made Normandy shoes in at least three different sizes. The shoes are listed in Table 1.

Figure M4. Images of original sketches of Coalport shoes from their pattern books. Most are shown here at about 30% full scale. *By courtesy of the Trustees of the Wedgwood Museum, Barlaston, Staffordshire, England.*

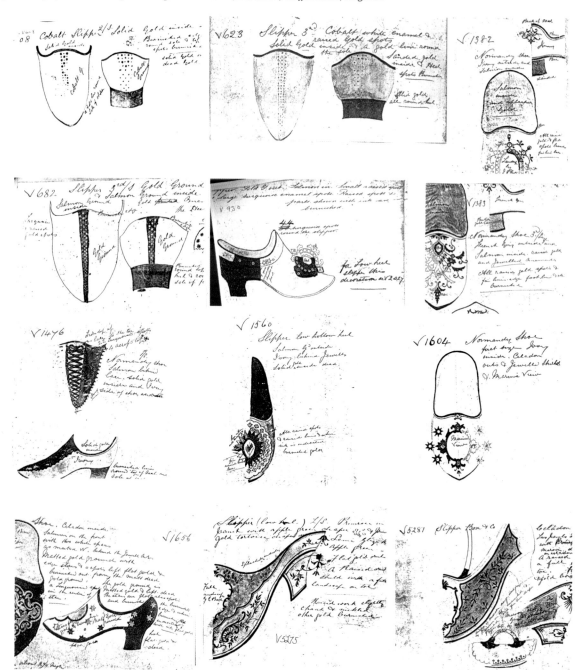

Table 1. Coalport Shoes and Slippers Made in the Late 1800s

Should not be assumed to be complete; occasionally, additional models show up. Boldface dates are from Coalport pattern books.

PATTERN #	DESCRIPTION (taken from Coalport pattern books unless otherwise noted)
V 608 (sketch)	**Slipper**. outside: cobalt; solid gold inside.
V 623 (sketch)	**Slipper**. outside: cobalt with white enamel and raised gold spots; solid gold inside; gold line around sole.
V 681	**Slipper**. outside: gold ground with turquoise and gold raised spots; salmon inside (Messenger, pg. 371).
V 682 (sketch)	**Slipper**. outside: gold ground with turquoise and gold raised spots; salmon inside; gold ornament on salmon ground inside heel opening.
V 696	**Slipper**. outside: gold ground with turquoise and gold raised spots; celeste (blue) inside.
V 930 (sketch)	**Slipper**. outside: gold ground with turquoise and gold raised spots; salmon inside; gold, jeweled ornament w. opal.
V 988	**Slipper**. outside: celeste (blue) ground with raised gold spots and acanthus design; white floral decoration and front lozenge painted with a landscape by J. Plant. **(1890)**
V 1382 (sketch)	**Normandy shoe**. outside: ivory ground with raised gold spots and acanthus design around lozenge with landscape by J. H. Plant; salmon inside.
V 1383 (sk.+ph.)	**Normandy shoe**. outside: French gray ground with raised gold and jeweled ornaments; salmon inside.
V 1476 (sketch)	**Normandy shoe**. outside: salmon ground overlaid with lace-like décor; ivory inside
V 1532	**Slipper**. same as V 681, but with opening in heel (Messenger, pg. 371).
V 1556	**Slipper**. apparently same as V1532 but with gold inside (Messenger, pg. 371).
V 1560 (sketch)	**Slipper**. outside: salmon ground with ivory behind jewels; solid gold inside; low hollow heel.
V 1604 (sketch)	**Normandy shoe**. outside: celadon with jeweled shield on front with marine view; gold ground (?); ivory inside.
V 1608	**Normandy shoe**. outside: ivory ground with raised gold and jeweled ornaments; blush pink inside.
V 1656 (sketch)	**Normandy shoe**. outside: salmon on front with areas of white and matted gold ground on remainder including heel; celadon inside.
V 1663 (photo)	**Slipper**. outside: ivory with raised gold spots and fine lines around jewels; blush pink inside.
V 1673	**Normandy shoe**. outside: ivory ground with raised jewels and gold work; salmon inside.
V 1717	**Normandy shoe**. outside: Rose du Barry ground with raised gold spots and broad bands around jewels; gold heel; ivory and splashed gold inside.
V 1885	**Normandy shoe**. outside: salmon with turquoise and gold raised spots; solid gold inside.
V 2111	**Normandy shoe**. outside: celadon ground, ivory behind jewels, burnished gold raised spots and fine lines; ivory inside.
V 2112	**Normandy shoe**. outside: ivory ground, jeweled with burnished gold, etc., as in V 2111; American blush pink inside.
V 2113	**Normandy shoe**. outside: ivory and Rose du Barry with raised gold spots and fine lines, burnished; ivory and splashed gold inside.
V 2175	**Normandy shoe**. outside: celadon ground with flowers painted in gold, petals of which are white enamel with center spot of red enamel; ivory and shaded blush pink from edge of inside.
V 2176	**Normandy shoe**. same as V 2175 but decorated with painted ivy in gold with berries in white enamel; all gold burnished.
V 2202	**Normandy shoe**, *high heel*. outside: American blush pink with shield in front with landscape; flat gold ground outside; ivory ground inside.
V 2215	**Normandy shoe**. outside: American blush pink, raised gold and jeweled with opal in center front; ivory inside with shaded salmon from edge.

PATTERN #	DESCRIPTION
V 2216	**Normandy shoe**. outside: celeste ground, landscape in shield on front, raised gold spots and fine lines; American blush pink inside.
V 2222	**Normandy shoe**. outside: American blush pink, border painted in gold, turquoise enamel; ivory inside with blended American blush pink from edge of inside.
V 2318	**Low heeled slipper**. outside: ivory, raised gold and jewels; American blush pink inside.
V 2349 (photo)	**Low heeled slipper**. outside: American blush pink on heel, jeweled star on toe with ivory behind, turquoise and raised gold spots, pearl center; solid gold inside.
V 2367	**Low heeled slipper**. outside: panels of gold painted ornaments with turquoise enamel spots, white enamel petals to rosettes, turquoise center spot; canary ground splashed with gold inside.
V 2498	**High heeled shoe**. outside: cobalt ground, raised ornament on toe with band of matte gold around, raised white and gold spots; cobalt inside.
V 2643	**Low heeled slipper**. outside: ivory ground, jeweled and raised gold ornaments with panels of turquoise and raised gold spots; white inside.
V 2810	**High heeled shoe**. outside: gold ground, rose shield with landscape, jewels in band, turquoise and round gold spots; blush pink inside.
V 2849	**Low heeled slipper**. outside: gold ground with turquoise and raised gold spots, rococo shield on front with landscape, raised ornament at heel, jeweled ornaments on band at edge; American blush pink inside.
V 3146	**Low heeled slipper**. outside: ivory and blush pink finish, raised gold and jeweled star on toe with agate stone in center, raised work between ivory and blush pink; straw color inside.
V 3150	**Low heeled slipper**. outside: ivory on toe and heel, raised gold star with jewels and agate stone at toe, gold ground above with turquoise and raised gold spots; blush pink inside.
V 3182	**Low heeled slipper, assumed**. outside: gold ground with turquoise and raised gold ornaments, very delicate blush pink behind jewels and raised ornaments on toe (assumed to be agate on an oval shield … see V4383); blush pink inside.
V 3202	**High heeled shoe**. outside: gold ground with turquoise and raised gold spots, lavender pink on back of heel and behind lace at front of toe, raised gold and jeweled ornaments; American blush pink and ivory ground on inside.
V 3204	**Shoe**. outside: ivory, raised gold and jeweled ornaments on front and band, raised gold ornaments; blush pink inside.
V 3240	**Low heeled slipper**. outside: ivory ground, panels of raised ornaments and flat printed gold spots, four agate stones on toe, printed gold vermacella; blush pink inside.
V 3327 (photo)	**Heeled slipper**. outside: burnished gold with turquoise jewels, raised gold spots, tooled geometric rim; gold inside.**(1893)**
V 3406	**High heeled shoe**. outside: ivory ground, printed gold ornament on toe, a panel at each side of gold diapers and red enamel spots; white and (undecipherable) splashed inside.
V 3410	**High heeled shoe**. outside: apple green ground, raised and gold ground and white enamel spots and raised gold spots; splashed gold inside.
V 3595	**High heeled shoe**. outside: ivory and chrome green, raised gold and jeweled ornaments (agate); white and splashed gold inside.
V 3857	**High heeled shoe**. outside: blush pink ground, raised gold and jeweled ornament (agate); primrose ground inside.
V 3917	**Slipper box and cover**. outside: blush pink ground, printed flat ornament on toe and panel of diaper on each side, solid handle; solid verge and splashed inside; same décor as V3406 but cover extra.
V 3918	**Slipper box and cover**. outside: splashed celadon and ivory, jewels and raised ornaments; ivory inside.

PATTERN #	DESCRIPTION
V 3919	**High heeled shoe.** apple green ground, printed gold band and flat ornament at heel, raised white and gold spots in shield.
V 3921	**Slipper box and cover.** outside: ivory ground, jewels and raised ornaments and panels of spiral printed flat ornaments on heel; white inside.
V 3930	**Shoe box and cover.** primrose ground, splashed inside, jewels and raised ornaments.
V 3931	**Slipper box and cover.** outside: ivory ground, raised gold and jeweled ornament in turquoise with little panels of spiral; white and splashed inside.
V 4036	**Low heeled slipper.** outside: celadon and ivory ground, agate stone and jewels and panels of diaper; splashed inside.
V 4040	**Low heeled slipper.** outside: ivory ground, raised rococo shield with agate stone, printed gold diaper.
V 4209	**Shoe box and cover.** same as V(undecipherable), apple green ground.
V 4303	**Slipper.** celadon and chrome green, a rococo shield with painted head and shoulders by F. Sutton, printed gold on heel and gold border at edge. (**1893**)
V 4371	**High heeled shoe.** solid ivory inside and outside, turquoise and gold raised spots, raised ornament on toe with agate stones and jewels.
V 4372	**Slipper box and cover.** Maroon ground and same decoration as V3930.
V 4373	**High heeled shoe.** shoe as in V3857 but with Mr. Walleys flowers for agate stone.
V 4383	**Tall heeled shoe.** outside: Venus pink on toe, same decoration as V3182 but with Mr. Walleys flowers instead of agate on oval shield, gold ground, etc., as in V3182; Venus pink inside and splashed.
V 4570	**Low heeled slipper.** outside; chrome green ground with a printed chrome diaper and a printed gold diaper over, printed raised gold shield with a full andscape by J. Plant, ivory on toe and primrose on heel; splash inside.
V 4587	**High heeled slipper.** chrome green on toe with printed chrome diaper under and gold diaper on top, raised rococo shield at front with painted group of flowers and printed gold ornament at back.
V 4597	**High heeled shoe.** maroon ground with maroon diaper under and printed flat gold diaper over maroon, primrose at heel, a raised rococo shield at toe with full landscape.
V 4598	**High heeled shoe.** outside: primrose ground with orange diaper under primrose ground, Venus pink at heel, a raised gold shield on heel with full landscape at front by J. Plant; ivory and splashed inside.
V 4610	**Slipper box and cover.** Venus pink on toe and back with primrose ground and orange diaper band under primrose and printed gold border on top, raised gold shield on toe with landscape by J. Plant, printed flat gold border under primrose band.
V 4620	**High heeled shoe.** ivory ground with a white shield at front with a painted spray of birds by T. Simpson, two maroon panels, raised work around shield and rococo work shield at back with a painted fly. (**1895**)

PATTERN #	DESCRIPTION
V 4692	**Low heeled slipper.** chrome green, ivory on toe and printed gold diaper on chrome green, ornamental shield on toe with landscape.
V 4756	**Slipper box and cover.** maroon ground, spray of raised flowers in gold with foliage, etc.
V 4780	**Slipper box and cover.** Venus pink ground, raised ferns and fly at heel in gold.
V 4792	**Slipper box and cover.** chrome green.
V 4793	**Slipper box and cover.** apple green.
V 4823	**Slipper box and cover.** chrome green.
V 4827	**Slipper box and cover.** Venus pink with landscape by J. Plant.
V 4839	**High heeled shoe.** outside: Rose du Barry ground; primrose inside.
V 4843	**Slipper box and cover.** ivory on heel and toe, primrose and apple green, full landscape in oval by E. (Ted) Ball. (**1895**)
V 4855	**Low heeled slipper.** outside: Rose du Barry ground with diaper of purple and gilt, ivory heel and toe, raised gold rococo shield with landscape painting in enamels by J. Plant (also in Messenger, pg. 371).
V 4930 (photo)	**Slipper box and cover.** printed crocodile diaper, green ground, same as V4756.
V 5181	**Low heeled slipper.** printed shaded hawthorn in dove color.
V 5182	**Slipper box with cover.** as in V5181, with printed cobalt wreath and gold band at edge and handle.
V 5188	**High heeled shoe.** printed birds, gold ground at toe, white and printed gold at heel.
V 5249	**High heeled shoe.** same décor as V5250
V 5250	**Slipper box and cover.** printed shield at front with flowers colored by W. Smith, one at heel and two on cover.
V 5251	**Low heeled slipper.** same décor as V5252.
V 5252	**Slipper box and cover.** printed gold panel at toe, top of toe and back of heel; group of flowers at toe and two on cover.
V 5267	**Slipper box and cover.** full landscape in oval shield at toe, two shields of (undecipherable) print gold diaper.
V 5273	**Low heeled slipper.** panel of printed lace, printed gold line diaper with gold sprigs forming diaper.
V 5275 (sketch)	**Low heeled slipper.** primrose in panel with apple green and printed gold tortoise diaper; full landscape, E. Ball.
V 5279	**Low heeled slipper.** primrose ground, chrome green panel; primrose and printed gold tortoise diaper; vig. landscape.
V 5281 (sketch)	**Slipper box and cover.** celadon; two panels with primrose, maroon on celadon; raised shield on toe.
V 5328	**Low heeled slipper.** primrose panels, printed diaper under in chrome green; raised ornamental shield w. full landscape.
V 5332	**High heeled shoe.** same as V5250.
V 6353	**Shoe, large middle and small.** Raised shield with landscape by E. Ball on toe, gold ground and raised red enamel and gold spots at front, printed gold diaper tortoise at back. (**21 November 1898**)

Conta & Boehme. Conta & Boehme, Possneck, Thuringia, Germany, 1814–c.1931.

Corbett, Bertha L. Born in Denver, Colorado, Corbett was a trained artist who created the Sunbonnet Babies. The Royal Bayreuth porcelain carrying the Sunbonnet Babies motifs are valuable collector's items; the factory's Sunbonnet Babies sabots are rare and command high prices.

Corbett moved to Minneapolis, Minnesota in 1884 to study under figure painter Douglas Volk at the Minneapolis School of Fine Arts. She became adept at quick portrait sketches when she accompanied a reporter for the *Minneapolis Journal* on interviews of famous actors and actresses on tour. She also studied under famous illustrator Howard Pyle at Drexel Institute in Philadelphia, Pennsylvania.

Corbett sketched the first Sunbonnet Baby for two young women who were china painters and shared her studio in Minneapolis. She expanded the concept to Christmas and Valentine cards illustrated by Sunbonnet Babies. These efforts were followed by the appearance of her creations in a small book, *Sunbonnet Babies*, published by Byron and Willard of Minneapolis in May 1900. The publication in 1902 of *The Sunbonnet Babies Primer* launched a career for Corbett that would span about a half century. Eulalie Osgood Grover wrote the text of the book and the illustrations were by Corbett. It was used throughout the United States to introduce children to the joys of reading. The collaborators produced a number of sequels in what became an extremely popular series.

Of interest to Royal Bayreuth Sunbonnet Babies collectors is this quote from Chamberlain: "Color reproductions of her oil paintings called the Sun Bonnet Series, a representation of the Juvenile Industry of the week comprising Washing Day [Monday], Ironing Day [Tuesday], Mending Day [Wednesday], Scrubbing Day [Thursday], Sweeping Day [Friday] and Baking Day [Saturday] *[NOTE: only six, not seven, days are mentioned here; Fishing Day (Sunday) is missing.]*, were published by J. J. Austin & Co., Chicago in 1904. This series was often framed for children's rooms and the designs were used on the Royal Bayreuth china. The *N. Y. Sunday World Supplement* brought them out again in 1907." McCaslin (*Book II*) has reported that neither she nor any other collector of whom she is aware has ever seen the Saturday Baking scene on any of the originally produced Royal Bayreuth pieces in any form, even though all seven original stone decals that had been long presumed destroyed in WWI were found and used in a 1974 reissue of 5,000 sets of seven plates. Just to muddy up the pond, the author notes that the Sunday fishing scene of Sunbonnet Babies Molly and May can be found with regularity on the originally issued Royal Bayreuth pieces, even though the fishing scene was not one of those published by Austin & Co. Austin issued

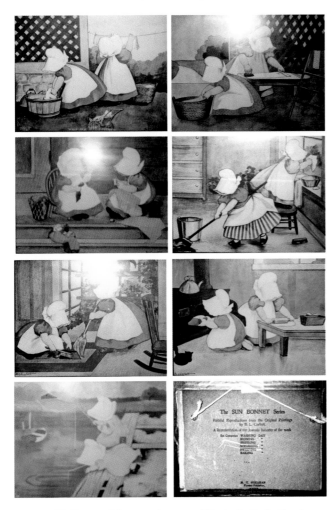

Figure M5. Photos of the reproductions of Bertha L. Corbett's oil paintings of the Sunbonnet Babies issued by J. J. Austen. The top six were published together as a series. On the front of each there is the title of the scene, Corbett's signature, and "Copyright 1904, J. J. Austen Co., Chicago." Shown in the bottom right image is what can be found on the back of each print: "The SUN BONNET Series/ Faithful Reproductions from the Original Paintings/by B. L. Corbett/A Representation of the Juvenile Industry of the week/Set Comprises WASHING DAY/IRONING DAY/MENDING DAY/SCRUBBING DAY/ SWEEPING DAY/BAKING DAY/M. T. SHEAHAN/Picture Publisher/ Boston, Mass." At the bottom left is the Fishing Scene that was issued separately. These images are provided for the collector who wishes to compare the Sunbonnet Babies scenes on Royal Bayreuth sabots and other Bayreuth pieces with the renderings in Corbett's original oil paintings. Note: These photos of the Austen prints were taken through the glass in the frames enclosing each, which accounts for the glare and the uneven resolution.

the fishing scene separately, and enterprising collectors must really search to locate it. All seven reproductions of the Corbett Sunbonnet Babies day-of-the-week series by Austin are shown in Figure M5 along with a photo of what can be found on the back of the six that were issued originally.

Among the characteristics that collectors find endearing with wares illustrated by Sunbonnet Babies are their involvement in both useful and mischievous tasks, and their faces always hidden by large bonnets. This latter distinction was Corbett's successful effort to prove that facial expression need not always be seen to communicate ideas and temperament.

Because of their great charm and wide distribution in publications, the Sunbonnet Babies are the creation for which Corbett is best remembered. However, she was a skilled artist in several media and her artistic creations extended to considerably more than Molly and May in their voluminous skirts and big bonnets. Corbett also worked in watercolors; painted portraits in oils and miniatures on ivory; made silhouettes and illuminated mottoes; and made fin-de-siecle girls. In August of 1910, she married George H. Melcher and moved with him to Los Angeles, California where she lived until her death.

Corona China. *See Hancock, Sampson & Sons.*

Cottard, F. E. *See Montagnon.*

Cyclone. *CYCLONE* is a bottom mark that is believed to have been used by a wholesaler of crested china manufactured by several different factories. The mark can be found with one of three sets of initials under it: *H.A.A.&S.*, *A.A.A.L.*, and *A.A.A.* The factories believed to have made the crested china are Taylor and Kent (usual trademark Florentine) and Wiltshaw and Robinson (usual trademark Carlton).

Dedham Pottery. Dedham Pottery, East Dedham, Massachusetts, 1896–1943. *See also, Chelsea Keramic Art Works.* The Dedham Pottery was preceded by the Chelsea Pottery US (1891–1895) and the Chelsea Keramic Art Works (c.1872–1889), all operated by members of the Robertson family. The Dedham Pottery specialized in a gray stoneware decorated with freehand cobalt blue motifs of animals, flowers, and fish. The Chinese-derived crackle finish was usually enhanced by rubbing black powder into the finely veined fissures in the glaze. Dedham is known to have made a very rare heeled slipper and two boot shapes, one a rare plain-cuffed boot that features an animal or floral motif in cobalt on its cuff, and a small boot with a painted tie on its front. The Potting Shed in Concord, Massachusetts began reproducing Dedham pottery about 1973. Their products are dishwasher proof and uniquely marked, in addition to their using new molds because the original Dedham molds were not available. Collectors should therefore not be confused.

Dell, William. William Dell Pottery *aka* Wm. Dell & Co., Cincinnati, Ohio, 1891–1892. The Cincinnati Art Pottery was in business from 1879 to 1891. William Dell was foreman of the company. By 1887, he was its superintendent and manager. When the company closed in 1891, Dell started his own company, making pottery from molds he acquired from them. He was in business for only about a year, making beautiful pottery, before he died at age thirty-five.

Emanuel, Max. Max Emanuel & Co., The Mosanic Pottery, Mitterteich, Bavaria, Germany, c.1882–1918. Some sources cite the company as one producing porcelain. Others cite the factory as having produced stoneware. It is assumed that the company did both. The author has not been able to track down the precise nature of the company's involvement in commissioning works from other factories, although Emanuel is reputed to have been living in London by at least 1914 where he purchased ceramics products made by other factories that carried Emanuel's trademark, "Mosanic". For example, a French faience clog has been found marked "Mosanic". It has been cast from the same mold and decorated with the same motifs as known Fourmaintraux clogs. Numerous other pieces have also been found with the Mosanic mark and references have been found to Max Emanuel having been in England when some or all of these pieces were commissioned. A curious black-painted shoe with two protruding heads has been found with a British Registration mark. Contact with the British Registry turned up the information that the design for the shoe was filed on 22 January 1903 by Max Emanuel and Co. of 41-42 Shoe Lane, London EC. It is assumed that this was a business address for Emanuel in England. What is not known is what factory actually manufactured the piece and whether Emanuel was living in England at this early date.

The main trade name bottom-marked on Max Emanuel items is *Mosanic*. Other trademarks that can be found on Max Emanuel pieces are *Maxim China* and *Unity China*. Items from this company can also be found marked simply *Austria, Czechoslovakia, Foreign,* or *Germany*, the first two incorrectly used after WWI because of the unwillingness of the British to purchase things German. Crested china models with impressed numbers are believed to have been made by Emanuel.

E. S. Germany. *See Schlegelmilch, Erdmann.*

Fairy Ware. *See Schmidt Victoria.*

Fenton Pottery. *See Bennington.*

Fenton (with three hooded heads as trademark). *See Hoods Ltd.*

Fielding & Co., S. S. Fielding & Company, Stoke, Staffordshire, England, 1879–1982. Fielding produced pottery from 1879 to 1982 including majolica. They changed their name to Crown Devon in 1905 although they used this name with "S.F. & CO" earlier. The company changed ownership in 1976 and was closed in 1982. The factory buildings were demolished in 1987.

Fielding produced a number of vellum patterns from about 1890 to about 1915. The Royal Devon pattern X543 was introduced in 1902 and it is the most sought after by collectors.

Fleury. Fleury, Paris, France, 1803–c.1847. The company manufactured products of hard-paste porcelain. From 1803 to 1835 it is believed to have been directed by Flamen Fleury. His products are known for their high quality. Reference to the company at a different address has been found as late as 1847.

Florentine China. *See Taylor and Kent.*

The Foley China. *The Foley China* is a trademark used from 1890 to 1910 by Wileman and Co., Foley Potteries and Foley China Works, Longton, Staffordshire, England. *See Shelley.*

Ford, Charles. Charles Ford, Hanley, Staffordshire, England, 1874–1904; branch of J. A. Robinson & Sons in 1910. *See Arkinstall & Sons.*

Fourmaintraux. Fourmaintraux family, Desvres, France, 1804–present. So many members of this family were involved in the pottery business that they are grouped here in a single entry for simplicity. The original family member who began the long line of potteries in Desvres was François-Joseph Fourmaintraux (spelled Fourmentraux in early records), who moved to the town in 1791. He married and then started his own pottery in 1804. Eventually, the firm was taken over by the oldest of three sons who had become potters, Louis-François. When Louis-François died in 1885, three of his six sons were already in the family trade. The three, François, Jules, and Emile, are important to shoe collectors because they made some of the most delightful of these figurals. Jules and Emile carried on their father's company and worked together from 1877 to 1887, specializing in the reproduction of old pottery items. During the decade that these two brothers worked together as the *Fourmaintraux Frères ("Brothers")*, they marked their wares with two script "F"s, underlined, with a number below. When Emile left in 1887, Jules continued his father's pottery until selling it in 1903 to François Masse.

Emile began a new company with his son, Gabriel, in 1899. From 1902 to 1934, their medium was fine porcelain, which they produced in a variety of forms classified as *objets d'art*. They added back items

in pottery as a result of the 1925 exposition that revitalized interest in the older type pottery forms made in the grand feu method. The mark they used consisted of the script letters "G" and "F" inside a circle with short, bent spokes coming from its perimeter. The company eventually evolved into the company G. & C. Fourmaintraux et Dutertre, which recently merged with the Masse factory and is now known as Masse-Fourmaintraux.

François Fourmaintraux married Mlle. Courquin in 1862. A year later, François started his own factory, introducing a new technique for replacing hand-formed square tiles by a press that would form them mechanically. François and his wife began producing specialty items for the retail trade in about 1872, the beginning of the time when collectibles bearing their mark started being manufactured. She supervised the décors, which were based on the old potteries of Delft, Nevers, Moustiers, and Rouen. The mark they used was a pair of script initials intertwined, F and C. The Fourmaintraux factory became "Charles Fourmaintraux" in 1934 and eventually evolved into S. A. Fourmaintraux-Delassus. In 1983 this company merged with M.C.M. (Mosaique Ceramique de Montplaisir) and the resulting entity now makes products whose mark is *DESVRES*.

Figure M6. Products of the Fourmaintraux-Courquin factory.

Fourmaintraux Brothers. Fourmaintraux Frères, Desvres, France, 1877–1887. *See Fourmaintraux.*

Fourmaintraux-Courquin. Fourmaintraux-Courquin, Desvres, France, 1872–1934. *See Fourmaintraux.*

Fourmaintraux, Gabriel. Gabriel Fourmaintraux, Desvres, France, 1900–1934. *See Fourmaintraux.*

Fraureuth. Porzellanfabrik Fraureuth AG, Fraureuth, Saxony, Germany, c.1898–1935. They produced figurines, decorative porcelain, dinnerware, and household accessories.

Gainsborough Collection, The. *See Lankester, Wendy.*

Gallé, Emile. b. 1846, d. 1904, Nancy, France. Gallé was a prolific designer, modeler, sculptor, artisan, and experimenter especially known for his brilliantly designed Art Nouveau art glass, though he also produced furniture and pottery. With Victor Prouvé and Louis Majorelle, Gallé founded the *Alliance Provinciale des Industries d'Art*, better known as the Ecole de Nancy arm of Art Nouveau. He owned a factory in Nancy that produced some of his work and that of his artisans on a large scale. The company numbered about 450 when he died, and his widow continued the business. It closed in 1931.

Gallé used local clay for his ceramic pieces. It was the first medium with which he experimented. His father, who was a potter, had taught him the basic principles of making and decorating ceramics. Emile Gallé perfected tin-based glazes and developed richly colored enamels. He experimented with other glazes and painting techniques to achieve a range of effects. While his resulting pottery was bright and creative, the forms tended to be somewhat crude, with a naïve quality. The medium did not offer Gallé the flexibility of the glass on which he was developing unique manufacturing techniques. He last exhibited his pottery in 1892 at the Salon du Champs-de-Mars.

Galluba & Hofmann. Galluba & Hofmann Porcelain Factory, Ilmenau, Thuringia, Germany, 1888–c.1932 (known to have been closed by 1937). They made decorative porcelain; luxury articles; figurines, including half-dolls; snow babies; kitchen items; souvenir china; and gift and novelty articles, including one of the widest selections of designs in miniature shoes and boots.

Galluba & Hofmann made one of the broadest ranges of shoe forms of any known factory producing them in the years near 1900. Coalport is known to have made over ninety different shoes, but production was very limited and they remain among the most difficult shoes for collectors to locate. Royal Bayreuth made over fifty shoe

forms, and some are very accessible to collectors today. But Galluba & Hofmann mass-produced porcelain shoes. It is testimony to the quality of the porcelain and the craftsmanship of the appliqués that so many have survived to this day in mint or nearly mint condition. Most of them, however, are unmarked. Thus, many people have them in their shoe collections but do not know who manufactured them.

Using the characteristics found on the few Galluba & Hofmann shoes that are marked, the author has constructed a list of the probable shoes and boots made by Galluba & Hofmann. They are recorded in Table 2. The few Galluba and Hofmann shoes found marked carry a logo registered in September 1905 with the German patent office. It consists of a shield containing the intertwined script letters "G" and "H", surmounted by a crown, with "GERMANY" written in a curve underneath.

Table 2.   Galluba & Hofmann Shoes & Boots

Should not be assumed to be complete … more keep showing up.

Number	Description		Typical Size	
1687	**TULIP**	BOOT	medium	4-3/8"L x 4-1/4"H
1698	**RIM RUFFLE & SCROLLS**	SHOE	medium	5-3/8"L x 2-3/8"H
1698A	**RIM RUFFLE & SCROLLS**	SHOE	medium	5-1/4"L x 2-3/8"H
1727A	**RIM RUFFLE & SCROLLS**	SHOE	small	4-1/4"L x 1-3/4"H
1717	**TULIP**	SHOE	large	6-5/8"L x 3"H
1717A	**TULIP**	SHOE	large	6-1/2"L x 2-7/8"H
1718	**TULIP**	SHOE	medium	5-7/16"L x 2-7/16"H
1719	**TULIP**	SHOE	small	4-7/16"L x 2-1/16"H
1784	**DAISY**	BOOT	large	5-3/16"L x 5"H
1785A	**DAISY**	BOOT	medium	4-3/8"L x 4-1/16"H
1786A	**DAISY**	BOOT	small	3-1/2"L x 3-3/8"H
1797	**SCROLLS & PLEATS**	SHOE	large	6-3/4"L x 2-3/4"H
1798	**SCROLLS & PLEATS**	SHOE	medium	assumed to exist
1799	**SCROLLS & PLEATS**	SHOE	small	4-1/2"L x 1-7/8"H
1808	**BLEEDING HEART**	SHOE	large	6-11/16"L x 2-13/16"H
1808A	**BLEEDING HEART**	SHOE	large	known to exist
1809	**BLEEDING HEART**	SHOE	medium	5-1/2"L x 2-1/4"H
1809A	**BLEEDING HEART**	SHOE	medium	5-7/16"L x 2-1/4"H
1810A	**BLEEDING HEART**	SHOE	small	4-3/8"L x 1-7/8"H
1830	**SCROLLS**	BOOT	large	*assumed to exist*
1830A	**SCROLLS**	BOOT	large	5-1/4"L x 4-7/8"H
1879	**SCALLOPED SCROLL**	SHOE	small	3-3/4"L x 1-3/8"H
1879A	**SCALLOPED SCROLL**	SHOE	small	3-3/4"L x 1-3/8"H
1880A	**SCALLOPED SCROLL**	SHOE	mini	3-3/8"L x 1-1/8"H
1884	**PLANTAIN LILY**	BOOT	large	5-1/4"L x 5-3/16"H
1885	**PLANTAIN LILY**	BOOT	medium	4-1/4"L x 4-1/4"H
1885A	**PLANTAIN LILY**	BOOT	medium	4-1/4"L x 4-1/4"H
1886	**PLANTAIN LILY**	BOOT	small	3-9/16"L x3-7/16"H
1923	**GERANIUM**	SHOE	large	6-1/2"L x 3-1/4"H
1924	**GERANIUM**	SHOE	medium	5-1/2"L x 2-5/8"H
1924A	**GERANIUM**	SHOE	medium	5-1/2"L x 2-5/8"H
1925A	**GERANIUM**	SHOE	small	4-1/2"L x 2-1/8"H
1926	**CLOVER & SWIRLS**	SHOE	large	6-1/2"L x 2-3/4"H
1926A	**CLOVER & SWIRLS**	SHOE	large	6-7/16"L x 2-11/16"H
1927	**CLOVER & SWIRLS**	SHOE	medium	5-7/16"L x 2-3/16"H
1950	**VIOLET & RIBBON**	SHOE	medium	5-1/4"L x 2-3/8"H
1951A	**VIOLET & RIBBON**	SHOE	small	4-5/16"L x 1-13/16"H
6210	**SCALLOPED SCROLL**	PAIR of SHOES	mini	3-3/8"L x 1-1/8"H
6311	**BORDER SHELL**	SHOE	mini	3-9/16"L x 1-5/8"H
6495	**DAISY**	SHOE	large	6-9/16"L x 3-3/16"H
A6495	**DAISY**	SHOE	large	*known to exist*
6496	**DAISY**	SHOE	medium	5-3/8"L x 2-5/8"H
6497	**DAISY**	SHOE	small	4-9/16"L x 2-3/16"H
A6497	**DAISY**	SHOE	small	*known to exist*
6498	**POPPY**	SHOE	large	6-3/8"L x 3-3/8"H
C6499	**POPPY**	SHOE	medium	5-1/2"L x 2-3/4"H
6500	**POPPY**	SHOE	small	4-7/16"L x 2-1/4"H
A6500	**POPPY**	SHOE	small	*known to exist*
6504	**SWEET PEA**	BOOT	large	*assumed to exist*
A6504	**SWEET PEA**	BOOT	large	*known to exist*

Number	Description		Typical Size	
C6504	SWEET PEA	BOOT	large	*known to exist*
6505	SWEET PEA	BOOT	medium	4-1/2"L x 4-1/4"H
6505A	SWEET PEA	BOOT	medium	4-1/2"L x 4-1/4"H
6506	SWEET PEA	BOOT	small	3-11/16"L x 3-5/8"H
6707	TEXTURED DAISY	SHOE	large	6-9/16"L x 3-1/4"H
6854	PEONY	BOOT	large	4-7/8"L x 4-15/16"H
6855	PEONY	BOOT M	medium	4-1/4"L x 4-1/4"L
6855	PEONY VARIATION (BUDS)	BOOT	medium	4-1/4"L x 4-3/16"H
6856	PEONY	BOOT M	small	3-7/16"H x 3-9/16"H
6857	BEAR CLAW	SHOE M	large	6-1/2"L x 3"H
6858	BEAR CLAW	SHOE M	medium	5-1/2"L x 2-5/8"H
6859	BEAR CLAW	SHOE M	small	4-1/2"L x 2-3/16"H
7224	TEXTURED PEONY	BOOT	large	5"L x 4-15/16"H
7225	TEXTURED PEONY	BOOT	medium	4-3/16"L x 4-3/16"H
7226	TEXTURED PEONY	BOOT	small	3-9/16"H x 3-1/2"H
7405	LADIES OXFORD	SHOE M		5-7/8"L x 2-13/16"H
7370	SCROLLS & BORDER SHELLS	BOOT M	large	4-15/16"L x 4-13/16"H
7416	SCROLLS & BORDER SHELLS	BOOT M	medium	4-1/16"L x 4-1/16"H
8232	FLORAL & MEDALLION CUFF	BOOT M	large	4-7/8"L x 5"H

M = at least one in the pattern and size specified has been found with the Galluba & Hofmann mark.

HISTORY. Galluba & Hofmann began when it was entered in the trade registry on 6 June 1888 as a porcelain factory and ceramic institute under the name "Bernhard Kuechler & Co.". The site was Langewiesner Strasse and the specialty was the production of fine porcelain figures. The factory also produced flowered objects and kitchen implements and was advertising "articles in the Copenhagen and Old Vienna Styles". Their products were sold in the United States and France as well as in Germany. Two years after its founding, the company employed seventy-nine people.

In June 1891, Hugo Galluba became a partner. It is assumed that Kuechler left at the same time because the name of the company now became "Galluba & Hofmann". In the decade preceding his join-ing the factory as a partner, Galluba had been an executive with the Ilmenauer Porzellanfabrik A.G. Galluba's experience is credited with the upswing of his namesake company. In 1894 at the World Fair in Antwerp, Belgium, the company was awarded a bronze medal for its products.

Figure M7 shows an announcement of 16 March 1896 "to all concerned" that was signed with power of attorney as per the court by E. Jaecklein and F. G. Albrecht. A translation from the German of the body of the announcement conveyed the following: *As the outcome of friendly discussions the previously joint owners of the firms Schumann & Klett and Galluba & Hofmann have agreed that Mr. Ad. Klett has become the sole owner of the porcelain studio of Schumann & Klett and has left the porcelain factory of Galluba & Hofmann whereas the messers Hugo Galluba and Alfred Teufel leave the firm of Schumann & Klett and continue to direct the por-celain factory of Galluba & Hofmann – which has for some time been under their direction – in unchanged manner. The operation of the two firms is in no way interrupted through this separation.*

The letterhead of this announcement has the company name, Galluba & Hofmann, and immediately under it a cartouched logo, "Fantasy pieces and figures of finer and finest genre. Kitchen items and inexpensive useful items for domestic and foreign market, etc." Their use of the word "fantasy" may have been in reference to the decorating technique they developed where they used extruded slip applied to pieces to give them the "wedding cake" look for which they became known. It may also have been in reference to the *novelty* nature of some of their wares.

The address for the company that was given in the announce-ment was the Showroom at the Leipzig Fair in the Exposition Palace, 3rd Floor, Rooms 101 and 102. In Ilmenau, the factory was located on Langewiesner Street.

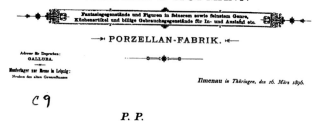

Figure M7. Letter formally announcing new management of Galluba & Hofmann factory.

By 1897, the number of employees had grown to over 500. In that year Galluba & Hofmann received the gold medal at the Saxon-Thuringian Industry and Trade Exhibition in Leipzig, Germany for their artistic accomplishments. Their growing renown was acknowl-edged by several visits to the factory by the family of the archduke. A porcelain clock entered into the 1900 Paris World's Fair brought an Honorable Mention to the company. Company products were also displayed at the Great Berlin Art Exhibition in 1911.

Siegismund Wernekinck was one of the better known artists from whom Galluba & Hofmann purchased models. He was especially known for his animal portrayals including a kangaroo group, a play-ing cat, and fighting stag beetles. Other independent artists known to have designed models for Galluba & Hofmann were Leuthäuser, Poertzel, and G. Mardersteig.

The factory successfully engaged in the field of porcelain technology, developing appliqué techniques as well as powerful colors, among which a yellow-brown was reported to have been particularly striking. The company invented "Marmorzellan", a type of imitation marble, and had it patented.

In 1912, the factory employed about 300 workers and artists. At that time there were four kilns for sharp firing and six muffle kilns. It is presumed that the company went bankrupt and porcelain production ceased some time after the beginning of the Great Depression in 1929. Röntgen has written the author that he has found the company mentioned in 1930 with 140 employees and in 1937 with the remark "company closed". Fiala reports that the porcelain decorating shop of Hertzer, Reinhardt & Gruebel was to be found in the factory buildings after 1932.

Figure M8. Products of the Galluba & Hofmann factory, Ilmenau, Thuringia, Germany.

Gemma. *See Schmidt Victoria.*

German Doll Company, The. *See also, Weiss, Kühnert.* The German Doll Company, Gräfenthal, Thuringia, Germany, 1999–present, a U.S. Subchapter S Corporation. Ohio businesswoman Susan Bickert purchased the entire contents of the Weiss, Kühnert factory in Gräfenthal in 1999. Among the contents were some 30,000 molds. With her German associate, Roland M. Schlegel, Bickert founded The German Doll Company and began production of a limited number of items made from the original Weiss, Kühnert molds. They are marked with their own company logo, a kiln-fired blue rolypoly clown, making it easy for a novice to distinguish the contemporary piece from the original. Experienced collectors would be able to tell the new from the old by the colors and glaze. Among their current products are limited edition pieces that are cast from the old molds for collectors' clubs and catalogs.

Gerz. Simon Peter Gerz, Grenzhausen, Palatinate, Germany, 1862–present.

Gibus & Redon. Limoges, France, 1872–1881. They made decorative porcelain, dinnerware, statuettes, large vases, pierced work, and items with angels/cherubs. The company excelled at "high-fired" porcelains and was known for the whiteness and quality of its porcelain. The city of Limoges sits on a deposit of kaolin, the ingredient in porcelain that provides its white color. The quality of this clay is exceptionally high.

Gibus & Redon was the second of three factories that evolved from the youthful friendship of three men from Limoges: Pierre Justin Gibus, born on 9 January 1821 in his father's bread shop, Alpinien Margaine, and Martial Redon. The latter two were sons of wood sellers, and each was five years younger than Gibus. All three lived in or near the Ponticauds quarter, one of the oldest parts of Limoges. It was bounded on one side by the Vienne River. Logs were floated down the river where they were gathered by

wood sellers who stacked them on the banks of the river port of the Le Naveix and distributed them to various clients including the porcelain factories that made up a large segment of this populous quarter.

In 1853, the three friends rented a building where they established a porcelain factory with three wood-fired kilns. By the age of thirty-two, Gibus was an accomplished porcelain technician. Among the three associates, the company bore his name alone and was called Gibus & Co. (1853-1872). Redon was probably in charge of management. Margaine was an artist who had attended the schools of design and modeling sponsored by the Society of Agriculture, Sciences and Arts and, "It was he who executed or directed the execution of works of porcelain whose beauty, elegance, purity of form, and impeccable taste characterize the production of this firm." (*Almanac of Limoges*, p. 160.) By 1861, Gibus & Co. employed 193 workers; in 1864, employees numbered 208, making it a factory of average importance. Their products, however, won acclaim with their contemporaries as well as at the Paris Exposition in 1855. From 1865 on, Gibus supplied the famous Charles Haviland factory with products to supplement the Haviland line, especially for the American market. Demand became so great that Gibus had to build a new factory. The new factory would open without Margaine, who resigned his position at the factory on 1 January 1872, probably due to illness. He would never again be professionally associated with his boyhood friends and he died on 3 December 1878.

The two remaining partners opened their new factory under their combined names: Gibus & Redon (1872–1881). They had three large coal-fired kilns, a work force of 250, and ranked fourth after Haviland, Alluaud, and Pouyat. At the World Exposition of 1878, the firm received accolades for its white porcelains in bisque and glazed finishes, as well as for the ornamentation on the pieces submitted. Note was also made of their contributions to the progress of the porcelain industry; they were among the first to introduce machines powered by steam engines to turn plates. Gibus retired in 1881 and died in 1897. Redon carried on the business as Martial Redon and Co. (1882–1896) until retiring in 1896. His product line evolved into utilitarian wares as well as pieces with elaborate patterns.

Gien. Faïenceries de Gien, Gien, France, 1822–present. The Englishman Thomas Antoine Edmé Hulm, also known as "Hall", began a pottery factory in Gien about 1 March 1822 in association with his brother-in-law Guyon. The factory was housed in a former convent that had been established in 1490 by Anne of Beaujeu. The company was registered as Hall & Guyon. Through name and ownership changes, years of glory and periods of decline, including bankruptcy in 1983, the factory has survived to this day. During its existence, the Gien factory has produced a full range of wares from plain white crockery and utilitarian tiles to elaborately decorated pieces. Indeed, the kinds of objects Gien made in pottery are astounding: from sconces to barometers, chandeliers to lanterns, fountains to knife rests, and musical instruments to dinnerware. Gien has won many awards for its pottery.

Gien reproduced patterns from Rouen, Delft, Moustiers, majolica, Faenza, Urbino and others beginning about 1856. Of special importance to shoe collectors is knowledge that from about 1876–1878 Gien made pieces with décors inspired by Longwy-style cloisonné glazes. If unmarked, these shoes are often attributed to Longwy when they instead were made by Gien or another factory. The Gien décor with which American collectors are most familiar is *bleu de Gien*, a classic Italian style in blue and white. When marked, the identification found on Gien is most often a representation of the coat of arms of the city of Gien, consisting of a castle topped with a crown of turrets under which is a banner with "Gien" in it.

Figure M9. Products of the Gien factory.

Goss. William Henry Goss (Ltd.), Stoke, Staffordshire, England, 1858–1929 (1858–1939). The company was known for the quality of its porcelain and hand-painted crests on those of its wares that bear coats of arms. Goss had learned his craft and the chemistry of ceramics at an early age when he worked for the Copeland Works, where he eventually became chief artist and designer. The porcelain in Goss pieces is among the thinnest that can be found. That so many pieces have survived for about a century is testimony to the superior strength, quality, and craftsmanship of the wares.

Pine has divided the Goss wares into three periods, with small overlaps in them. The First Period, 1858–1887, covers the products manufactured by William Henry Goss during the time when he owned and operated the company. The Second Period, 1881–1934, is the range during which his sons were involved in the business. The Third Period, 1930–1939, delineates the period in which the Goss mark was used on wares made by other factories.

The heraldic china for which the company is especially known was introduced in the Second Period as the result of an idea by Adolphus, son of William. He believed that there was a tourist market for small souvenir china ornaments bearing the coat-of-arms of the town being visited. Now known as crested china, these ornaments would become the major products of the factory during the Second Period. The spectrum of models and crests was extensive. The models were chosen because they had some unique connection to a town and the original crest on the piece would be that town's coat of arms. For example, the riding shoe of Queen Elizabeth I was housed at Horham Hall in Thaxted, England. Goss made a miniature model of it and cast it in porcelain. The first pieces carried the coat of arms of Thaxted. When the coat of arms represents the town in which the historic artifact was found, it is called a *matching crest*. As the demand for crested china spread, most items produced by Goss were made with crests from other towns. Today, pieces with matching crests are generally the rarest and thus more valuable. All had hand-painted crests whose painters were carefully trained before being allowed to work on a piece for market. Nearly every Goss piece is clearly marked, usually on its base. The crested china pieces have the factory Goshawk with outstretched wings, the company's name, and usually a description of the piece.

Goss is known to have made eight shoes during its Second Period and two during its Third Period. All are shown in this book. Table 3 lists the Goss shoes with details on each. The Princess Victoria First Shoe originally came with a small leaflet called *The News* and titled "Her Majesty's First Little Shoes". It is reproduced in Figure M10.

Table 3. W. H. Goss Crested China Shoes

Goss was the originator and is the best-known manufacturer of heraldic china. A crest from the town or city for which the piece was designed is called a matching crest. Crested china with matching crests is more valuable.

Name of Shoe	First Made	Dimensions	Bottom Inscription
1. PRINCESS/QUEEN VICTORIA'S FIRST SHOE *Matching arms: SIDMOUTH or H.M.QUEEN VICTORIA*	late 1880s	4-1/16" L x 1-5/16" H	**pre 1901:** "MODEL, EXACT SIZE, OF FIRST SHOES WORN BY PRINCESS VICTORIA – H. M. THE QUEEN – MADE AT SIDMOUTH 1819" **post 1901:** replaced "THE QUEEN", above, with "LATE QUEEN (WHO DIED JAN. 22ⁿᵈ 1901) …"
2. BOULOGNE WOODEN SHOE *Matching arms: BOULOGNE-SUR-MER*	1909	4-3/4"L x 1-1/2"H	"MODEL OF WOODEN SHOES WORN BY THE FISHERWOMEN OF BOULOGNE SUR MER & LE PORTAL RᴰNᴼ 539421" *(registered 1909)*
3. DINANT WOODEN SHOE *Matching arms: DINANT* *(rare with this crest because of war)*	1914	2-7/8"L x 1-5/8"H	"MODEL OF WOODEN SHOE WORN AT DINANT"
4. NORWEGIAN WOODEN SHOE *Matching arms: NORGE (NORWAY)*	1914	4-3/16"L x 1-1/8"H	"MODEL OF NORWEGIAN WOODEN SHOE"
5. LANCASHIRE CLOG *Matching arms: LANCASHIRE*	1916	3-3/4"L x 2-1/8"H	"MODEL OF A LANCASHIRE CLOG. COPYRIGHT"
6. DUTCH SABOT *Matching arms: HOLLAND or ANY DUTCH TOWN*	2nd period	3-1/4"L x 1-1/2"H	"MODEL OF DUTCH SABOT"
7. QUEEN ELIZABETH'S RIDING SHOE *(rarest of Goss shoes) Matching arms: THAXTED*	1921	4-3/16"L x 1-5/8"H	"MODEL OF QUEEN ELIZABETH'S RIDING SHOE ORIGINALLY AT HORHAM HALL, THAXTED"
8. SLIPPER WALL POCKET	2nd period	3-7/8"L x 1-1/16"H	None
9. ANKLE SHOE ("slipper" in Pine book)	3rd period	2-7/8" L x 1-5/8"L	None
10. JOHN WATERSON'S CLOG *Arcadian factory model with Goss mark*	3rd period	4-1/8"L x 1-5/8"H	None

HER MAJESTY'S FIRST LITTLE SHOES.

THE exquisite taste displayed by Mr. William Henry Goss, of Stoke-on-Trent, in his parian and porcelain wares, whether classic and ornamental, or adapted for ordinary domestic use, both in design and material, has been endorsed by prize medals at various of the world's great exhibitions. In one report we read:—"Few displays of porcelain are to be seen in the exhibition which excel those made by Mr. Goss. In the parian statuettes, vases, tazzi, &c., and other ceramic materials under notice, the perfection of art manufacture seems certainly to have been reached."

Mr. Goss is a Fellow of the Royal Geological and of several other learned societies, a chemical expert, an accomplished antiquarian, and the author of a number of valuable biographical, scientific, and literary works.

There is always something touching in looking at the shoe of a little child; for who can forecast the rough and often thorny paths the little pilgrim may have to tread!

Mr. Goss, accidently, in the following manner, got to hear of the Queen's first shoe, which he has now copied and reproduced in porcelain—imitating form, material and colour. The story we give, although it is a story, is quite true.

Her Majesty's father, the Duke of Kent, went to live at Sidmouth, in 1819, to get the benefit of the Devonshire climate. While there, a certain local shoemaker received the order for the first pair of shoes for the infant Princess Victoria. But instead of making two only he made three, while he was about it, facsimiles, and kept one as a memorial and curiosity. It has been preserved to this day, and is now in the possession of his daughter, who is the wife of Mr. Goss's porcelain agent at Sidmouth.

Hearing of this, Mr. Goss borrowed the shoe, and made an exact copy in porcelain. The dainty little shoe is four inches in length, has a brown leather sole, white satin upper, is laced and tied in front with a bow of light blue silk ribbon, and bound with the same round the edge, and down the back of the heel.

In 1820 the shoemaker received the Royal Warrant; and that, also, is preserved with the interesting little shoe.

This little porcelain model, so suggestive, will arouse the loyal thrill of love and blessing in thousands of British hearts, simple little Cinderella sort of thing as it is; while to Her Gracious Majesty herself, it must touch a minor chord that vibrates back to the far reach of memory.

A. J. S.

Figure M10. Leaflet issued with Goss model of Queen Victoria's first shoes.

Grafton China. *See Jones, Alfred B., and Sons.*

Hampshire Pottery. Hampshire Pottery Company, Keene, New Hampshire, 1871–1923. James Scholly Taft and his uncle James Burnap established the Hampshire Pottery in Keene in 1871, first producing utilitarian products such as crocks, jugs, butter churns, and pots. In 1878, the company began producing majolica wares, and in 1883 they entered the art pottery market. Taft's brother-in-law, Cadmon Robertson, joined the company in 1904. He was the creator of Hampshire's famous matte glazes. Robertson became so important to the business that when he died in 1914, Taft would plod on without him for only two years before selling the pottery. The new owner closed the factory in 1923 because the expense of bringing in fuel for the kilns made the operation uncompetitive. The glazes on Hampshire Pottery generally dictate their value. Taft's name or initials are commonly impressed into wares, but the early pieces are not marked.

Hancock, Sampson, & Sons. Sampson Hancock & Sons, Stoke, Staffordshire, England, 1858–1937. The company began manufacturing earthenware in 1858. After the company's founder Sampson Hancock died on 9 May 1900, the factory was taken over by his sons. They made all types of domestic pottery and later introduced a high-quality semi-porcelain used for a wide range of products. The company is believed to have ceased production of crested china miniatures in the early 1920s. The company's most common trademark is *Corona China*. Among twenty-three other trademarks, the company's products may also be found with bottom marks *Alexandra*, *British Manufacture*, *Triood*, and *Victoria China*; some of these may be whole-

salers' marks placed on products purchased from several factories.

Hautin and Boulanger. Hautin and Boulanger, Choisy-le-Roi (Seine), France, 1836-1934. An earthenware factory was begun in 1804 by a gentleman named Paillart. He and Hautin operated the factory from 1824-1836. In 1836, Louis Boulanger and Hyppolite Hautin took over the factory and it became Hautin and Boulanger. They were succeeded in 1863 by Hyppolite Boulanger who initiated the factory's work in majolica. Majolica production ceased in 1920 and the factory closed in 1934.

HB. *See Hubaudière.*

Heber & Co. Heber & Co. Porzellanfabrik, Neustadt, Bavaria, Germany, 1900–1922. The factory produced figurines, dolls, doll heads, household porcelain, and giftware.

Heinz & Co. Porzellanfabrik Heinz & Co. (1900–1972)/Heinz & Co. Porzellanfabrik GmbH (1994–present), Grafenthal-Meernach, Thuringia, Germany. The factory was established on 6 October 1897 as Theodor Wagner & Co. It was acquired on 3 March 1900 by Friedrich Heinz who with his family apparently ran the company until 1972 when it was nationalized and the facilities appropriated for use as storage buildings. In 1994, about four years after the reunification of Germany, the facilities and property were restituted to the Heinz family. Among their current specialties are figurines of animals, birds, and children. The author's husband and German friend met the current owner, Mrs. Hess, when

Figure M11. Composite of shoes taken from the pages of an early Heinz & Co. catalog, c. early 1900s.

they visited the factory in 1998. Mrs. Hess was born a Heinz. She has a license agreement with Alberta's Molds, Inc. of Atascadero, California. Under the agreement, Alberta can sell certain forms through its mail order business for laymen artists. In a 1999 conversation with the former owner of Alberta, it was learned that he had gone out of business but that his employees had bought out part of Alberta, including the Heinz molds. By arrangement with Heinz, the American personnel go to the factory in Germany, select useful master molds, ship them back to the States, and make new masters from the Heinz molds. Occasionally, they modify the master molds to simplify their use.

There were no shoes in the Alberta catalog that Mrs. Hess had at her factory. Mrs. Hess did, however, have an old Heinz catalog from the early 1900s. On three pages of it she found a total of a half dozen shoes. She generously donated those pages. They are reproduced in the illustration in Figure M11. The numbers below each shoe are those that appeared in the catalog.

Henriot. Henriot, Quimper, France, 1778–c.1984 (Les Faïenceries de Quimper). *See also, Hubaudière.* The lineage of the Henriot factory began in 1778 when Guillaume Dumaine established a second pottery in Quimper, where there were deposits of fine clay as well as plentiful wood from nearby forests to fuel kilns. The factory passed through several family generations with their associated marriages. On the death of Pierre-Jules Henriot in 1884, his son Jules Henriot, only eighteen at the time, became the sole director of the factory. In spite of societal unrest and economic difficulties, Jules grew the company until it rivaled the Hubaudière establishment, also in Quimper. Henriot's products were very popular, with visitors using the newly opened rail lines to Brittany bringing home souvenirs, including those from the Henriot factory. Between WWI and WWII, both Henriot and Hubaudière expanded and innovated. Jules turned over the factory to his two sons in 1944. In 1968, it was merged with Verlingue's HB factory, the two being called Les Faïenceries de Quimper. Although they were housed under the same roof, the Henriot and HB groups continued to produce the products in the designs for which they each were known, and they also continued to use their own marks. The entire operation was purchased in 1984 by an American couple that eventually integrated the Hubaudière and Henriot factories.

Figure M12. Products of the Henriot factory.

Heubach. Gebr. Christoph & Phillipp Heubach (1843–1904)/ Gebr. Heubach AG (1904–1945), Lichte, Thuringia, Germany. The Heubach factory had both predecessor owners and successor owners and continues in operation today, but the period of most interest to collectors was the time when the company was in Heubach hands. The early Heubachs made household and decorative porcelain and figurines. They may be most famous, however, for the broad variety of dolls with expressive faces that they made beginning in 1910. A small group of shoes made by Heubach has been identified. The most valuable of them are the baby-in-a-tramp shoe series and snow shoes with hand-painted designs.

Hewitt and Leadbeater. Hewitt and Leadbeater, Willow Potteries, Longton, Staffordshire, England, 1905–1919; Hewitt Brothers, same location, 1919–c.1925. The primary trademark used by Hewitt and Leadbeater was *Willow Art China*, but they used over seventy additional trademarks on various items. Among those that may be found on crested china shoes are *Alexandra China* (for an unknown wholesaler) and *The Milton China*. The latter was a trademark used by the Hewitt Bros. at their Willow Potteries works on china produced for a London wholesaler (G.G.&Co.). The trademark *Wy Not?* with the question mark was used by Robinson & Leadbeater. *Wy Not* without the question mark was a trademark used by Hewitt and Leadbeater.

Hirsch, Franziska. Franziska Hirsch (Decorating Shop), Dresden, Saxony, Germany, 1894–1914. Hirsch ran a porcelain decorating shop in Dresden that specialized in décors in the Meissen and Vienna styles. Among her décors found on shoes are hand-painted, small florals against a white ground. In 1914 the shop was owned by Fanny Koppel, and in 1930 it was purchased by Margot Wohlauer.

Hoganas. Hoganas Ceramics, Hoganas, Sweden, 1797–c.1980.

Hoods Ltd. Hoods Ltd., International Works, Fenton, Staffordshire, England, 1919–c.1964. The company manufactured earthenware and made crested china from c.1919 until probably only the early 1920s. Their registered trademark consisted of three hooded heads. It can be found with *Triood* or *Fenton Stoke-on-Trent* written beneath. Their products are identical to those of Corona China.

Houry, Jules-Charles. Jules-Charles Houry, Limoges, France, second half of 1800s. Houry is known to have had a studio for ceramic decoration in the second half of the 19th century in France. He decorated faiences including the appliqué of flowers for vases, bowls, clocks, etc. He won prizes at expositions where he exhibited and served on judging committees: London, 1862; Vienna, 1873; Philadelphia, 1876; Paris, 1878, 1889, and 1900; St. Petersburg, Madrid, etc.

Hubaudière. Maison Bousquet-de la Hubaudière *aka* Faïencerie de la Grande Maison (Hubaudière) *aka* de la Hubaudière *aka* HB, Quimper, France, 1690– c.1916, 1922–c.1984 (Les Faïenceries de Quimper). *See also Henriot.* Jean-Baptiste Bousquet came to Quimper from southern France in about 1699. His son Pierre, an experienced faience maker when he was in Marseilles, established the first faience factory in Quimper, c.1707. In 1731, Pierre took in his son-in-law as his assistant and in 1739 Pierre Clément Caussy joined the group. He provided technical skills learned from his family, long in the pottery business. When Caussy died in 1782, the factory passed to his son-in-law, Antoine de la Hubaudière, and remained in the family until 1917 when the potter Jules Verlingue from Boulogne-sur-Mer purchased it, bringing it back into production in 1920. His son, Jean-Yves Verlingue, took over the HB factory in 1952. The Verlingue HB factory joined with the Henriot factory under one roof in 1968, though both continued to use their own designs. The combined operation was named *Les Faïenceries de Quimper.* An American couple, Paul and Sarah Janssens, formed a company in 1984 that purchased the combined HB and Henriot potteries. Beginning about 1882, the HB factory decreased its output of wares in the Rouen décor and increased its production of wares with Breton décors.

Figure M13. Products of the HB factory.

Hunt, B.F.&S. Benjamin F. Hunt & Sons, Elbogen, Bohemia, Austria (presently Loket, Czechia), 1893–1902. Hunt was a wealthy American businessman, treasurer of the Boston toy company Horace Partridge Company, when he bought into the Carl Speck porcelain factory in Elbogen, Austria in 1893. With his twenty-one-year-old twin sons Horace and Homer, Hunt operated the new business as Benjamin F. Hunt & Sons. They manufactured fine china in the Carlsbad area of Bohemia, specializing in high-quality souvenir china. The senior Hunt spent a great deal of his time in Bohemia while his sons operated the wholesale and retail outlets in New York and Boston. The firm was prospering when it inexplicably announced in December 1902 that it was going out of business, that Hunt senior would remain at the Elbogen factory, and that his sons would pursue other lines of work. Adolph Persch purchased the Elbogen factory in 1902 and operated it as a branch until closing it in 1937.

Ilmenau Porcelain Factory. Ilmenauer Porzellanfabrik AG (1871–1934), Ilmenau, Thuringia, Germany, 1777–present. They made decorative porcelain; table, coffee, and tea sets including in the popular strawflower pattern; figurines; and gift and novelty items including thimbles, writing utensils, pipe heads, and a range of miniature shoes.

The Ilmenau Porcelain Factory can trace its beginning to the factory founded in 1777 by Christian Zacharias Gräbner. From then until the present, there have been at least eleven different factory names and/or ownership changes. In this text, the firm will be referred to as the Ilmenau Porcelain Factory, its name during production of the shoes shown herein.

Figure M14. Products of and attributed to the Ilmenau Porcelain Factory, c.1900. Note the similarities in decorating techniques to Galluba & Hofmann, its sister porcelain factory in the city of Ilmenau.

HISTORY. The first attempts at porcelain making in Ilmenau were made in the first half of the 18th century, when Duke Ernst August von Sachsen (Saxony)-Weimar, in whose territory Ilmenau was located, granted permission for the construction of a porcelain factory. It was built in 1737 but failed to make porcelain, turning out only fayence. Although the secrets of making porcelain had escaped from the Meissen factory with factory workers a few decades earlier, the intricacies of the processes were not well understood by many. Another four decades would pass until the founding of the first successful Ilmenau porcelain factory.

In 1777, the ruling duke Karl-August granted concessions to porcelain entrepreneur Christian Zacharias Gräbner (1777–1782) in order to gain the privilege of having a porcelain factory in his own territory. The concessions granted to the founder of the factory and, in part, to later leaseholders, give testimony to the importance to the ruler of the prestige of having porcelain manufactured in his district. The concessions dealt with the ability to obtain wood from the state forest, the arrangement of favorable payment agreements and extensive credit, and the exclusion of any other porcelain establishments in the Ilmenau district.

Ilmenau was part of the Duchy of Saxony-Weimar. It was surrounded by other small states. Every border was a tariff border where raw materials and wares being brought into the Duchy were taxed. A decisive factor in the profitability of 18th century German porcelain factories was their proximity to needed raw materials. Feldspar was mined in a town near Ilmenau in the Saxony-Weimar district, cutting transportation and tariff costs. The material used to protect the porcelain from open fires was secured from Martinroda beginning in 1786. But to obtain kaolin of the needed quality, it was necessary to shoulder the added cost of bringing it from the Zettlitz mines in the state of Bohemia. Eventually, by the close of the 1700s, wood had to be brought in from Langewiesen, which belonged to Schwarzburg-Sonderhausen. The mills producing the cleaned and mixed materials of the porcelain were set up in the Ilm valley to use waterpower as the energy source.

The original porcelain factory went through several owners in the 1800s. Gräbner was continually in debt, necessitating a takeover of the factory by Duke Karl-August of Saxony-Weimar (1782–1786). He gained legal ownership of the factory in 1786 and in July of that year leased it to Gotthelf Greiner for six years (1786–1792). Greiner already owned porcelain factories in Limbach and Grossbreitenbach. In spite of favorable developments in the factory under his direction, he chose not to renew his lease when it expired. The factory was then leased to Christian Nonne (1792–1808) who later purchased it, in 1808, with his son-in-law, Ernst Karl Roesch. They operated the company as Nonne & Roesch (1808–1813) until Nonne's death. Under them the factory flourished and became one of the most important businesses in the city, employing about 100 at its height. Among their products were blue and white medallions with the classic themes modeled after the jasper ware of Josiah Wedgwood, coffee services with Vedouten painting, and portrait cups in the Bordueren mode.

Roesch and his successors operated the business as the Ilmenau Porcelain Factory (1813–1871). With time and succeeding managers, the business declined and indebtedness increased. In 1871, Hermann Stuercke, co-owner of the Adolph Stuercke banking house, forced an auction of the factory and simultaneously created a group of people interested in becoming stockholders. When they won the factory at auction, Stuercke, with 224 of the 400 total shares, became the main stockholder. The name of the enterprise now became the Ilmenauer Porzellanfabrik A.G. (1871–1934). It was the first Thuringian stock company in the porcelain business. A great upswing in business resulted in the number employed rising to 479. Although employment numbers would be affected by economic factors, between 300 and 500 were employed by the factory until 1973.

In the closing years of the 19th century, the Ilmenau Porcelain Factory A.G. produced cups and other objects with flower motifs. The factory patented several processes including relief gilding, matte-gold, and matte finishes. To this day, many objects made by the factory at that time retain remarkably bright gold accents. The markets of this era were primarily in England and the United States.

The outbreak of WWI had a catastrophic effect on business. Exports to both enemy and neutral countries were blockaded. Drafting of workers into military service made the conduct of the porcelain business problematic. The difficulty of obtaining coal, now used in the kilns instead of wood, and the needed raw materials increased constantly. The beginning of the global economic crisis in 1929 foretold cutbacks and shortened work hours. In the following year, the amount of business done by the Ilmenau Porcelain Factory sank by 50 percent. The company was particularly hard hit because its major markets were in England and the United States, the latter especially hard hit by the Great Depression. By 1932, the output of the porcelain factory was only 13.4 percent of that of 1928.

Between 1932 and 1934, a way out of the weak market was sought by switching from inexpensive export porcelain to quality porcelain. Porcelain with the popular cobalt blue decoration and rich gilding became a specialty. The year 1934 saw the arrival of a new director, Emil Lentner from Meissen, and a new name, Ilmenauer Porzellanfabrik Graf von Henneberg A.G. (Ilmenau Porcelain Factory Count von Henneberg A.G.) (1934–1948).

After the outbreak of WWII, export was intensified. About 1942, some production was changed to the provision of products needed for the war effort. In the first post-WWII years, the factory produced almost exclusively for reparations to the occupying Soviet Union. The Supreme Head of the Soviet Military Administration of Germany appropriated the ownership of the factory on 17 April 1948, taking the company out of private hands. With nationalization came a name change to VEB Porzellanwerk Graf von Henneberg (1948–1973). The product lines, as just before WWII, consisted mainly of household porcelain, often richly decorated.

In the fall of 1973, porcelain production was moved from the old buildings into new quarters in Eichicht and with the move came the newest name, VEB Henneberg Porzellan (1973–1991). By 1990, some 1700 were employed in the porcelain business there, ranking the enterprise next to Kahla as one of the great porcelain producers of the former DDR, or German Democratic Republic. Since 1991, the porcelain business has been in private hands again.

Several other porcelain factories and porcelain decorating shops were established over the years in Ilmenau. At one time or another, eight porcelain factories and a dozen porcelain-decorating shops have existed in Ilmenau. Only what is referred to herein as the Ilmenau Porcelain Factory remains. Although the work force numbered only about 400 by 1995, this single porcelain company remains one of the largest employers in the region. Among the products for which there is high demand is the tableware made there.

Irice. Irice is a designation used by New York importer Irving Rice on the wares he brought in from and had made in such countries as Czechoslovakia and France. This importer appears to have been active in the pre-WWII era.

Ivora Ware. *See Ritchie, William & Son.*

Jones, Alfred B., and Sons. Alfred B. Jones and Sons Ltd., Grafton China Works, Longton, Staffordshire, England, 1900–present. Jones used the trademark *Grafton China* and the company is thus commonly referred to as Grafton, though a dozen other trademarks can be found on their wares. Grafton was a major producer of high-quality genuine porcelain. They rivaled Shelley as the primary Goss competitors for the higher-end market share. By 1906, the company was producing crested china and continued with these items probably through most of the 1920s.

Jonroth. *See Roth, John H.*

Keltic. *See Taylor and Kent.*

Kister, A. W. Fr. A. W. Fr. Kister Porzellanmanufaktur (A. W. Fr. Kister Porcelain Manufactory), Scheibe-Alsbach, Thuringia, Germany, 1846–1972; successors: 1972–present. Kister hired first-rate artists and sculptors. The factory attained an international reputation for its por-

celain figurines and won many international awards between about 1870 and 1914. Its products included high-quality figurines of the Meissen type, busts of poets and composers, tomb ornaments, dolls' heads, jointed dolls, and other toys including Snow Babies. They even developed and produced a doll that could be immersed in water. The company was nationalized in 1972, becoming VEB Porzellanmanufaktur Scheibe-Alsbach. In 1975, it became a branch of VEB United Decorative Porcelainworks Lichte in Lichte, Germany. The factory was privatized in 1990 with the dissolution of the German Democratic Republic (East Germany) and was purchased in 1995 by the Royal Bayreuth factory in Tettau, Germany.

Kusnetzoff. Kusnetzoff, Novocharitonowa and other cities, Russia, c.1800–present. T. J. Kusnetzoff founded a porcelain factory in Novocharitonowa in about 1800. The company remained family owned through the generations, building factories in other Russian cities and absorbing many smaller factories. It is believed to exist to this day.

Kutscher, Wilhelm. Schwarzenberger Porzellanfabrik Fr. Wilhelm Kutscher & Co., Schwarzenberg, Saxony, Germany, 1908–1931. They are known to have made household and decorative porcelain, gift articles, and crested china. Their crested china sometimes carries a bottom mark *Made in Saxony,* but more often is unmarked.

Lamm, Ambrosius. Ambrosius Lamm (Decorating Shop), Dresden, Saxony, Germany, 1887–c.1949. Lamm established a decorating shop that specialized in décors of the Meissen and Vienna styles. His shop was known to have changed hands by 1928, when Rudolf Pitschke was its owner.

Lankester, Wendy. Wendy Lankester, *The Gainsborough Collection,* Kent, England. Lankester, Figure M15, is a contemporary researcher and sculptor of miniature historic shoes cast in finest bone china and painted under her direction by master painters from well-known English bone china factories. Lankester learned her pottery skills at The Hammersmith School of Art in London in her early years. She has worked in earthenware, stoneware, all forms of studio pottery, and on the potter's wheel. Her creativity led to her modeling and sculpting her original designs in clay. Lankester launched her *Gainsborough Collection* with four limited-edition figural shoes in February 1984. Hers was the first such specialist collection ever created and she was the first to research and produce authentic replicas of actual shoe styles worn during various historical periods. The limited-edition shoes were modeled to look as though they actually had been worn. The *Gainsborough Collection* (Table 4) is thus a three-dimensional picture of the history of footwear, manufactured in the finest bone china. Unlike the resin shoe series that her models inspired, Lankester's shoes were never mass-produced; all the beads, buttons, bows, and buckles were made by hand and separately applied after the casting. By the year 2002, Lankester had ceased production of her *Gainsborough Collection,* destroyed all the molds but one, and was immersed in her love of landscape painting. The one mold not destroyed was that for *Sophie,* which had mysteriously disappeared many years ago from the factory commissioned to cast it.

Lankester's carefully researched shoes are faithful porcelain interpretations of historic fashions. For example, the shoe she has titled "Early Stuart Rose Shoe" is, surprisingly, a man's shoe. Her meticulous design and sculpture was based on a portrait of Richard Sackville, 3rd Earl of Dorset, painted by William Larkin in 1613. His shoes were shown with enormous rose poufs of intricately formed ribbons, whose expense was decried by moralists of the era as an extravagant self-indulgence. Lankester's models of these poufs are a remarkable example of the perfection of the porcelain makers' arts.

Lankester's "Frederica" is modeled after the shoe worn by Princess Frederica of Prussia, a scale sketch of which was published on 6 December 1791. She had become the Duchess of York when she married the Duke of York, second son of George III, in November

Figure M15. Shoe designer and modeler Wendy Lankester working in Kent, England in 1999 on a wax sculpture of an historic shoe. *Photo by Jeffry Alan Bradway.*

1791. Her feet were reputed to be only 5-7/8" long and 2" wide at the broadest point. The publication of the 1791 sketch sparked a fad for miniature ceramic shoes among the wealthy.

Unique for its size and the story of its creation is Lankester's cowboy boot. At nearly 6" in length and just over 6" in height, it is considerably larger in scale than many of her other shoes. Lankester was commissioned in 1987 by Thomas Goode & Company of Mayfair, London to produce a cowboy boot in fine bone china specifically for the American market. Goode toured the United States once or twice a year with special promotions of English china and glass. They particularly targeted ladies' luncheon clubs at prestigious hotels in the States. The stock market crash on "Black Monday" in the autumn of 1987 caused Goode to cancel the planned tour and only fifty cowboy boots were ever produced. Decorated in "Buffalo Bill" colors, the motifs depict the spread eagle, a longhorn, stars, and traditional lightning flashes stitched as underlays and overlays. In addition to Lankester's *Gainsborough Collection* hat logo, the bottom marks on the fifty boots include the initials of Dan Smith, one of the top ceramic artists at the Royal Doulton factory and a part-time painter for Lankester, and an elephant, Goode's special logo permitted only on items specially commissioned by them.

Leake, William. William Leake was one of many craftsmen who came from Staffordshire, England to work at United States Pottery, the Bennington, Vermont factory of Christopher Webber Fenton. (*See Bennington*). Leake is credited with having designed in the mid-1800s the tiny Bennington boots and shoe shown within this text. Spargo reported that Leake can be assumed to have been a potter of uncommon ability because many of his pieces match the quality of anything of their kind ever produced at any American pottery.

Limoges. Limoges is a city in France. Indigenous kaolin of superior quality has provided the basis for a thriving porcelain industry

for over two centuries; by the mid-1700s, Limoges was the center of the industry in France. Thus, a mark including the word "Limoges" indicates the city in which the item was made, not the factory that produced it. In the time since porcelain manufacture began in Limoges, at least ninety factories and decorating shops are known to have operated there, upwards of forty at one time. If a piece of porcelain from the city of Limoges is also marked "France", it likely was made after 1891, the year in which the U. S. McKinley Tariff Act became effective; this act required products coming into the U. S. to be marked with the country of origin. Some bottom marks include the name of the American import company instead of the French manufacturer, accompanied simply by "Limoges". NOTE: Beginning in the late 1990s, the U. S. market was flooded with porcelain objects from China. A significant percentage of them carried a mark that included the word "Limoges", usually accompanied by the word "China". Many secondary market sellers have erroneously characterized such pieces as "Limoges", a name that is correctly used only for products made in the French city of Limoges.

Longchamp Faïence Factory. Longchamp Faïence Factory, Burgundy, France. An old pottery factory was located in Longchamp, near Dijon. At the end of the 19th century, Robert Charbonnier took it over, creating the Longchamp Faïence factory. About 1914, Gaétan Moissand, who married Robert Charbonnier's daughter, took over operations of the factory. Henceforth, operations remained in the hands of the Moissand family.

Majolica formed a large part of the output of the Longchamp factory. One of the specialties of the factory was majolica with elaborate, large-scale appliqués. The company did a good business in cemetery flowers, with every petal hand-made. Also characteristic of Longchamp are decorative platters ornamented with large appliqués of such fruits and associated foliage as apples, pears, grapes, and currents. Longchamp also produced trompe-l'œil plates for shellfish and asparagus, some of which were both painted and appliquéd. Faveton has attributed three majolica shoes to Longchamp: a woman's pump with ruffled rim and large appliqué of roses; a flat-heeled skimmer with toe appliqué of a large six-petal apple blossom and leaves; and a child's shoe with two pairs of open eyelets aside an open vee with a toe appliqué of a large magnolia-like flower and leaves.

Longwy. Societe des Faienceries de Longwy et Senelle *aka* Emaux de Longwy (The Enamels of Longwy), Longwy, France, 1798–present. The Longwy pottery works dates back to 1798, when an 18th century convent was appropriated to create plates and other wares with republican scenes. With the advent shortly thereafter of Napoleon's new Empire, different motifs had to be found and vengeful slogans turned into imperial eagles. While passing through the region, Napoleon enhanced the reputation of the town and its pottery factory when he chose table services for the new houses of the Legion of Honor that he had created for the orphans of war after the battle of Austerlitz. But it was only after the Second Empire (Napoleon III, 1852–1870) that the vision of Fernand and Hippolyte d'Huart would bring to the factory a décor that would make it famous.

At great expense, the d'Huart brothers enticed away the Italian Amédée de Caranza, director of the ceramic factories of the Emperor of Japan. Not only did Caranza introduce the then popular Persian and Oriental themes to Longwy products, but he also created a new decorating technique that resembled the cloisonné enamels for which the public had such fondness. This décor, first introduced in about 1875, became known as the enamels of Longwy, although Gien produced wares at about the same time with the same technique. In greatly simplified terms, a design is produced in grease pencil on the object to be decorated. The separate areas of the design are then filled in with color. During kiln firing, the grease lines, also called "resist lines", prevent the colorful enamels from flowing across, resulting in the cloisonné effect in relief. At Longwy, the formulas for the approximately eight

Table 4. Wendy Lankester Shoes
The Gainsborough Collection

"Authentic replicas of period shoes individually handmade in English Bone China"

HISTORICAL FASHIONS in strictly limited editions of 200**	first issued	issue price*
A. HAUTE COUTURE (app. 6-1/2"L x 3-1/2"H)		
A001 Edwardian Sandal Shoe 1902	Feb. 1984	$395
A002 Early Stuart Rose Shoe 1613	Sep. 1985	$395
A003 French Regency Shoe 1775	Mar. 1986	$395
A004 Medieval Rose Window Shoe 1380	Aug. 1986	$395
A005 Late Stuart Brocade Shoe 1690	Oct. 1986	$395
B. MINIATURE (app. 4-1/2"L x 2-1/2"H)		
B001 Victorian Ladies Bootee 1890s style	Feb. 1984	$195
B002 Satin Bar Shoe 1920s style	Feb. 1984	$195
B003 Snakeskin Court Shoe 1930s style	Feb. 1984	$195
B004 Gibson Shoe 1900s style	May 1986	$195
B005 Stiletto Mule 1950s style	Oct. 1986	$195

PERIOD FASHIONS unlimited editions**	first issued	issue price*
M001 Sophie – 1740s style	July 1994	$125
M002 Marie – 1740s style	July 1994	$125

PERIOD FASHIONS unlimited editions**	first issued	issue price*
M003 Frederica – 1791s style	Apr. 1995	$125
M004 Nell – 1665s style	Apr. 1995	$115
M005 Carmen – 1680s style	Apr. 1995	$135
M006 Suleyman – 1545s style	Aug. 1996	$135
M007 Ming – 1644s style	Aug. 1996	$135
M008 Alice – 1850s style	Aug. 1996	$135
M009 Georgina – 1912s style	July 1998	$135
M010 Chloe – 1935s style	July 1998	$135

SPECIAL RELEASES*		
• (American) Cowboy boot, limited edition of 50	Oct. 1987	$495
• Queen Charlotte's shoe of 1761, Millennium project for City of Charlotte, limited to 2,000	Oct. 1999	$179

* The secondary market has not yet established resale values.
** Painter's initials on bottoms: DF = Dave Fuller & JF = Jane Fuller, painters of limited editions; DS = Dan Smith, painter of unlimited editions and cowboy boot.

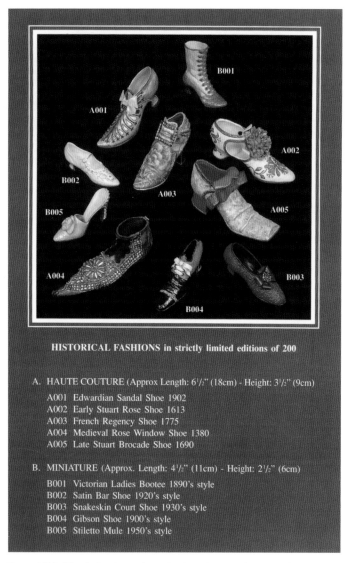

HISTORICAL FASHIONS in strictly limited editions of 200

  A. HAUTE COUTURE (Approx Length: 6¹/₂" (18cm) - Height: 3¹/₂" (9cm)

    A001 Edwardian Sandal Shoe 1902
    A002 Early Stuart Rose Shoe 1613
    A003 French Regency 1775
    A004 Medieval Rose Window Shoe 1380
    A005 Late Stuart Brocade Shoe 1690

  B. MINIATURE (Approx. Length: 4¹/₂" (11cm) - Height: 2¹/₂" (6cm)

    B001 Victorian Ladies Bootee 1890's style
    B002 Satin Bar Shoe 1920's style
    B003 Snakeskin Court Shoe 1930's style
    B004 Gibson Shoe 1900's style
    B005 Stiletto Mule 1950's style

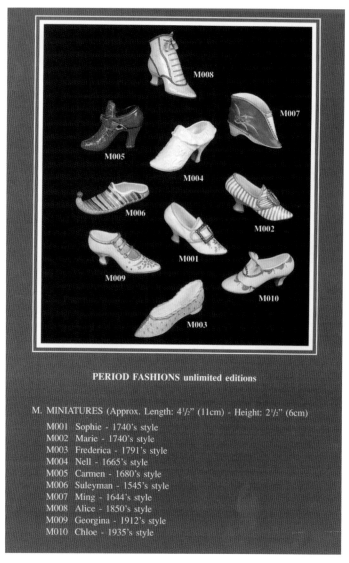

PERIOD FASHIONS unlimited editions

  M. MINIATURES (Approx. Length: 4¹/₂" (11cm) - Height: 2¹/₂" (6cm)

    M001 Sophie - 1740's style
    M002 Marie - 1740's style
    M003 Frederica - 1791's style
    M004 Nell - 1665's style
    M005 Carmen - 1680's style
    M006 Suleyman - 1545's style
    M007 Ming - 1644's style
    M008 Alice - 1850's style
    M009 Georgina - 1912's style
    M010 Chloe - 1935's style

Figure M16. Wendy Lankester limited edition Historical Fashion Shoes.

Figure M17. Wendy Lankester Period Fashion Shoes.

hundred available colors are a closely guarded secret. But it is known that the factory has used precious metals such as platinum and gold, which alone can give the rich depth to colors such as purple. In addition to being known for its brilliant colors in Art Nouveau and Art Deco motifs, Longwy is known for its crackle glaze. As soon as pieces leave the kiln, a low murmur is heard as thousands of nearly invisible cracks begin to appear in the glaze. It is a deliberate effect obtained by applying an enamel whose coefficient of expansion differs from the base pottery. The effect is emphasized by wiping the surface with a sponge soaked in China ink or raw sienna.

The Longwy factory only made one shoe form, a clog, though they made it in both rights and lefts. Any other shoe form with a Longwy type décor has to be assumed to be from another factory. Some are known to have been made by Gien. The Belgian factory of Boch Frères Keramis also produced cloisonné-enameled pottery well into the 20th century. Their floral patterns and colors were in the Art Nouveau tradition. Their resist lines were intentionally brushed on so that after kiln firing they would appear to be irregular with some enamel running into adjacent areas. The purpose was to give Boch Frères wares a studio pottery appearance. The technical hallmark of Longwy and Gien, however, is always precisely controlled resist lines. They are never irregular, nor do they allow the flow of enamels from one cloison, or cell, to another. Roberts lists another eleven early 20th-century factories that made cloisonné-enameled ceramics.

Figure M18. The Enamels of Longwy, products of the Longwy factory (except for the shoe on the front right, which is illustrative of shoes commonly misidentified as Longwy).

Manufacture Royale et Impériale de Nimy. Manufacture Royale et Impériale de Nimy, Mons, Belgium, c.1789–c.1950. The company manufactured faience (pottery) for over 150 years. Mouzin Lecat, whose name appears on some marks, is reported to have directed the company from 1851 to 1898 when much majolica was manufactured.

Mardorf & Bandorf. Porzellanfabrik Arnstadt Mardorf & Bandorf, Arnstadt, Thuringia, Germany, 1906–c.1924. Although some authors mention the existence of a small porcelain factory in Arnstadt that is believed to have been founded in 1790, little if anything is known about it and it has no relevance to this book. Therefore, "Arnstadt" herein refers to the *porcelain* factory there of Mardorf and Bandorf that produced decorative porcelain, technical and sanitary porcelain, toys, and dolls, much of it intended for export. It is this factory that is the source of most of the variegated green shoes and

many of the variegated green décors incorporating pink pigs, red devils, and similarly fashioned items.

Figure M19. Products of the Mardorf and Bandorf factory.

The merchant Arthur Mardorf from Coburg and the porcelain manufacturer Paul Bandorf from Elgersburg appeared at the royal court on 3 November 1905 to found "an open trade company" for the purpose of the production and running of a porcelain factory in Arnstadt. They were to be the sole partners and the company was to be called Mardorf & Bandorf. They constructed new buildings at Friedrichstrasse 22 in Arnstadt in 1905. Production was begun immediately after completion of the main building in 1906. Mardorf ran the business side. Bandorf took care of the technical and artistic functions.

Born in April 1866, Johann Gustav Paul Bandorf became an artist and modeler. His father had owned a porcelain factory in Beutelsdorf, located between Rudolstadt and Kahla. It is assumed that this is where Paul, as he was known, learned to use porcelain manufacturing as an outlet for his artistic skills. He is believed to have left his father's firm in 1895 to work elsewhere in the porcelain industry. Bandorf was officially accepted as a citizen of Arnstadt on 12 April 1907, though this occurrence has also been reported as having occurred on 20 May 1908. He and his wife Anna rented accommodations until 1910 when they moved into their newly built home at Roonstrasse 4 (now Thomas Mann Strasse). Bandorf lived there until his death on 17 November 1926. For reasons of health, Bandorf had departed as a partner in 1910. His brother Otto Bandorf took his place shortly thereafter. Otto was a porcelain maker from Ilmenau, Thuringia and he is known to have been in Arnstadt in 1912. From 1913 until his death in 1947, Otto Bandorf lived with his family in his own house at Rabenhold 4. However, he stayed with the Arnstadt company only until 12 December 1914. At that point, Mardorf took over and ran the company by himself under the Mardorf & Bandorf name. He sold the company on 5 June 1919, at the conclusion of WWI. Mardorf rented housing in Arnstadt from 1907 until about 1921, when he purchased a home at Lindenallee 1 in Arnstadt. He died there in 1925.

When Mardorf sold the factory in 1919, it was continued by a limited partnership company, Thüringer Braunstein and Mineralmahlwerke, Inc., which had apparently signed a contract for the takeover on 18 September 1918. The contract seems to have taken effect on or about 5 June 1919. The name of the company was changed to "Porzellanfabrik Arnstadt/Mardorf & Bandorf Kommanditgesellschaft" in about 1921. The 1931/32 Arnstadt city directory no longer listed any porcelain factory in Arnstadt. Court documents showed that the owners had financial problems in the

Mardorf & Bandorf, Porzellanfabrik, Arnstadt
Spezialität: Billige, aparte Füllartikel.

Nr.					per Dtz.
1637	Aschenschale	ca. 8½	cm hoch	M	3.75
1639	Maurer als Zigarrenbehälter	14	„ „	„	3.75
1640	Frau als Zigarrenbehälter	14	„ „	„	3.75
1667	Gefäß mit Hund und Spiral-Wackelschwanz .	10	„ „	„	2.80
1668	Gefäß mit Schwein	11½	„ „	„	2.80
1670	Schweine-Barometer	15	„ „	„	3.75.—
1721	Mann und Frau mit Gefäß	12½	„ „	„	3.75
1725	Schweine am Baumstamm	9	„ „	„	3.75
1731	Esel-Barometer	15	„ „	„	3.75
1739	Aschenschale	11	„ „	„	3.75

Mardorf & Bandorf, Porzellanfabrik, Arnstadt
Spezialität: Billige, aparte Füllartikel.

Nr.		per Dtz.	Nr.		per Dtz.
658	Junge am Topf	M 3.75	1654	Katze am Schuh	M 3.50
1341	Gießkanne mit Blumenbelag .	2.80	1693	Kinder auf Schlitten	3.75
1390	Körbchen mit Blumenbelag .	3.30	1716	Korb mit 2 Schweinen	3.30
1533	Sechseckiger Topf mit 2 Vögel .	6.60	1717	Korb mit 2 Schweinen, kleiner	
1543	Flasche mit Kind	3.75		als Nr. 1716	1.—
1574	Water-Closet mit Holzdeckel .	6.—	1718	Korb mit 2 Schweinen, kleiner	
1576	Water-Closet, kleiner als Nr.			als Nr. 1717	0.75
	1574	4.20	1713	Korb wie 1716 mit 2 Hasen .	3.30
1577	Water-Closet, kleiner als Nr.		1719	Korb wie 1717 mit 2 Hasen .	1.—
	1576	3.60	1720	Korb wie 1718 mit 2 Hasen .	0.75
1580/p	Körbchen mit Jiexzweig .	6.60	1738	Hufeisen	2.—
1635	Aschenschale mit Dackel und		1741	Tolletten-Eimer mit Korbhenkel .	4.80
	3 Kücken	3.75	1746	Blumentopf mit Korbhenkel .	3.75
1652	Hund als Zahnstocherhalter .	2.80			

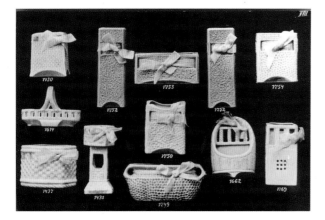

Mardorf & Bandorf, Porzellanfabrik, Arnstadt
Spezialität: Billige, aparte Füllartikel.

Nr.					per Dtz.
1169	Viereckige Vase mit Band	ca. 12	cm hoch	M	3.50
1429	Viereckiger Blumenkübel mit Band wie Nr. 1430	10	„ „	„	4.25
1430	Viereckiger Blumenkübel mit Band, kleiner als Nr. 1429	8½	„ „	„	3.—
1431	Kleiner Blumenständer mit Band	14	„ „	„	4.20
1437	Sechseckiger Blumentopf mit Band	8½	„ „	„	4.—
1614	Durchbrochener Blumenkorb	9	„ „	„	3.—
1662	Wandkorb mit Schleife	12	„ „	„	2.25
1748	Jardinière mit Band wie Nr. 1749	7	„ „	„	6.—
1749	Jardinière mit Band größer als Nr. 1748 . . .	7½	„ „	„	8.—
1750	Blumenkübel mit Band	10	„ „	„	4.—
1752	Vase mit Band	15½	„ „	„	2.25
1753	Jardinière für Vase Nr. 1752 passend . . .	6	„ „	„	2.75
1754	Jardinière für Vase Nr. 1752 passend . . .	10	„ „	„	3.25

Mardorf & Bandorf, Porzellanfabrik, Arnstadt
Spezialität: Billige, aparte Füllartikel.

Nr.		per Dtz.	Nr.		per Dtz.
938	Katze am Korb	M 1.75	1868	Schuh mit Katze	M 1.85
1288	Aschenschale mit Hund . .	„ 2.—	1869	Tragkorb mit Katze . . .	„ 1.85
1558	Vase mit Foxterrier . . .	„ 1.60	1870	Kübel „ „ . . .	„ 2.—
1833	Schweizerkörbchen mit Hahn .	„ 2.—	1875	Katze mit drehbarem Kopf .	„ 2.50
1847	Vase mit Pudel	„ 1.60	1876	Hase „	„ 2.50
1851	Schuh „	„ 1.75	1901	Tragkorb mit 2 Eulen . . .	„ 2.—
1854	Schweizer-Körbchen mit 2		1902	Schuh mit 2 Eulen . . .	„ 2.—
	Hasen	„ 2.—	1908	Gefäß mit 2 grotesken Eulen .	„ 2.—
1855	Pilz mit 2 Hasen	„ 4.20	1942	Korb-Vase mit Katze . . .	„ 3.—
1867	Konservenglas mit Katze . .	„ 1.85	1943	Schuh „ . . .	„ 3.25

Figure M20. Pages from c. 1910 Mardorf & Bandorf catalog.

early 1920s and sought to find a means for settling their debts. It is believed that porcelain production had actually ended in 1924, although it would be not be until 28 December 1937 that ownership was converted to Kunze Kommanditgesellschaft Arnstadt.

The author had long suspected Arnstadt to be the location of the factory that made all the variegated green shoes and many of the variegated green wares incorporating pink pigs and other members of the animal kingdom. Contact with the local museum in 1997 uncovered a number of materials that became important in the sleuth work. Helga Scheidt, director of the Schlossmuseum Arnstadt, reported in an article she wrote in 1996 and relayed to the author that "up until now no porcelain of this Arnstadt manufacturer (Mardorf & Bandorf) has been found ... Only four still extant pages from a small catalog of offerings show porcelain of the factory. They were quite remarkable creations that were manufactured in Arnstadt." The museum came into the possession of these catalog pages in 1960. At that time, the museum received from Erika Bandorf, daughter-in-law of Paul Bandorf, several documents from Paul Bandorf's family, now housed in the museum under "The File Paul Bandorf of the Palace Museum Arnstadt".

Of the materials given to the museum, only the four catalog pages in black and white provide a clue to some of what the factory manufactured. The catalog pages are believed to be c.1910, placing them in the period between the founding of the company and the beginning of WWI in 1914, when manufacture of decorative porcelain was temporarily suspended. The catalog pages are reproduced in Figure M20. Remarkably, four of the items were shoes, two of which looked like some in the author's possession; however, the items in question had animal appliqués that had not been found and the resolution of the reproduced catalogue page left uncertainty about the in-mold characteristics. Moreover, the author had never seen the most unusual shoe on these catalog pages, one with an in-mold basket-weave pattern. The hunt began. The author has since found two of the pictured items, both in variegated green. Just as important, one of the newly located items confirmed that the shoes already in the author's possession were indeed Arnstadt products. It was marked with a unique millstone mark. Several similar shoes with other unique "Germany" marks were subsequently found. Along with scale sketches that allowed examination of the design details in the molds, the unique bottom marks allowed construction of a sort of family tree and the tying together of what is probably most of a series of shoes produced by Mardorf and Bandorf. The author has seen enough surprising things in this business to avoid betting her life on anything deduced in this manner, but she believes that placing a wager on Arnstadt being the source of the majority of the variegated green porcelain would have reasonable odds in its favor.

Martinroda. Porzellanfabrik Martinroda Friedrich Eger & Co. GmbH, Martinroda, Thuringia, Germany, 1900–present. The porcelain printer Friedrich Eger and his son Hermann founded Friedrich Eger & Co. in 1900 in the small community of Martinroda, which is about eighteen miles from Erfurt, the capital of Thuringia. They fired up their kilns and made their first production run of porcelain at Christmas, 1900, with a work force of 60 employees in the factory complex shown in Figure M21. Their primary market was the United States. Among the wares they produced were vases, castor sets, reticulated plates, demitasse sets, and articles with an Oriental motif. Production was discontinued during WWII.

Hans Ziehm and former staff members resumed the production of porcelain in June 1946. The post-WWII company began exporting its porcelain in 1949. By 1969, employees numbered 125. Eighty percent of their products, primarily gift articles, were exported to Belgium, The Netherlands, the United States, Canada, Australia, New Zealand, Denmark, Sweden, Norway, Switzerland, Finland, Greece, Italy, and other countries. Among the decorative effects in which they specialized was a cobalt ground with an overglaze décor.

The company was nationalized in 1972 and called VEB Porzellanwerk Martinroda. It became a subsidiary of VEB United Porcelainworks Lichte in Lichte in 1975. Production was completely suspended in January 1977 when the company was taken over by the Porcelain Factory Ilmenau and converted into a decorating department of that firm. Under a unified Germany, the company was returned on 1 October 1990 to two brothers and a sister who were great-grandchildren of the founder. All three are now involved in the factory operation. Their grandmother was born an Eger.

During a trip into Thuringia in 1997 to the Eger factory, photos of porcelain shoes and boots then in production at the factory were taken that are shown in the composite Figure M22. Among the shoes

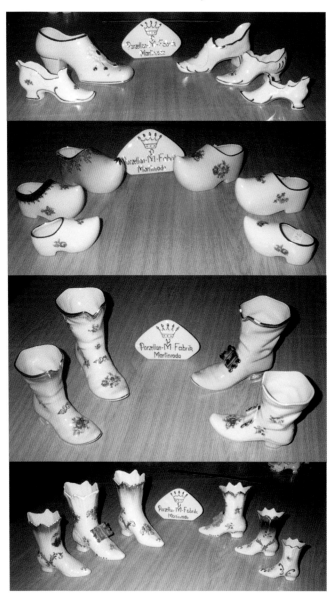

Figure M22. Shoes in contemporary production at the Martinroda factory Friedrich Eger in 1997.

Figure M21. The porcelain factory Friedrich Eger & Co., Martinroda, in the year 1900.

in this composite are two shoes known to have been originated at the Galluba & Hofmann factory in Ilmenau that closed in the 1930s. Martinroda is only a few miles from Ilmenau. It is impossible to refrain from speculating that some or all Galluba & Hofmann molds may have been purchased by the Eger factory.

Maxem China. *See Emanuel, Max.*

Mehlem, Franz Anton. Steingutfabrik Franz Anton Mehlem, Bonn, Rhineland, Germany, 1836–1920. They produced goods in both pottery and porcelain. The forms they manufactured included household items, dishware, and decorative items, as well as technical and sanitary products. The Mettlach company of Villeroy & Boch purchased the Mehlem plant in 1921 and closed it in 1931. A plate with the Mehlem factory logo has been found with the same airbrushed ground and a similar floral transfer as a clog that may have been made in Austria. Both are shown in the following illustration.

Figure M23. An apparent mystery awaiting resolution: a plate with the factory logo of a German company and an unmarked clog that may have been made in Austria, both with the same type of décor.

Meissen. Staatliche Porzellan Manufaktur Meissen *aka* Royal Porcelain Manufactory, Meissen, Saxony, Germany, 1710–present. Porcelain was experimentally created by Johann Friedrich Bottger in 1708, which led to the founding in Meissen of the first European porcelain factory. Through nearly three centuries it has had many name changes, the most recent of them listed here. It is owned by the State of Saxony. Meissen figurines with meticulous detail, dinnerware, and decorative porcelain are among the valued products of this factory.

Meissen marks, the most famous of which is the crossed swords trademark introduced in 1723, have been voraciously copied through the years. For shoe collectors, the task of identifying an authentic piece of Meissen is easy. Meissen has made only one stand-alone shoe form, the crushed heel slipper, though they have made it in two sizes, with lefts and rights in each, and in upwards of some 94 different décors. Unlike any other crushed heel slipper the author has seen, the Meissen slipper has a very thick base, making the larger size heavy enough to be used as a paperweight. The real question facing shoe collectors with a Meissen slipper is its date. The factory was unable to supply the date when its slippers were first produced (nor the name of the modeler). One therefore needs to be a student of Meissen marks to adequately analyze them for production era.

Meissen slippers made prior to 1973 are not normally found with an identifying number. However, the factory did code the slippers in their record books and in their catalogs. For example, Meissen showed the slipper in their 1913/1914 catalog as part of a porcelain ensemble

called "Neuer Ausschnitt". The factory had adopted a new numbering system in 1913, and it was reflected in this catalog, where the left and right slippers in the larger size were listed as form number 408 and the left and right slippers in the smaller size were listed as form 409. Prior to 1913 and going back into the 19th century, the slippers were numbered 1 and 2 for the left and right, respectively, of the smaller slipper and 3 and 4 for the left and right, respectively, of the larger slipper. But the author has never found any of these numbers actually visible on pre-1973 slippers, so a collector will have to obtain a reliable text on Meissen marks to determine the manufacturing period for these slippers.

In 1973, the factory instituted new five-digit form numbers to be able to computerize their inventory. These numbers are impressed on pieces produced from 1973 onward. They have reported the following: the small left is 53519 and in 1997 was available in 65 décors; the small right is 53520 and in 1997 was available in 94 décors; the large left is 53521 and in 1997 was available in 78 décors; and the large right is 53522 and in 1997 was available in 37 décors. When the author found a post-1973 small right Meissen slipper with the clearly impressed numbers 52320 (instead of 53520) and inquired about it to the factory, she was firmly told that unless the number had been misread, it was the result of a wrong die being used by the worker making the impression because 52320 belongs to an oval box! Just to make things more interesting with Meissen slippers, the author has found a large left slipper with either a 38 or a 58 impressed into its bottom. Those numbers, the factory responded, were not model numbers but numbers given to the molder of the slipper making it possible to identify sloppy work at a later date.

Figure M24. Early Meissen figurine of young woman and dog.

Table 5. Minton Shoes and Slippers

Model #	Date	Description (Descriptions in quotes are from Minton pattern books)	Size
	1840	Matchstriker: Pair of china cuffed boots and bootjack mounted on rococo base	
	1854	China candle holder shaped like a foot with a Roman sandal	
1791	c.1870	Low-heeled slipper	3-1/2"L
2640	c.1870/80	"Flower Holder": Normandy shoe on oval base, a cupid sitting on front, second cupid standing at back of shoe	10-1/2"L x 7-3/4"H
2656	c.1870/80	"Flower Holder, Cupid & Slipper": same as 2640 except that the cupid at front has been replaced by roses that spill onto base	10-1/2"L x 7-3/4"H
2657	c. 1870/80	"Flower Holder, Two Cupids & Slipper & Spray of Flowers": same as 2640 except that a spray of flowers has been added to base	10-1/2"L x 7-3/4"H
2663	c.1870/80	"Flower Holder, One Cupid & Slipper, Not-Flowered": same as 2640 except has only the cupid standing at rear of shoe	10-1/2"L x 7-3/4"H
2670	c.1870/80	"Flower Holder Shoe": medium heeled shoe with in-mold buckle at top of high vamp	6"L x 3-1/2"H
2677	c.1870/80	"Flower Holder": two shoes that appear to be attached, similar to 2670.	6"L x 3-1/2"H
2680	c.1870/80	"Flower Holder, as 2663 with Bow in front of shoe extra": has large fluffy, applied bow on vamp. *Note difference in dimensions*	10-3/4"L x 8-1/2"H
3591-25	c.1891/1902*	Large, heeled slipper	6"L x 2"H
3591-26	c.1891/1902*	Small, heeled slipper, same shape as 3591-25	4-1/2"L x 1-1/4"H

*A second source cites these shoes as having been made from 1920-1950. The model numbers would suggest that the earlier dates might be more reliable.

Mettlach. *See Villeroy & Boch.*

Millar China. Importer's mark occasionally found as part of a bottom mark, especially on souvenir china. It has been found as "Millar China, Made in Germany" and as "Millar China, Made in Austria." This may be the importer George V. Millar & Co. of Scranton, Pennsylvania, whose importer mark has also been found on wares made by Haviland & Co. of Limoges, France.

Milton China, The. *See Hewitt and Leadbeater* and *Wiltshaw and Robinson.*

Minton. Minton, Stoke, Staffordshire, England, 1793–present. In their long history they have made an enormous variety of wares in porcelain and pottery. Included were shoes in several designs. They are listed in Table 5.

Moehling, Johann. Johann Moehling, Aich, Bohemia (now Doubi, Czechia), 1849–c.1875. Moehling produced both yellow ware and majolica. He was among the earliest Central European potters to produce majolica, with his later works showing crisp modeling and skilled craftsmanship in the application of various colored glazes. Most of his work is marked, and that mark is an impressed letter "A" enclosed within a square outline. The left and bottom bars of the square are often invisible to the naked eye.

Montagnon. Various Montagnons, Nevers, France, pre-1859–1978. Antoine Montagnon used marks between 1875 and 1899 that include a green bow. In one version, there are the capital letters "M" and "A" above the green bow, with the "A" rotated so that it is perpendicular to the "M". This mark was used from 1875 to 1889. From 1889 to 1899, "AMONTAGNON" was spelled vertically through the center of the bow. Gabriel Montagnon used his initials GM from 1899 to 1937. The artist F. E. Cottard used his initials superimposed on the bow. Jean Montagnon used his initials JM from 1937 to 1978.

Moreau. Jules and Léon Moreau, Malicorne, France, c.1918–1931. From 1899 until 1918, Gustave Leroy ran a Malicorne factory named "Bourg-Joly". Disabled by his military service, Gustave was forced to sell his factory. He and his wife sold it to the widow of Jules Moreau. Jules Moreau had married Marie Juliette Béatrix, sister to Marie Angèle Béatrix, who married Léon Pouplard. The latter two were the principals in the Pouplard-Béatrix factory in Malicorne. The widow Moreau placed her sons Jules II and Léon in charge of the factory. They ran it until 1932 when Léon retired. Jules II took over the operation and ran it with his sons until he died in 1959. The factory remained in the Moreau family until 1993 when it was sold to Jean-Pierre Fouquet.

Figure M25. French faience coin banks, likely from the Jules and Léon Moreau factory.

Morimura/Morimura Bros. The Morimura Bros. was an American importing company that had its roots in Japan. Ichizaemon Morimura was born in October 1839 in Tokyo, Japan. He began in poverty and worked his way to eminence in business, running the Morimura Bank, a factory, and in 1876 Morimura Kumi (Morimura Brothers), an exporting business in Tokyo. At one point, he had his younger brother learn English and sent him to New York to set up a retail and wholesale branch office of Morimura. In 1904, Ichizaemon initiated his plan to make fine decorative porcelain when he established Nippon Toki Kaisha Ltd. in the village of Noritake near the center of Japanese ceramics manufacture, Nagoya. He began exporting ceramics products from his factory to the United States in 1910. But it was not until 1914 that his factory succeeded in manufacturing porcelain dinner plates. It is therefore assumed that the fine porcelain sabots made by this company that are marked *Nippon* were made between this date and about 1921, when this word was generally replaced by *Japan*. In 1918, the Morimura factory employed 2500 people, about half of whom were young women. It was modern by the standards of that era. Although a large part of their business consisted of small items, one hundred people were employed in the painting, which specialized in hand painting of excellent quality on larger wares. The Nippon M-wreath, maple leaf and RC marks of this factory are on wares among the most highly regarded by collectors. *See also Nippon.*

Nippon Toki Kaisha Ltd. was officially renamed the Noritake Company in 1981. However, the "M" within the wreath that stood for Morimura was replaced by an "N" for Noritake in 1941 at about the time that the company's export facilities were closed.

Mosanic. *See Emanuel, Max.*

Nautilus Porcelain. Nautilus Porcelain Co., Possil Pottery, Glasgow, Scotland, 1896–1914.

Nippon. Nippon is an alternative name for the country of Japan. The McKinley Tariff Act of 1890 that took effect 1 March 1891 required goods coming into the United States to be marked with the country of origin. From 1891 until 1921, manufacturers in Japan commonly incorporated *Nippon* in their identification marks, indicating that the piece had come from Japan. After 1 August 1921, all wares from Japan were to be marked *Japan* by a U. S. Customs ruling.

The only shoe forms with an authentic *Nippon* incorporated into their marks that have been seen by the author are two sizes of a Dutch shoe. All of them have been marked *Hand Painted* with the green circular wreath surrounding a script "M" that identifies them as having been imported by the Morimura Bros. from their factory in Japan, a mark they used beginning in 1911. The Nippon wares marked with this M-wreath or with a maple leaf or RC are the most artistically finished and of a higher quality than other porcelain marked Nippon, making them the most desirable to collectors. *See also Morimura/ Morimura Bros.*

Figure M26. Group of matte finish Japanese porcelain in the *Nile Dhow and Palm* pattern bearing a Morimura *Nippon* (c. 1911–1921) mark.

Nippon Toki Kaisha Ltd. *See Morimura.*

Norton Pottery. *See Bennington.*

Oldest Volkstedt Porcelain Factory. Aelteste Volkstedter Porzellanfabrik *aka* Oldest Volkstedt Porcelain Factory, Volkstedt (since 1923, part of Rudolstadt), Thuringia, Germany, 1762–present (with various names and owners).

Perrin. Veuve Perrin Factory, Marseilles, France, c.1740–c.1795. Claude Perrin founded the factory in about 1740. When he died in 1748, his widow took over the business until 1793, after which their son Joseph ran the factory until about 1795.

Plant, R.H. & S.L. R.H. & S.L. Plant Ltd., Tuscan Works, Longton, Staffordshire, England, 1880–present. The company has been known for its tea and breakfast china, and for its miniatures. It is known to have made crested china from at least 1908 to 1925. The company's most common trademark was *Tuscan China.*

plaster mold companies. A number of companies make plaster of paris molds for use by hobbyists and by industrial and commercial firms. The novice collector needs to be alert that such molds exist, because products made from them by hobbyists are often mistaken for those produced professionally. Among the companies that have made or continue to make plaster molds are Alberta's Molds of Atascadero, California (*See Heinz & Co.*); Holland Mold, Inc. of Trenton, New Jersey; Atlantic Mold of Trenton, New Jersey; Duncan Enterprises of Fresno, California; Kimple Mold Corp.; the Kleine Company; and Byron Molds.

Porcelain Factory Victoria. *See Schmidt Victoria.*

"Porcelle". *See Ritchie, William, & Son.*

Porquier. Porquier, Quimper, France, 1809–1905. Charles Porquier succeeded his father-in-law as owner of a pottery factory in Quimper. In 1869, the widow of his son Clet-Adolphe, Augustine Carof Porquier, took over the factory and soon forged a partnership with Alfred Beau, a photographer and painter. To respond to an increasing interest in local costumes, customs, and folklore, Beau designed over two hundred country scenes of local people in local dress going about their traditional lives. These scenes were hand-painted on the Porquier wares. They celebrated Beau's Breton heritage and reflected Celtic humor and fanciful thoughts. Beau left in 1903 and the factory closed in 1905; about 1913 Henriot purchased the marks and models of Porquier, reissuing Porquier-Beau designs from approximately 1918 to 1930. The company mark from 1872–1903 consists of a capital "P" with a capital "B" superimposed over it at right angles. The son of Augustine, Arthur Porquier, reissued in about 1900 some small items with the "AP" mark used occasionally by his father, Clet-Adolphe, years earlier.

Figure M27. Products of the Porquier factory.

Porsgrund. Porsgrunds Porselænsfabrik A/S, Porsgrunn, Norway, 1885–present. Founded in Norway's historic porcelain-making city of Porsgrunn in 1885, the factory fired up its first porcelain on 10 February 1887. It produces dinnerware, coffee services, table accessories, picture frames, and figurines, many designed by well-known Norwegian artists. Only one shoe shape is known to have been manufactured by them: a simple, low-heeled clog. It was, however, sold in a large number of patterns and motifs.

Pouplard/Béatrix. Pouplard/Béatrix, Malicorne, France, 1891–1952. Born in Angers in 1865, Léon Pouplard married Marie-Angèle Béatrix of Malicorne in 1888. He became an apprentice in the Béatrix family factory in Malicorne, taking it over in 1890. He introduced designs using Breton figures and decorations inspired by those created by Alfred Beau at the Porquier factory in Quimper. From 1891 to 1898, the factory mark consisted of two capital letters, "PB", with the "P" backwards, apparently to resemble the Porquier factory mark. A lawsuit forced Pouplard to change his mark. From 1898 it was "PBx", a mark believed to have been used until he closed his factory in 1952, two years before he died, leaving no heirs.

Figure M28. Products of the Pouplard/Béatrix factory.

PV. The mark "PV" appears on some French products, such as certain sanded majolica shoes. It is the mark of the distributor Mitteldorfer Strauss of New York. Established in 1907, they filed for this copyrighted symbol on 2 February 1929, claiming use since 15 February 1928.

Quimper. Quimper is a city in France. *Quimper* (pronounced "camp-pair") is used by some as a generic term for French faience (pottery that is tin enamel-glazed) that is hand-painted in the mode of potteries in the city of Quimper, especially with images of a Breton man and woman. Quimper is located in the northwestern-most part of France. Its natives are Celtic in origin and their culture and customs are reflected in their art works. *See Henriot, Hubaudière,* and *Porquier.*

Rieber, Josef. Josef Rieber & Co., Selb, Bavaria, Germany, 1868–c.1920. Josef Rieber & Company was a porcelain decorating shop established in Selb in 1868. About 1920, Rieber purchased the Porcelain Factory Julius Rother in Mitterteich, Bavaria, Germany (founded in 1899) and renamed it *Porcelain Factory Josef Rieber & Co.* The same year, Rieber moved its factory headquarters to Mitterteich and closed the shop in Selb. The Mitterteich factory became a limited stock company in 1932 and went out of business in about 1978. The Rieber decorating shop used several variations of the intertwined letters "J" and "R", believed to have been used on pieces decorated in the period from 1910 until about 1920.

Ritchie, William, & Son. Wholesale stationer and retailer William Ritchie & Son Ltd., Edinburgh, Scotland registered their trademark "Porcelle" in 1910. This bottom mark was used on crested china from c.1910 to c.1924. Ritchie obtained most of his models from Birks, Rawlins and Co. (*Savoy* trademark) and Arkinstall & Sons (*Arcadian* trademark). Ritchie also registered the trademark *Ivora Ware.* Ritchie used this trademark on domestic wares he had manufactured by Birks, Rawlins & Co (*Savoy* trademark). *See Arkinstall & Sons* and *Birks, Rawlins and Co.*

Robinson & Leadbeater. Robinson & Leadbeater Ltd., Wolfe Street, Stoke-on-Trent, Staffordshire, England, 1850–1924. Established in 1850, the company specialized in Parian statuary (bisque porcelain) that imitated marble. Their extensive and well-produced range

of busts is popular with collectors. When the craze for crested china hit, the company developed and made a number of forms. Their crested china shoes typically carry the bottom mark *Wy Not? Crest China.* Robinson & Leadbeater became insolvent in 1904, was taken over by Harold Taylor Robinson (Arcadian China) in 1906 who formed it into Robinson & Leadbeater Ltd., and became a branch of J. A. Robinson in 1910. NOTE: *Wy Not* without the question mark was a trademark used by Hewitt and Leadbeater.

Robinson, J. A. *See Arkinstall & Sons.*

Roth, John H. John H. Roth & Co. aka JONROTH, Peoria, Illinois (1909–1970), Florida (1970–present). John H. Roth started with Wheelock, for whom he was a buyer for fifteen years before George Wheelock bought out Roth's one-fifth ownership. This provided Roth with the financial resources to start his own business in competition with Wheelock. Roth was a major supplier of souvenir china. He was succeeded by a son and grandson, the latter of whom moved the business to Florida in 1970.

Rouen. Rouen is a town in France. It is also the name given to a décor. Many French faience pieces can be found with "Rouen" written alone or as part of a bottom mark. They also can be found with a Rouen town crest and a bottom mark including "Rouen". Often, these pieces were made in the late 19th or early 20th century and were not made in Rouen. Some or many were likely made in Desvres, France. *See Fourmaintraux.*

Royal Bayreuth. Königlich Privilegierte Porzellanfabrik Tettau GMBH (Royally Privileged Porcelain Factory Tettau GMBH), Tettau, Bavaria, Germany, 1794–present. In the United States, products of this porcelain company are known as Royal Bayreuth. The factory's primary products have been dinnerware, tea and coffee sets. But the company also produced some of the most interesting novelty items. The animal, floral, vegetable, and other unusual figurals, including shoes, were made at the factory from about 1885 to WWI. The company originated the extraordinary *tapestry* finish that can be found on products from dining pieces to shoes. In spite of attempts, other factories were unsuccessful in duplicating the process. Tapestry finish products in the triple rose pattern are shown in Figure M29. Only a close-up can adequately show the texture and delicate décors on the surfaces of these pieces.

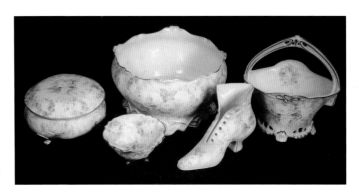

Figure M29. Royal Bayreuth pieces in the company's three-rose motif tapestry finish.

Dees reported that the most important products of the Tettau factory were dishes for everyday use and coffee, tea, and chocolate services whose shapes were truly diverse and of "astonishing variation", all meant to appeal to urban middle class and country families, and that their value was previously less than that of Thuringian factories, but did not merit this evaluation. He continued that from the 1820s and 1830s, the Tettau factory produced porcelain superior to other factories, "those of Meissen not excepted". At later dates in the factory's history, he noted that the quality of Tettau porcelain varied depending on management and technicians.

Royal Bayreuth is highly collectible. It is also a category that requires study if one is to become knowledgeable about the factory's products because an enormous range of wares has been produced over the years, much of it marked but some unmarked. In the United States, the Royal Bayreuth Collectors Club was formed to share information and provide a centralized group for the collection of history on the factory and its products.

The factory was burned in a devastating fire in 1897, and a new factory was built on the same site. The fire destroyed important records and molds and this may be the reason why certain shoe shapes known to have been produced in the 1885–c.1897 era are not found with color combinations and décors that would date them as post-1897. Since about 1990, the factory has produced low-cut ladies' oxfords and high-tops in a white high-gloss glaze, usually with decals of over-all florals. They all carry a unique bottom mark easily identifying them. The mark consists of a lion with crown and shield under which is *Königl. pr. Tettau* and a script "*T*" around all of which is a circle of print consisting of *Tettau Antiquariat* at the top and *Anno 1890* at the bottom. These shoes are in current production and can be purchased at factory outlets in Germany for about $20 each.

Royal Porcelain Manufactory. Royal Porcelain Manufactory and State's Porcelain Manufactory, Berlin, Germany, 1763–present.

Royal Rudolstadt. New York and Rudolstadt Pottery, Rudolstadt, Thuringia, Germany, 1882–1918. The New York company Lewis Straus & Son was either the co-owner or owner of the porcelain factory and the sole importer for the United States.

Royal Worcester. Worcester Porcelain Company *aka* Royal Worcester Spode Ltd., Worcester, England, 1751–present. The products of the Worcester Porcelain Company, first deeded in 1751 and first called Royal Worcester in 1862, are among the finest products made in this medium. Through the years the company has employed top ranked modelers and painters. James Hadley, responsible for moving the product line from one with a Japanese influence to one in the Victorian mode, is considered by many to have been one of the finest designers and modelers. For shoe collectors, it is the eight models produced at the end of the 1800s that are of great interest. Most of the models were made in more than one décor and all that the author has seen have been clearly marked with the company's logo for the late 1800s, a circle with "51" (for 1751) inside with a crown above it. The year of manufacture was incised into the bottom, indicated by a letter of the alphabet, written as a year beneath the circle, or stamped with a letter of the alphabet beneath the circle, with the letter representing a specific year. *Royal Worcester England* was added to the logo in 1891 and the shape of the crown was changed. Beginning in 1892, a series of dots and other symbols was used with the logo to designate the date of manufacture. These can be found in standard reference works of Royal Worcester as well as in several texts on marks.

Sandon (letter to author in 1998) speculated that Hadley may have designed some of the Worcester shoes, "…but it is not possible to know…" George Owen, whose pierced work on standard factory models has never been matched, produced some of the most sought-after Worcester works including some shoes. Sandon wrote that he "…once saw a pair of them in a fitted box with the original price on them of 22/-6d".

An historic set of negatives exists showing all eight Royal Worcester shoes in their biscuit form, just after their first firing. Although not dated, these black and white photographs probably were taken in the 1880s and probably not all at the same time. Some of the negatives may go back to the 1870s when the first of these shoes was produced. Given that the negatives are over a century old, it should not be surprising that prints made from them would be grainy and not exhibit crisp resolution. Nevertheless, they constitute an important record for shoe collectors and are reproduced in Figure M30. The numbering system, of which these shoes are a part, was devised about 1862 as a

method of identifying ornamental shapes within the factory. One can only speculate why the numbering of the first four shoes is not in order. A current Worcester Museum curator has suggested that one reason may be that the designer added the numbers after the mold maker had made and numbered the molds.

Any designation by any author, including this one, of rarity to any Worcester piece is based on personal experience, because the factory has advised that *no surviving factory records exist* relating to the number of objects produced from a particular mold, whether it be figural shoes or some other Worcester product. In this Figure, the descriptions of each shoe and the dates when they were first produced are taken from the Sandon text. Not taken from this text is the judgment about rarity, which many shoe collectors would challenge. Writing to the author in 1998, Sandon said, "It is not possible to know how many [shoes] were made but they are all very rarely seen nowadays." All Royal Worcester shoes are difficult to find. In the author's experience, the rarest are No. 700, the embossed slipper, and No. 763, the pierced shoe. Some of the other shoes in certain décors are uncommon for their particular molds.

Royal Worcester made a clog in 1962 and several shoes for a Compton and Woodhouse collection in the 1990s.

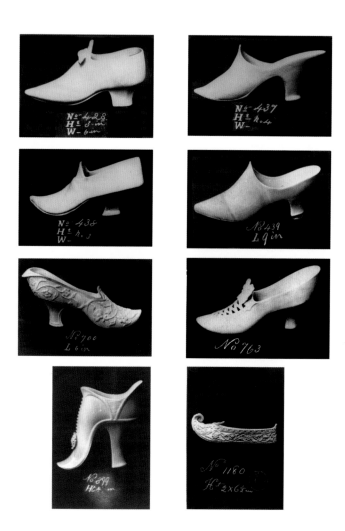

Figure M30. Prints of historic negatives of Royal Worcester shoes taken c.1880s. From left to right, top to bottom with the years in which they were introduced, they are: No. 428, Slipper number 2, 1874; No. 437, Shoe number 4, 1874; No. 438, Shoe number 3, 1874; No. 439, Shoe number 1, 1874; No. 700, Embossed slipper, 1879; No. 763, Pierced shoe, 1880; No. 899, High-heeled shoe, 1882; and No. 1180, Indian slipper shoe (can be found both as shown and pierced), 1886.

R. S. Prussia. *See Schlegelmilch, Reinhold.*

R. S. Germany. *See Schlegelmilch, Reinhold.*

St. Clément. St. Clément, France, mid 1700s–present. There have been potteries in the towns of Lunéville and St. Clément, about eight miles away, since the 1700s. Since that time there have been various owners and, at times, mergers. Factory marks appeared about 1820, with St. Clement spelled out in blue. St.C initials appeared c.1892.

Satsuma. Satsuma is the name of a province in Japan. Satsuma is also the name by which is known a genre of pottery that typically has an ivory crackle glazed background with simple to elaborate designs on it, often heavily enameled, and with a great amount of gold and silver enamel. The subject matter may be simple florals or detailed scenes involving samurai warriors, Japanese royalty of the old times, or geishas, as shown in some of the wares in Figure M31. Pottery was first made in the province of Satsuma in the 1600s. In the 1850s, the export of Satsuma pottery increased dramatically. A cross within a circle is the genuine mark of the province of Satsuma. It may be found in gold on the body or lid of the piece, or in red if on the base. The cross within a circle is the crest of the Shimazu family who ruled Satsuma at one time. From about 1880 to about 1925, a large number of factories were producing Satsuma for export to Europe and the United States. From 1926 to the present, wares incorrectly referred to as Satsuma have come from other places in Japan. They are characterized by being less carefully made and having enamels applied by a heavy hand. The province of Satsuma is now called the province of Kagoshima-ken.

Figure M31. Variety of Japanese wares. Front, left to right: pair of pottery Satsuma shoes reported to have been copied in the 1980s using the original molds and décor; two sizes of porcelain Kutani cups, late 1800s; Satsuma pottery ladies' oxford. Back, left to right: 19th century pottery Satsuma vase; pierced, pottery Meizan vase, c.1900; 19th century, tall pottery Satsuma vase; 19th century pottery Satsuma covered box.

Savoy China. *See Birks, Rawlins and Co.*

Saxony. *See Kutscher, Wilhelm.*

Schäfer & Vater: Schäfer & Vater Porzellanfabrik, Rudolstadt, Thuringia, Germany, 1890–c.1962. The company was founded by Gustav Schäfer and Gunther Vater in 1890. They used local clay that was rich in kaolin, resulting in wares with a velvety texture and a fine grain. The factory made some of the most imaginative designs and used unusual fabrication techniques, as shown in some smalls in Figure M32. The mark on much of this factory's porcelain is either missing or impressed so lightly that it is almost impossible to decipher. The mark is a 9-pointed star inside of which is a script "R" and above which is a crown.

Figure M32. Products of the Schäfer & Vater factory.

Scheidig, Carl. Carl Scheidig Porzellanfabrik (1906–1972)/ VEB Gräfenthaler Porzellanfiguren (1972–1990)/Porzellanfiguren Gräfenthal GmbH (1990–c.1997), Grafenthal, Thuringia, Germany. Carl Scheidig established his porcelain factory in 1906, where he manufactured figurines, decorative porcelain, giftware, collector's items, and technical porcelain. The factory is known to have made at least one shoe, designed as a Royal Bayreuth look-alike. It is shaped like a Bayreuth's men's shoe with the protruding tab. But in the Scheidig model, the tab is bent under and attached to the back seam of the shoe. Although not pictured in this book, the author has seen this Scheidig shoe painted in the same two-tone brown, with dark brown sole edges as was often painted on the Bayreuth shoe. The Scheidig shoe is pictured in this book in white with gold trim, as it is usually found in the secondary market. Impressed into the right side of the heel are the numbers "3586". When the author's husband and German friend visited the Porzellanfiguren Grafenthal factory in May 1998, it was in receivership. The factory outlet that was also operated as a museum was, however, open. The museum portion displayed mostly figurines from the 1910 to 1960 period, when the company name was Carl Scheidig Porzellanfabrik. The outlet had a single shoe, airbrushed in a graduated taupe color, which the author's husband purchased. Impressed into the right side of the heel were the numbers "3586". It was the same shoe as described above, but it had been made in recent years. The outlet manager said that it was the last of the shoes to be produced from that mold and that the mold was being destroyed.

Schierholz. *See von Schierholz.*

Schiller, W., & Son: *See W.S.& S.*

Schlegelmilch, Erdmann. Erdmann Schlegelmilch Porzellanfabrik, Suhl, Thuringia, Germany, 1881–1938. The factory produced high-quality porcelain that typically was marked either "E. S. Germany" or "E. S. Prov. Saxe.".

Schlegelmilch, Reinhold. Reinhold Schlegelmilch Porzellanfabriken, Suhl, Thuringia, Germany, 1869–1932, and Tillowitz, Silesia (presently Tulovice, Poland), Germany, 1894–c.1947. Schlegelmilch opened a porcelain factory in Suhl in 1869. From the late 1870s to the early 1900s, the Suhl factory's common mark was a wreath and star accompanied by "R S Prussia". Suhl was in the Thuringian region of the part of Germany known as Prussia until the conclusion of WWI. A common mark for the Tillowitz factory was a wreath and star with "R S Germany". Collectors must be alert to the fact that a large number of wares have been manufactured in Asia, beginning in the 1970s, bearing fake "R S Prussia" marks.

Schmidt, Carl. Carl Schmidt Porcelain Factory, Schleusingen, Saxony, Germany, founded 1863. Known for figurines and other porcelain wares.

Schmidt Victoria. Porzellanfabrik Victoria *aka* Porzellanfabrik "Victoria" Schmidt & Co. *aka* Charles Schmidt & Co. *aka* Schmidt Victoria, Altrohlau, Bohemia (now Stara Role, Czechia), 1883–1945. The Charles Schmidt porcelain factory was established in 1883 in Altrohlau, near Karlsbad (or Carlsbad), then in Bohemia (Karlsbad, Bohemia is now Karlovy Vary, Czechia). The region around Karlsbad was the center of the Bohemian porcelain industry in the late 1800s and early 1900s. Many companies included either Karlsbad or Carlsbad in their marks, even though they were not located in the city. Thus, some Schmidt Victoria marks include "Carlsbad" as a part of the logo. Most Schmidt Victoria models can be found in luster finishes. One of the company's hallmark lusters was shaded from a pale yellow through orange to rust. The company also used lusters in mother-of-pearl, pink, a dull orange, and blue. Schmidt Victoria was one of the largest German exporters of crested china, made especially for the British market. It sold well into the 1920s. They also made souvenir china with both colored views and those in black and white. Schmidt's *Gemma* trademark was often used on these miniatures. The mark is a simple shield with diagonal bars containing "GEMMA". A crown may appear above the shield. Below the shield there may be no designation or there may be "Austria", if the piece was made before WWI, or "Czechoslovakia", for the newly formed country after WWI. *Fairy Ware* was a trademark used by another Schmidt factory. It occasionally can be found printed over the Gemma mark. It is believed that Gemma was an earlier mark and was not used after WWI. *Fairy Ware* models are often identical to Gemma models. Among the other trademarks used by Schmidt Victoria are *Alexandre, Empire, Empire Gem, Empress China, Durbar, Elite, Ness China, Rococo,* and *Victoria.* Certain unmarked Schmidt Victoria shoes are often misidentified as Royal Bayreuth.

Schoenau, Bros. Gebr. Schoenau, Hüttensteinach, Thuringia, Germany, 1865–1920. The Bros. Schoenau operated from 1865 until they merged in 1920 with another company in their town, Swaine & Co. Prior to the merger, Schoenau produced tableware and household and decorative porcelain. After the merger, the combined companies were named *Gebr. Schoenau, Swaine & Co.* (1920–1954), added dolls' heads to their product line, and later moved to Köppelsdorf, Thuringia, Germany. In the Spring 1939 catalog of the Leipzig Fair, they announced, "Gift articles and tableware for domestic use and export, table lamps in modern and antique shapes". The company was nationalized in 1954 and named *VEB Sonneberger Porzellanfabriken* (1954–1990).

Sergent, T. T Sergent, Paris, France, ~1865 – ~1890. Thomas Victor Sergent opened his own ceramics shop in Paris in about 1865. He is classified as a "19th Century French Follower of Palissy" who produced works in the Avisseau tradition. Sergent produced beautifully decorated majolica. On shoes, his mark commonly consists of the impressed first initials of his name, "T.S."

Shelley and **Shelley China.** Wileman & Co., Foley Potteries and Foley Works, 1860–1925; Shelley Potteries Ltd., 1925–present,

Longton, Staffordshire, England. J. F. Wileman and J. E. Shelley founded Wileman and Co. in about 1860, but from 1883 on, the factory was run exclusively by the Shelley family. From 1890 to 1910, the company used *The Foley China* as its trade name. The use of *Foley* as a trade name by other firms was causing confusion, so Wileman and Co. decided to use the name of the owners, Shelley, in its trademark. From about 1910 to about 1924, the company used *Late Foley* with its new trademark *Shelley.* The company's name was legally changed to Shelley Ltd in 1925, although the new mark using just *Shelley* was likely used prior to 1925. The Shelley family began producing crested china in 1903. Its high quality placed it in direct competition with Goss. Shelley stopped producing crested china sooner than other British firms and probably did not manufacture this ware after about 1923.

Spode. Spode, Stoke-on-Trent, Staffordshire, England, c.1762–present. The originator of the company, Josiah Spode I, is responsible for what are viewed as two of the most important developments in the English ceramics industry. In 1784 he perfected blue underglaze printing on pottery from hand-engraved copper plates. Then, in the closing years of the 1700s, he perfected the formula for Fine Bone China, deemed by some the single most important development in the history of English ceramics. After working for Spode II for nineteen years, William Copeland became a partner in the London showroom in 1805. When Josiah Spode III died, William Taylor Copeland assumed control of the company in 1833, a Copeland family association that continued for 133 years. There have been several corporate ownership changes since 1976, but the original Spode factory continues to produce china. Examples of older Spode are shown in Figure M33 along with a contemporary shoe.

Figure M33. Products of the Spode factory.

Spode is known to have made only one shoe form, a Fine Bone China slipper inkwell. It was made in 1824 in at least three patterns. They are known as Pattern 3993, crimson ground with pattern of a bird with leaves raised and gilded; Pattern 4054, Saxon blue ground with pattern of a bird with leaves raised and gilded; and Japanese Silk. A search of the pattern books in the Spode archives produced no record of the number of patterns in which this slipper was made, nor even a sketch of the slipper itself. There also are no records to indicate how many were made.

In 1984, Spode reproduced a number of its old wares, shown in Figure M34. One was the 1824 slipper inkwell. It was not cast from the original mold; rather, a new mold was made so that the shrinkage using modern kiln techniques would yield a slipper of the same final size as the original. It is estimated that approximately fifty of these may have been made. In 1996, Spode made two miniature versions of the outside of the 1824 slipper for a Compton & Woodhouse collection of shoes, one of which is shown in Figure M33. Several other contemporary versions made by Spode have been seen recently with various décors.

Figure M34. Copy of 1984 Spode catalog showing reproductions of old Spode wares. The reproduction inkwell slipper is 5-13/16"L x 1-9/16"H in Spode pattern 4054.

Stadtlengsfeld. Porzellanfabrik Stadtlengsfeld (1889–c.1945)/ branch of VEB Thuringian Porcelainworks (c.1945–1950)/VEB Porcelainwork Stadtlengsfeld (1950–present), Stadtlengsfeld, Thuringia, Germany, 1889–c.1945. Prior to WWII, the factory produced table and household accessories, decorative porcelain, giftware, and hotel porcelain. Since WWII, it has produced household, hotel, and decorative porcelain. The "Excelsior/Germany" mark with sword crossed with two keys was used 1894–1904.

Staffordshire. Staffordshire is a region in England. In the 19th century, an enormous amount of porcelain and pottery was made in Great Britain; in Staffordshire alone, there were over two thousand master potters. When the word *Staffordshire* is used to describe a piece of pottery, it denotes a type of décor not a particular factory.

Swaine & Co. Swaine & Co., Hüttensteinach, Thuringia, Germany, 1854–1920. In its more than sixty years in operation, the company produced tableware and household, decorative, and technical porcelain. In 1920, they merged with the Bros. Schoenau from the same town. *See also Schoenau, Bros.*

Swan China. Swan China was a trademark used on Charles Ford products. It is not believed to have been used after 1925. *See Ford, Charles* and *Arkinstall & Sons.*

Sunbonnet Babies. *See Corbett, Bertha L.*

Taylor and Kent. Taylor and Kent Ltd., Florence Works, Longton, Staffordshire, England, 1862–c.1964. The company specialized in tableware and novelties, but they produced crested china only between 1900 and 1925. The most common trademark of the company was *Florentine.* Other trademarks used by them that are found on crested china shoes are *Albion China, Atlas Heraldic China, British Manufacture, Coronet Ware, Cyclone, English Manufacture, Florentine China,* and *Keltic.* The *Albion China* trademark is usually found combined with *T.C.&P.,* a Scottish wholesaler for whom Taylor and Kent manufactured items at their Florence Works.

Thoune. Thoune (also Thun, Thonne, and Thuner majolica) is not the name of a manufacturer but rather the name given to pottery made in the Thoune region of Switzerland, an area formerly known as Heimberg. Pronounced "toon", the earthenware so designated usually is intricately slip-decorated and painted in white, yellow, orange, green, and blue. Typically, the background is dark, often a deep brown. Edelweiss, often part of the theme décor, became a design element in about 1881.

Thoune, or Heimberg, pottery had three distinctive development phases. In the first, from 1800 to 1860, the pottery was utilitarian but intricately decorated and colorful, often against light backgrounds. It is referred to as "Old Heimberg". In the second phase, from 1860 to 1880, the pottery was decorated with a rich palette, usually florals, against a dark ground. It is referred to as "Paris Ware" after the World Exhibition in Paris in 1878 to which much was sent and sold. In the third phase, from 1881 to 1914, Edelweiss flowers were introduced into the designs, reputedly to satisfy tourists who wished to take back an object that would invoke memories of their visit. In this last phase, geometrical patterns also were often used.

Most of the factories making Thoune pottery were small. The artist potter whose works are most in demand is Johann Wanzenried, whose wares were produced in the 19th century. Thoune pottery manufacture declined rapidly in the early 20th century with the influx of the then more desirable porcelain, primarily from German factories. Thoune pottery is once again in production to satisfy tourist demand and upwards of twenty Swiss firms make Thoune pottery in the present day.

Tielsch, C. C. Tielsch & Co., Altwasser, Silesia, Germany (now Walbrzych, Poland), 1845–1945. They made household, hotel and decorative porcelain. In 1918, the majority of the Tielsch stock was acquired by C. M. Hutschenreuther of Hohenberg, Germany.

Triood. *See Hoods Ltd.*

Tuscan. *See Plant, R.H. & S.L.*

Ulysse à Blois. Ulysse à Blois, Blois, France, 1862–1891, 1891–1927. Born in Blois in 1826, Jean Judes Ulysse Besnard studied painting in Paris before returning to his hometown in 1858. He shortened his name to Ulysse in about 1861. For much of 1862, he experimented with the technical aspects of producing pottery, leading him to establish his own pottery works by the end of the year. For the mark he would use on his pottery, Ulysse chose a shell, the symbol of St. James. Within it, he placed a cross and the Roman version of "U", a "V". From 1862 to 1891, he used a Roman numeral above the shell to indicate the month of production, and Arabic numerals on each side to indicate the year of production. His products ranged from the large to the small, from important decorative works to the incidental wares for retail, from Rouen designs to Italian Renaissance styles. Ulysse sold his factory in 1887 to Emile Balon, though he remained associated with it until 1891, after which Balon modified the shell and cross mark to say "Ulysse à Blois, E. Balon Succ.", meaning that Balon was the successor of Ulysse, and he used this mark until 1927. Ulysse died in 1899. The firm eventually passed through several Balon family members, closing in 1953.

Unger, Schneider & Cie. Unger, Schneider & Cie (1861–1887)/ Carl Schneider's Heirs (1887–c.1972), Gräfenthal, Thuringia, Germany. The company produced figurines, dolls' heads, religious articles, household and decorative porcelain, and souvenirs. A number of bisque figurines with shoes as part of the design have been found with the company's impressed distinctive mark of a large capital "G" with one or two arrows through it vertically.

Verlingue, Jules. Jules Verlingue, Boulogne, France, 1903–1920. *See Hubaudière.*

Victoria. *See Schmidt Victoria* and *Victoria China.*

Victoria China. James Reeves Victoria Works, Fenton, England, 1870–1948. They were primarily a pottery manufacturer that made dinnerware and ornamental pottery. They made crested china in the early 20th century, including several shoe models. The *Victoria China* trademark used by Reeves often has *J. R. & Cᵒ* under the logo. These initials are believed to represent a china wholesaler. *Victoria China* was also used to mark some Sampson Hancock & Sons and some Taylor & Kent items.

Vieillard. A. Vieillard & Cie, Bordeaux, France, 1845-?. David Johnson founded a factory in Bordeaux in 1836. He produced creamware and soft paste porcelain. He apparently had a partner, J. Vieillard. A. Vieillard succeeded the original owner(s) in 1845. His products were described as very good. His mark is very rare.

Villeroy & Boch. Villeroy & Boch, Mettlach, Saarland, Germany, 1836–present. Villeroy & Boch was formed with the merger in 1836 of Nicolas Villeroy and Eugen Boch, both of whom had earthenware factories, Boch's being in Mettlach. The company is especially known for its earthenware and stoneware beer steins, mugs, tiles, figurines, and household wares. They also produced some majolica at their Schramberg facility. Between 1850 and 1880, Villeroy & Boch manufactured figurines and figural objects, some in soft paste porcelain and some in stoneware/earthenware. A devastating fire in 1922 destroyed molds used in the manufacturing process and a large part of the archives. Among the records destroyed were those that covered the 1850–1880 period. A very large Dutch shoe held by a girl in Dutch dress is pictured on the cover of the October 1953 *Hobbies* magazine and attributed in an article inside to the Villeroy and Boch factory. It is possible that the attribution is true, but only if an example can be found and its markings are clear can this be verified. The example of this piece in the author's collection has no manufacturer's mark. The only shoe forms the company is known with certainty to have made are the two shown in Figures M35 and M36; and a molded, flat-heeled large contemporary slipper that is clearly marked with the company logo and "Naif Christmas".

Voigt, Reinhold. Bartholomé, Stade & Co. (1910–1919)/Porzellanfabrik Gräfenroda – Ort Reinhold Voigt (1919–c.1972)/VEB Porzellanfabrik Gräfenroda (c.1972–unknown), Gräfenroda, Thuringia, Germany. Reinhold Voigt purchased the factory in 1919. The company was nationalized about 1972 and at some later time it was merged with VEB Porcelain Manufactory Plaue in Plaue, Thuringia, Germany.

von Schierholz. Christian Gottfried Schierholz (1817–1829)/C. G. Schierholz & Söhn (1829–1905)/C. G. Schierholz & Söhn, Porzellanmanufactur Plaue GmbH (1905–1912)/von Schierholz'sche Porzellanmanufactur Plaue GmbH (1912–1972, where from c.1945–1972 the firm was under government trusteeship)/VEB Porzellanmanufaktur Plaue (nationalized: 1972–1990)/returned to former proprietors (1991–1996)/purchased by Royal Bayreuth of Tettau, and is now called Porzellanmanufaktur Plaue GmbH (1996–present), Plaue, Thuringia, Germany.

Throughout its history, von Schierholz has produced high-quality porcelain for dinnerware, table accessories, figurines (see Figure M37), luxury decorative items, and technical wares. They made exquisite candelabra (see Figure M38) and chandeliers, ornately embellished with figurines and hand-made floral appliqués; pierced work; appliqué lace detail; and hand-painted wares. The factory has been one of the few to make lithophanes, beginning from at least 1890. One of the marks used by the factory that dates to about 1890, consisting of two parallel lines crossed at a right angle by a third line, is often confused with a mark used by Sitzendorf.

Figure M37. Masterful figurine representing one of the four seasons made by the von Schierholz factory about 1890, marked in blue with a pair of parallel lines crossed with a second pair at a slant.

Figure M35. Villeroy & Boch drinking boot, c. 1885–1905. It was made in 15 cm and 17 cm high sizes with capacities of 0.75 liters and 1 liter, respectively. Several of the design features are in high relief and platinum was used in the painting décor. It was designed by Christian Warth from Birkenfeld. Image is from a catalog of the era.

Figure M36. Villeroy & Boch Blumenvase (flower vase), c. 1900. It was made in two sizes, 5 cm and 13 cm high, in hand-painted stoneware. It was designed by Matthias Hein from Saarhoelzbach/Mettlach. Image is from a catalog of the era.

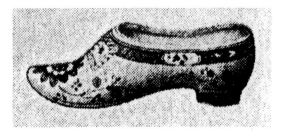

Figure M38. A pair of meticulously crafted candelabra made by the von Schierholz factory about 1880, marked in blue with a pair of parallel lines crossed with a third line at a perpendicular.

W (framed by either a diamond or square) **British Made.** *See Williamson, H. M.*

Weiss, Kühnert. *See also German Doll Company, The.* Weiss, Kühnert & Company (1891–c.1972)/VEB Gebrauchsporzellan (VEB Utility Porcelain) (c.1972–1990)/Porzellanmanufaktur Gräfenthal (1990–1995), Gräfenthal, Thuringia, Germany. Five men whose skills were important to the process of making porcelain established the Weiss, Kühnert & Company porcelain factory in 1891. They were the capsule turner Christian Weiss, the mold pourer Theodor Kühnert, and the porcelain painters Johann Fischer, Carl Scheidig, and E. Baumann. Ninety-five percent of their wares were exported. These included figurines; dolls and half-dolls; vases; cabinet pieces; Snow Babies; an enormous variety of novelties and useful objects such as salt and pepper shakers, eggcups, pitchers, oil & vinegar sets, and toothbrush holders; and a large assortment of figural shoes. In a 36-page catalog, c.1920, it has been reported that individual items numbering over two thousand were illustrated.

The company was run by a succession of family members of the original owners until somewhere in the vicinity of WWII. The company was nationalized in 1972 and directed to produce only a limited range of items, leaving some thirty thousand molds in the attic. In 1990, after the return of nationalized industries to private ownership,

Table 6. Weiss, Kühnert & Company
Shoe Model Numbers & Descriptions

There is more than one size in some of these shoes. Where that occurs, the factory gave different model numbers to the item(s). It is assumed that the lower number would represent the larger models, with higher numbers representing form-offs, or smaller versions. Bold-faced numbers were not pictured in the catalog pages available to the author, but have been attributed to Weiss, Kühnert, herein. Bold-faced names are for easy location of WK shoes with animals or figures.

No.	Description
1472	large, 12-bead centerline, piked toe, pinched heel slipper
1488	small, 12-bead centerline, piked toe, pinched heel slipper
1800	strap shoe, rectangular cutout, low at back of heel
1919	small pair attached low-cut clogs w/ pointed toes, lifting ring
1?78	medium pair attached low-cut clogs w/pointed toes, lifting ring
2088	strap shoe, high vamp
2112	Normandy shoe with leaves & grapes on vamp
2165	Normandy shoe, no ruching, something on vamp
2189	Normandy type, something on vamp
2210	high-top shoe, pointed toe, in-mold leaves & grapes
2259	Normandy shoe with cherries on vamp, very large
2260	Normandy shoe with three berries & leaves on vamp
2439	high-top shoe, pointed toe, grapes & leaves on vamp
2596	high-top boot with in-mold cherries on paneled top
2621	pair: **boy clown** standing inside tramp ankle shoe, dog looking out from vamp
	girl clown standing inside tramp ankle shoe, dog looking out from vamp
2647(?)	strap shoe, rectangular cut-out, high at back of heel
2864	high-top ladies lace-up shoe, in-mold laces & tie
2877	high-top ladies lace-up shoe, in-mold laces & tie
2978	snub nose type
2979	high vamp, low sides, up-turned toe
3216	pair: **Dutch boy** holding large **Dutch shoe** w/grapes
	Dutch girl holding large **Dutch shoe** w/grapes
3217	pair: **Dutch boy** holding large **Dutch shoe** w/grapes
	Dutch girl holding large **Dutch shoe** w/grapes
3263	man's cap-toe, lace-up ankle work shoe
3314	cuffed boot, **dog** (?) on back
3315	cuffed boot, **dog** on front looking at **cat** inside cuff

No.	Description
3316	cuffed boot, **dog** on vamp looking away from boot
3406	pair: **boy pierrot** sitting on toe, fox on left side
	girl pierrot sitting on toe, rabbit on right side
3407	pair: **boy pierrot** sitting on toe, fox on left side
	girl pierrot sitting on toe, rabbit on right side
3408	pair: left & right facing, pair of **cats** playing with ball, mice on rear quarters
3409	pair: left & right facing, pair of **cats** playing with ball, mice on rear quarters
3470	pair: left & right facing **pheasants** (?) w/rabbit on rear quarters
3471	pair: left & right facing **turkeys**, chick on back quarters
3472	pair: left & right facing **cockatiels**, bird in flight on rear quarters (parakeets??)
3493	pair: left & right facing **pheasants** (?) w/rabbit on rear quarters
3494	pair: left & right facing **turkeys**, chick on back quarters
3495	pair: left & right facing **cockatiels**, bird in flight on rear quarters
3542	pair: left & right facing pair of **roosters** w/a chick on rear quarters
3543	pair: left & right facing **mallards** (?), bird in flight on rear quarters
3544	pair: left & right facing pair of **geese** w/gosling on rear quarters
3546	slipper (partially obscured in catalog illustration)
3580	man's high-top lace-up shoe, in-mold laces & tie
3683	small shoe w/**cat** curled across front
3703	cuffed boot, **dog** (?) on back
3704	cuffed boot, **dog** on front looking at **cat** inside cuff
3705	cuffed boot, **dog** on vamp looking away from boot
3717	fancy high-top boot, medallion on side
3718	ladies low-cut oxford
3735	ladies' low-cut oxford
4122	pair: left and right facing strap pumps w/4-leaf clovers
5441	pair: **boy pierrot** sitting on toe, fox on left side
	girl pierrot sitting on toe, rabbit on right side
5442	pair: left & right facing, pair of **cats** playing with ball, mice on rear quarters
5481	pair: left and right facing strap pumps w/4-leaf clovers
5490	pair: left & right facing **pheasants** (?) w/rabbit on rear quarters
5491	pair: left & right facing **turkeys**, chick on back quarters
5492	pair: left & right facing **cockatiels**, bird in flight on rear quarters (parakeets??)
11141	pair: **in-mold Dutch boy** holding large **Dutch shoe** w/grapes
	in-mold Dutch girl holding large **Dutch shoe** w/grapes

a couple tried to reestablish the Weiss, Kühnert & Company factory, which they had named Porzellanmanufaktur Gräfenthal. Their efforts ended in bankruptcy in about 1995. The thirty thousand molds in the attic were retrieved by Susan Bickert of The German Doll Company when she purchased them in 1999.

The Weiss, Kühnert factory made a wide range of figural shoes, over fifty of which have been identified because of their appearance in a 1920s-vintage catalog. They include a group of animal shoes that demonstrate the mold-maker's art of designing the animals to be part of a two-piece mold, thereby reducing the labor-intensiveness of separately molding the animals and then attaching them before kiln-firing. Many of the Weiss, Kühnert shoes are illustrated in the body of this book. In Table 6 is a list of the Weiss, Kühnert shoes known by the author to date. Such a list is helpful to the collector because nearly all Weiss, Kühnert shoes are unmarked by factory of origin. Uniquely, however, most have the impressed mold number in their body, often on a backside, and often have "Germany" impressed nearby.

Weller. Weller Pottery, Fultonham and Zanesville, Ohio, 1872–1948. The company that Samuel A. Weller founded made an enormous range of wares over the years, including art pottery. During its existence, Weller employed a large number of decorators, many of whom signed their works with their initials, their last name, or first initial and last name. Jacques Sicard (Sicardo) was a well-known artist who worked for Weller before returning to France. The only shoe form seen by the author that can be attributed to Weller was signed by Sicard. It is a large sabot with a graduated yellow-to-orange glaze and an applied cicada. A similarly colored vase with an applied cicada has been seen by the author, signed "Sicard, Marseille".

Wheelock. C. E. Wheelock & Co., Peoria, Illinois, 1888–1971. The company originally started as a pottery, primarily making utilitarian wares. They entered the importing business during the souvenir china craze and became a major source of commemorative and souvenir china, most of it made in Germany.

Williams, H. M. H. M. Williams and Sons, Bridge Pottery, Longton, Staffordshire, England, 1858-1941. The name of this company has been found spelled both this way and *Williamson*. *See next entry.*

Williamson, H. M. H. M. Williamson and Sons, Bridge Pottery, Longton, Staffordshire, England, 1858–1941. The company used a "W" framed by either a diamond or square with the words "British Made" as a bottom mark that can be found on its crested china. It is believed that the mark was used for only a short time beginning about 1900.

Willow Art China. *See Hewitt and Leadbeater.*

Wiltshaw and Robinson. Wiltshaw and Robinson Ltd., Stoke, Staffordshire, England, 1890–present. The company made earthenware and porcelain. They introduced crested china in 1902 as "Carlton Heraldic China", making them the first of the big competitors of Goss in the crested china market. They produced crested china into the late 1920s. The most common trademark of the company is *Carlton China*. Among the twenty other trademarks known to have been used by the company are *Cyclone* (for a wholesaler) and *The Milton China* (for a wholesaler G.G.&Co.), the latter more often found on factory models made by Hewitt and Leadbeater.

Worcester Porcelain Company. *See Royal Worcester.*

W. S. & S./W. Schiller & Son. W. Schiller & Son, Bodenbach, Bohemia (presently Podmokly, Czechia), c.1885–1885. W. Schiller & Son made both porcelain and pottery. The predecessor company, Schiller & Gerbing, was in existence from 1829 to c.1885 when part of the company split off into W. Schiller & Son, an operation only in existence for about a year. The other part continued on as Gerbing & Stephen, c.1895-1898, until the Gerbing family took on operations in 1898.

Wy Not. *See Hewitt and Leadbeater.*
Wy Not? *See Robinson & Leadbeater.*

Glossary

airbrushing. A method of applying paint using a pencil-sized spray gun with an attached paint container and air supply. Paint flow is controlled through adjustable nozzles. The technique allows many effects including a gradual change in the density of the applied color and the gradual blending of different colors so that there is no obvious place where the color changes from one to another. The watercolor artist Charles Burdick invented the airbrush in 1893.

bocage. Term used in ceramics to describe slip forced through a sieve and applied and painted to resemble moss or grass, translates to "woodland" a variation of boscag from the old French "boscage".

bone china. Porcelain made of china clay (kaolin) and Cornish stone with 45%-50% calcined bone. Typically, it is kiln fired to about 2400°F. It is a soft-paste porcelain with high translucency.

boscage. Variation of bocage, usually referring to a mass of growing trees or shrubs or the pictorial representation of wooded landscapes.

decal or decalcomania. A design or logo printed on a film of varnish and applied either under or over glaze to the ceramic piece.

delftware. Pottery coated with tin-enameled glaze (white) and decorated in blue.

DEP. abb. for déposé, meaning trademark **dep**osited with the patent office. The abbreviation can be found on German as well as French wares. The presence of DEP usually suggests a manufacturing date after about 1900 and before about 1918.

embossed. Design heavily raised from the body of the piece created during the casting or molding process.

faience (Anglicized), **faïence** (French). Pottery coated with a tin-enamel glaze, the spelling used for French and Italian wares.

fayence (German). Pottery coated with a tin-enamel glaze.

grand feu. A glazing and decorating technique where the green ware is fired once, coated with glaze, and allowed to dry. The décor is painted on the powdery raw glaze and then fired for the second time, bonding the glaze to the piece and activating the mineral salts in the décor. A major drawback was the difficulty or impossibility of producing certain colors.

ground. A term used by decorators to indicate the back*ground* color.

impressed. Indentation into the body of the piece made by a tooled shape.

incised. Indentation into the body of the piece made by a hand-operated scratching device.

luster or **lustre.** A décor made from metallic salts applied over a base glaze, then refired at a lower temperature than the bisque firing. Typically, lustres are thin, soft, and easily scratched. Older lustres are usually deep, solid colors; newer lustres tend to be more iridescent.

majolica. Majolica is a heavy pottery, lead or tin-glazed over bright colors, with cobalt, turquoise, and lavender in highest demand. Introduced in Great Britain at the Great Exhibit of 1851, it reached its height of popularity in the Victorian era. It is often unmarked.

MIB. abb. for Mint In Box.

MIG. abb. for Made in Germany.

MIJ: abb. for Made In Japan.

MOJ: abb. for Made in Occupied Japan.

moriage. Décor formed by trailing slip, or liquid ceramic, onto the body of the piece before or after glazing.

petit feu. A glazing and decorating technique where the piece was fired a total of three times: first, the green ware was fired to its biscuit stage; second, the biscuit was coated with glaze and fired again; third, the décor was applied using paints mixed with a colorless flux and then fired for last time. One advantage was the ability to produce the purples, pinks, and certain greens not possible with the *grand feu* method.

raised and cut up. Term used when paste is modeled on the surface of the ceramic object. See Spode inkwells for an illustration of the effects of this process.

scroddle. Marbleized clay.

sewertile. Sewertile pottery was made off-hours from left-over clay by craftsmen in the sewertile factories of the United States beginning in the 19th century, but primarily in the first half of the 20th century. Most was made in the sanitary pipe factories of Ohio. Generally of red clay, the rich glaze was achieved by throwing buckets full of salt into the kiln at the height of its firing.

spatter. A decorating method of early English origin performed by striking a paint-full brush against a stick over the piece to be colored.

sponge. A decorating method developed in the mid 1800s that used a cut sponge thinly covered with paint to apply color to the piece being decorated.

stamp or stamped. Décor or logo applied using a rubber stamp to create an outline that might then be filled in with hand painting. Intricate stamps have been used to form the border outlines and major design motifs of some wares.

stenciling. Design achieved by painting through openings in a template.

stoneware. Pottery that has been kiln-fired to about 2400°F, the same temperature as bone china. It is extremely hard and durable.

tin glaze, or tin-enamel glaze. White enamel formed from silica, lead, and tin compounds to provide an opaque surface to cover the color of the clay foundation, providing a background through which the clay color would not bleed and thus would not interfere with the colors then applied in the décor.

transfer. Design printed on special tissue paper, cut out and laid on the piece to be decorated, and kiln fired to set the design. Whether the paper is removed before or burned off during the kiln firing depends on whether the design was printed with a slow drying ink or a dry transfer. An additional firing is usually required to set a glaze applied over the transfer. John Sadler, an engraver from Liverpool, England, is generally credited with creating the process in about 1752.

yellow ware. Yellow ware is made from natural buff-colored clay. It was first made in England and Scotland in the 16th and 17th centuries. It was also made in such other European countries as Germany, Holland, and France. Immigrants coming to the United States found the same type of clay and began making pottery wares from it, beginning in the 19th century. Its advantages are durability compared to fragile and porous redware, and relative lightness compared to the heavier stoneware.

References

Books and Periodicals

Almanac of Limoges. Limoges, France: 1879.

Alsford, Denis B. *Match Holders, 100 Years of Ingenuity.* Atglen, Pennsylvania: Schiffer Publishing Ltd., 1994.

Andacht, Sandra. *Collector's Value Guide To Oriental Decorative Arts.* Dubuque, Iowa: Antique Trader Books, 1997.

Atterbury, Paul; Ellen Paul Denker; and Maureen Batkin. *Miller's Twentieth-Century Ceramics.* London: Octopus Publishing Group Ltd., 1999.

Ayers, Tim, ed. *Art at Auction, The Year at Sotheby's 1981-82.* London: Philip Wilson Publishers Ltd., 1982.

Barret, Richard Carter. *Bennington Pottery and Porcelain, A Guide to Identification.* New York: Bonanza Books, 1958.

Bernard, Roger, and Jean-Claude Renard. *La Faïence de Gien*, English translation by Denis Mahaffey. Gien, France: Société Nouvelle des Faïenceries de Gien, c. 1990s.

Bigelow, Marybelle S. *Fashion in History, Apparel in the Western World.* Minneapolis, Minnesota: Burgess Publishing Company, 1970.

Bly, John. "Ask John Bly." *Country Homes & Interiors.* English periodical, June 1998.

Bowers, Sharon; Sue Closser; and Kathy Ellis. *Czechoslovakian Pottery, "Czeching" Out America.* Marietta, Ohio: Antique Publications, A Division of the Glass Press, Inc., 1999.

Bunt, Cyril G. E. *British Potters and Pottery Today.* Leigh-on-Sea, United Kingdom: F. Lewis, 1956.

Chamberlain, Georgia S. "Sunbonnet Babies and Overall Boys." *Spinning Wheel.* April 1955.

Cox, Warren E. *The Book of Pottery and Porcelain.* 2 vols. 1970. Revised ed. (2 vols. in 1), New York: Crown Publishers, Inc., 1979.

Cushion, J. P., in collaboration with W. B. Honey. *Handbook of Pottery and Porcelain Marks.* 5th ed. revised and expanded. London, England: Farber and Farber Limited, 1996.

d'Albis, J., and C. Romanet. *La Porcelaine de Limoges.* Paris: 1980. (Translated for the author by Jeffry Alan Bradway. *The Porcelain of Limoges*)

Danckert, Ludwig. *Directory of European Porcelain; Marks, Makers and Factories*, trans. Rita Kipling. London: Robert Hale Ltd., 1995.

Dees, Dr. K. Otto. *Die Geschichte der Porzellanfabrik zu Tettau und die Beziehungen Alexander v. Humboldts zur Porzellanindustrie (The History of the Porcelain Factory at Tettau and the Relationship of Alexander von Humbolt to the Porcelain Industry).* Saalfeld, Thuringia, Germany: Weidmannischen Printers Corporation, c. 1920. (Translated from the German for the author by Robert Hall.)

Degenhardt, Richard K. *Belleek, The Complete Collector's Guide and Illustrated Reference.* 2nd edition. Radnor, Pennsylvania: Wallace-Homestead Book Company, 1993.

Dietrich, Judy. "Collecting British Delft." *The Hudson Valley (Rhinebeck, New York) Antiquer*, vol. 4, no. 9, June 1996.

Dreyfus, Dominique. *Emaux de Longwy.* Paris, France: Editions Charles Massin, 1990.

——. *Longwy, Les Marques, Les Signatures.* 3rd edition. Longwy, France: 1992.

Encyclopaedia Britannica, 11th ed., s.v. "Ceramics."

Ende, Jean-Louis. "The Long Life of the Enamels of Longwy." *Reader's Digest* (French edition*).* February 1995. (Translated for the author by Jeffry Alan Bradway.)

Ettinger, Roseann. *3000 Shoes from 1896.* Atglen, Pennsylvania: Schiffer Publishing Ltd., 1998.

Faience de Gien, La. *L'Estampille*, no. 184. Fontaine-lès-Dijon, France: Editions Faton, September 1985. (Translated for the author by Jeffry Alan Bradway.)

Faveton, Pierre. *Les Barbotines.* Paris, France: Editions Charles Massin, n.d.

Fiala, Claudia. "Porzellanfabrikation in Ilmenau – Tradition und Vielfalt." Pp. 221–236 in *Ilmenau: Beiträge zur Geschichte einer Stadt.* Herausgegeben von der Stadt Ilmenau unter Leitung von Silke Leisner. Ilmenau, Thuringia, Germany: Ilmenau-Hildburghausen, 1995. (Translated for the author by Robert Hall as "Porcelain Production in Ilmenau – Tradition and Variety." *Ilmenau: Contributions to the History of a City.* Published by the City of Ilmenau under the direction of Silke Leisner.)

Gannon, Michael. *Black May, The Epic Story of the Allies' Defeat of the German U-Boats in May 1943.* New York: Dell Publishing, a Division of Random House, Inc., 1998.

Gilchrist, Martyn. *Whistles.* Buckinghamshire, UK: Shire Publications, Ltd., 2000.

Gillard, Michèle-Cécile. *L'Age D'or Gien des Faïences.* Paris: Charles Massin Editeur, n.d.

Gleeson, Janet. *The Arcanum.* London: Bantam Books, 1998.

Grafton, Carol Belanger. *Shoes, Hats and Fashion Accessories, A Pictorial Archive, 1850-1940.* Minneola, New York: Dover Publications, Inc., 1998.

Grover, Eulalie Osgood, author, and Bertha L. Corbett, illustrator. *The Sunbonnet Babies Primer.* Chicago: Rand McNally & Company, 1903.

Hales, Sarah. "Meissen Figures." *The Collector.* England: Barrington Publications, June/July 1999.

Harran, Jim & Susan. *Collectible Cups & Saucers, Identification & Values.* Books I & II. Paducah, Kentucky: Collector Books, 1997 and 2000.

Hibbert, Christopher. *Napoleon, His Wives and Women.* New York: W. W. Norton & Company, 2002.

Hobbies 47, no. 11, January 1943.

Hobbies 58, no. 8, October 1953.

Hunting, Jean & Franklin. *Collectible Match Holders for Tabletops and Walls.* Atglen, Pennsylvania: Schiffer Publishing Ltd., 1998.

Huxford, Sharon and Bob. *The Collectors Encyclopedia of Weller Pottery.* Paducah, Kentucky: Collector Books, 1979. Values updated, 1999.

——. *Schroeder's Antiques Price Guide, Fourteenth Edition.* Paducah, Kentucky: Collector Books, A Division of Schroeder Publishing Co., Inc., 1996.

Karlin, Elyse Zorn. *Children Figurines of Bisque and Chinawares, 1850-1950.* West Chester, Pennsylvania: Schiffer Publishing Ltd., 1990.

Knight, F., 71 engravings by. *Scroll Ornaments of the Early Victorian Period.* Orig. pub. c.1847. New York: Dover Publications, Inc., 1978.

Kovel, Ralph M. and Terry H. *Dictionary of Marks – Pottery and Porcelain.* New York: Crown Publishers, Inc., 1953.

Kovel, Ralph and Terry. *Kovels' New Dictionary of Marks.* New York: Crown Publishers, Inc., 1986.

Krombholz, Mary Gorham, in collaboration with Cynthia Erfurt Musser. *The Story of German Doll Making, 1530 – 2000.* Grantsville, Maryland: Hobby House Press, 2001.

Lankester, Wendy, "A Story of Ceramic Shoes, Part 1: BC – 1800." *Antique Collecting* (Antique Collectors' Club, Woodbridge, Suffolk, England) 20, no. 5 (October 1985): 62–65.

——. "A Story of Ceramic Shoes, Part 2: 1800 to Present Day." *Antique Collecting* (Antique Collectors' Club, Woodbridge, Suffolk, England) 20, no. 6 (November 1985): 15–20.

Larkin, Leah. "Germany's White Gold." *German Life.* October/November 2000.

Lee, Ruth Webb. *Victorian Glass.* Wellesley Hills, Massachusetts: Lee Publications, 1944.

Lehner, Lois. *Lehner's Encyclopedia of U. S. Marks on Pottery, Porcelain & Clay.* Paducah, Kentucky: Collector Books, A Division of Schroeder Publishing Co., Inc., 1988.

Lesur, Adrien. *Les Poteries et les Faïences Françaises.* 3 vols. Paris: Tardy, 1957–59.

Liu, Aimee, and Meg Rottman. *Shoe Time.* New York: Arbor House, Timber Books, 1986.

Mali, Millicent S. *French Faïence Fantaisie et Populaire of the 19th and 20th Centuries.* United Printing, 1986.

——. *CA, A French Faïence Breakthrough.* Harbor Springs, Michigan: Carpenter Printing, 2000.

——. *The Old Quimper Review,* pub. biannually; Vol. VI, No.1, March 1995; Vol. IX, No.2, October 1998; Vol. X, No. 2, October 1999; Vol. XI, No. 1, March 2000. Box 377, East Greenwich, Rhode Island.

Margulis, Marilyn Irvin. "A Living Link to Christmas Past." *Antiques & Collecting Magazine,* December 2001.

Martin, Courtenay. "Art & Sole." *San Antonio Express-News,* 25 March 1999.

McCaslin, Mary J. *Royal Bayreuth, A Collector's Guide.* Books I & II. Marietta, Ohio: Antique Publications, 1994 and 2000.

McDowell, Colin. *Shoes, Fashion and Fantasy.* London: Thames and Hudson Ltd, 1989.

Messenger, Michael. *Coalport 1795 – 1926.* Woodbridge, Suffolk, England: Antique Collectors' Club, 1995.

Miller, Judith & Martin, eds. *Miller's Antiques Checklist, Art Deco.* U.S.A.: Viking Penguin, 1991.

——. *Miller's Antiques Checklist, Art Nouveau.* London: Reed Consumer Books Limited, 1992. Reprinted 1994.

Murray, D. Michael. *European Majolica, with Values.* Atglen, Pennsylvania: Schiffer Publishing Ltd., 1997.

Newark, Tim. *The Art of Emile Gallé.* Quintet Publishing, 1989. London: Grange Books, 1995.

Newbound, Betty and Bill. *Collector's Encyclopedia of Wall Pockets: Identification and Values.* Paducah, Kentucky: Collector Books, 1996.

Nichelason, Margery G. *Shoes.* Minneapolis, Minnesota: Carolrhoda Books, Inc., 1997.

Nicholson, Paul T. *Egyptian Faience and Glass.* Shire Egyptology Series no. 19. Buckinghamshire, U. K.: Shire Publications Ltd., 1993.

O'Keefe, Linda. *Shoes, A Celebration of Pumps, Sandals, Slippers & More.* New York: Workman Publishing, 1996.

Ormsbee, Thomas H. *English China and its Marks.* Deerfield Editions, Ltd., 1959. New York: Deerfield Books, Inc., 1967.

Pine, Nicholas. *The Concise Encyclopedia and Price Guide to Goss China.* Ed. by Norman Pratten. Hampshire, U. K.: Milestone Publications, Goss & Crested China Ltd., 1992.

——. *Goss and Other Crested China.* Shire Album no. 120. Buckinghamshire, U. K.: Shire Publications Ltd., 1994.

——. *The Price Guide to Crested China.* Hants, U. K.: Milestone Publications, Goss & Crested China Ltd., 1992.

——. *The 2000 Price Guide to Crested China.* Hants, U.K.: Milestone Publications, Goss & Crested China Ltd., 2000.

Poole, Julia E. *English Pottery.* Fitzwilliam Museum Handbooks. Cambridge, England: Cambridge University Press, 1995.

Pratt, Lucy, and Linda Woolley. *Shoes.* London: V & A Publications, 1999.

Raines, Joan and Marvin. *A Guide to Royal Bayreuth Figurals.* New City, New York: n.p., 1973.

——. *A Guide to Royal Bayreuth Figurals, Book 2, Including Price Guide.* New York: Lawton York Corporation, 1977.

Ramsey, L. G. G., ed. *Antique English Pottery, Porcelain and Glass.* New York: E. P. Dutton & Company, Inc., 1961.

Roberts, Alan A. "Ceramic Cloisonné, The European Tradition." *Antiques & Collecting.* April 1990.

Röntgen, Robert E. *The Book of Meissen.* 2nd ed. Atglen, Pennsylvania: Schiffer Publishing Ltd., 1996.

——. *Marks on German, Bohemian and Austrian Porcelain, 1710 to the Present.* Updated and revised edition. Atglen, Pennsylvania: Schiffer Publishing Ltd., 1997.

Salley, Virginia Sutton, and George H. Salley. *Royal Bayreuth China.* Portland, Maine: Portland Lithograph Company, 1969.

Sandon, Henry. *Royal Worcester Porcelain from 1862 to the Present Day.* 3rd ed. London: Barrie & Jenkins, 1978.

Sater, Denise M., ed. "Wintry Snow Babies Give Joy Year Round." *Antiques & Auction News,* 29 no.1. Mount Joy, Pennsylvania: Joel Sater Publications, 2 January 1998.

Scheidt, Helga. "Die Porzellanproduktion in Arnstadt" (pp. 91–101) and "Der Modelleur Paul Bandorf" (pp. 102–104). These articles, part of a larger booklet published in 1996 by the Geschichtsverein (Historical society) and of unknown title, were provided to the author in 1997 by Scheidt, director of the Schlossmuseum Arnstadt in Arnstadt, Germany. (Translated from German for the author by Robert Hall.)

Scherf, Helmut. *Thüringer Porzellan, Geschichte, Fabriken und Erzeugnisse.* Herausgeber, Germany: Kreisheimatmuseum Leuchtenburg, 1992.

Schwarzbach, Fred. "Case of Mistaken Identity: Hard news about soft paste." *Antique Week,* Eastern Edition; 22 November 1999.

Sotheby's. "Important Chinese Export Porcelain and Chinese Works of Art from the Collection of the Late Mildred R. and Rafi Y. Mottahedeh." *Sotheby's Preview.* sothebys.com, New York: 19 October 2000.

Spargo, John. *The Potters and Potteries of Bennington.* Southampton, Long Island, New York: Cracker Barrel Press, 1926.

Speltz, Alexander. *The Styles of Ornament.* (Unabridged and unaltered republication of David O'Connor's translation from the second German edition.) New York: Dover Publications, Inc., 1959.

Squire, Geoffrey. *Dress and Society 1560 – 1970.* New York: Viking Press, Inc., 1974.

Stefano, Jr., Frank. *Pictorial Souvenirs & Commemoratives of North America.* New York: E. P. Dutton & Co., Inc., 1976.

Stewart, Tabori & Chang, pub. *Shoes.* New York, 1999.

Swann, June. *Shoemaking.* Shire Album 155. © 1986. Buckinghamshire, U. K.: Shire Publications Ltd., 1997.

——. *Shoes.* London: B. T. Batsford Ltd., 1982.

Van Patten, Joan F. *The Collector's Encyclopedia of Nippon Porcelain.* © 1979. Paducah, Kentucky: Collector Books, A Division of

Schroeder Publishing Co., Inc., 1994.

———. *Collector's Encyclopedia of Nippon Porcelain, fifth series.* Paducah, Kentucky: Collector Books, A Division of Schroeder Publishing Co., Inc., 1998.

———. "R. S. Prussia Reproduction Alert." *The MidAtlantic Antiques Magazine.* Henderson, North Carolina, June 1998.

Vogel, Janice and Richard. *Conta & Boehme Porcelain, Identification and Value Guide.* Ocala, Florida; Poßneck Publishing Company, 2001.

———. *Victorian Trinket Boxes, A Handbook with Price Guide for the Collector.* Ocala, Florida: Poßneck Publishing Company, 1996.

Wendl, Martin, and Ernst Schäfer. *Altes Thüringer Porzellan.* Erfurt, Germany: Druck-und-Verlagshaus Erfurt, 1995.

Wilcox, R. Turner. *The Mode in Footwear.* New York: Charles Scribner's Sons, 1948.

Williams, Laurence W. *Collector's Guide to Souvenir China, Keepsakes of a Golden Era, Identification and Values.* Paducah, Kentucky: Collector Books, A Division of Schroeder Publishing Co., Inc., 1998.

Willis, Alf, *The Charlton Standard Catalogue of Coalport Collectibles.* Toronto: The Charlton Press, 2000.

Yalom, Libby. *Shoes of Glass, 2.* Marietta, Ohio: The Glass Press, Inc., dba Antique Publications, 1998.

Catalogs and Pamphlets

A. A. Importing Company. *Catalog 68, Year 2000 Edition.* St. Louis, Missouri: A. A. Importing Company, © 1999.

The Boot & Shoe Trades Journal. Weekly record of the leather industries. London, 29 April 1882.

Butler Brothers. *Our Drummer.* Catalog no. 455. New York, Butler Brother, Spring 1903.

Alfred J. Cammeyer Illustrated Catalog and Price List of Boots, Shoes, Slippers and Rubbers. New York, Spring & Summer, 1894.

The Jean and Kenneth Chorley Collection, Sale 7614. New York: Christie's New York, 25 January 1993.

Dedham Pottery Catalog, 1938.

W. L. Douglas Shoes for Men, Boys & Youths, Women, Misses and Children. Brockton, Massachusetts: Wholesale Catalog, Spring and Summer, 1909.

Franco, Barbara. *White's Utica Pottery, Munson-Williams-Proctor Institute Exhibition Pamphlet, Nov. 9, 1969-Feb. 8, 1970.* Utica, New York Public Library, photocopy (ref: 738.37).

James Huggins & Bro. *Boots, Shoes and Rubbers Catalogue.* New York, 1889.

LaMode Illustree, Journal de la Famille. Paris: 2 December 1888.

Mardorf & Bandorf Porzellanfabrik factory catalog, 4 pages. Arnstadt, Germany, c.1910.

Montgomery Ward catalogs, 1872–1914. Montgomery Ward catalogs are archived at the University of Wisconsin's American Heritage Center in their Coe Library, P.O. Box 3924, Laramie, Wyoming 82071-3924. The archive contains all catalogs from the first, issued in 1872, through the 1980s, with only two 1980s catalogs missing. The catalogs are available on microfilm through an interlibrary loan. The 1872 catalog is a single sheet listing the names and prices of 163 items. The Fall/Winter 1874–75 catalog has a few illustrations. The Fall/Winter 1878 "Illustrated" catalog is the first to be so designated and is full of what appear to be steel engravings of items for sale. A sense of the growth of catalog sales can be gained by the increasing size of the catalog: 540 pages in 1890, 814 pages in 1898, and 1038 pages in 1899. In each year there was a Fall/Winter and a Spring/Summer catalog. The years 1872–1914 represent the time span of catalogs reviewed by the author to search for ceramic shoes sold through this outlet, and to establish an earliest date for the manufacture of certain styles of shoes. Announcement that the company was going out of business was made on 28 December 2000.

Parker Holmes & Co. Fall Catalogue 1902. Boston. (A wholesale catalog of boots, shoes, rubbers, etc.)

The Famous Queen Quality Shoes for Women. Boston: Thomas G. Plant Co., Manufacturers, 1902.

Chas. A. Roberts. *The Bradford Comfort Shoes Catalogue.* Haverhill, Massachusetts, c. 1913.

Shoe and Leather Reporter. XXXVII, no. 10. New York: 6 March 1884.

Sotheby's. *English and Continental Ceramics and Glass.* London: Sotheby's, Tuesday, 15 November 1994.

Spode. *The Story of the Original Fine Bone China.* Stoke-on-Trent, England: Spode, c.1990.

J. S. Taft & Company. *Introducing Hampshire Pottery.* Reprint of a c.1905 catalog of the Keene, New Hampshire pottery's product line. On page 18 the reprint shows the Hampshire Pottery boot with form number 406.

Unterwegs auf der Thüringer Porzellanstraße. Brochure describing the Thuringian Porcelain Road. Saalfeld, Thuringia, Germany: Förderverein "Thüringer Porzellanstraße" e. V., c. 2000. (Translated for the author by Oliver Osterwind.)

Vogel, Janice and Richard, eds. *Conta & Boehme Product Catalog.* Ocala, Florida: Poßneck Publishing Company, 2001. (Reproduction of catalog believed to have been issued about 1912–1917.)

Weiss, Kühnert factory catalog, 9 assorted pages. Gräfenthal, Germany, c.1920.

Communications

Boland, Robert M. Artist, theatrical expert, professor emeritus, and former chairman of the Department of Fine and Applied Arts, Berkshire Community College, Pittsfield, Massachusetts. Communication to author of 19 May 2003 on research into painting techniques.

Caraty, Denis. Member of Société: Faïenceries de Gien, Gien, France. Several communications with the author in June 2002 regarding the identification of shoes made by the Gien factory.

Cook, Wendy. Curator of the Museum of Worcester Porcelain, Worcester, England. Letter to author of 23 August 2001 responding to questions about the numbering and production runs of Royal Worcester shoes.

Copeland, Robert. Historical Consultant to Spode, fifth generation from Spode II's first partner, William Copeland and author of books on historic ceramics. Letters to the author of 19 June 1996, 6 August 1996, and 4 September 1996 on Spode and its inkwell slippers. Mr. Copeland is also the photographer of the Spode inkwell slippers.

Dreyfus, Huguette. President of the Association of Collectors of Old Faiences and Enamels of Longwy and mother of the late Dominique. Letters to the author of 6 December 1998, 29 January 1999, 20 July 1999, 14 October 1999, and 9 December 2002 regarding Longwy products. (Translated for the author by Jeffry Alan Bradway.)

Halvorsen, Josef. Sales Manager of Porsgrund Porcelain Factory, Porsgrunn, Norway. Letter to author of 3 September 1996 regarding only shoe known to have been manufactured by this company and its production dates.

Herold, Alfred. Executive at Königl. Priv. Porzellanfabrik Tettau GmbH (Royal Bayreuth factory). Letter to author of 11 August 1997 verifying that Royal Bayreuth sold white blanks, including shoes, to small shops to be decorated and put through secondary kiln firing. (Translated for the author by Michael Osterwind.); letter to author of 20 January 2003 verifying that a smaller version of the ladies cap toe oxford is a copy of a Royal Bayreuth shoe, and not made by the RB factory.

Lankester, Wendy. Researcher, creator, designer and modeler of historic shoes comprising the Gainsborough Collection and author on the history of shoes. Correspondence with the author as a result of contact beginning in January 1996 on English porcelain factories and on the technicalities of porcelain manufacture. Letters of 14 April 1996, 30 April 1996, 27 May 1996, 5 September 1996, 28 September 1996, 23 November 1996, 30 March 1997, 31 August 1997, 20 August 1998, 15 October 1999, 5 March 2000, and 7 March 2001.

Mali, Millicent. Researcher, author, collector and authority on French history and French faience. Letters to author of 18 April 1997, 7 June 2002, 17 June 2002, 24 June 2002, and 12 June 2003 concerning French faience.

Meslin-Perrier, Chantal. Conservateur en Chef du Musée, Musée national Adrien Dubouché, Limoges, France. Letters to author of 13 February 1997 and 9 April 1997 on products of Gibus & Co./Gibus & Redon. (Translated for the author by Jeffry Alan Bradway.)

Osterwind, Michael. German industry executive. Materials from two trips: one week in Thuringia and Bavaria with visits to several museums and factories including Royal Bayreuth, April 1997; one week in Thuringia visiting sixteen factories and museums, May 1998. Letters to the author on numerous aspects of German porcelain factories, 11 July 1996, 15 January 1997, 4 April 1997, 4 May 1997, 16 June 1997, 19 July 1997, 15 May 1998, 12 June 1998, 8 July 1998, 14 August 1999, 20 February 2000, 15 May 2001, 21 May 2001, and 4 September 2001.

Rainka, Ron. souvenir china dealer. Conversations on many occasions on the collectibility and values of souvenir wares.

Röntgen, Robert E. author of book on porcelain marks. Letter to author of 14 June 1997 on his research into unidentified porcelain marks and responses to inquiries on German porcelain factories.

Sandon, Henry. Former curator of The Museum of Worcester Porcelain and author on Royal Worcester. Letter to author of 25 February 1998 responding to questions about historic negatives of Royal Worcester shoes of the late 1880s, their rarity, and their designer or designers.

Schärer, Herr. Archivist with the Royal Porcelain Manufactory, Meissen. Letters to author of 3 February 1997, 29 May 1997, 16 June 1997, and 13 August 1997 responding to questions on Meissen slippers, Meissen patterns, marks, and dating system. (Translated for the author by Michael Osterwind.)

Schneider, Ester. Curator of Keramik-Museum Mettlach, Mettlach, Saar, Germany. Letter of 23 January 1997 regarding identification of shoe forms made by Villeroy and Boch. (Translated for the author by Michael Osterwind.)

Stefano, Frank. Author of text on souvenir china. Letter to author of 6 August 1997 verifying existence of marked Royal Bayreuth souvenir china.

Strauche, Carola. Presiding Board Member of the Thüringer Porzellanstraße e.V., Saalfeld, Germany. Letter to author of 3 August 1999 explaining the nature of the sites available for visits along the Thuringian Porcelain Road in Germany.

Wojtkowski, Thomas C. Notes on Thuringian factories from trip in May 1998.

Index